MYTH AND LANGUAGE

MYTH
&
LANGUAGE

Albert Cook

INDIANA UNIVERSITY PRESS
Bloomington

Library of Congress Cataloging in Publication Data

Cook, Albert Spaulding.
    Myth and language.

    Bibliography: p.
    Includes index.
    1. Myth. 2. Language and languages. 3. Lévi-Strauss, Claude.
4. Greek literature—History and criticism. 5. Folk literature—History and
criticism. I. Title.
BL304.C66   401'.9   79–84259
ISBN 0–253–14027–7   1   2   3   4   5   84   83   82   81   80

To Jean and William Sylvester,
Flora and Samuel Levin

splendent usu

CONTENTS

PREFACE

THIS book has arisen out of the pressing conviction that both the area of myth and the structure of language bear importantly on our most intimate and challenging concerns. This conviction is widely shared; less widely shared is the view that, at least for explaining literature, myth and language are necessarily interrelated. An examination of myth alone, or of language alone, will not go very far towards accounting for the odd power and special comprehensiveness of the achieved literary work: we must somehow try to look at both together and trace their interaction. And without some understanding of these processes we cannot effectively assess the role of literature in society generally.

To be sure, I cannot claim to have got very far towards doing this myself. What I offer in *Myth and Language* is not a step-by-step argument defining modes of interaction for myth and language. Rather, in each part of the book I take a series of probes as far as I can. These probes converge: the delimitation of Lévi-Strauss and the delineation of large phases for the interaction of myth and language in history do provide some further horizon for addressing the complexities of Ovid and Blake, while the separation of lyric poetry and philosophy and historiography out of their union in Homer moves into another phase by redefining myth. Such indeed has been the generally accepted view, though a comparable transposition of implied verbal attention in the elementary forms of proverb, riddle, and parable has rarely if ever been noticed.

In any case, anyone who writes at all comprehensively about myth must waver before George Eliot's implied indictment when she cast as the would-be author of a Key to All Mythologies a vague, senescent Mr. Casaubon, whose irrelevance and dilatoriness shade into impotence. Perhaps in this figure she was exorcising her earlier contributions to the vein of the Higher Criticism. But she cannot so cleanly separate her argument from the dream of her creation. Nor can we; and it should help to try to understand why, even if only partially.

All translations are mine, except where otherwise noted. All bibliographic citations will be found in the List of Works Cited, in accordance with the form of citation now common for the social sciences.

ACKNOWLEDGMENTS

I should like to thank those who have read and commented on all or part of the manuscript: Lionel Abel, Edward Ahearn, Charles Boer, Gerald Bond, Clint Goodson, Flora Levin, Samuel R. Levin, Thomas McFarland, Irving Massey, Charles Segal, and Herbert Schneidau. Saul Myers, my research assistant, and Angelika Webb, my secretary, were also resourcefully helpful in the preparation of copy.

Two research establishments, to which I owe thanks, accorded me their facilities while I was working over parts of the book: the Fondation Hardt in Geneva and the Camargo Foundation in Cassis.

I am grateful to the editors of *Arion*, *Boundary 2*, *Helios*, and *MLN*, who published sections of the book in their journals.

My wife, Carol, remains the sort of marvelous companion and adviser whose very presence makes possible the conception of such undertakings as this book.

Überhaupt gibt es so viel Ähnlichkeiten in der Welt und darin liegt etwas Beruhigendes, allerdings etwas Aufregendes, denn man sucht sie.

—Franz Kafka,
Briefe an Felice

(In general there are so many similarities in the world, and therein lies something that calms, and indeed something that excites, because people seek them out.)

MYTH AND LANGUAGE

INTRODUCTION

1.

To organize all aspects of life, to explain the relation between this-worldly activities and other-worldly ones, to reassure himself on every front, man everywhere in the beginning had recourse almost exclusively to myths. For the earliest societies science as well as religion, rules of kinship and exchange as well as who the dead are and how to treat them, the course of the seasons and the meaning of dreams, the management of plants and animals along with the cure of psychic illness —all come into place through individual myths and systems of myth. And in modern societies, too, the patterns derived from myths may be found to underlie our deepest personal histories and motivations, "the unconscious." Myths stubbornly pervade the way we treat one another and organize the space around us; they charge our works of art with urgent meaning.

Myths must be formulated in language, and myth must be discussed in language. But myth, in Jolles' suggestive characterization, provides an answer to a question we do not have. Myth handles material that lies in some way out of the reach of natural language, with a technique that for Freud is an emotional dynamic and for Lévi-Strauss an intellectual dialectic.

A myth, however, or what amounts to a myth, provides a technique for handling the unknown, for naming the unknown without offering a solution. Science, on the other hand, proceeds to name an unknown in order to solve it. But even the mythography of Freud and that of Lévi-Strauss, which explain myth as an emotional or an intellectual process, posit as the source or motive of this process something that does really remain an unknown: the unconscious or the savage mind. The myths that order the phenomena later studied by natural science also celebrate the connection between the phenomena and an unpredictable source. In the interpretations of Girard, Burkert, and Bataille, sacrifice rituals not only solidify society and perpetuate its means of food production or food gathering; they also carefully preserve a willful evasion of the

1

extreme facts that the myths about sacrifice codify: they insist on the unknown.

Insofar as myth must be communicated in language, and insofar as myth—a particular myth, or "myth" in general—necessarily constitutes the central reference for statements of or about it, then myth is continuous with language. But myth, as that area which resists formulation, a permanent and powerful unknown, is also discontinuous from language, however much the principles ordering myths may be deduced to resemble the principles ordering a language. Lévi-Strauss bases himself on this discontinuity when he calls ritual a paralanguage and myth a metalanguage (9, p. 84).

As for language itself, the whole question of how to render a structural account of linguistic performance must not only always be supplemented by a theory of truth-functions for sentences and modes of reference for the lexical items that make up sentences (as well as for sentences themselves). All these questions, structure, truth-function and reference taken globally, interact—at least in the most intense forms of utterance, "literary" statements as well as "myths"—with a sort of "monstrous a priori" where the interplay of emotion and the resolution of contradiction are given names of only negative definition (the unconscious), or of hypostatized beings (*daimones*). Bateson calls the hypothetical center in consciousness for such activity the "black box," the source that we may speak of but which is impenetrable to us.

The strategies for getting from myth to language, and from language to myth, are elaborate. And these strategies have undergone massive change in the course of human history. It is not only artful language, poetry, whose history can be related to changes in the interaction between myth and language; philosophy and historiography and other forms of formal human discourse become possible, it would seem from the historical evidence, only after and through a shift in the interaction between myth and language.

We may take myths, Greek or primitive, and subject them to the patterns of Freudian or Jungian analysis to lay bare their emotional content. We may also follow Lévi-Strauss and factor the events they recount into series of binary algorithms in order to diagram the thought-process they represent. But even if a writer like Marcel Detienne uses Lévi-Strauss's techniques to go beyond Lévi-Strauss's Frazeresque concentration on seasons and the fertility of crops and people, still, in order to give these patterns their full dimension, we should have to understand further how myth interacts with language. Freud "discovered" the unconscious; but the unconscious is known through its interactions with the ego as much as the ego is known through its manipulations of the unconscious. Similarly, the most comprehensive constructions about myth in language, literary works, would have to be understood in a reciprocity between the two systems. Otherwise, we would be left with the transmutation of myth into literature unexplained, which is in fact precisely where we are left after all of Lévi-Strauss's masterly demonstrations. Or else we would translate literary functions back into simplified mythic functions, and come out with something like Northrop Frye's quasi-Jungian categories.

Without a theory of the mediation between myth and language, we should effectually be caught in the false antithesis of honoring Apollo on the one hand, in a blind subservience to something like the god's urgency, or just reading his hieroglyphic on the other hand, losing the urgency.

The system of myth has an inseparable relation to the system of language, and we owe it to Lévi-Strauss, on the one hand, to have shown us how complexly the myths of a culture can be read as a sort of grammar of implied ideas. On the other hand, the form of myth, even as Lévi-Strauss analyzes it, cannot be wholly free of the form of language. Myth is not only analogous to language; it must inescapably enter language in order to be transmitted.

Language itself, seen just as a system of rules for producing syntax patterns, can be described as content-free; myth never can;[1] the content of language can be assigned to a separable lexicon, standing available to the speaker when he would invent a sentence, for which he would need given words.

Within the system of myths, there may be a systematic definition of the contents of the given "words"—the figures like Apollo and Dionysus or the story "bits" that Lévi-Strauss calls mythemes, the killing of the Python by Apollo or the sewing of Dionysus into the thigh of Zeus. Myth itself, once formulated within a society, is a given system, a sort of lexicon, where the relations between words are more fixed than in language: the words "Dionysus" and "Zeus" may be combined in a sentence much more freely than the mythemes about them can be.

We are, from as far back as we can know, a story-telling kind. And story-telling persists in our society for conveying what would seem to be otherwise inexpressible in language. So that under all the phases of interrelation between myth and language there is continuity. From very far back we also transpose our stories. Myth is another name for such a transposition; "mythos" originally means "story," a story in language. The possibility of writing down language is inseparable, already in Egypt and indeed as far back as the caves of the Paleolithic, from the impetus to communicate in something like language the elements of myth.

But of course if there are phases, there have to be techniques for moving from one phase to another. The very holistic character of myth would necessitate a very large linguistic gesture to effectuate the movement from one phase to another. And so myth cannot, in the last analysis, be fully accounted for as a sort of metalanguage, thinking itself through the group that possesses it. In Lévi-Strauss's posited faculty of mythmaking in the savage mind, the group is possessed by its myths. If so, it could not have transmuted them. We need a better account of the process than to say simply that myths die (Lévi-Strauss 9, pp. 301–18), even if the myth is shown to develop into legend, romance, or novel.

The transition from "oral" to "written" culture, for example, could be seen as a "cause" of change in the relations between myth and language. Or else it could be seen as an "effect," and literacy itself could be envisaged as a supremely powerful social by-product of redefining the relation between myth and language.

Without assignment of cause or effect, the purpose of this book is to examine some of the sensitized interaction between myth and language. My aim here has not been to provide a systematic account of myth, and so to define it. Rather, I have tried to see as far as I could into the interaction between myth and language at points where this interaction manifests itself with special salience.

While I do feel that the sections of this book bear on one another, I have organized it in such a way that they do so paratactically: I have not produced a step-by-step argument; points are argued separately. In Part One I examine Lévi-Strauss's systematic and penetrating account of myth as a communicative system, and seek to show that the usefulness of his binary procedures is, in effect, confined to only one aspect of a corpus of myth, an aspect that manifests itself most exclusively and pronouncedly during just one particular phase of culture, the Neolithic. In the second chapter I sketch a typology of cultural phases, distinguishing them by the relation between myth and language, with particular attention to literary forms.

In Part Two, again somewhat paratactically, I set up three examples of how the Greeks redefined the relation between myth and language as they moved from the elaborate oral culture of Homer to the literate, analytical culture where an Aristotle was produced. Heraclitus strips Homer's binary system of both meter and story to turn it into an instrument of thought; Pindar dynamizes a celebratory context by applying an arbitrary constellation of given myths to a particular occasion; and Herodotus applies a vast sorting process at once diachronic (historical) and synchronic (anthropological) to human behavior, wherein religious observances, both myths and rituals, are only incidents, one of the many attributes of the Egyptians or the Scythians. Some sense that Herodotus was redefining myth must have been felt by those who much later gave the names of the Muses to his nine books. The last chapter of Part Two examines how Ovid—heir several hundred years after Herodotus to a rich tradition of Greek and Roman myth, religion, philosophy, poetry, and history—plays fast and loose with the intrigue, the mystery, and even the absurdity of his mythic material.

In Part Three I again shift ground to look at the intimate dependence of the most elementary literary forms and procedures—proverb, riddle, parable, and metaphor—on a transposition into language of concerns associated with myth. At the end I try to make a case for the persisting vitality of mythic procedures in literary forms, and equally, by implication, for the necessity of literary forms to keep the mythic procedures alive.

2.

Greece offers a powerful example of how the change in the technical uses of writing within a society goes hand in hand with a deep alteration of its whole world outlook. On the one hand, as Walter J. Ong reminds us (pp. 119–22), sound is "in certain ways a preferred field for the movement from inertness to intelligence." There is found "increasing exploitation of voice as one moves up the evolutionary scale," and man's uses of sound are more "interiorized" than those of porpoises, bats, and apes, since sound serves man for interpersonal relationships rather than for marking objects or territories. Still, the cultures we loosely characterize as oral tend to lack a sense of history and a capacity for the sort of abstract induction that the Prometheus of Aeschylus, at roughly this transitional point, may be taken to symbolize. It is one thing to set fire on a stable hearth in a cyclic system—that is the Neolithic revolution. It is another thing to think back retrospectively to a stage where fire is included in a series of other general notions—that is the birth of philosophy, and Heraclitus, whatever his fire doctrines may mean, may well have been a necessary prelude to Aeschylus.[2]

The oral-aural, as Marshall McLuhan has taught us, tribalizes a society. The individual in such a society lacks what we think of as a special personal identity; he is defined wholly and comprehensively by his membership in a group. Ideas transmitted by word of mouth tend to follow the circumstances of auditory communication, and consequently they are centered; the hearer is in the middle of the sound waves. Everybody hears an oral announcement, proclamation, or recited poem at one time, inescapably caught in the group, as again Ong deduces. Ideas transmitted to the eye through written documents do not have this gripping simultaneity. They are as sequential as letters on a page, and they must be apprehended by a reader in separation from the group. To the oral culture in Greece one could connect everything in Homer's conditions from ring composition, parataxis, and the formula to the closed world of staple societal virtues; whereas writing, once it has been firmly established by Plato, triumphs in the sequential, encyclopedic-taxonomic definitions of Aristotle. He is, however, still early enough to have defined an ideal city as one small enough for all the citizens to live within earshot of a single herald.[3]

So much is by now commonplace, and commonplace for good reason. In one sense it is the purpose of this book to flesh out this commonplace. But we must also beware of commonplace. There are a number of considerations we must raise before falling back on the distinction between oral and written.

Greece, to begin with, is unique as well as exemplary. As Havelock has pointed out, following Jeffery and I.J. Gelb, only in Greece are sounds further abstracted to become an alphabet of phonetic representation rather than just the given cluster-representations, morpheme by morpheme, of hieroglyphics; or a syllabary; or some combination of the two. Linear B was a syllabary, like every other form of writing in the world before the remarkable Greek adaptation of a Phoenician syllabary to produce the phonetic alphabet. The Greeks were not just literate; they were literate in a special way that allowed them (or at least occurred with) their special development.[4] Greek literacy in itself differs from Hebrew or Chinese literacy as markedly as oral does from written in those cultures at various stages.

Moreover *oral* is not parallel to *written* as a descriptive term for cultures.

All language at any stage of culture is fundamentally oral. It has a phonological base, and it is built up first, and inescapably, from sound structures that may be omitted but are always present, not only for some pioneer of silent reading like Saint Ambrose but for any denizen of a highly literate culture.

The sound structures of natural language are supplemented, at least for poetry at any stage of culture, by further arbitrary sound structures. It is by sound structures that verse is defined, and even the "thought-rhyme" of Hebrew parallelism has complementary sound-structures above those of the natural language. Poetry also tends to occur in a specially selected diction and an especially modified syntax, in the *Kunstsprachen* or artificial languages that constitute Homer's Ionic-Aeolic or Dante's Tuscan. These special languages were never spoken anywhere, like the artificial language of Wordsworth or Pound that masquerades as a natural language, much as art song pretends to be folk song, by being supposedly but arbitrarily (in ways definably different from natural language) confined to "natural" dictions or rhythms.

In these *Kunstsprachen*, the special features of diction and syntax are always complemented and marked by special rhythmic features: the oral-aural component of rhythm and meter is as inseparable from these features as the phonological component is from natural language. This is true for the earliest Indo-European texts, the *Ṛgveda*, composed in staple meters and in a language whose very name for itself means artificial or confected (Sanskrit, *samskṛta*).

Oral, then, a term we may use loosely to characterize a stage of culture before widespread literacy, applies strictly (in the necessarily prior synchronic analysis) to all languages, natural or artificial, whether transmitted by mouth or by page. *Written* is not a term symmetrical with *oral* synchronically, though it too may be used for loose diachronic designation. *Writing* refers, strictly speaking, not to language, but to a special technique for transmitting language. And this would be true even of the "writing" of Derrida, which posits an epistemological rift between the "voice" and the "phenomenon" of a sort that in the phenomenology of perception any assignment of words to objects must involve a "primal writing" (*archi-écriture*) in the mind of the perceiver (1, pp. 81ff, pp. 164ff). This process would have to be distinct from that of calling up the words and producing the sentences of a language, natural or artificial.

Writing is a technique that is defined by its social context: by the uses to which the technique is put and by the classes of people who employ it, often in early societies a particular group of scribes or priests. These, in Dumézil's "first function" of Indo-European society, are frequently members of the same large group as the singers or bards who recite, though priests and poets may constitute separate sub-groups. Calchas in Homer does not do the work of Demodocus, but he possesses a special knowledge of past, present and future, as the bard has a special knowledge of mythos. The *Rgveda*, of course, is a body of hymns; and so it is the property of a priestly class. Writing serves as a class function for the transmission of documents like sacred texts, inventory records, and laws—before it is used in any form to record poems—though the sacred texts do already provide a form of relationship between myth and language.

Looking ahead from a prevailingly "oral" culture, Havelock distinguishes three states in Greece from Homer to Aristotle: craft literacy when literacy belonged just to a class of scribes, recitation literacy when the ability to recite from a text was transmitted in schools, and finally a socialized literacy when texts would be freely and privately read. A vase from the early fifth century B.C. depicts recitation in school but the conning of a text is not represented in art until about 400 B.C., on a grave stele. As Jeffery notes in tracing the uncertain progress of inscriptional alphabets in archaic Greece, the verb for reading, *epilegesthai*, is derived by Chantraine from *legein* in its primary sense of "gathering" the word letter by letter: *"il s'agit d'assembler, de recueillir pour comprendre."*

Looking backward from the "oral" societies of which we have record to Neolithic and even Paleolithic times, we find no stage of society of which we can confidently assert that it lacked "writing" for some use. Leroi-Gourhan (2) deduces the very possibility of language itself from the duality of interaction between hand and mouth. This procedure would lead not only to speaking but, through the use of the hand for instrumental work, directly to writing, through the fashioning of tools, to the cave paintings which he argues must be taken as proto-hieroglyphics, at once picture and writing at a time when picture and writing

were indistinguishable. If all writing systems we know begin as ideo-
graphs that become hieroglyphics, then going backward in time, one
could not arbitrarily stop somewhere short of the cave paintings in
defining a hieroglyph. For this "oral" people there is arguably a "writing" that consists of imaging animals and human sexual symbols on a
wall, and possibly also of tallying up a count of moons by scratching
"numbers" on a bone, for purposes from which we have no way of
divorcing the legal, the "religious," or the "mythical."

Scripta manent. The cave paintings do remain, and they are writing
at least in that sense. If there is arguably no stage of human culture
since the Paleolithic in which writing did not exist, then one of the
exchange-systems in any conceivable society would be the special assignment of some linguistic communications to a preserving code. Writing,
too, would be defined in its societal context as an exchange. And any
exchange, as Mauss has taught us, can be defined in a society only by
defining all the institutions of the society. Writing is always in the
picture.

At the point where a society would allow anything whatever—rather
than, say, just laws or records—to be transmitted in writing, the society
becomes self-conscious about its institutions. In this ethnological sense,
without reference to the particular psychological conditions under which
writing is apprehended, the birth of "sociological" literacy is the birth
of philosophy. Neolithic questions about the nature of fire and the sun
are quickly replaced, before Socrates, by the questions of epistemology
and ontology in which man becomes the measure of all things (whatever
that phrase of Protagoras' may specifically mean).

The self-consciousness that breaks the dominance of the cyclic in time
and the tribal in space also seeks to redefine—to incorporate or scrap
but in any case to retransmute—the tales into which the cyclic in time
and the tribal in space were both hypostasized and coded. Language
begins to perform a new function in its inseparable relation to myth.
There may have been series of "chthonic revivals" in Greece before the
one in the sixth century B.C., when we suddenly see special attention
given to chthonic deities over Olympian ones, but we know about that
wave of revivals because it was subjected to a kind of linguistic examination which has preserved it for us. It is the *post*-Homeric Pindar who
defines poetry in its function of preserving the tales of the heroes,
sometimes with an unfair slant, as Pindar (*Nemean* 7) charges against
Homer.

Cox follows Gogarten in reading the Pentateuch itself as a de-mythologizing in its humanization and abstraction of the Old Testament Jehovah. In Greece, too, humanization and abstraction tend to go together, though differently. There, too, de-mythologizing and the redefinition of myth are performed at about the same time in history, and sometimes by the same writer.

Language is haunted by myth, and the act of defining myth is an act of something like exorcism. To define myth and to invoke its power require a strategy that calls for more than the vast and algorithmic circular definitions of Lévi-Strauss, whereby the myth simply reflects both the underlying thought-processes and the institutions and procedures of the society. In a further strategy the dynamic of interaction between language and myth should be examined without either separating them or fusing them unduly. It is the aim of this book to move toward such a strategy.

PART ONE
THE SOCIAL CONTEXT

1.

LÉVI-STRAUSS, MYTH,
AND THE NEOLITHIC
REVOLUTION

*Mental processes are queer. (It is as if one said: "The clock
tells us the time. What time is, is not yet settled. And as for
what one tells the time* for—*that doesn't come in here.")*

*Ask yourself: Would it be imaginable for someone to learn
to do sums in his head without ever doing written or oral ones?
—"Learning it" will mean: being able to do it. Only the question arises, what will count as a criterion for being able to do
it?—But is it also possible for some tribe to know only of calculation in the head, and of no other kind? Here one has to ask
oneself: "What will that be like?"—And so one will have to
depict it as a limiting case. And the question will then arise
whether we are still willing to use the concept of 'calculating in
the head' here—or whether in such circumstances it has lost
its purpose, because the phenomena gravitate towards another
paradigm.*
  —LUDWIG WITTGENSTEIN,
   Philosophical Investigations

1.

PHILOSOPHERS like Hegel and Schelling devised world-constructs, explanatory systems that were intended to hold generally for psychological
processes, social organization, historical successions, as well as for questions about epistemology and ontology. This all-embracing aim may
still be traced in the explanatory procedures of such semi-empirical
thinkers as Marx and Freud. It may even be seen in the enterprise of
later philosophers, who turn to the roots of verbal behavior for explanation. Wittgenstein does so by asking questions about what happens
before the fact of the word. Heidegger locates his inquiry in the task of
spelling out the implications of verbal usage after the fact. And it may
be said that Derrida tries to combine these two procedures by deriving
an epistemology from the conditions for using and transcribing verbal
utterances. All these philosophers, in their various ways, address myth

and questions about myth, at least by implication; and usually they do so explicitly.

In a sense the anthropologist has taken this lead and engaged himself in the old enterprise of providing a world-construct. Instead of doing so directly, however, the anthropologist asks what principles of organization underlie some alien culture, a culture in some ways radically incapacitated for asking this question about itself. The subject of world-construct has thus found a new home by distancing or disguising itself as the Other. It is Tylor or Radcliffe-Brown, Mauss or Malinowski, Lévy-Bruhl or Lévi-Strauss, who provide generalizing classifications or organizing principles for a society other than their own.

In the home culture of the anthropologist, to be sure, there are survivals, practices that resemble those of the alien, more primitive culture. There must be survivals, since the whole anthropological enterprise finds its justification in the analogy or homology between Us and Other. But the Herodotean process of comparing Us and Other, Greek and non-Greek, is not carried through much more systematically than it was by Herodotus. And so all the comparison between Us and Other is kept in the form of something like an enthymeme, a logical proof in which one premise remains unexpressed.

Such an enthymematic presentation of the likeness between Us and Other still, in its very form, leaves unexamined, or insufficiently examined, what the differences between the two cultures in question may amount to. And in not assessing how far or in what respects the likeness holds, the anthropologist is finally not in a position to assess it any more than he can assess the differences. In particular, he may assume too quickly that the function of myth remains fixed for both cultures in its relation to language and other central features of a society. He may assume that myth is either simply present or simply absent.[1]

Lévi-Strauss throws into relief both the difference between our own thought processes and the primitive's, and the fundamental likeness between them. He does this by choosing as the object of his investigation a society where the "divergence" (that is, the difference) from his own society will be the most "marked" (*accusé*) by the rules of his (different) method, and will thus reveal a system (*réseau*) of basic and universal laws (*contraintes*) (RC; p. 11). This "supreme gymnastics" of seeking likeness by applying difference finds the likeness as a kind of deep structure under a surface structure of different social facts. Lévi-Strauss's procedure, however, locks likeness from difference as form from content, and fixes him in a series of discontinuities. Therein an adequate account of the interaction of myth with language is radically attenuated in the very process of elaborating the structures of a mythic system by itself.

The realm of myth, finally, like the realms of art and religion, does not lend itself easily to the subject-object distinction on which Lévi-Strauss insists to justify mythology as his object (HN, p. 563), because the sign-systems in those realms attempt, by their very coherence and economy, to provide a means for bypassing that distinction. As Adorno says, "The subjectifying and the objectification of music are the same" (1958, p. 145).

2.

In *Structural Anthropology* Lévi-Strauss systematized Radcliffe-Brown's analysis of kinship classes. He proposed that a ratio of relationships among kin, rather than the relationships themselves, could serve as a formula that would order any known set of kinship rules: "The relation between maternal uncle and nephew is to the relation between brother and sister as the relation between father and son is to that between husband and wife" (p. 40). In that same work and elsewhere he defined totemic systems as modes of classification: a totemic system serves to mediate one or more ways of relating the general to the particular. The *Mythologiques* subsume both these procedures, that of ratios and that of classificatory modes, showing how myths include and deploy kinship and totemic systems, along with much else. Much earlier he had presented the Oedipus myth as providing a ratio to account for and contain an instability, "to find a satisfactory transition between this theory (mankind's autochthonous origin) and the knowledge that human beings are actually born from the union of man and woman. Although the problem obviously cannot be solved, the Oedipus myth provides a kind of logical tool which relates the original problem: born from different or born from same? By a correlation of this type, the overrating of blood relations is to the underrating of blood relations as the attempt to escape autochthony is to the impossibility to succeed in it" (L-S 1, p. 212).

In the *Mythologiques* likeness and difference, or homology and contrast, between individual items (mythemes) of a mythic story generate the binary oppositions that permit the ordering of elements in nature

and culture, while at the same time revealing the rigor of the ordering
principle. Thus the opposition between earth and sky is mediated by
water (belonging to the earth) and by the fire of the sky, brought to
earth in cooking fire. Water is the inversion of fire in the South American mythic systems with which he begins, but also, *homologously*,
through all the transformations in the mythologies of the tribes of the
Great Plains and the Pacific Northwest. Water is the opposite of fire
because water produces raw vegetable food and the fire cooks animal
food (either by *boiling* in *water* or by roasting directly, the former raising a possible confusion with the *rotten* as an intermediate natural term
between the natural raw and the cultural cooked). Each contains in
itself the binary opposition of a creative side and a destructive side.
Water is the realm of the dead in the Bororo myths, and a place where
one drowns or gets inundated as well as where fish and plants are
produced. The cooking fire mimics the approach of the celestial fire to
earth, but then (RC, p. 289 and *passim*) this implies the danger of
universal conflagration: "Thus closes a vast system, the invariant elements of which can always be represented in the form of a combat
between earth and sky for the conquest of fire" (HN, p. 535). While
Lévi-Strauss scrupulously limits himself to his American terrain, his
analyses permit and even encourage extrapolation to myths from other
terrains. Here, then, is an explanation for the resonance of a Prometheus
myth in any culture. The fire-stealer also brought to men an ignorance
of when they would die (an inversion of knowing that one is mortal)
and paid a penalty for providing cooking fire by having his liver eaten
raw.

Mediating terms are the operators of the combinatory process. As
both fire and water mediate between earth and sky, so the zoologic
order mediates between the cosmic and the social (RC, p. 327). The
mediating term, say the act of cooking, does not disappear, though it is
sometimes suppressed, as the wife of the jaguar (RC, p. 83) is necessarily suppressed after having served between man who used the raw
and the jaguar who knew the cooked. The new term could be taken as
the locus of a whole system; marriage, a union of earth and sky in
miniature (RC, pp. 328–29), produces a birth. Birth, in turn, itself
serves as a new mediating term in this ongoing dialectic. The five senses
are five interrelated codes, where taste, in its rapport with the alimentary
mediation of nature and culture, holds a privileged position (RC, p.
164). The binary contrasts, mediated, allow for transpositions from set

to set, "from noise-making (*vacarme*) to eclipses, from eclipses to incest, from incest to unruliness (*désorde*), and from unruliness to the colored plumage (*la couleur*) of birds" (RC, p. 312). This process serves to "bear witness to the fact that there is an isomorphic relation between two types of order, which may be either the cosmic order and the cultural order; the cosmic or meteorological order and the social order; or one or other of the orders above and the zoological order, which is situated on an intermediate level in relation to them" (RC, p. 316).

Moreover, the armature of an entire system including paired terms is convertible, at a further, second level of abstraction, into the armature, point for point, of another. The system (S_1) whose axis is the cooking fire (uniting sky and earth) can be transformed into a system (S_2) on the axis of meat, his diagrammed analysis of myths about the origin of obtaining meat as food. This system offers paired oppositions where the role of edible pigs in one myth corresponds to the role of bird plumage in another on the axis of ornaments (S_{-2}), whose own inverse is the system aligned upon honey (S_{-3}) (HA; pp. 29–32). Fire in the myths about meat is a means; in the myths about tobacco fire is an end, organized on another axis (S_3). A parallel opposition is found in the myths and ceremonies surrounding honey (S_{-3}), set systematically into relation with bird plumage and also with game, whose supply the honey ceremonies are supposed to ensure (HA, pp. 29–32).

And at still another, third level, the whole series of myths encompassing the "second-level" systems, the Bird-Nester (*Dénicheur des Oiseaux*) series of Brazil, the Canadian Star-Husband series, and the Plains Star-Husband series, form a vast closed system, transformable, through the deformations (HN, pp. 528–31) they evidence, each into the other ("*Le Mythe Unique*," HN, pp. 502–58). "A group of myths constitutes in itself a code, one of a power superior to each of those it utilizes . . . a veritable intercode" (HN, p. 38). Thus (Lévi-Strauss says in partial refutation of Max Müller) "the myth does not admit of reduction by any single code taken by itself, nor does it result from the addition of several."

The procedure of analyzing the sacred, from James' *Varieties of Religious Experience* through Durkheim, Mauss, and Malinowski, is carried by Lévi-Strauss to the point of absence or neutralized immanence.[2] He maps the whole perceptual universe of myth as an unconscious science not different as a primitive theory from Frazer's sympathetic and imitative magic, though far more powerful in the manifold calculus of its applicability. Lévi-Strauss's system provides the relational calculus among items in a myth's story. However, in his system we lack —he would say we must lack—a specific meaning for, or even a flexible relation between, the elements of a story and the sense of mystery that accompanies the sacred. No meaning is offered, for example, to explain the metamorphoses in which the myths abound. Now a metamorphosis is an awesome thing. This sense of mystery that arises when the boundary between animal and human is in some way crossed is still exploited in the considerable literature of metamorphosis (Massey 1). When Maba (Honey), the wife of M_{233}, changes into a bee, Lévi-Strauss charts algorithms which may link marital exchanges to the gathering of a complex natural product; but he does not offer a reason why the myths so consistently choose transformations between the animal kingdom and the human as a means of expressing this food-gathering notion. Whatever reticulations of significance may be activated between the wife and the bee, there is a radical discontinuity between the two, definable in terms of the different human existence in and awareness of time, as well as between nature and culture, as this difference touches on the sacred. Lévi-Strauss takes Kroeber to task (HN, p. 95) for assuming that myths reflect ethnographic reality, rather than dialectical relations that "often violate that reality," but his own demonstrations of dialectical relations themselves become a simple delineation of an ethnographic reality whose functional circularity is offered as a proof of its all-inclusiveness, at least within a given culture. Still, the bearing towards time and death is not simply either parallel to or derivable from attitudes towards nurture and kinship and astronomical phenomena, but rather—this is only the conventional view, which must be accorded its weight—the other way around. Lévi-Strauss is moving onto a terrain where the distinction between functionalism and structuralism is reciprocally definable; yet the opposition between diachrony and synchrony must finally yield before the preeminence of time in any human existence, and myths are framed to address the riddle of mortality.

It is not, as Hartman says (1, pp. 19–20) that Lévi-Strauss fails to deal with repetition, but rather that he reduces repetition to mere recursion.[3] All the psychological force inherent in repetition is lost, all that makes repetition so important to Freud and Lacan. The force of striving in myths is lost too, and the succession of generations becomes just a formulable demographic balance (HN, p. 244).

Thus, the tribal groups among whom myth is alive are deprived of their history (which, given the ahistorical nature of nonliterate, "cold" societies, would be difficult to retrieve in any case). And they are also deprived of any equivalent for history, by having their myths translated into an atemporal dialectic, reducing analogies between their functions and our religion or art to spatial ones (the analogy between the zones of a city and the interlocking sections of a tribal hut pattern) or simply functional ones (the use of noisemaking at certain seasons or as a protest against a mating incongruous with social rule).

In Van Gennep's own discussion—it is from his compendium (2) that the last practice is illustrated—the *rites de passage* take place on thresholds, spirit-haunted loci where space and time converge in a moment that is unique for the individual undergoing the rite even if periodic in the society. It does not bear on this question to say of an abstract model of such a process that consciousness or unconsciousness does not affect the nature of the model (L-S 1, p. 273).

Literate societies, with the self-consciousness towards the nonrecursive aspect of time that written records spanning past rememberable generations may develop, produce a literature with a "tradition" that can change its frames of reference as well as its formulas. In any society each poem is ultimately fixed in time, and correspondingly the order of words is fixed in it. This can happen even in an "oral" society: the Ṛgveda is handed down orally in a fixed state. The necessarily temporal character of language is invariant with respect to means, having a fixed order in a given poem (even if the poem was composed by a process wholly or partly improvisatory), but variant with respect to end. In preliterate societies, on the other hand, in the myths or in poems with unchanging frames and formulas, the single nonrecursive destiny of a given man is unself-consciously doubled by a recursive conception of time. Myth in a tribal society performs some of the functions later assigned to written literature; but myth, too, must be recounted in language, where the temporal character of the language cannot be abrogated; it *does* matter what order the events of a myth are told in. It is not just that Lévi-Strauss redefines the syntagm of temporal order as a paradigm of logical relations, but rather that the linguistic formulation of myth, variable as it is spoken now one way and now another, is variant with respect to means but invariant with respect to end: the myth, as Lévi-Strauss abundantly demonstrates, can only obscure one of its elements and leave a "gap" in the story that one may fill out elsewhere in the "field" of the mythic system.

Lévi-Strauss's insistence on the preeminence of the mythic paradigm has its counterpart and converse in the theory of Propp (p. 20), who takes the presence of story "functions" (roughly equivalent to Lévi-Strauss's "mythemes") to constitute an underlying morphology in which "the sequence of functions is always identical." Propp outlines a supposedly invariant sequence in the Russian fairy tale of thirty-one steps. But when it turns out that a single function can have a double or treble meaning, that no tale perfectly preserves the order, that any function may be omitted (p. 64); that, further, the functions may even "switch positions" (p. 97); then the supposedly invariant time-order becomes quite variant, and the argument must be reduced to the weak form of identifying type-clusters in stories, the sequence amounting to not much more than that a hero must leave home before he returns, and that if he is tested by a villain his trials may involve trickery but will certainly happen between these two events, and before his efforts are crowned by marrying the princess.[4]

Such analyses as Lévi-Strauss offers would not, then, make his relational operations a substructure; rather they would be a tested series of relational constructs whose object would have disappeared, as the myths themselves cannot. His recourse to a sort of graph where the "decades" are given either cardinal or fractional reading according to position happens exactly to reproduce the Pythagorean triangle (the tetroktys) or one version of it ("*La Balance Egale*," OMT, esp. pp. 289–91). In centralizing ratios he may anyway be said to be Pythagoreanizing Cassirer, and there is a sort of residual Pythagoreanism in the uneasy mystique with which he introduces the musical analogies and title-groupings that order the text of the entire first volume in the *Mythologiques*.

The giant advance he furnishes in our power to analyze myths has been made, for the time being, at the cost of obscuring and ignoring questions that should be asked about the sacred or mana or the numinous. Of course Lévi-Strauss has maintained, in his critique of Jung (L-S 8, p. xxxii), that such questions would frustrate his relational analyses by an attention to semantic questions. The analogy with linguistics is meant to hold here; Saussure would have been similarly frustrated in his linguistic theory if he had not bypassed the priority of semantic questions.

Now, in linguistics the phonological, lexical, and syntactic components can be discussed separately. But in a myth there is no point when an item, a name, or a mytheme, does not carry both lexical and syntactic content, as Lévi-Strauss himself on occasion asserts. "Apollo" signifies many things and embodies (the syntax of) many stories.

Thus, the achievement of the *Mythologiques* leaves us not only with the question of how all this deep-thought correlation underlying myths bears upon the sacred; even more important, we would have to ask how Lévi-Strauss's algorithms of mediation among mythemes accord with the generation of such binary, or ternary systems in the accounts given of the sacred by prior cultures. And we would have to explain, as well, the tendency in such cultures to intensify key terms. Even in the economic relations of the Polynesian society that Marcel Mauss analyzes, the *hau*, or spirit, clings to the goods passed along an exchange network. And if all systems in a society are interrelated, then the *hau* would be present or relatable to any item—and consequently to any mytheme. Indeed, Sahlins (p. 1011) goes further than Mauss, as against him and implicitly also Lévi-Strauss, to demonstrate the non-distinguishability for the Maori of spiritual and material in the *hau*.

The jaguar of the *Mythologiques* is just such an intensified key term, explained by systems of relations (S_2 and S_3 of HA, pp. 37–42). The jaguar functions globally by both a likeness to, and a difference from, man. Both likeness and difference are bound up together in a single figure whose numinous presence is guaranteed by what amounts to his figurative supersession of the law of contraries, though Lévi-Strauss analyzes the stories in ways that make it seem as though a thought process is actively factoring out all contradictions. The jaguar also gathers his functions comprehensively into himself, of relating implicitly to all the categories of the South American systems (as of course any figure could be made to do by relational analysis), since he eats raw meat, teaches the cooking of meat (M_{12}), gathers wild honey (M_{188}), and has tobacco coming from his body. The ara-birds eaten by the jaguar (M_{7-12}) are changed into serpents eaten by a divinity (M_{300a}, M_{303}), a divinity who may himself be a form of the jaguar, in what Lévi-Strauss speaks of as possibly the older Aztec level of the myth. The jaguar generates fear (as in M_{14}, RC, pp. 82–83), and the recounted myths are full of fear, flight, danger, impulsive marriages, risks, deaths, and transformations—at once connecting and disconnecting the intensifying terms—of woman into frog or bear or buffalo, of man into bird or porcupine. The trickster figure of North American mythology—who is an allomorph of the jaguar—does not just serve as a mediator, his function in Lévi-Strauss's structural analysis; he also preserves the ambivalence between terms. And, concordantly, he acts the beneficent demiurge, by bearing the quasi-moral onus of a name, Coyote or whatever, that points up not just a successful transfer between categories but the thorny impossibility of carrying a transfer through cleanly.

"The false antinomy between logical and prelogical mentality . . . once dispelled, it remains no less true that, contrary to Lévy-Bruhl's opinion, [its] thought [that of the savage mind] proceeds through understanding, not by confusion and participation" (L-S 3, p. 268). Thus Lévi-Strauss dismisses one false antinomy (in the process, however, dangerously collapsing the dialectic between the likeness of primitive thought to our own and the difference) only to replace it with another. Affectivity, and indeed spirituality, does enter into the *classification* systems; for "confusion and participation," the "distinctions and oppositions" of early societies, spiritual or affective elements often intrinsically constitute what is classified. The Yin and Yang of the Chinese function as such comprehensive systems of classification. So do the Muntu ("human being"), Kuntu ("modality"), Kinto ("thing"), and Hantu ("place and time") of the Yoruba (Jahn, p. 100 and *passim*) and the even more comprehensive terms Ntu and Nommo. The cosmic opposition between good and evil, or creation and destruction, is incorporated, sometimes ambivalently, in the Indian Brahma, Shiva, and Vishnu; in Iranian mythology, and in early Chinese mythology. The Urubu divide their universe into "hard" and "soft," thus categorizing discourse, conduct, kinds of life, and aspects of the world. Overriding categories for the Navajo are round and linear. The connection between the disposition of the body and spiritual states in *yoga* (the term itself indicates "conjunction") goes back to the earliest recoverable state of Indian thought, to the third millennium B.C. (W. Norman Brown in Kramer, pp. 304–305). *Mudra*, the conventionalized hand gestures, "are among the oldest known religious phenomena in India."[5]

Lévi-Strauss does attempt to account for such phenomena in his discussions of magic, religion, and sorcery.

> In contrast with scientific explanation, the problem here is not to attribute confused and disorganized states, emotions, or representations to an objective cause, but rather to articulate them into a whole or system. The system is valid precisely to the extent that it allows us to understand the intellectual condition of man, in which the universe is never charged with sufficient meaning and in which the mind always has more meanings available than there are ob-

> jects to which to relate them. Torn between these two systems of
> reference—the signifying and the signified—man asks magical
> thinking to provide him with a new system of reference . . . but we
> know that this system is built at the expense of the progress of
> knowledge, which would have required us to retain only one of the
> two previous systems (L-S 1, pp. 176–78).

Shuttling, as ever, between the likeness and difference of the logical to
the prelogical, Lévi-Strauss allows at once too much and not enough
to the classification of spiritual elements: too much, because the mere
logical relations are given a comprehensiveness of reference they cannot
attain to if their referents are re-translated into terms of exchange; not
enough, because it is the spiritual elements, after all, precisely as systems
of understanding, that they are classifying.

Lévi-Strauss, for what would seem to be quite arbitrary reasons (unless it is simply a deep-rooted assumption that the spiritual element in
myths must be eliminated as a continuation of Frazer's implied attack
on Christianity), pulls up short whenever there is an opportunity to
apply his combinatory systems to the spiritual element that is demonstrably a main constituent of myths, inseparable and finally untranslat-
able. Instead he asserts—in the last analysis, quite categorically—that
the preparation and gathering of food, as these activities are resumed
in the exchange-system of the market whereby a homogeneity of diet is
diversified, dominate every aspect of the myth: "cosmic, meteorological,
zoological, botanical, technical, economic, sexual, social, etc." (HN, p.
287). Only in passing does he concede that drinking water and the
cooking fire stand outside this defining system and that the market itself,
the locus of Mauss's principle of the centrality of exchange-systems to
a society (HN, pp. 245–64), acts as a "reducing mirror" (HN, p. 265).
Through all this analysis and qualification, water and fire, even when
they are extended into the heavens, remain confined to their function
of furthering or restricting nurture. For Lévi-Strauss, neither the Flood
nor a Conflagration, whether apocalyptic or perpetual, would be anything but a mask for these processes.

Yet man does not live by bread alone. The miracles of multiplying
bread in the New Testament deal wholly with nurture, yet must be defined in their sign-system (quite apart from whether they are true or
false) by categories other than nurture. An analysis of this spiritual
element in the New Testament would, of course, have to deal with this
asserted transcendence directly. In such an analysis, the elements of

myth subsumed in the account of Christ's life would have to be analyzed without final reference to nurture or exchange. In effect, the text of the New Testament tells us this quite directly, offering an overriding (and binary) opposition between the nurture which is perishable and that which is not: "Labor not for the meat which perisheth, but for that meat which endureth unto everlasting life, which the Son of man shall give unto you: for him hath God the Father sealed" (John 6:27).

This passage follows on a distinction between the act of eating and the act of observing "signs" (*semeia*, John 6:26; rendered as "miracles" in the King James Version). The verb *sphragizo* closes the circle of this allegation, since it is itself a sign. "Seal" (*sphragizo*) includes within itself a whole structurable repertoire of senses from pre-Christian uses, going back at least as far as the Babylonian Third Millennium, when seals were already common, indicating by their use: property, authority, relation to god, kingship, proper linguistic designation, and plenipotentiary legitimation (Kittel, vol. 7, pp. 939–54 sub voc.), while the physical seal itself indicates "an object with a sign, picture, letter, word, or combination of these elements." It also serves linguistically as a nonce-hieroglyphic.

The seal was later used in pre-Christian practice to close off objects or mark them as secret or holy or precious or valuable. In both the Old and the New Testaments the seal serves as a designation for circumcision, with all that rite's constellation of anthropological signification. And it was used, too, for the sealing of graves.

No one of these significations or uses is irrelevant to the New Testament verse quoted above. This verse is itself assumed and redeployed in the seven seals of Revelations. In Austin Farrer's reading of the latter, a series of relational transformations logically equivalent to those offered by the *Mythologiques* takes priority over, and neutralizes, the ascription of particular readings to the mythemes of Revelations, such as the number 666 or the four horsemen, around which generations of interpreters have ramified confusions. Farrer notably both anticipates and transcends the *Mythologiques*: in Farrer's interpretation, as distinct from the practice of Lévi-Strauss, the images themselves, while relational, are neither neutralized nor reduced to their material equivalents: they are a syntax as well as a paradigm: "In a long concatenation of images, each fixes the sense of the others, and is itself determined by them" (p. 18). Thus they do not disappear into their paradigmatic function, as the jaguar of Lévi-Strauss tends to do.

3.

Lévi-Strauss's jaguar shuttles back and forth between technological-nurtural significance and a merely relational or mediatory function. A central weakness in Lévi-Strauss's analysis is that he assigns a zero significance of "saturation" to the plurisignificant terms that, for reasons discussed by Cassirer, tend to occur in the very accounts of myth he addresses. For him a term like *mana* is only a sort of smoke-screen permitting the cybernetic function, the symbolic function as he calls it, to proceed uninterrupted.[6] "In the system of symbols that every cosmology constitutes, it [mana] would be simply a *zero symbolic value*" (L-S 9, p. 1, italics Lévi-Strauss's). In this drive to disambiguation, Lévi-Strauss thus leaves aside a fundamental attribute of the terms he handles, thereby parting company with the information theory he draws upon. If put through the entropy and redundancy formulas of information theory, terms like *mana* would still offer enough content to contain a message. And, in fact, it is an inescapable ethnological datum that they do contain a message in their social context, indicating, if nothing else, the presence of the sacred.

Nor does it follow, as Lévi-Strauss asserts in his critique of Jung (L-S 8, p. xxxii), that to invest a store of such archetypal symbols with significance precludes understanding or performing Lévi-Strauss's rational transformations. This is the crux of the issue between Lévi-Strauss and his predecessors. He feels not only that the algebraic power of his combinatory operations will supplant other explanations, but that the items entering into combination are, in effect, thereby voided of separable content. Actually, Jung could have failed—like almost everybody else! —to see the cybernetic function of the unconscious, and it would still be at least logically possible to read Jung's significations into the terms. Lévi-Strauss insists, rightly, that the terms, the mythemes, must constantly be seen in relation to one another. But, it is still the case that their "charge" must be preserved, if we are to see the proportional force of those relations in the light of their actual significance; if their syntax, ultimately, is to carry the full sense they "intend."

Lévi-Strauss's initial analogy for his "linguistic" procedures is the Jakobson-Troubetskoi system of phonetic contrast in natural language. Now, this system applies predominantly to lexical elements, whereas myth is predominantly syntactic. And, it is revealing that Lévi-Strauss overdefines their system as "precisely permitting the definition of a language by a small number of constant relations" (L-S 8, p. xxxv), whereas in fact the system does not permit the definition of a language at all, but only a schematic description of its *phonological* component.

In ordinary language, once the contrastive value of a *phonetic* component is activated, it becomes *phonemic*: the raw sound is *combined* with another raw sound and thereby invested with sense. Before the fact, this assignment is arbitrary. After the fact, once it has entered into combination, it is fixed. The function of the contrast between voiced and silent terminal dental in *led* and *let* is fixed, and constant, and (most important) not susceptible of further combination as involving this pair; the contrast is single.

Now a mytheme is already invested with sense, as Lévi-Strauss himself says (L-S 1): it never floats neutrally the way raw, unassigned phonetic sound does, though Lévi-Strauss's concentration on its relational combinations makes it seem to do so. Indeed, a mytheme would have to be invested with sense—to be already a sort of charged constant —to enter into so many series of permutations, something that also cannot happen to a contrastive phoneme, which is absolutely free before being assigned a function and absolutely fixed to just that one function afterwards.

Having rendered the sense of a mytheme as its relational function, he can then permit the interchangeability of signifier and signified in myth (HA, p. 421). The sense itself is left floating in a sort of limbo. The two functions, of mirroring the structure of the society's culture and of mediating the technological and astronomical practices by which it controls nature, never come into the trans-societal signification at which, within the cultures, they are "intentionally" aimed. Yet in a full linguistic account the mythic terms must be accorded "the sacred" linguistically, independently of whether or not credence is assigned to it. In the process Lévi-Strauss spells out, the syntax of myth must always at best be underdetermined in its structural translation.

Myth is linked to language more complexly than a simple initial contrast can account for; the link is not a void (HN, p. 579). Myth must always be coded into language or into some communicative system of iconic cues. We have no other way of knowing about it. And this is the crucial difference between myths and Lévi-Strauss's cybernetic equivalent for a Freudian or Jungian unconscious. It is confusing, and a kind of exaggeration, to say that syntagmatic chains in myth "contain no definite meaning" (RC, p. 307) and are only accorded sense when a paradigmatic ensemble is imposed thereupon, linking them to other syntagms in other myths. To reveal relational substructures is not to cancel the initial syntactic structure of temporal presentation, inescapably primary.

Lévi-Strauss sets himself the goal of "transcending the contrast (*l'opposition*) between the tangible (*sensible*) and the intelligible by operating from the outset at the sign level" (RC, p. 14), "where logical properties, as attributes of things, will be manifested as directly as flavors or perfumes." By so doing, he would have his lexical-relational constructs, in effect, cancel out their own mediation. Drawing on the process from the "arbitrary character of linguistic signs" to their relative "motivation" (the marking of a word by morphemic combination, *in* plus *amicus* giving *inimicus*), he characterizes his own abstractive procedure—the context is that of primitive numbering and categorization, but it also applies to his analyses of myth—as the simple reverse (L-S 3, pp. 156–57). "For Saussure, therefore, language moves from arbitrariness to motivation. The systems we have been considering so far on the other hand go from motivation to arbitrariness." But the sign, in myth or any other linguistic construct, does not lose its "motivation" by being set into the "arbitrariness" of combinatory patterns. There is at no point a state of myth like the "noise" or "chaos" of possible, undifferentiated phones.

Nor does all sense really escape from his lexemes through the levels of systemic combination; throughout the *Mythologiques* the lexemes do in fact stubbornly retain the Frazeresque function of putting the seasonal world into perceptible order so that agriculture, food-gathering, and hunting can proceed in successful patterns.

A total transfer would be necessary for such a lexical system to come into being, and Lévi-Strauss's astonishing inference is that such would have had to have taken place. His creation *ex nihilo* is none other than language: in the beginning was the word; "language could only have been born at a stroke . . . the whole Universe, at one stroke, became *significative*" (L-S 8, p. xlii, italics and capitalization Lévi-Strauss's).[7]

His mythic system thus is seen as a floating linguistic function, one that lacks fixed significant content for its lexemes while it contains a whole systemic set for modes of connecting nature and culture in a society. Such a system is at once pre- and post-linguistic. Its likeness to, and its difference from, natural language are kept in a state of irresolution by systematically excluding a consideration of its interactions with natural language. Lévi-Strauss bypasses the whole fundamental question of the linguistic substructure of plurisignificance and the sequent mode of its linguistic presentation, by a vague reference to "subject matter" (*contenu*): "I propose to give the name *armature* to a combination of properties that remain invariant in two or several myths: *code* to the pattern of functions ascribed by each myth to these properties; and *message* to the subject matter of an individual myth. . . . I can define the relation between the Bororo myth (M_1) and the Sherente myth (M_{12}) by stating that when we move from one to the other, the armature remains constant, the code is changed, and the message is reversed" (RC, p. 199). At this point he proceeds to the derivation of some "second-level" transformations between myths, translating them into mathematical equations, a process whose concentrations of abstract properties continue to leave obscured the mode of their interaction with language. He goes on to make the arbitrariness of the *contenu* in the myth explicit: "The truth of the myth does not lie in any special (*privilégié*) content. It consists in logical relations which are devoid of (*dépourvus de*) content or, more precisely, whose invariant properties exhaust their operative value, since comparable relations can be established among the elements of a large number of different contents" (p. 240). And so they can, as he, with remarkable expansiveness, teaches us. But the exhaustiveness of this function in spelling out relations does not render entirely arbitrary the plurisignificance of the contents that are thus shown to be entering into combination.

Oddly enough, Lévi-Strauss distinguishes a third level of linguistic function for myth, above *langue* and *parole*, which operates to free it from those functions rather than to provide the ground for its combining with them:

> . . . *langue* belonging to a reversible time, *parole* being non-reversible. If those two levels already exist in language, then a third one can conceivably be isolated. . . . It is that double structure, altogether (*à la fois*) historical and ahistorical, which explains how myth, while pertaining to the realm of *parole* and calling for an explanation as such, as well as to that of *langue* in which it is expressed. . . . [there] can also be an absolute entity on a third level which, though it remains linguistic by nature, is nevertheless distinct from the other two (L-S 1, pp. 205–206).

How myth may be both "linguistic" and distinct from the constitutive features of language is precisely the question, and we owe thanks to

Lévi-Strauss for having brought us to the point of asking it, however suspended his own answer may be.

Within mythic thought itself, he sees the plurality of systemic levels as the price paid for the passage from the continuous to the discrete (RC, p. 34); though, if we accept his analysis, it is not clear why the plurality of levels between systems is not equivalent to normal concessive or other qualifying conjunctions that indicate the relation between one sentence and another in ordinary discourse. It may well be that metaphor itself rests at least partly on logical relations (RC, p. 339), but it is hard to see how myth "proves" this, even if it exemplifies the process. Nor is it clear why, if mythic systems are to be assigned no credence (HN, p. 571), metaphor can be seen as returning language "to its initial purity," unless Lévi-Strauss is once again shifting back and forth between the likeness of such logical discourse as his own to mythic accounts and their difference. Still, he does not bring to bear on an analysis of the shift between language and myth anything like the discriminatory subtlety which he applies to the myths themselves.

Lévi-Strauss maintains a barrier between conscious thought and unconscious, when a connection between them always obtains in language as elsewhere. On the one hand, he accords equivalent combinatory powers to both conscious and unconscious. On the other hand, he wants to retain the conceptual element of the counters in mythic thought as a blank by virtue of their operation below the level of consciousness: "scientific thought . . . works with concepts . . . mythic thought . . . with significations; and if the concept appears as the operator of the opening of the whole *ensemble*, signification appears as the operator of its reorganization" (OMT, p. 290). And again he has explained, "Images (*l'image*) cannot be ideas (*idée*) but they can play the part of signs or, to be more precise, co-exist with ideas in signs and, if ideas are not yet present, they can keep their future place open for them and make its contours apparent negatively" (L-S 3, pp. 20–21). Here he goes on to characterize as "bricolage" the combination of idea and image in mythic thought, a perpetual Penelope's web where the weaving always changes the figures. Even this fluidity in analysis, which any plurisignificant image may lend itself to, is now and then criticized for the ambivalence of its connections: "this regression of culture towards nature often appeals to procedures of a metalinguistic order: confusion of signifier and signified, or word and thing, of figurative and literal sense, or resemblance and contiguity" (OMT, pp. 62–63).

Plurisignificance, however, must be taken whole to be understood. It must be viewed not as confusion, but as a Gestalt, a matrix of connections that cannot be fully accounted for by being reorganized into binary series. After the analysis has provided all its explanations, the tendency to form a matrix would still not have been explained. And this tendency seems always to characterize myth, whereas a counter tendency towards specification of terms manifests itself in languages. The Egyptian Hathor is such a matrix, the good world cow who equals the sky who also equals: water, the woman Nut, a roof, the bad Eye of Atun, and the Eye of Re. All of this, as Kramer sensibly concludes (p. 21) "proves that the combination of various concepts of the sky was accepted as valid at the very beginning of Egyptian history." The dual god Ometeotl of the Aztecs is both a Master and a Mistress (p. 449), and as Lévi-Strauss quotes the Arawak proverb (OMT, p. 103), "Every thing has its jaguar."

Lévi-Strauss is a sort of anti-Mallarmé. Mallarmé endowed the word *flower* with a generalizing power which "other than the known petals" (*autre que les calices sus*) gave the "absent one of all bouquets" (p. 368). Lévi-Strauss is curiously dizzied by the very same sort of term (which is as central to myth as it is to poetry), "a sense very blurred (*flou*), almost empty. . . . a word like 'flower' or 'stone' designates an infinity of very vague objects, and the word only takes its full sense at the interior of a phrase" (L-S quoted in Charbonnier, p. 101). Here he characteristically, if casually, uses the primacy of syntax to empty diction of its significative function, performing upon ordinary language what he tries to perform upon myth, a concreteness-misplacing disambiguation.

As his procedure now stands, Lévi-Strauss diagrams the structural relations of his mythic "bits" so fully that he deprives himself of the capacity for bringing all of them, in turn, truly into relation with their function in a society's discourse, verbal and non-verbal. By factoring plurisignification into oppositions he posits a saturation point of about ten informational items (five times two) for a term, or series, when in fact many more can on occasion be accommodated.

If myth is "open" like *langue*, in the sense that it admits of further combinations according to its laws (RC, p. 7), still a given area of myth like the Greek or the Pacific Northwest would be a closed system, a formed set or network of lexical relations. The *langue* does not constitute such a set, since its lexical entries can always be differentiated from its syntactic rules, whereas the system of a myth must combine the lexical and the syntactic: the sequence of events attributed by syntactic combination to Apollo is identical with the sum of lexical entries under the word "Apollo." The relation between myth and language can only be worked out by inspecting the continuities between myth and language as well as the discontinuities.

Lévi-Strauss's own vast articulation of these gives us every reason to expect that the articulations between myth and language would not be a simple homology, but rather would contain a complexity no less rich than that which his analyses reveal within a mythic system. The simple nomenclature of rudimentary processes—like *metaphor* and *metonymy* or *symbolic*, *real*, and *imaginary*, even as algebraized by Lacan (HA, pp. 246–49 and *passim*)—cannot serve as a full analytical instrument. We must account for the function of myth within culture in some more comprehensive way than as an object sometimes explicit and sometimes implicit in its relation to ritual (HN, p. 598). This last characterization dismisses with a truism a vast, complex historical and comparative terrain, much as does his classification of science as metonymic and art as metaphoric in its interesting, but not definitive, penchant for miniaturization (L-S 3, pp. 20–29). "Myths travel the same road but start from the other end. They use a structure to produce what is itself an object consisting of a set of events (for all myths tell a story). Art thus proceeds from a set (object plus event) to the *discovery* of its structure. Myth starts from a structure by means of which it *constructs* a set (object plus event)" (p. 26). This circular process of definition is clarifying only so far as it goes. It would not really help to explain how art, and especially literary art, appropriates and transforms myth.

4.

To put myth and language into a relationship which is alike in that it always has those two primary components but different as to the conditions of their relationship would help account for both the likeness and the difference between primitive and modern society. Shamanism, for example, resembles psychoanalysis both functionally (it effects a cure) and structurally (it manages the type-patterns of the unconscious). It differs though, both in the account it gives of the mythic element and in the way the mythic element in the unconscious is managed by the structures of the ego. Establishing such a two-termed relationship between language and myth would provide the ground where the "literary side," the content, of myth could be understood interactively, and also the mythic element in literature. Just such an understanding is lacking in Lévi-Strauss's rather pedestrian collaborative analysis of Baudelaire's *Les Chats*. This analysis ends where it should have begun, with the question of why power resides in the implicit analogy between inanimate and animate, then between the cat and the woman. What kind of hieratic interest is invested in a cat? How does the tangential domestication of awe-tinged power in a modern city differ from the sacralization of such animals in Egypt, often evoked by Baudelaire? Lévi-Strauss is content just to categorize the rhyme-words, and other pairings of words, mostly by grammatical classification. But whole sets of further, more powerful relationships, some of them of the very sort analyzed in the *Mythologiques*, are suggested (and left unmentioned by Jakobson and Lévi-Strauss) in the bald juxtapositions of those very rhyme-words: *austères, saison, maison, sédentaires, volupté, ténèbres, funèbres, fierté, attitudes, solitudes, fin, magiques, mystiques*. Which do we take for granted; the binary grammatical tendency of verse, or the power residing in the implicit predications lying below the surface of its rhyme-junctures? Neither should be taken for granted, but either is obvious without the other; it is their *interaction* we cannot avoid asking about.

It is such interaction that, ultimately, must provide both the grounds for definition and the justified source of attention to both myth and literature.

In the lexicon that Lévi-Strauss provides us for myth itself, where relations are paramount, no modalities are admitted: possibility, contingency, likelihood—to say nothing of Jungian "synchronicity"—which haunt the savages, and radically define us as we lay out our lives, cannot be accounted for. "The sun is new every day," says Heraclitus (Diels 22. B6), echoing old myths of the Near East that have parallels in such other cultures as the Aztec. It is the regularity of the sun, transferred from the contingent to the certain as well as from the discontinuous to the continuous (contingency is not just a form mediating between these two), that makes possible stability and the planning of life. This in turn, we may infer, allowed for the mapping of astronomical and therefore vegetational certainties to bring about "the Neolithic revolution." It is not philosophy in just a quasi-Whorfian sense, or just a classificatory relationship, that determines these messages as well as these codes, when "from Paraguay to the banks of the Amazon, honey and the Pleiades are interconnected both linguistically and philosophically (*dans la langue et dans la philosophie*)" (HA, p. 271).

Ritual, a code of language and gestures, thereby carries a comparable message. Ritual includes thought, as well as running a course between continuous and discontinuous differently from both myth and language (HN, p. 607), both of which it embodies and so also resembles. If laughter is caused by success of symbolic connection and anxiety by failure (HN, p. 609), then symbolic connection itself must carry a message which involves a fixing of probabilities for an outcome of something beyond a statistical analysis. Manners, diets, utensils (OMT, p. 421) may isolate persons and transform signification by suppressing the charge between the poles of ambivalent terms. They may serve as instruments of measure, like the canoe of the South American sun-and-moon myths, which keeps a proportion between separating men and uniting them, a proportion the loss of which would make them impotent or insane. Manners, though, must be defined in a gestural and verbal context of language. They must be coded to gain signification. Signification already resides in the canoe; it has already taken symbolic form. Manners are random; we may use them on given occasion or not; they are "casual." The canoe is always part of the myth system. It is hieratic.

On all these matters the myths themselves often include a metalinguistic commentary. Tests occur in the grail legends, for example, and in the Gilgamesh epic. And tests may be taken as metalinguistic comments, within the myths themselves, on what their events signify. In such myths the knowledge and ignorance of the persons are ultimately inclusive categories. There is a fundamental connection between riddle and incest (Paz, pp. 32–33, following Lévi-Strauss), not only in the cerebral solutions provided for kinship matrices in early societies, but in the questions asked. A myth is the inverse of a riddle, in Jolles's treatment of both myth and riddle as "simple forms" of expression. The Quest is itself a question laid out on a temporal (and also spatial) form. In a society where the Bible is the Book of God and God created the world, there is a tradition that takes physical nature as a text to be deciphered; in this sense the unknown time of the future and the unknown space of a new country would be a thicket of unsolved significations, a Forest of Broceliande, involving *danger*—the Chapel Perilous.

5.

I have moved, of course, into the forms of a society in some senses literate, and therefore into a radically different period of incorporating myth into the linguistic accounts of a society. It is such periodization, however, which implicitly underlies the *Mythologiques* themselves. And the periods ought to be defined as changes in the mode of interrelation between language and myth, rather than simply by a before-and-after or whole-and-part, where beforehand the society wholly explained its existence by myth and was unconscious of the process, while afterward our society, capable of consciousness, preserves mythic gestures as residues. More characteristically, civilized practices are seen as inversions of primitive ones: we should eat silently, where noise while eating is desired in some primitive societies; we think of the world as corrupt and ourselves as pure and drink through straws, the savage conversely seeing himself (OMT, pp. 418–419) as corrupt and the world as pure.

It is possible, indeed, that the same substructure of unconscious mythic transformations underlies our eating habits and our perception of the universe, and that this unconscious structure functions in a way comparable to the function of myth in pre-literate societies. But for such a comparison to be more than casual, for it to hold with the same complexity of correspondence that Lévi-Strauss's analyses hold for North and South American Indian mythology, we should have to subsume all our verbal structures—mathematics, philosophy, legal systems, comic discourse, poetry, grand opera, and of course also the expansive discussions of the anthropologist—into the reticulations of unconscious structures. And this would, very likely, be impossible. Our highly literate uses of myth do admit of such a modality, as Freud knew; and yet taken by themselves the mythic structures are to some degree incidental. They must interact with the ego's instruments, with language and all its mechanisms of sublimation.

The mind, if inescapably binary in its deployment of mythic units, must also inescapably use language to accomplish that deployment, and it uses language in fundamentally different ways at different points in social development.

Literature can only be understood, in its relation to myth, as a product of a comprehensive consciousness that deeply defines and expresses these phases.

By cyberneticizing myths, Lévi-Strauss has stayed, after all, within the assumptions of Cassirer, for whom myth is a symbolic form that resembles the permutations of language and thus both reflects and structures the epistemological process. "The problem of the origin of myth," he rounds out (HN, p. 539), "thus is bound up with (*se confond avec*) that of thought itself, for which the constitutive experience is not that of an opposition between self and other but of the other apprehended as an opposition. If this intrinsic property were lacking— the sole one, in truth, which is absolutely given—no constitutive act of consciousness of the self would be possible. Not being apprehendable (*saisissable*) as a relation (*rapport*), being would be equivalent to nothingness." This last attribution may also be transferred to his own myth analyses, purely relational within their own closed system, but not, for all that, apprehensible in their interactive relations with formulating language. So they stand on the verge of offering only an empty series, or of being open to the assertion that they correspond in no way with reality but merely exhibit a process of thought—of equating being with nothingness.

In Lévi-Strauss's system, language, deprived of its constitutive function for the very subject he is investigating, shrinks to its phatic attribute of courtesy or insult, its function of disjunct naming, on his scale of song-speech-signal (HA, p. 328). Music itself, which serves ambiguously as a rhetorical marker in the organization of *The Raw and the Cooked*, a mid-point as he teaches us between language and myth, loses its full function of structuring the affections significantly when the pole of language is thus weakened. This Principia Mythologica does not offer us a language equivalent to the realm explored by Wagner, but rather an application of language thereto, a functional examination rather than in any sense a homologue. The analogy offered between music and "any language" (RC, p. 24) will not hold because the system of musical language is more simply generated than any natural language. Musical language is exhausted by the significative function of its sequences: it offers only a syntactic axis, and nothing that corresponds to a lexicon (unless the tonal associations of certain instruments and the significations of Greek modes or modern key signatures be taken for a feeble equivalent).

Music suspends, as myth does not, such aspects as the performative, the constative, and the metalinguistic in language by making them equivalent: a piece of music, by exhibiting the bare bones of its structure, is metalinguistic; it designs the mood it manages and evokes; and it carries through the illocutionary intention of evoking the state, which lacks any other content but itself, into which it places the auditor. Music, not because it draws its materials from an arbitrarily selected hierarchy of sounds and is therefore "cultural" in origin, but because of the internal relations of its own syntax, is a sort of dead center between myth and language, sharing and identifying any of the properties of each, but not admitting of the relational extrapolations they demand of us.

Ritual draws music to itself, whether the monodic "molima" of the pygmies or the polyphony of a Bach Cantata. Silence, as the suspension of both music and language, is equally drawn to ritual; it clears the terrain before a *dromenon*. It is this function which is invariant for silence, not the reversible silence or noise before eating but the silence surrounding a noise before eating or cooking (RC, p. 293), the silence before prayer, and also the silence of the auditors at a sung mass. The Orphic initiate, like initiates all over the world, has a silence enjoined upon him; he must keep "an ox on the tongue," (as this phrase of Aeschylus' is sometimes interpreted). Moreover, if all myth has an astronomical correlative, it begs the question to say that the opposition between silence and noise refers in particular to the solar cycle. All of Lévi-Strauss, in this sense, begs the question. The myths are seen in relation to many recursive social processes. He does not see them in the light of what they most fundamentally express, the sacred; nor does he allow for their interactions with what they most intimately utilize, language.

2.

THE LARGE PHASES OF MYTH

1.

AN interaction between myth and language can be postulated for mankind as far back as we have any trace, at least to the Paleolithic. And a change in that interaction may be the crucial factor, overriding the related transition into various kinds of writing, for other changes in human society. The change from hunting and gathering to the earliest agriculture—the Neolithic revolution—may be correlated with, if not confidently derived out of, a change from a goddess-centered unicity of myth to a splitting into periodicities, complete with creation-myths, and all the vast, interlocking binary series of Lévi-Strauss's demonstrations.

In the long history of this development back to the Paleolithic, and in its profound and complex ramifications into all aspects of human existence, it is to pass over the whole question of possible phases to assert (HN, p. 560) that the difference between myth and literature is one not of kind but of degree. Rather, literature constitutes an elaborate repository of achieved techniques for articulating and coordinating in language some of the more advanced stages of the interaction between the human psyche and myth. As has been perceived especially in our own time, but arguably at least since the Renaissance, literature draws intimately on myths and also activates a power for which myth itself constitutes a vocabulary. These attributes go far towards explaining at once the strange directness of the literary effect and the strange indirectness of the literary message as we attempt to decode it hermeneutically from its offered structures of language.

Literature in its various stages offers a repertoire of kinds for the relation between myth and language; there are other kinds, of which ritual is also one. For the survival in imaginative literature of a "primitive" consciousness, as Wayne Shumaker says (p. 54), "the language

37

of literature resembles primitive language not only in being extremely concrete but also in tending to register percepts in *Gestalten*. . . . The writer's eye tends instinctively to see objects in groups or against backgrounds." Olga M. Freidenberg traces an interaction between image and mythic thought at early stages of Greek culture. The long controversy of how far and how fully ritual may be coextensive with myth may itself be rephrased as the question of how the communicative structures of a ritual, the expression and self-expression and collective affirmation residing therein, may be taken as another kind of relation between myth and language. Literature, visual art, the evocative side of music, and ritual, are all linguistic models for structuring a matrix of givens to some degree unknown: the area of myth.

In early society all features of institutionalized life stand in relation to myth: medicine, social classes, age groups, funeral customs, the management of dreams, the determination of decisions. These institutional practices can be related, of course, to systems of exchange and kinship, but the latter cannot be given the special priority ethnographic investigation tends to give them. And literature itself even in the most sophisticated societies oscillates between an explanatory function and a shamanistic one, of which the "pleasure" attributed to it at least since Horace is a sort of debasement, "Poets wish to teach or to give pleasure" (*aut prodesse volunt aut delectare poetae*). Or else "*delectare*" is a term crying out for some such explanation as Freud's of what unknown force may lie behind the giving of pleasure.

In fifty thousand years of interaction between myth and language, there would have to be many overlappings and interfusions. One phase would not disappear soon, if ever; nor would another phase begin abruptly. For these reasons, and also because of our possibly permanent perplexity about the earliest stages of human development, the periods or modes I am about to delineate should be taken not as absolutely differentiated sequences in time, but rather as thought-types (*Gedankentypen*) in Max Weber's sense, abstract structures for the means by which language, or some communicative form, accounts for and orders the unconscious terms of myth. Delineating the large phases of myth may serve to emphasize the implications of a shift from unicity to a cyclic and binary organization. And for the later phases it will help explain the power of ironic attitudes to see them as a motive force for the dialectical handling of myth.

2.

The first such period that we may posit—the most arbitrary and abstract of all because the evidence is so puzzling—would be the unicity of a Mother cult which would include all mythic expressions, statements, and rituals.[1] The earliest representational artifacts we know, and they date back to the Paleolithic, are figures of squat, heavy-breasted females, or semi-abstract ones (Marshak), presumably maternal, presumably divine. These are scattered broadly over Europe and Asia, and date back to a time before the Western Hemisphere is known to have been inhabited.[2] In Europe itself these Venusses of Willendorf undergo many metamorphoses, becoming stylized, with occasionally fused phallic heads, throughout the whole of Europe from Kiev to the Adriatic, as Gimbutas demonstrates. Zuntz finds Persephone figures distributed widely through the Greece of the Bronze Age and earlier; he offers many parallels and amplifications for the figures discussed by Gimbutas. The earliest goddess figures have an even wider distribution, from Siberia to the Bay of Biscay. Such figures later become the Great Mothers of Crete and the Near East, the idols of the Cyclades, the Inanna of the Sumerians, the Ishtar of the Babylonians, all the later Cybele figures, and perhaps also the "Stone Grandmothers" (*kamyennayi babi*) of the steppes.

There are in Greece itself before Homer many traces not only of a Mother cult, but also of one that would suggest the unicity of such a "first period" in the remote past for the interrelation of myth and language. West (1, p. 37) indicates that "the scarcity of husbands" in mythology could be derived from the wide distribution of the Mother cult. One could also derive the scarcity of males from the overriding inclusiveness of such a cult, dispensing with the need for other than the replaceable, anonymous figures whom the later, emasculated priests of Cybele embodied. For Empedocles (B 128, B 130), Aphrodite represents the earliest phase of culture.[3]

In the earliest conceivable form of a Mother-bound unicity between language and its object in myth, the duality and arbitrariness of the phonetic process would not have been translated into a duality and arbitrariness of even a syllabary's correspondence to abstract sounds (assuming that the earliest spiral writing recorded by Gimbutas is not yet this). Homer himself, who fuses the literate and the pre-literate, the

present and the past, and also such abstract "thought-types," may preserve a reminiscence of such a first period in the divination of Calchas,
who interprets a snake (a chthonic being related to the Mother, and not
exclusively phallic) as a separable portent (*teras*) as it creeps out from
under the plane tree by the altars of Aulis (*Iliad* 2.303–332). Calchas'
act of interpretation is pre-oracular, and non-cyclic, a reading of nature
perhaps not different in kind from an early hieroglyphic or even a wall-
painting—though at the end he includes it in the cyclic reckoning of a
time-count, "nine years and a tenth." At an earlier point, in Neolithic
life, it is distinctly possible, and more in line with our evidence than is
the contrary, that the duality and combinatory arbitrariness of myth as
Lévi-Strauss analyzes it had still not been developed so as to enter the
language (or the traceable perception). At the earliest period we have
no male figures clearly identifiable as equal in function to females, and
also no clear mapping in the sex differences perceptible in the cave
animals.[4] Burkert (2, pp. 92–96) would include hunting magic in the
sphere of the "Mistress of the Beasts" (*potnia theron*) as she is earlier
called and perhaps still earlier represented on Minoan and Mycenean
gems. But the patterns of ritual killing that he deduces cannot be associated to any other pattern: it would seem that the very fact, on the
evidence he adduces, that animals were killed ritually in Paleolithic
society at least as early as men would rule out a confident reading of a
sacrifice-syntax at this period, in which animals are a euphemistic substitution for men (Girard). They could be, in history, a reversion mask-
ing as a substitution. And yet no such patterns could be read out.

If animals are included in the sphere of the Mother, however, then
there would be a tinge of the "first period" much later—say in such late
Roman examples as the grouped animals in the hunting scenes, inter-
spersed with erotic scenes, of Imperial mosaics at Piazza Armerina.
Nor would the mystique of the leopard-skin coat in modern times be
wholly attributable to the dominant hunter's proud ownership of his
women, or wholly dissociable from the "Mistress of the Beasts," since
the fur coat is an icon of self-assertion as much as of submissiveness.
The "ethologist's" insistence on spatial territoriality or on ritual fighting,
or even on communicative systems, as explaining the animal nature of
man, may be taken not only as an assertion of scientific verity but as a
reversion in a scientistic spirit to an identification of man and animal,
something to be found in the myth-charged inclusion of animals in human mythic forms, going all the way back to the skin-wearing 'priest'

of Trois Frères. La Fontaine and Lewis Carroll offer sophistications for the mythic handling of animals, but the first phase lingers on, and none of these uses can be wholly dissociated from the animals of Altamira and Lascaux, or even from the dissociation-by-identification of the ethologist, who resembles the Paleolithic hunter in the focussing attention he accords his animals, as well as in his attribution of Paleolithic habits to modern man. But the "rituals" of animals, as Lévi-Strauss demonstrates (HN, p. 610), always differ from those of men in their handling of continuities and discontinuities.

The myths Lévi-Strauss analyzes are those of a second phase, in which a thought process constantly produces discriminations between continuities and discontinuities. In the world dominated by the Mother there are as yet no such dominant periodicities, even if Marshak has shown evidence for some correlation of plant and animal seasons and an awareness of the phases of the moon. Sumerian mythology, which makes so much of a central female figure, also refers to a time when activities dependent upon periodicities, pastoral and agriculture, did not exist, in the "Myth of Cattle and Grain" (Grimal, p. 62). To project a sex system back on the statistical and spatial occurrences of male and female in the cave animals would be to project backwards our own sense of their necessary interaction, in social process and also in mythology. But as Turner points out (p. 16), "the cyclical repetitive view is itself only one among a number of possible processual alternatives." We can be confident, for the first phase of the relation between myth and language, of just one strikingly predominant hieratic figure, the Mother, who is, in Erich Neumann's phrase, at the "origin of consciousness."

This focus—an abstract "thought-type" as always—of all mythology into one dominant myth, and all notational processes into either one-for-one image or one-for-one tallies instead of abstract phonetic constructs, characterizes what is not only the earliest, but also by far the longest, period of interaction between myth and language. We can define this period in terms of negatives—no cycles, no crops, no social classes. (This condition of social equality Diamond finds still in African tribes at the Neolithic level.) In all this there is only one positive: a unitary focus of all charged perception upon one figure, the nurturing female.

To call the Mother "analogous" in some way to the process of the seasons, or even of the generations, is to project upon her the very periodicity which would have been, and did presumably become, the condition for transition to the next stage,[5] the cyclic universe of "oral" cultures, which has provided the central repository of elements for Frazer, Eliade, and Lévi-Strauss, among many others. Analogy is already a two-termed process: it involves congruence between something and something else. The Venusses offer not congruence but centralization. The language that coexisted with such a (hypothetical) unitary perception would be "participative" to an almost uncontrollable degree. The unity of man with beast would be a fearful threat, at a time before the structuring of human society into totemic groups to control the threat and so structure the random acts of hunting and socialization into interrelated periodicities. Nothing in the earlier society could help being related to the central myth (the Mother), and at the same time no terms in the language could find the means for mediating, or performing transformations upon, the myth. General and particular would mirror each other without the categorizations of a "savage mind." The only possible writing would be the pre- or sub-hieroglyphics of cave paintings, the one-by-one tallies of moons scratched on a bone that Marshak has deciphered. To perceive and record the waxing and waning of the moon, or even to associate deer with spring leaves as on some artifacts he analyzes, is still a long way from plotting and calculating annual periodicities.

3.

Such categorizations of the typical and recursive features of nature and culture would require mediations and transformations. With them would come duality, in both language and myth, a duality which would be the most notable and perdurable achievement of the "Neolithic revolution," as distinct from the unicity of a (hypothetical or actual) first period. Whether the transition be hypothetical or actual, Lévi-Strauss has confined his attention to that part of the inhabited world where till recently few physical traces of Paleolithic culture have ever been found,[6] and only an occasional possible survival in tradition, like the parallel between M_{311} and M_{86a} where the "paleolithic common heritage" (HA, p. 378) does involve a female sun god.

Having come across the Bering Strait, all the Indians of North and South America are at once sealed-off originals at a second stage of development, much like the Nambikwara whom Lévi-Strauss idealizes, and a "new" people, incorporating the myths they must presumably have brought with them in the flora and fauna of what, for them too, would have been a new world, adapting or developing forms that would correspond to the Coyote and salmon in the North, the jaguar in the South, the frog in either. Lévi-Strauss's plea for a complicated pre-Columbian history (L-S 2, p. 218) would give the detail of, but not mitigate, the essential lateness and homogeneity of the peoples he studies.

The lateness and the homogeneity of the North and South American Indian groups, all of whom lack a complex Paleolithic development and most of whom did not develop a civilization, as the Mayans and Aztecs did, serve him conveniently to make their phase, and style, of conjunction between myth and language do duty for all.

The transition from the first phase to the second, indeed, may be said to have taken place through the activation of those very mental processes the understanding of which we owe to Lévi-Strauss. Once savage *thought* had codified by coordination and abstraction the periodicities in nature that would permit those techniques of food production and stable habitation usually called Neolithic, it follows both that the mythological constructs would use those processes of comparison and contrast, of coordination and abstraction, and that they would center for their subject matter on the very periodicities which permitted the revolution: on the relations between nurture and the agricultural, astronomical, and animal seasonal sources whose structuring allowed them to be predicted. The form and the content of such a stage in human culture would not only resemble each other—the form being that very mode of operation which would permit the content to be understood— they would also tend to locate the boundary between nature and culture at the very point where such operations of transformation took place. The Western Hemisphere, as a sort of natural laboratory, offers for study a vast array of tribes at roughly the same post-Neolithic but precivilized stage. These savages resemble us in that we, too, are the recent heirs of a technological revolution and may therefore be especially sensitized to the substructure of their stage.

In the second period the dialectical relationship between myth and language has the binary simplicity that Lévi-Strauss implies: the language of myth proceeds in his combinatory patterns, while the thought of myth proceeds almost randomly, but not indifferently, on a time-sequence whose only regularity is periodic, as Eliade among others has defined the time-sense of pre-literate cultures. In the second period the

cyclic predominates not only over perception, and over such codified
behavior as ritual, but also over linguistic accounts. Pre-literate is here
pre-literary although not exclusively "oral" (since what may be identified as a form of writing is already in use) but rather pre-alphabetic
and pre-syllabary.

All that we think of as characteristic of tribal society or an oral stage
is present in this second period for the relation between language and
myth, where binary patterns provide the interaction between the terms.[7]
Not only are social, economic, cosmological, and religious activities interdependent; their interdependence is factored by systems of transform-
ing definition, as Lévi-Strauss has elaborately analyzed them. The recursiveness of seasons and life cycles, à la Frazer, takes a central role in
ordering all human activity and explanation; patterns of reciprocity are
set up among members of the family and various social classes and sub-
groups. Our ethnographic inquiries have tended to center on the description and coordination of these reciprocities, and to undervalue, as a
simple binary opposition of positive or negative poles, the ambivalence
of seeking and shunning which is embodied wherever the sacred appears,
and in the very word *sacer* (holy/cursed) itself. A binary analysis serves
to pattern this ambivalence, but the myth also preserves the ambivalence
undiminished (unfactored) and transfers it into the language, as a term
in the vocabulary. This vocabulary is one of single negations—*arete* or
its lack, *timé* or its lack, *aidos* or its lack. We are at the stage of the
shame culture, of a directness of response unanalyzable by codes, or
even Aeschylean myths, of jurisprudence. And we are also at the stage
of social classes; the king is sacred in himself, and a carrier and guarantee through his ritual death and/or incest/chastity of proper seasonal
recursiveness; the king is the key person for a network of reciprocal
social duties. We have left Diamond's first level of a classless, nomadic
society behind, and entered at least his second level, where a priest-king
centers the tribe, though Diamond's groups of "militaristic federations,"
"extensive primitive democratic nationalities," "conquest proto-states,"
and "aristocratic warrior-oriented pastoralists," all would most likely
exhibit our "second period" characteristics with respect to the handling
of myth by language.

These groupings, successively applicable to specific modern African
tribes in his analysis, are all more or less simultaneously applicable to
the societies pictured in the Homeric poems. His categories, too, are
"thought-types," and a given situation may present a fusion of several

types, as a given statement in language about myth may do for the large-scale phases I am sketching out.

Homer, the very model for Greek society and our own of an early harmonious organization, of an "Olympian" religiosity, functions mainly on the second-phase level of automatic reciprocity. So powerful and persistent a hold did this principle have over men's minds that Plato felt a need to draft laws against it. In this communal society founded on *timé*, *arete*, and *aidos*, the Olympian gods work through a system of checks and balances. The model of the good society is the agriculture of the Neolithic revolution, though (as still in our own society) there remains the ritual hunt, and the Autolycos myth preserves, as Burkert (2) demonstrates, some traces of the ritual uses of wolf and boar. A standard image in Homer for the incursion of violence into a group is the seizure of a domestic animal by a lion, a scene also found often in Mycenean art (Vermeule, 1975). There is, in the *Iliad* at least, a constant and pervasive binary organization traceable from the balance of epithets in a single line to the overall organization of the poem (Whitman).

The cosmos engraved by Hephaistos in gold on the shield of Achilles frames formally, and takes for granted, such an enclosed society, alternating between the "two cities," one of peace and the other of war, as the description of the peaceful city shows, with its cycle of marriages, plowings, and rituals; a circle broken, and then closed, by a blood-price for murder:

> On it he wrought two cities of articulate men,
> Lovely ones. In the first were marriages and festivals.
> Brides from their chambers under glittering torches
> They were leading through the city, and the loud marriage song
>   was rising.
> Young men, dancers, whirled about. And among them
> The flutes and the lyres kept up the din. And the women,
> Each one standing at the door of her court, admired them.
> The people were gathered in the marketplace. There a dispute[8]
> Had arisen, and two men disputed over the blood-price
> For a man who had been killed. . . .
> And he made upon it a soft fallow, a fertile ploughland,
> Broad and thrice-tilled. There were many ploughmen upon it
> Who wheeled their yoke-beasts and drove them this way and
>   that.
> But when they had turned and reached the limit of the field,

Just then would a man come up to them and give them a cup
Of honey-sweet wine, and they would turn back to the furrows,
Pushing on to reach the limit of the deep fallow.
. . . And the king among them in silence
Stood holding his sceptre at the furrow, glad in heart.
Heralds off apart under a tree were dividing up a feast
And preparing a great ox they had sacrificed.
                                   (*Iliad* 18.490–99, 541–47, 556–59)

Homer is so resolutely Olympian, so thoroughly binary in his presentation and reciprocity-minded in his social outlook that it would be possible to urge, as both Rohde and Nilsson do, that his is a special, ideological slant editing out the darker, chthonic survivals. These are to be found not only in the chthonic revivals after his time but in the life he and his contemporaries knew, which he makes a point of not presenting. Such a displacement in favor of an encompassing binary scheme, such a totalizing definition of order and interaction, whether evasively or not, triumphs in having the language handle a new, multiple Olympian scheme of myth. The earlier myth-system—Cimmerians and Circe and the Cyclops, Linos and Demeter and Dodona—is secondary, if powerful, in Homer, however many layers there may be under a given myth, and however long a time-span may cover the events that the poems telescope.

For the second stage to incorporate the unicity of the first, however, would always present a problem: as understanding and formulating the myth always does anyway. The Mother-goddess of the first phase, insofar as she is identified with the caves of Paleolithic home burial, may be identified with the tomb and the womb together. So long as the Mother holds a unicity of dominance over the drift of the hunting culture, the ambivalence of her sacredness is not faced: the terror in the erotic life, of child or adult, still mingles with the delight. But to the binary consciousness, terror and delight remain unstable even when they are coded. With Slater we may read this instability into Greek family life and Greek mythology as they reflect one another. In Greek mythology there is the unusually high incidence of powerful, threatening women, and the reactive pattern of suppressing them or sublimating them ("we find . . . Athene and Artemis being transformed, over the centuries, from mother-goddesses to youthful virgins," p. 12); with consequent substitute formations in a mythology of adoptive homosexuality that embraces both Zeus (Ganymede, Pelops) and Achilles (Patroklos): "pederasty . . .

became an almost vital institution, diluting the mother-son pathology, counteracting rivalry between father and son, and providing a substitute father-son bond" (p. 59).

In the given mythology itself, an instability resides between the emergent hero and the powerful woman: Perseus before Danae, Andromeda, and Medusa; Oedipus before the Sphinx who was summoned from distant Ethiopia to punish his father's erotic pursuit of a boy, and then before Jocasta. Heracles, "the glory of Hera," is threatened by Hera, and also pervasively in his marital stability as in his mind, a side of him emphasized by the recent compendium on him (Pauly-Wissowa, Suppl XIV, 1974, 185–190) as well as by Slater. The Python, like the dragon of Neumann's widespread Ouroboros myth, while it has the phallic attributes of the snake, associates unstably, as the chthonic snake does, with the Mother (Fontenrose, pp. 21, 46–76): the *drakaina* nurses the monstrous Typhoeis (whom Hera bore), fusing three Mother-centered beings, since Typhoeis is planted deep in the earth at the base of a mountain, both earth and mountains being associated with the Mother (who herself shifts from person to process to ground in Hesiod's account, *Theog.* 820–46). In the *Philebus* (12b) Plato produces an exchange where "pleasure (*hedone*) is her truest name" for Aphrodite, but Socrates replies by invoking his own fear in the face of the names of the gods.

That the dualities of mythography in the second phase cannot fully handle the dominant unicity of the first makes for a power in the myth as well as for incapacity in the language: something remains unexplained and unincorporated, persistently uncontained in the categories which from the beginning, at any phase, are devised to name the uncontained. A (hypothetical) first phase can often be traced in the psychology of anyone born of woman, with Neumann; and in the poetic activity designed to capture and order the force of the myth, with Graves (p. 9): "the language of poetic myth anciently current in the Mediterranean and Northern Europe was a magical language bound up with popular religious ceremonies in honor of the Moon-goddess, or Muses, some of them dating from the Old Stone Age, and. . . . this remains the language of true poetry."

However, the Mother, who dominates the first phase in the relation of myth to language, whose effect inhabits the unconscious of the psychic life, is always manifested only as a survival in the cultures of which we have any record, all of which have already entered the second phase of reciprocity, which assigns the function of some kind of writing to a given class. The record-keeping of Mycenean times certainly precedes Homer, and the "oral" Homeric text itself mentions writing, the mana-loaded or "dire" signs (*semata lugra*) carried by Bellerophon (*Iliad* 6.165. The word *sema* has a wide meaning in Homer.). Literacy itself, the abstract universalization of writing for theoretical functions, usually betokens the third phase found in "written" cultures (though my phases, as I sketch them, do not sharply divide at discernible times in the technology of writing). More exactly, the threshold of literacy usually betokens the second phase, a sensitized period when the hieroglyphics of the Egyptians, the ideograms of the Chinese, the runes of the Germanic north, the syllabary of the Phoenicians, or the developing alphabet of the Greeks characteristically accompany the codification of periods and cycles. Then come questions about the beginning, and so creation myths; the fact that creation myths deal with the beginning has led many thinkers to place them at the beginning of myth-making, in spite of the fact that there are no traces at all of construable creation myths in the first phase (when one could construe hunting rituals and sacrifices, with or without relation to the Mother).

In his own third-phase abstract questioning about pre-Homeric but post-Atlantic times, Plato speaks of men (*Critias* 109d–110a) who are defined as being mountain dwellers and without any technique for writing (*oreion kai agrammaton*):

> The names they were willing enough to give to
> their children; but the virtues and the laws of
> their predecessors, they know only by obscure
> traditions; and as they themselves and their
> children lacked for many generations the
> necessities of life, they directed their attention
> to the supply of their wants—Mythology and the
> inquiry into things ancient come into cities along
> with free time, when men see that the necessities
> of life are provided for.
>
> (Jowett, revised)

Plato here links enabling mastery of the necessities of life (*ta anankaia*), much as Lévi-Strauss does—though of course without either the elaborate analysis or the logical connection—to the act of ordering myths reasonably (*mythologia*) and of inquiring into the far past.

4.

Such an inquiry as Plato's here, pursued systematically, takes us into a third phase of abstract sifting, a phase distinct from the second. The "inquiry" (*anazetesis*) of the *Critias* is here a fair synonym for the "inquiry" (*historie*) of Herodotus, and the enterprise suggested as possible here is the one systematized by Herodotus, though he applied it more to recent events than to those of Plato's remote antiquity (*ton palaion*).

The second phase is included, and subsumed wholly or partly in the abstraction of the third phase, so that Lévi-Strauss's assertion of comprehensiveness for his myth-analysis does in fact have some force. Yet even in the second phase, to which his chief examples adhere, there is much room for manipulation. Day and night, tides and seasons, are reversed in the Salish land of the dead (HN, p. 405), which retains those cyclic and combinatory characteristics of ordinary economic and social life. So does the Land of the Dead in the Egypt of the Book of the Dead, which includes the second phase of a thought that is comparably cyclic and combinatory. Isis and Osiris do permute earth, sky, and water, in the patterns of a seasonal ritual. However, the Egyptian mythology also transvalues the reciprocities of the second phase into the abstractions of a third phase: in their Land of the Dead a different kind of pattern may also be apprehended, a predominant one. It is, to begin with, the boundary between life and death, and not that between nature and culture, which makes for the main distinction in Egyptian myth. The cyclic no longer predominates. What predominate, rather, are elaborate preparations whose exact fulfillment will guarantee the dead man's participation in a society that resembles the earthly society in particulars, but which heightens and regularizes those particulars, placing a heavier emphasis on such terms as triumph, strength, vengeance, and the divine. The gods enter into combinations of remarkable abstractness and complexity, as do also the Sumerian gods. Man himself is organized as a fusion of several entities much more fully coordinated than the *melea*, the *thymos*, *ker*, *psyche*, and *noos*, of the human psychological plurality in the Homeric poems. In the Book of the Dead man has (Budge, pp. lviii–lxxiv) a *khat* or physical body, a *sahu* (spiritual body), an *ab* (heart), a *ka* (double), a *ba* (soul), a *khaibit* (shadow), a *khu* (intelligence), "a translucent intelligible casing or covering for the body," and a *sekhem* or form, which persists in heaven, as does the *ren*, or name.

Lévi-Strauss has made the choice of further limiting his implied exclusivity of analysis by attending to just those aspects of the Western Hemisphere that are uncontaminated by development into a third phase, the period of reworking the dualities of myth and the systems of language into an overarching, self-consistent explanation. He deals only tangentially with the Aztecs, the Toltecs, the Incas, and the Mayans, all of whom evolved their second phase 'binary' mythology into the abstractness of what I am (hypothetically) calling a third phase. Nor will Lévi-Strauss deal with the Navajo mythology "not only because of its richness and complexity, but because successive generations of *indigenous* thinkers [italics mine] have elaborated it into a theological and liturgical form which profoundly modifies the perspective in which the analyst must place himself" (HN, p. 475). ("Must," we would add, if he wishes not to account for other phases.) Still, at the same time Lévi-Strauss does posit an isomorphic didacticism between Navajo mythology and that of the Utes (and consequently with those of the whole hemisphere). However, since the Navajo are more conservative, having gone through less acculturation than other groups of North American Indians, it is possible that their "theology," by carrying the myth over into a third phase of abstract comprehensiveness, preserves the full form of its mythologies, leaving as a diminished form the second-phase economic and technological and kinship orientations of the myths Lévi-Strauss analyzes. It is also possible, since he goes along with the nearly universal opinion that the Western Hemisphere was peopled by migrations across the Bering Strait, that the Navajos, who place a great emphasis on such female figures as Sky-Woman, preserve traces of the Paleolithic mother cult, of a first period too, something that other traditions, such as the matrilineal descent of the Iroquois (RC, p. 331), may also echo.

It would be wrong to call the third-phase Egyptian terms for man and his attributes simply abstractions. Rather, they are *unambivalent* general terms that subsume the entities of myth—the cow and the sun and all the others—and restructure them into a sort of homogeneity. The language exemplifies, and implicitly declares, the unity of the mythic perception, while standing off from the mythemes of the mythic story.

Egyptian myths provide the integers for the hieroglyphics that record the language, but only as a syllabary, wherein some elements are also soon phoneticized. Whether or not a given hieroglyphic has lost its pictorial character in favor of phonetic representation, the language now combines the hieroglyphics in patterns that draw on single elements of myth for their pictographs. Myth and history are still not differentiated. For Herodotus Arion is still on a par with Croesus, but inquiry (*historie*) dominates the linguistic terms, levelling them in a "third-phase" rigor and simplicity which may even be detected as far back as the comprehensive male-god dominations in Sumerian, Akkadian, and Hittite mythology. Hindu *Maya*, and the *yugas* of macro-history would also be third-phase abstractions, where the complexities of myth have entered a simpler order, though only subsumptively: all the second-phase polytheism continues and is carried along. Complex, and distinguishable, formulations and attitudes towards the process of history were gradually developed over the slow transition from second to third phase in Egypt, Mesopotamia, Persia, and Israel (Dentan). These were later refined into dialectical interpretations of time itself, notably in Greece by Plato and Aristotle but also by Gnostic Christianity, Islam, China, and India (Campbell). As Puech says of the Gnostic view (p. 40), "we might speak of a game among three opposing conceptions, the first representing time by a circle, the second by a straight line, the third by a broken line."

This third phase is often labelled simply "the birth of philosophy." This can be misleading, since it suggests a closed system for the abstract questions asked, rather than an exploration of the ways the abstractions restructure the mythic material, which can be taken to be logically as well as temporally prior to them. The jaguar, whose second-period manifestations Lévi-Strauss analyzes, would seem to have had a long history of pre-Columbian iconography. Its incorporation into the Aztec calendar both for a recursive day, Ocelotl, the fourteenth, of its twenty-day/thirteen day week, and as the third before our own of a macro-historical 676-year period, provides also a third-phase systematization of seasonal phenomena at once more abstract and simpler than the second-phase ones Lévi-Strauss discusses at such length.

The Oedipus myth is a second-phase phenomenon, susceptible to the sort of analysis Lévi-Strauss gives it. After the "birth of philosophy" in archaic Greece, it enters a different grid of identification, so that for Sophocles moral and intellectual questions, themselves identified, provide the definition for the mythic material which is conceived as feeding into them. Pindar (*Olympian* 2, 38–43) is one of the first to mention the life-course of Oedipus, who for Homer is just a hero who activated "a Mother's furies" (*Odyssey* 11. 280). The chorus of the *Oedipus Rex* closes with a big, unanswerable question about the meaning of the cycle of a unique life. To invoke Jolles again, the inverse of the myth is the riddle which, in Norse mythology, too, is a death test. Only very late in our accounts does the riddle of the Sphinx get any verbal formulations or solution. In Sophocles it remains a puzzle. As for the puzzle—in spatial terms, the maze—its solution or the quest out of a maze, themselves[9] provide the sort of resumptive, simple terms by which linguistic structures, usually poetic ones, take over the mythic material.

Lévi-Strauss repeatedly goes to a late third-phase formulator, to Plutarch, for points not only about Greek myth but (a hundred years after the "Isis and Osiris" has ceased to be a truly primary source) for Egyptian myth as well. Detienne finds in the myths surrounding Adonis and the Phoenix something other than a seasonal myth; rather, a division between bread and perfume or necessity and luxury; thus he already offers terms that simplify by abstractions within "culture" the complexity of the mythic materials, even though he reproduces Lévi-Straussian contrastive diagrams for his components on the one hand and disavows as "ideology"—thus vainly trying to precipitate them away—all the spiritual correlatives of the phoenix on the other (p. 68). Samson's reading of honey in the Bible as a riddle explaining and paralleling himself—the honey in the carcass of the lion for "Out of the eater came forth meat, and out of the strong came forth sweetness" (Judges 14.14) —offers a semi-abstract emblem that transforms a second-phase binary set, lion and honey no doubt functioning somewhat as jaguar and honey do in Lévi-Strauss's interpretation.

The very exemplary comprehensiveness of Homer's presentation of reciprocities and periodicities, culture reflecting nature and men reflecting gods, amounts to an abstract view of the second phase, one already on the way to something new. The third phase develops mainly in Greece, indeed, by resisting (and also, in this light, by furthering) the dominance of Homer. Apollo leaves Hector (*Iliad* 22.213) after Zeus has Hector's fate fall in the scale-pan, and Athene deceives Hector by urging him to continue the fight (239–46), a deceit which he later recognizes. The reciprocities are those of a tribal culture; but the acts of understanding, and the complex interactions, are "psychological," and to that degree they are abstract. They are in no way referred to reciprocities or periodicities, after the initial connection in which Zeus has been induced to favor Achilles instead of the Trojan, the beginning of this series. The fact that Hector himself recognizes the series shows his sophistication as well as his credulity. Similarly, the anthropomorphism in Homer, whereby the interactions among the gods are a distorted mirror of the *social* forces among humans, is more sophisticated than the dark dominance of pre-Olympian gods even while it is an instance of persisting pre-literate concretizing. Hector says, in the face of the observed portent when the eagle (bird of Zeus) drops the snake (of primordial chthonic force), "There is one bird-of-omen (*oionos*) best: to ward off for the fatherland" (*Iliad* 12.243). The abstract connection between the fatherland and the bird—here rendered as a metaphor or nonce-term for patriotism and tribal fidelity—itself amounts to an abstract thought, even to a touch of irony. This connection drops aside shortly when we are told that in trying to break the Achaian phalanx they "relied on the portents and on their might" (253), putting omen and personal force on an easy and unexamined par.

"Difficult it is for the gods to appear distinctly" (20.131), the poem says, and it maintains an unstable balance between the pattern of reciprocities and the intense examination of them. The very act of trying to understand dark forces removes them from their darkness. Thus Homer through a nascent abstracting capacity renders the unknown that resides in the myth. He makes of the myth a way not given or predictable, but a free play of fixed forces. We know that Zeus is susceptible to influence, but not that Thetis will now prevail over him and now Hera, though the norms of daughters' behavior towards fathers and of wives' behavior towards husbands serve as guides, and revelations, for the individual instance.

Athene is in some ways an allegory of intelligence; Hypnos, sleep, is fully allegorical. Homer's literary sophistication in constantly recombining events to create new structures evidences the exercise of abstract thinking. Notice for instance his including in his narrative the detail that when the embassy approaches Achilles in Book 9, he is playing the *klea andron*—celebrating the very glories of men that are Homer's subject, and from which Achilles is absenting himself—on a lyre plundered from the sack of Andromache's father's city. Eetion's own downfall in that very sack, as his bereft daughter Andromache has earlier said, intensifies her total wifely devotion to Hector, whom Achilles will also destroy once he has reentered the battle. In being recombined, these tribal ideas are already being transcended.

In the face of such sophisticated connections, and in the face of the fact that hoplite warfare would seem to have been introduced within decades of the final formulation of the poems, one cannot be confident that the fusion of societies over a millennium which Homer offers has the randomness of a similar, less complex fusion in the songs of the Yugoslav guslars, second-phase curiosities surviving on the margin of our fifth- or sixth-phase civilizations. As Snodgrass still further shows, Homer offers us what has to be taken as a conflation of different epochs in time. Homer's time fusion presents a more complex picture than the simple ancestor sequence and blind anachronistic synchronicity an oral tribesman might recite. In the Homeric poems the idealized past would have had to be a partial, and differentiated, basis for the present there shown, if only because the poet carefully centers on a selected, compact time-scheme for the particular events of both *Iliad* and *Odyssey*.

The sense of alternate verbal expression as it coexists with formula in Homer, if applied to Homer's poetry (as I and others have applied it, Cook 1966), may be taken for the beginning of a third-phase possibility (the alternate expression) on a second-phase base (the repository of formulas): "The tongue of mortals is twisted; there are many stories in it / Of all sorts, and much range on this side and on that" (*Iliad* 20.248–49). From the second phase on, it is in literature that the clearest interactions between myth and language occur.

A step further (or a step aside, for Hesiod, since the time of Herodotus, has been taken as contemporaneous with Homer) and we have the distinction between true and false as applied to poetry at the beginning of the *Theogony* (28). The focus of the *Theogony* on celestial phenomena, and of *Works and Days* on the management of the seasonal cycle, keeps Hesiod's purview in the second phase, though the tendency towards allegorizing abstraction (as in his possible Babylonian originals), the classification of human existence into the non-cyclic protoanthropological phases of "the five ages of man" (*Works and Days*, 106–201), and the appearance of the allegorized Prometheus story in both poems all take on the abstract and reflective attributes of a third phase. The comparison of either Prometheus passage in Hesiod with any of the hundreds of myths recounted by Lévi-Strauss in the *Mythologiques* would throw this "new" abstract and reflective aspect into relief.

Texts vary in their relation to the religious institutions of the people among whom they were produced. Homer, in the theory of Rohde still affirmed by Nilsson (1952, 135–136), may well have neglected some aspects of contemporaneous religion; and he may have over-emphasized others by the very act of codification. His text, once it had come finally into being, had scriptural attributes, though it did not have the ritual function of the *Rgveda*, the eschatological-prescriptive character of *The Book of The Dead*, the elaborately institutionalized role of the Chinese *Five Classics*, or the enshrinement in the Temple and the attribution to divine inspiration of the Pentateuch. If I were trying to define the interchanges between language and religion, instead of those between language and the manifestations, intricately but not directly religious, of myth, then I would be obliged to focus on the distinctions between these various texts, each of them scripturally marked for particular kinds of significant linguistic exchange. As it is, they all share not only a common typology as "scriptures"; but, in terms of the hypothetical phases here outlined, they are all "second-phase" texts on the way towards the abstractness of a third phase. It may be, indeed, that this is the condition for a scripture's coming-into-being. Even so, the third phase would be independent of Cassirer's phase-definition (pp. 71–77), for Cassirer attributes "polynomy" uniformly to this phase. "Every deity unites in itself a wealth of attributes, which originally belonged to the special gods that have all been combined in one new god." But there are cultural differences in "polynomy." The elaborately substitutive Egyptian pantheon differs from the discretely named and only partially overlapping Greek gods. Then there is the rudimentary early Chinese mythology whose varieties very soon evolved into binary opposition (both sexual and abstract) between yin and yang—not to mention the severe and triumphant monotheistic Jahweh, abstract but personal, of the Old Testament.

Religion as a social institution makes the myth accessible to the individual psyche through ritual. Religion stabilizes. A text, in so far as it is scriptural, records that stability. But a text also provides, in stability, the ground for possible change. The Greek lyric poets do not have to perform the radical act of revising Homer that Heraclitus and Xenophanes felt it necessary to do. After the birth of philosophy, a permutation of philosophy into religion produces many odd fusions of phase, in such phenomena as the Gnostic notion that the First Man was androgynous, a notion with many parallels (Nock and Festugière 9: xx I. 9, 20): "Mind is god, being male-female (ho de Nous ho theos, arrenothēlus ōn. *Hermetica* A9). Here the first phase of unicity—something like the phallic mother statues that Gimbutas describes and that Freud's unconscious is said to image—and the second phase of binary reciprocity between male and female, and a third phase of "mind," reassigning the abstract Nous of Plato and Aristotle to a mythical context, all converge in a harmony at once total and vapid.

The third, abstract phase undergoes various systematizations up to the Middle Ages. Philosophy after Plato, as part of its program, stays with abstractions. Literature, on the other hand, gains its force just from the evocation produced through the subsumption of earlier phases, from a sense of access to myth as well as from an understanding of myth. The Beatrice of Dante, like the Laura of Petrarch and the lady of all the troubadours, subsumes the Goddess and sublimates her through the Christian immortality of soul, the Christian equality of the souls of women, and the Christian emphasis on the virginity of the Mother (a major transmutation of the force of the Goddess into something both sublimated and abstract). In the *Divina Commedia* Dante organizes an approach to this exalted first-phase figure, using all the patterns of the second phase: a precise dating on the seasonal cycle, a precise set of locations in the `cosmology, and an exact concurrence of Holy Week and Jubilee Year for the momentous journey. At the same time, of course, the overriding systematization, from the abstractness of the style to the sequence of theological categories and dialogues of philosophical definitions, concatenates the poem (with none of, say, Sophocles' energic adaptiveness) into a third-phase coordination.

The assertion of congruence between a beloved object and the sense of the deity can be traced pervasively in many cultures, as Dronke has impressively done, going back to the Egyptian love lyric (I, p. 9). One may trace it back even further, conjecturally, to some form of the feeling for the Mother. Of course in moving ahead in time through abstract phases, as Dronke says when contrasting Byzantine love poems with Guinizelli, "the feeling is similar; the differences of expression are startling" (I, p. 58)—so startling that they may comprise a difference of feeling, a plane of Apollonian equanimity in which it would be possible to assert, with the early medieval *lai de l'oiselet, "dieus et Amors sont d'un acort"* (cited, p. 5). Dronke's "mystic," "noetic," and "Sapiential" strains all become possible only in a third phase of trans-cyclic abstraction which had been firmly established in Egypt, his earliest example, for a good millennium by the time of the Chester Beatty Papyrus (1160 B.C.).

All these structures of expression are convergent in Dante, who radiates a feeling of plenitude that derives intellectually (Nardi, pp. 69–72) from Averroes' notion of the sufficiency of knowledge to desire.[10]

5.

When the act of language consciously allows for and virtually names, instead of merely subsuming, the unconscious element in the mythic process, we have already moved into a fourth period; or we can postulate one. The correspondences between myth and social fact are carefully preserved: in being preserved, they enter into delicate, ironic relations with the linguistic forms, which differ from them not only in constructing conscious accounts but in being both firmly sequent in a temporal order and rigorous in their linear conformity to rule. All the rationalizations of mythic forms in the Renaissance, from Pico della Mirandola possibly through Blake, are of a fourth period, distinct from Dante's conscious restructuring of what he would not regard as unconscious, when the analogy—of the Sun to God, of Beatrice to St. John—carefully hypostasizes likeness (Cook 1966, pp. 222–28) and through careful rhetorical structures purges oppositions into hierarchical levels.

The allegorizing of the classical gods, which can be traced back to the Stoics (Seznec, p. 84, citing Decharme) is an enterprise of assimilation-by-abstraction, adapting classical gods to more abstract, conscious purposes. The long tradition of visual iconography allows for many conflations like those in the "Prudentia" or "Three Ages of Man" ascribed to Titian: "The first, borrowed from medieval morality, represents the three phases of Time as encompassed in Prudence; these are purely intellectual concepts, personified in human form. The second, issuing from the Oriental cults of the late Empire, depicts Time as a mythical force made up of three ravening beasts" (Seznec, p. 121, citing Panofsky).

The frequent references to "Venus" in Renaissance poetry, in Ronsard, and in Shakespeare take both the "intellectual" idea of love and the fact of love as a mythical force still further, beyond such allegorization; they subject the conflation of classical god with the feeling of love to the delicate, dissecting irony of poetic artifice, as though to say that the relations within the love-sphere are as delightfully formal as the very manner in which the poem at hand can attribute the name of a deity disbelieved by the poet to the idea of love and the force of love.

Such a displacement suggests the richness that love's own displacements may delicately, and at the same time urgently, create. The *Venus and Adonis*, operating at every point in the self-delight of such a "fourth-phase" irony, hovers between being a case study in male passivity and a twitching of the veil over the mythic mystery. The terror of the boar in the poem—which is derived from, but also displaced from, the terror of the chthonic animal in the ritual hunt—is also tamed. The boar is prettified. The relation between love and death is desperate, as the poem keeps insisting, and at the same time it is virtual, as the net of artifice around the myth implies.

Such a deployment of contingencies does the fourth or "ironic" phase of the relation between myth and language permit. "I'll say yon grey is not the morning's eye, / 'Tis but the pale reflex of Cynthia's brow" (*Romeo and Juliet*, II, v, 192–20). The lightness of the erotic and its urgency here both show in the virtuality of a moon-goddess, "Cynthia," who cannot be wholly dissociated from the Mother, since she is seen as so encompassing that her mere reflection gives the grey light to the entire sky. Naming her underscores both the inventiveness and the false-hood of someone whose love even before Juliet was accompanied by a poetic effusion verging on vacuity.

This ironic shuttling between the main thrust of artifice-disbelief and a considerable byplay of communicative suggestion is already taken beyond Lyly in *A Midsummer Night's Dream*. Four of Shakespeare's five last plays invoke only the pagan gods, with a consequent initial, and fundamental, irony of credence (Cook, 1976). The very raptness of the Emissaries to the oracle in *The Winter's Tale* (III, i, 1–21) must be distanced by our near certainty that Shakespeare could not assign credence to such a consultation. But the irony permutes, and we are further distanced, when Leontes is instantly punished by the death of his son for the statement of his own flat disbelief, "There is no truth at all i' the oracle" (137)—though of course his refusal to believe is a moral act entailed by his denial of his queen, and the mystery of connection between the cyclic life of a ritualized king and his moral being is precisely the theme of the play. The cyclic life is evidenced not only by the pastoral of Act Four but also by the fact that at the end this is the only one of all Shakespeare's plays where the next generation—the son of one king and the daughter of another—take over to rule, in undeflected though deeply interrupted cyclic succession.

Shakespeare may well have learned the manipulation of such irony from Ovid, in whom this fourth phase of restructuring an abstracted mythology may be detected, as I shall later argue at length. But the overarching power of the Christian revelation mostly delayed until the Renaissance any further use of what is most essential in Ovid. His third-phase feature of abstracting the mythology into near-allegory served just as a convenient moral repertory for the *Ovide moralisé* of the Middle Ages (Seznec, pp. 91ff).

6.

The operations of language upon myth through flexible literary arti-fice become so delicate at this point that the delineation of phases is even more arbitrary. Still, when the irony becomes pervasive enough, it invades the syntactic assertions of the language, and we can say that the fourth phase gives way to a fifth, in which the irony self-consciously becomes a sort of paradigm, just as the third phase may be defined as the application of another reasoning process back to the myths (rather than a Lévi-Straussian binary extension of the myths by complemen-tarities of stories that keep filling in the contradictions). In the fifth phase not only the myths themselves but the process of myth formation may come under examination. This is the time when both anthropology and the depth psychology of the "unconscious before Freud" came into being, characteristically by examining and interpreting the body of myth. In one sense this enterprise continues the *Poetic Theology* of Pico della Mirandola, and Romantic attitudes do tend to intensify Renaissance attitudes (Cook, *Thresholds*, forthcoming). But there is a difference. Pico merely wished to apply his abstractions to the classical gods, taking their accessibility to allegorization as a justification for their identifica-tion with an intellectual process. His suspension between disbelief and belief, his "functionalism" with respect to the classical myths, could be translated into the cursory irony of Ronsard or Shakespeare.

In Blake, however, there is no suspension. The act of language self-ironically provides ironic combinations for the entities of myth. Blake both derives these figures from his long tradition and invents them through a quasi-theologized inspiration.

More sternly logical than any poet, let alone the playful Ovid, Saint Augustine believed in the classical gods; he believed that for the most part they were devils masked under the classical names. Petrarch and Pico della Mirandola, on the other hand, did not believe in their real existence, but in their function as naming psychological and spiritual states. Typological interpretation of the Bible since Philo and before, expanded to become the fourfold series (literal, allegorical, moral, ana-gogical) adapted by Dante, became the vehicle for extending the allegorical reading from scripture to everyday life. Milton only complicates and virtualizes these procedures, and his long poems exist rhetorically as commentary on Scripture.

Blake transforms all these modes of relating an implied language of statement to myth. It cannot be said that he believes in his Zoas, as Saint Augustine or Milton or even Blake himself believes Scripture. Yet it cannot be said that he disbelieves in them. Nor are these entities exactly masks for devils or psychological states: rather they are revelations of the spiritual powers and psychological states themselves. *The Four Zoas* is not a commentary on Scripture, but a sort of transposition of scripture-like meanings into a different form which Blake believes has the force of scripture in any case. And still *The Four Zoas* is legitimized by a scriptural epigraph, given in Greek as though to insist on its literal origins, "We wrestle not against flesh and blood, but against principalities, against powers, against the rulers of the darkness of this world" (Ephesians 6:12).

Irony can be made to serve, in Blake's prose, as a transform between belief and disbelief. Consider the following sequence of Blake's abstractions, which proceed from the Bible, where myths have maximum credence:

> As a new heaven is begun, and it is now thirty-
> three years since its advent: the Eternal Hell revives.
> And lo! Swedenborg is the Angel sitting at the tomb;
> his writings are the linen clothes folded up. Now is
> the dominion of Edom, & the return of Adam into Paradise;
> see Isaiah XXIV & XXV Chap:
> Without Contraries is no progression. Attraction
> and Repulsion, Reason and Energy, are necessary to
> Human existence.
> From these contraries spring what the religious
> call Good & Evil. Good is the passive that obeys Reason.
> Evil is the active springing from Energy. Good is
> Heaven, Evil is Hell
> . . . . .
> The voice of the Devil

> All Bibles or sacred codes have been the causes of
> the following errors.
> 1. That man has two real existing principles Viz:
>   a Body & a Soul.
> 2. That Energy, called Evil, is alone from the Body.
>   & that Reason, called Good, is alone from the Soul.
> 3. That God will torment Man in Eternity for following
>   his Energies. But the following Contraries to these
>   are True.
>   1. Man has no Body distinct from his Soul for that
>   calld Body is a portion of Soul discernd by the
>   five Senses, the chief inlets of Soul in this age.
>   2. Energy is the only life and is from the Body and
>   Reason is the bound or outward circumference of
>   Energy.
>   3. Energy is Eternal Delight
> *The Marriage of Heaven and Hell*, Plates 3 and 4
> (Erdman p. 34).

Here the law of contraries, felt since Heraclitus to be intimately bound up with a rejection of myth and with a re-definition of its proper role, is at once adduced and violated. For Devil read Angel and for Good read Evil. Yet this irony, which rests on turning normal terms topsy-turvy (an extreme of the normal ironic statement, saying the opposite of what is meant), rests on an entirely different assertion of "contraries," one based on the ambivalence of mythic entities and their reflection and/or source in the psychic life of the unconscious (Cook 4), where indeed love and hate for the same object at the same time can coexist. Blake would go further and assert that this kind of contrary coexistence is necessary to progression.

Here we have an ambivalence of Blake's own towards the Devil (really an angel) who scorns the "Bibles or sacred codes" which produce what the "Devil" calls "error." However, the Devil also adduces the principle of Contraries, which has just been brought in as essential by Blake, implying that the second set of three propositions above is true and the first, Bible-derived set false—a mutual exclusion which establishes the logical law of contraries rather than the Blakean law of Contraries-for-the-sake-of-progression. Taken this way, the "Devil," though a source of the key Blake maxim, "Energy is Eternal Delight," is himself not (ironically) an Angel, but diabolical in his violation of the key Blakean law. He is Urizen (Your-reason).

Moreover, all these contradictions—subtler than the law of contraries

as here stated may allow for without recombination—are in a sense
applied to the beginning of these statements. Blake is ambivalent, and
ambivalent in his very ambivalence, towards the Swedenborg who is
introduced here as an "Angel" associable to either the "new heaven"
or the "Eternal Hell" (either successive or contrarily complementary
simultaneous entities). Blake's allegorical interpretation of Swedenborg's
relation to the events surrounding the Resurrection is at once a blas-
phemy and a sort of apocalypse, as the reversion to Old Testament
prophecy underscores ("Now is the dominion of Edom") and the seemingly undercutting and overriding authoritative earnestness of the scriptural quotation from Isaiah.

Isaiah 24 and 25 are a prophecy-lament for an Israel in desolation,
an equivalent for Blake's "dark Satanic mills," here brought in obliquely
so as not to overwhelm the possibilities of ironic definition. These
ironies at once replace and reaffirm the Christian Bible, by assigning
plus words to minus valuation, *angel* and *heaven* to *devil* and *hell*. This
is done in such a way as to conflate the values. So Blake's title indicates
—through a metaphor which is drawn from Old Testament typology
(Israel as an unfaithful wife in the prophets) and New (the Church as
the bride of Christ).

Even in prose Blake does not offer a simple ironic reversal. In the
Marriage some of the same terms are used unironically. In particular
the references to Christ and the Judgment seem to stand in a sort of
suspension between ironic and unironic uses. Nor can it be said that
the ironic application of a term like *angel* randomly occurs in context
with the unironic use, since the effect is to produce a sort of endless
series.

The process of using contraries to undermine the principle of contraries is reminiscent of Heraclitus, but Blake goes farther, interfusing
mythic evocations with his interpretations as he goes on to produce the
Prophetic Books.

Wagner, too, may be said, without all Blake's intricacy of definition
or his fertility at recreating a mythology, to operate in such a fifth phase
of the relation between myth and language, a phase that may be called
paradigmatic because the main action of all Blake's prophetic books is
to work through and test out combinations of abstractly defined mythic
entities. The *leitmotif* is not ironic: it is at once wordless and combinatory, and Lévi-Strauss himself—not in what he analyzes, but in the
procedure of his own analysis—is comparably paradigmatic, and be-

longs to the fifth phase. In fact he repeatedly compares himself to Wagner, and asserts his derivation from Freud and Marx. Marx's prophetic use of Hegel, and the inclusion of a Utopia myth (not too different from the second-phase Hesiod, or Genesis, or Book of Manu) in a historical-dialectical paradigm, may be associated to the fifth phase, though the reference to myth in Marx is only vestigial. Prometheus, to be sure, holds meaning for him. In Freud, however, myth is essential: without the equivalent of Oedipus, no unconscious; without the paradigm of analysis, no explanation of its mechanisms of evolution.

7.

In the speed-up of modern times the phases could come on more quickly, and we may differentiate still further a sixth hypothetical phase, in which the paradigmatic activity of the fifth phase is itself subjected to reexamination and set to work reflexively so as to produce, even at random, new "mythic" combinations in language. Some such intention lay behind the harnessing of the unconscious by the programmatic surrealists. Here the act of language, by buckling with, and buckling under to, the unconscious determinants of the process of language, at once celebrates and questions the theoretical foundations of both myth and language, triumphantly reconnecting them in an act of dissolution. Such a series of transformations—a paradigm of a paradigm—Per Aage Brandt finds implicitly to underlie surrealism as it harnesses the conscious law of contradiction to move up and down his defined levels of verbalization and the unconscious: the text, sleep, and dream.

Consider the very possibility that such a poem as this one by the surrealist Benjamin Péret could exist:

26 POINTS A PRÉCISER

A André Masson.

Ma vie finira par a
Je suis $b - a$
Je demande $cb - a$
je pèse les jours de fête $\dfrac{d}{cb - a}$
Mes prévisions d'avenir $\dfrac{de}{cb - a}$

Mon suicide heureux $\dfrac{de}{(cb - a)\,f}$

Ma volonté $\sqrt[a]{\dfrac{de}{(cb - a)\,f}}$

Ma force physique $\sqrt[a]{\dfrac{de}{(cb - a)\,f}} + h$

Mes instincts sanguinaires $\sqrt[a]{\dfrac{de}{(cb - a)\,f}} + h - i$

Les cartes ont mis dans ma poche

$$\left(\sqrt[g]{\dfrac{de}{(cb - a)\,f}} + h - i\right)^{j}$$

Elles ont retiré $\left(\sqrt[g]{\dfrac{de}{(cb - a)\,f}} + h - i\right)^{j} + k$

. . . .

Avec mon sexe je fais l'amour

$$\dfrac{\dfrac{m}{n}\left(\sqrt[g]{\dfrac{de}{(cb - a)\,f}} + h - i\right)^{j} + kl + o}{\sqrt[t]{(pq + r)\,s}}$$

La longueur de mes cheveux

$$\dfrac{\dfrac{m}{n}\left(\sqrt[g]{\dfrac{de}{(cb - a)\,f}} + h - i\right)^{j} + kl + o}{\sqrt[t]{(pq + r)\,s}} - u$$

Mon travail du matin

$$\dfrac{\dfrac{m}{n}\left(\sqrt[g]{\dfrac{de}{(cb - a)\,f}} + h - i\right)^{j} + kl + o}{\sqrt[t]{(pq + r)\,s}} - u\,v$$

Mon travail de l'après-midi

$$\dfrac{\dfrac{m}{n}\left(\sqrt[g]{\dfrac{de}{(cb - a)\,f}} + h - i\right)^{j} + kl + o}{\sqrt[t]{(pq + r)\,s}} - uv - w$$

Mon sommeil

$$\left(\dfrac{\dfrac{m}{n}\left(\sqrt[g]{\dfrac{de}{(cb - a)\,f}} + h - i\right)^{j} + kl + o}{\sqrt[t]{(pq + r)\,s}} - uv - w\right)^{x}$$

Ma fortune

$$\left(\frac{\dfrac{m}{n}\left(\sqrt[g]{\dfrac{de}{(cb-a)\,f}}+h-i\right)^{j}+kl+o}{\sqrt[t]{(pq+r)\,s}}-uv-w\right)^{x}-y$$

Ma date de naissance

$$\left(\frac{\dfrac{m}{n}\left(\sqrt[g]{\dfrac{de}{(cb-a)\,f}}+h-i\right)^{j}+kl+o}{\sqrt[t]{(pq+r)\,s}}-uv-w\right)^{x}-\frac{y}{z}$$

A comparable strategy in this sixth or transumptive phase is that of D.H. Lawrence. While he is of course no surrealist, there is a constant undercurrent of subliminal reactions that governs the actions of the characters in his novel. They themselves discuss the paradigms of inter-action, evoking or submitting to the mythic forces whose flow they in some sense determine. Personal identity and fusion into the anonymity of Man or Woman stand in a constant dialectic, awareness of which is necessary in order to survive. The later Lawrence tipped the scale towards anonymity and celebrated the dissolution of a woman's identity into anonymous Woman. But the protagonists of *Women in Love* and *The Rainbow* would have insisted on the permutability of the terms, and the process is one for which the culminating visual image of the rainbow may be taken to stand: the possibility of a realized future hinging on the proper combinations of the past. As all the phases are subsumed in the transumptive sixth phase, one may find not only the seasonal-binary of the second phase here and the abstract discourse of the third, the ironies of the fourth phase become the paradigms of the fifth. One may also, and still, see in Woman the Goddess of the first phase, doubly operative as a pervasive survival and as an element for recombination, as Rachel Levy's title can be taken to suggest, "Religious Conceptions of the Stone Age and Their Influence on European Thought." The influence persists; nothing is ever lost. The Paleolithic itself may be exalted, as Gary Snyder has done, citing the larger brain-size of Paleolithic man and basing pieces of a credo on practices hypothesized by anthropologists.

On such a vitality of origins did Charles Olson insist, to take still another sixth-phase practitioner. In his critical writings, what I have called the transumptive process admits of a "proprioceptive" recon-

structuring of its entities, into pairs of fourfold attributes (1, p. 12):
millennia (field), process (act), time (quantity; spatialization of society
into the demographic and technological), and result (person). Here the
figures of myth are rounded out to the abstractions of social and psychological theory. In Olson's system there remains of myth only its axis of
combination—and axes are also pivotal in Lévi-Strauss's reading of
myth. The procedure underlying myth is not transposed into a third-
phase abstract philosophy but itself used for a sort of transumptive
myth-making, an energic mediation between myth and language where
the story-properties of myth have been stripped away while the canons
of logic are used only for their combinatory energy.

The aphorisms of Nietzsche have a comparable structure of mediation, and in this abstract typology of phases he, too, like Blake, could
be assumed into the transumptive, sixth phase. Nietzsche's aphorisms,
however, unlike Blake's, are reflexively self-critical of the act of language itself. They both overshoot the function of language and fall short
of it, without direct recourse to the myths he scorned Wagner for invest-
ing with too full a credence. He preserves the myth, the lion or the
camel of Zarathustra or Zarathustra himself, only for short-term and
casual interaction between myth and language.

This practice had already begun during the powerful transition in
Greece from the Homeric world to that of pre-Socratic philosophy.
Nietzsche could well have subscribed to many of the aphorisms of
Heraclitus, whom he frequently mentions. In this connection, for the
relation of myth to language, he himself could well have said (though
no doubt more ironically than Heraclitus): "Hen to sophon mounon
legesthai ouk ethelei kai ethelei Zēnos onoma." (The wise is one thing
alone; it does not wish and wishes to be called the name of Zeus.)
(Diels 22. B 32). The aphorism of more than merely proverbial weight
was invented by Heraclitus in Greece, and perhaps also by Confucius
in China. For Heraclitus it went hand in hand with a powerful "bracketing" of myth. The aphorism gained philosophical power as it transmuted
the relation between myth and language. The "language games" and
aphoristic paragraphs of Wittgenstein continue this process, inescapably.

PART TWO

THE CLASSICAL EXAMPLE

3.
HERACLITUS AND THE CONDITIONS OF UTTERANCE

1.

IN Greece the long process, begun by Homer, of redefining the relations between myth and language could only continue by rejecting him. However sophisticated we may find Homer he makes little or no distinction between "fact" and "fiction," "abstract" and "concrete," or even between "general" and "particular." For the Greece Homer dominated, if one asks "What is history?" the answer is Homer; "What is poetry?" Homer again, and those like him, his followers, the *Homeridae*. And also, to "What is philosophy?" the answer is still Homer. Though "religion" remains (but Homer also has a scriptural tinge), archaic Greece notably provided an impetus still unexhausted for redefining myth in relation to language by separating off poetry from philosophy and from history. The possibility of history, and philosophy, as for developing poetry, emerges in an exemplary way as Greece tests for itself the definitions of myth.

The values codified in Homer and his place in Greek tradition make him for all practical purposes the sort of tribal figure against whom Havelock asserts Plato to have had to exercise his major revisionist force. Simultaneous homage and refutation are to be found as early as Xenophanes, who says that all men have learned with Homer (*kath'-Homeron*) from the beginning (Diels 21 B9) but directs the brunt of his own revising attack against Homer.

Heraclitus' radical revision of the relation between myth and language in Homer not only alters the approach to myth but recasts the structures of the language which is used to handle the questions he asks, where Xenophanes had stayed within the epic and elegiac meters. Heraclitus recasts literary form, continues the process of releasing formal expression from the tribal bonds of meter, challenges myth, discovers a powerful tool of philosophy in applying the principle of contradiction, and redefines the *daimon* in myth while vitalizing the bases of language, all in one verbal act. His immediate predecessors had provided a basis for questioning myth—Xenophanes by challenging a blind acceptance of the Homeric gods, and Anaximander by abstracting the cyclic time of a Homeric world-view into a principle of compensatory justice, "justice . . . payment . . . according to the arrangement of time" ("diken . . . tisin . . . kata ten tou chronou taxin" [Diels 12 B.1]).

Philosophy tends to abolish myth from its domain. But in activating itself philosophy also oddly activates myth; it reestablishes and revitalizes the relationship between myth and language in the very act of questioning language or myth. As Pavese said, "The peoples which have had a rich mythology are the peoples who have then avidly philosophized: Indians, Greeks, Germans."[1] And the last person in the world to do so had made a similar connection: Aristotle. The principle of wondering inquiry to which he attributes the inception of philosophy is said to serve equally for myth: "Therefore even he who loves myth is sort of a philosopher too; for myth is composed of wonders." ("dio kai ho philomythos philosophos pōs estin. ho gar mythos synkeitai ek thaumasiōn." *Metaphysics* 982 B 17–19).

2.

A tribal group-domination, both one phase of myth and a permanent tendency for mythic systems, already loses its grip on the verbal expression of the lyric poets. They are dedicated to the primacy of personal pleasure (Sappho, Alcaeus) and to a private perception that in Alcman could still also lend itself to the cult hymn. The fusion of the private and the cultic achieved a full elaboration in Pindar and Bacchylides, without breaking the hold of the tribal group, whereas the much later artifice hymns of Callimachus are already at another stage. They center on gods as different from the Aphrodite of Empedocles or even the Venus of Lucretius as these are from the Venus of Shakespeare. The discursive lyric stayed close to the tribal code in Solon's presentation of proverbial principles and Theognis' more expansive series of advisory aphorisms.

The codification of myth, first in Hesiod, and later, more scientifically, in Pherecydes, indicates anxiety about its stability. By the time of Plato the word *theologia* has been invented,[2] and attention is focussed on what may be deduced directly from the unifying idea of a single divine originator. Much later, in the work of Apollodorus and Plutarch, the impulse to codify myth will have become exhaustive and detached from the force of myth.

Pythagoras certainly did found a cult, one based on correspondences between the most abstract translinguistic systems, mathematics and music. A calculating process, to which Lévi-Strauss has given a quasi-mathematical form, underlies mythic systems, and music characteristically accompanies public rituals of homage to mythic beings. In Pythagoras all the mythic figures themselves have disappeared, it would seem, but mathematics and music, each defined in terms of the other, in effect replace them and become the basis for a cult. The cult's practice carried along with it the dietary stipulations that, again according to Lévi-Strauss, characteristically accompany and reflect mythic systems.

In Pythagoras' new abstract system, the parts of the world are defined and ordered according to an assigned number, itself placed in a system, the Pythagorean triangle of ten. This is formed by placing one dot, then two, then three, then four, adding up to ten. The triangle takes over many of the functions of the Olympian system. The presence of music, and the emphasis on it, attests to the dominant power of the oral-aural.

Mathematics, if applied to music, identifies the oral and the visual. And visible entities are what the mathematics of Pythagoras is taken to plot, actual geometric figures in space to which numbers are assigned, as for the "Pythagorean theorem." Greek mathematics was not to sever itself from perceptible figures until more than a generation later, and the visual itself remained a puzzle for Greek philosophers after Pythagoras, from Heraclitus through Plato and Aristotle.[3]

The abstractions of Pythagoras remained close to hearing and sight. Pythagoras is compared to Homer as a cult-guide (Plato, *Republic* 600 a, b), looking backward; looking ahead, the Pythagorean circle was often compared to Plato's Academy (Burkert 1, p. 74). Plato speaks of the opposition in Pythagoras, like that in Homer, between the public (*demosia*) and the private (*idia*), an opposition which is not, however, schematized in Homer.

A similar tension obtains in Heraclitus, accompanying a similar transposition of mythic systems, one that alters their content while attempting to retain their power. Heraclitus regards a private consciousness (*idian phronesin*, 22 B 2) as an illusion: but in the very act of asserting the community of the logos he divorces himself from the tribal community of persons: it is just the many (*hoi polloi*) who make this error about the private consciousness.

3.

The protracted effort to derive a cosmology from what we have of Heraclitus' statements has resulted, I should like to demonstrate, not so much in error, which would be a strange consequence of so much intricate and intelligent thought.[4] Rather, it has resulted in a misplacement of emphasis so considerable as to obscure the philosophical character and direction of utterances that are nothing if not pointed. If Heraclitus is already obscure, *skoteinos*[5] in the attribution of antiquity, it would not help to further obscure the thrust of the kind of statement he makes. To do so would, in fact, obscure the conditions of his obscurity.

First of all, how did Heraclitus see himself with reference to the cosmological and other concerns of his contemporaries and predecessors? We have, as it happens, a number of his statements about them, considerably more than we have from any other pre-Socratic philosopher. That alone should alert us to Heraclitus' concern to distinguish himself from them, not so much by refining their doctrines, though he may be said to refine Anaximander and Anaximenes if not others anonymously.[6]

Every one of Heraclitus' explicit statements about writers involves not the rejection of a specific doctrine but, arguably, the attribution of a total wrongheadedness of approach. Of these statements the most comprehensive is:

> πο-
> λυμαθίη νόον ἔχειν οὐ διδάσκει· Ἡσίοδον γὰρ ἂν
> ἐδίδαξε καὶ Πυθαγόρην αὖτίς τε Ξενοφάνεά τε καὶ
> Ἑκαταῖον.

> Learning many things does not teach thought, for it would have taught Hesiod and Pythagoras, and also Xenophanes and Hecataeus.   (Diels B 40)

The sense of *manthano* ("learning") in *polymathie* ("learning many things") must be active[7]—the acquisition of concerted bodies of intellectual skill, and not the miscellaneous information which, for one who has *noos* ("thought"), would be a necessary raw material for *philoso-phoi*. The *philosophoi* are to inquire about many things quite thoroughly (*eu mala*):

χρὴ γὰρ εὖ μάλα πολλῶν ἱστο-
ρας φιλοσόφους ἄνδρας εἶναι καθ᾽ Ἡράκλειτον.

> Those men who love wisdom must be thorough inquirers into many things.   (B 35)

The four thinkers mentioned in B 40 have not been taught by their *polymathie* to have *noos*, presumably because they have stopped inquiry (B 35, *historas*) short of that point of unity which for Heraclitus is equivalent to wakefulness and to intelligence—to understanding that the *logos* is *xunos* (B 1).

Bollack (*ad loc*) asks what sets these particular four writers into relationship. But first we need to know in what respect each of them may be said to have *polymathie* and yet to lack *noos*.

For Hesiod, the broad classification of his extant work into theology and husbandry provides such a split. The distinction between men and gods, so important to Heraclitus, would then not be correctly perceived along Hesiod's lines because the principle that unifies men and gods would not have been discovered. So that even within the *Theogony* Hesiod would be in error, as B 57 tells us, the word *didaskalos* recalling the *ou didaskei* of B 40:

διδάσκαλος δὲ πλείστων Ἡσίοδος· τοῦτον
ἐπίστανται πλεῖστα εἰδέναι, ὅστις ἡμέρην καὶ εὐφρό-
νην οὐκ ἐγίνωσκεν· ἔστι γὰρ ἕν.

> Hesiod is a teacher of the greatest number. They are convinced this man knew a number of things, who did not understand day and night; for they are ore.   (B 57)

This statement must be taken as a criticism of the theological-philosophical adequacy of the *Theogony*, where we hear of the origins of day and night. Hesiod has not sought the principle of unity underlying what men have taken as entities distinct enough to be given the different names "night" and "day."

It is just such a doctrine of seeming unity that Pythagoras, the second figure in the list, is reputed to have offered, and there would seem to be

no definite areas into which one might divide his *polymathie*. Music and
numbers, however, are obvious candidates, and even though Pythagoras'
system would seem to have defined each in terms of the other, Heraclitus' assertion would have to be taken as undercutting Pythagoras'
claim of their unity. Such is the force of his other statements about
Pythagoras. The longest of these, B 129, begins with seeming praise and
descends to a pejorative anticlimax, the penultimate word, again, being
polymathie:

Πυθαγόρης Μνησάρχου ἱστορίην ἤσκησεν
ἀνθρώπων μάλιστα πάντων καὶ ἐκλεξάμενος ταύτας τὰς
συγγραφὰς ἐποιήσατο ἑαυτοῦ σοφίην, πολυμαθίην, κακο-
τεχνίην.

> Pythagoras, son of Mnesarchos, pursued inquiry most of all men,
> and having chosen out these writings made them his wisdom, his
> much-learning, his bad skill.   (B 129)

Historie is the desired activity of the *philosophoi* in B 35. "All men" is
a double-edged expression if this context of praise is correlated with
Heraclitus' other statements about collective humanity. The act of choosing (*eklexamenos*) gave Pythagoras a skill-wisdom which was merely
private; *heautou sophien*, in a pejorative context, is pretty much equivalent to the *idian phronesin*, "private perception," that the *hoi polloi*
mistakenly suppose they can rely on (B 2).

It is the very claim to unity, when in fact his particularity is finally
to be defined as bad skill, *kakotechnie*, that must make Pythagoras the
"tutelary chief of liars" (B 81, in which the term *archegos* carries some
suggestion of religion and hence of his cult,[8] and the rare word *kopidon*,
cognate with a term for knife, perhaps refers to bad distinctions rather
than to the unachieved unification of his system).

The third in the list, Xenophanes, is also said to have made an assertion of proto-pantheistic unity, and his demythologization is similar in
tone to Heraclitus' own. All the more reason he should be rejected with
the others, since even his remarkable scientific observations, like the
deduction of much higher primitive sea levels from his discovery and
identification of shell fossils (Diels 21.A 33), do not add up to any
unified view and so would not teach him *noos*.

Hecataeus followed Hesiod in compiling genealogies, which constitute
a summary of past time; and he followed Anaximander, the first map-

maker, by writing a geography which located peoples in space. In some sense, taking Heraclitus' list as cumulative, Hecataeus would most fully exemplify *polymathie*. But the genealogies and the geography could not possibly be set into unitary relation, and so Hecataeus too is a disappointment: a comedown from the unifier Pythagoras even while he is a scientific advance beyond him.

Heraclitus' fondness for ratios and proportions should indicate that some sets of relations among the four figures are being posited in B 40, as the term *autis* ("moreover") further invites us to see.[9] One set, that provided by Bollack and Wismann (pp. 151–152), concentrates on both domains and procedures:

> The four names present, in the whole extent of science, four exemplary types. All the forms of knowledge are there: the organization of the divine in Hesiod, the numerical constitution of the world in Pythagoras, the renewal of theological thought in Xenophanes, the systematic inquiry into the life of men in Hecataeus.
>
> A complex network of relationships is established among them, to diversify the nature of the term they have in common: a numerous knowledge (*le savoir nombreux*).

Like Plato after him (Havelock), Heraclitus rejects the Homeric universe. He not only passes over its content in silence and replaces its network of explanations with a rigorously different one (as I shall argue); he also attacks Homer with vehemence:

τόν τε Ὅμηρον ἔφασκεν ἄξιον ἐκ τῶν ἀγώνων
ἐκβάλλεσθαι καὶ ῥαπίζεσθαι καὶ Ἀρχίλοχον ὁμοίως

Homer deserves to be cast out of the contests and flogged, and Archilochus likewise.   (B 42)

If there were an intellectual competition like the athletic games, then it would be apparent that Homer is so unworthy as to be disqualified, and to be struck with a cudgel, just as Homer has Thersites struck (*Iliad* 2.212–277), and for the same reason, his ideas. The verb Heraclitus uses is the very one Xenophanes uses in having Pythagoras say a dog should not be struck that way (Xenophanes B. 7.4–5). And lest we should think that a Thersites-like simple opposition to the Homeric universe would suffice, Heraclitus includes Archilochus identically in his condemnation: counter-assertion in satiric iambs deserves the same

treatment as assertion in heroic hexameters. Homer, like the Pythagoras
of B 129 and the Hesiod of B 57, is a compound of skill and folly. He
is "the most skilled and wisest of all the Hellenes" ("tōn Hellēnōn
sophōteros pantōn," B 56), but he is easily deceived by mere boys, as
men tend to be, with respect to the knowledge of the visible ("tēn
gnōsin tōn phanerōn") when confronted not with a holistic Olympian
view of the universe but a simple and specific problem, a riddle about
fleas, the point of B 56.

Heraclitus further blames Homer (B 105) for saying that no man
can escape his fate (*Iliad* 6.488), coupling that expression to the "born
in a single night" attributed to Hector and Polydamas (18.251) so as
to conclude that Homer is an "astrologer," a term which here is pejorative. And the term must also be pejorative when he applies it to Thales
in his sole direct reference to any Milesian philosopher (*protos astrolo-
gesai*, B 38). Plutarch places Heraclitus' further refutation of Hesiod in
a similarly astrological context when he says that Heraclitus castigated
Hesiod (*epeplexen*) for not knowing that the nature of any and every
day was the same:

περὶ δ' ἡμερῶν ἀποφράδων εἴτε χρὴ
τίθεσθαί τινας εἴτε ὀρθῶς Ἡράκλειτος ἐπέπληξεν Ἡσιόδωι
τὰς μὲν ἀγαθὰς ποιουμένωι, τὰς δὲ φαύλας, ὡς ἀγνοοῦντι
φύσιν ἡμέρας ἀπάσης μίαν οὖσαν, ἑτέρωθι διηπόρηται

> Heraclitus castigated Hesiod for making some days good and oth-
> ers bad, as not knowing the nature of every day to be one.
> (B 106)

Taken with Heraclitus' implied rejection of merely astronomical evidence in Hesiod's corresponding mistake about the identity of day and
night (B 57), the whole force of Heraclitus' testimony about pre-Socratic and other astronomical cosmology is negative. And if this were a
positive rather than a negative statement of Heraclitus', it would be his
sole positive statement about any named person, with the exception of
a single one:

ἐν Πριήνηι Βίας ἐγένετο ὁ Τευτάμεω,
οὗ πλείων λόγος ἢ τῶν ἄλλων.

> In Priene was Bias son of Teutames whose *logos* was greater than
> that of others.   (B 39)

This is positive however one reads it, though it may also be double-edged. If we read *logos*, as most commentators do, in its rare sense "fame, report," then Bias surpasses all others in Priene without incurring the unwelcome fate of Hermodorus, killed for his excellence by the Ephesians (B 121). Bias' preeminence would then have the character of a Homeric *arete*, which also generates fame. If we read *logos* in its more usual sense, Heraclitean and general, of "statement" or "coherent conception," *logos* unifies into one viewpoint the *logoi* of this lesser-known figure, who is always included in the somewhat unstable list of the legendary Seven Wise Men. The actual *logoi* of Bias must have had something of the gnomic character we find in his sayings (probably legendary), as reported by Stobaeus from Demetrius of Phalerum (Diels 10.3). If so, then they were homelier versions of the "tribal" thought whose loftier formulation is to be found in the Homeric poems. In such a Homeric world *logos* in the sense of fame resolves into *logos* in the sense of thought. Merit and responsibility are as indissociable from one another, Adkins points out, as abstract formulation would also be from them. Such an identity of these two senses of *logos* would certainly render impossible any achievement of a true Heraclitean *logos*. Though common (*xunos*), this Homeric *logos* would keep people asleep, whereas Heraclitus elsewhere (B 2) contrasts sleep with the wakeful awareness of philosophical unity.

At this point I am close to reading too much into Heraclitus, the pitfall of all his unitary interpreters (Hegel, Nietzsche, Heidegger), when they are not following the misplaced emphasis of those who give their rigorous attention only to the cosmological statements. But we have no choice, before such a barefaced statement as B 39; we must risk reading too much in, or we shall certainly read in too little.

This exhausts the list of Heraclitus' references to his predecessors and contemporaries. Brief though it is, however, it is unusual for existing at all. Heraclitus is the only one of the pre-Socratics who refers to other thinkers by name.

Such interreference as we may deduce in Heraclitus is to the ideas rather than to names. Parmenides, for example, is alleged to be refuting Heraclitus' principle of reconciling opposites,[10] a doctrine which for Heraclitus himself finds close parallels in the pairs of opposites attributed to Pythagoras (Diels 58 B5). But he does not name Pythagoras in this connection, or the Thales from whom he may have adapted the doctrine of water-transmutation (B 31). If he takes over notions about thunder and lightning, and even the notion of *Dike* from Anaximander, the former are too much in the mainstream of cosmological speculation, and the latter is too common in the Greek vocabulary, to be attributed to a particular interdependence of two thinkers. When Heraclitus does mention another thinker, his main concern is to dissociate himself, in both doctrine and practice. This concern, unique in his time, should lead us to seek a corresponding uniqueness in his doctrines and practice. And we should examine all his statements as closely as we have the cosmological ones. Those happen most to resemble in concern the very thinkers from whom he is trying to dissociate himself, naming some quite forcefully and passing over others, above all the Milesians, in silence.

4.

The particular originality of Heraclitus in his historical context should be seen first in his form, the separate utterance. Whereas what has come down to us from antiquity of the other pre-Socratics is in the form of fragments, the utterances of Heraclitus are almost surely entire statements. These single aphorisms are for the most part not fragmentary, even though a few of them are longer than aphorisms. And certainly many are lost. Most writers since Aristotle have looked past the individual aphorisms and applied them one to another to make them yield a doctrine. This procedure, while correct and to some degree unavoidable, has often had the effect, definitely avoidable, of re-directing the thrust of the individual utterance.

Each of his aphorisms stands free. It is Heraclitus' startling originality to make them do so, a view which has been defended at least since Diels. With a master-stroke Heraclitus liberates philosophical statement from the continuous discourse in which Anaximander, Anaximenes, and very probably Thales, resemble Homer. Heraclitus harnesses what we may presume was by his time the folk tradition of the proverb and makes it do duty, singly and succinctly, for the enunciation of whole philosophical propositions.[11]

In producing the schematically balanced aphorism Heraclitus may be said to have detached the semantic skeleton from the Homeric hexameter, leaving behind the numbing rhythmic overlay. The sort of counterpoise and ratio, or chiasmus, that Heraclitus characteristically offers in his aphorisms may be seen as a special version of the tendency in Homer to balance epithets off against another, by setting two in one line. Similarly, when Heraclitus asserts the unification of opposites, he in effect takes the elaborate schematic contrasts that Whitman and others have found in the *Iliad*[12] and universalizes them by detaching them from a narrative context.

Binary contrasts are deeply characteristic of mythic thinking generally, as Lévi-Strauss has shown us; and parallelism, whether in meters or not, is deeply characteristic of poetic expression generally, especially in early cultures. Binary schemes without myths, parallelism without poetic lines—Heraclitus takes these over as a usable common denominator from the oral culture that preceded him and transposes them into a form of great simplicity and great power.[13]

Heraclitus' statements differ from conventional proverbs in posing puzzles rather than merely offering experiential solutions. They are like riddles; he is called *ainiktes*,[14] and at least once he does quote a particular riddle, the one about Homer, "wisest of all the Hellenes" (B 56): Homer indeed is wisest in his presentation of Olympian myth, but less clever than the boys who offer him a riddle about fleas.

In those terms Homer's world of myth is closed off from the boys' world of riddle. Now, as André Jolles (p. 129) argues, "Myth is an answer in which a question has been comprised; riddle is a question that postulates an answer." Heraclitus has found not a simple form but a simple trans-form of expression. The answer the aphorism offers comprises a question about what is really being said, and in such a way that the aphorism is also a question whose answer is given as well as postulated. The world of myth is demythologized, the world of riddle is departicularized. Myth here is not an inversion of riddle any longer, and one riddle loses some of its point's particularity by getting the contextual frame of the hyperbolic and itself paradoxical contrast between wise Homer (more than men) and the boys (less than men) of B 56. B 51 is like a riddle *plus* its solution:

οὐ ξυνιᾶσιν

ὅκως διαφερόμενον ἑωυτῶι ὁμολογέει· παλίντροπος
ἁρμονίη ὅκωσπερ τόξου καὶ λύρης.

> They do not know how what is borne apart is borne together, a
> back-turning harmony, as of a bow or a lyre.   (B 51)

Taken by themselves, the bow and the lyre have some of the character of a Homeric simile. But taking them as themselves illustrating the principle they enunciate, as *palintropos*,[15] they are solutions to the riddle, "turning back" the expression upon itself. "In what way can a thing that is borne together be at the same time borne apart? Answer: a bow or a lyre."

In their sometimes explicit insistence on a contextual framework the gnomic statements of Heraclitus resemble that riddle aimed towards the future: the oracle. Oracles became quite prominent during the period of tyranny, colonization, and imperial threat of the Asia Minor into which Heraclitus was born. Heraclitus' one statement about oracles says, on the face of it, what everybody knows about oracles, that they give their indications in cryptic form:

$$\text{ὁ ἄναξ, οὗ τὸ μαντεῖόν ἐστι τὸ ἐν}$$
$$\text{Δελφοῖς, οὔτε λέγει οὔτε κρύπτει ἀλλὰ σημαίνει.}$$

> The lord, he whose oracle is the one in Delphi, does not speak or conceal but gives a sign.   (B 93)

But this speaking is referred to as not speaking (as therefore a *legein* that lacks some essential attribute of a Heraclitean *logos*), and the cryptic utterance is declared not to be cryptic (*ou kryptei*, when in accordance with another aphorism, "nature loves to hide itself," "physis kruptesthai philei," B 123).

B 93 shares the very characteristics of the oracle it describes: it does not conceal and it does not speak; it indicates. Now it is extremely unlikely that this statement is merely a commonplace about oracles. Any Greek knows that the oracle does not give a plain answer. What happens at Delphi which (contrary to expectation) is not speaking and not concealment is (as everybody knows) an indication about the future. In some sense this model would have to serve for all utterances, including preeminently those of Heraclitus himself, which are inferior to those of the oracle in issuing from a man rather than a god (*ho anax*—the God as superior), but presumably superior in that they do *legein*; they comprise the Heraclitean *logos*, in a way that a mere oracle, always applied to a specific future situation, would not.

The dialectic above, where the act of defining the oracle both does and does not define the utterance in which the definition is made, provides its own self-sufficient context while talking about another context.

The oracle context has at least six constituents: the god, the prophetess, Delphi, the consultant, the utterance, the future event. All these constituents must be translated into a single pointing of direction (*semainei*), as the self-sufficient statement before us, it announces, cannot be. Neither can we translate this statement into the later distinction between syntax (implied by *legein*) and diction (*semainein* much as the term comes to imply for Plato [*Cratylus* 393a]), though again that distinction cannot be declared to be absent. Nor, since the oracle comes from a god, can we exclude the Homeric sense of *semainein*, "command" (*Iliad*, 1.289, etc.). Heraclitus has here produced a statement which at once exemplifies and qualifies what it says. Consequently, it is more like an oracle than a riddle; though oracle tends to meld with riddle,[16] it is also more like a riddle than any oracle. And it is more bare-faced and commonplace in phrasing than a riddle or an oracle ever are.

The proverb is oriented towards the past; it summarizes common experience, and Heraclitus was used in antiquity as a source of proverbs, some of his aphorisms (B 130–135) coming down to us in a collection of proverbs. The riddle is oriented towards concrete objects that can be named: fleas or whatever. The oracle is oriented towards the future: it hints at a definite result in future time. Heraclitus' statements are undefined as to time, and yet they bring together past, present, and future in their melding of these simple verbal forms, much as the seer Calchas is said to have done in the *Iliad* (1.70). Oracle, too, tends to meld with proverb: the proverbs *meden agan* and *gnothi seauton* are attributed to the Delphic oracle. But they are also attributed to this or that person (including Bias) in the list of the Seven Wise Men (Diels 10), and Heraclitus is their successor.

The riddle, Aristotle says, enables one to make a statement through metaphor which one would not be able to make by a combination of terms ("tēn tōn onomatōn synthesin").[17] He has also defined the essence (idea) of the riddle as putting the statements in question (*legonta hyparchonta*) into impossible combination. And it is perhaps no accident, since Aristotle is our source in both instances, that the word he uses for "combination," *sunapsai*, is the same which Heraclitus himself (presumably) uses in the nominal form for the beginning of B 10: "synapsies hola kai oukh hola," "combinations are whole entities and not whole entities."

Heraclitus' form of the riddle bypasses what could be called metaphor; it tends to pass on to the simile,[18] a form that makes logical con-

nections more explicit. Its combinations are whole entities, but, rid-
dlingly, they are at the same time not whole entities: they advertise the
fact that there is a process by which they require completion. We must
supply a thought-process to the statement about the oracle at Delphi,
or else we are left with a useless commonplace on our hands. The plain
sense remains apparent, "How could anyone escape what never ducks
under (or never sets)" (B 16). But on the other hand, concealment is
a law, "Nature loves to hide herself" (B 123).

5.

Now, the thought process which we apply to B 93 is a critical one:
to make the statement mean more than a commonplace about the oracle
it must pointedly question what a statement is (including itself), what
an oracle is, and how an oracle relates to a statement. The process
underlying this single sentence already coils within itself the elenchic
and contextual process by which Socrates, pretending to be puzzled,
asks what *arete* is.

The development of such an elenchic process begins before Plato.
According to Montgomery Furth, it is the only way we can solve Parmenides' seeming self-contradictions:

> First, it is of the essence of Parmenides' procedure, as I under-
> stand it, that *he is not at this point putting forth an ontology of his
> own*, but is practising dialectical criticism upon that being put forth
> by Betathon; his own word for his argument is *elenchos* (B 7.5),
> which we must assume means for him, as it presently was to mean
> for Socrates, the technique of refuting an opponent by reasoning
> from a premise that the opponent accepts to a conclusion that he
> must regard as intolerable, such as an explicit self-contradiction or
> the negation of some proposition that (for whatever reason) he
> cannot deny, and thus forcing him to abandon the premise.
> [p. 118]

Applying Furth's perspective to B 93, we may say that Heraclitus is
"practising dialectical criticism" not upon what an interlocutor puts
forth, but upon what he himself is putting forth. While not so Platonic
in his elenchic procedure as Furth's Parmenides, Heraclitus does provide an *elenchos* of the statement upon itself. We test the meaning of
"the Delphic oracle does not speak or conceal but gives a sign" by what
it says, by asking in what sense it itself does what it describes (a proce-

dure quite different from just seeing how many meanings it has). From the suspended contradictions of Heraclitus' method we know he does not regard an explicit self-contradiction as impossible.[19] In this elenchos he has seen the possibility of coming at explicit contradictions not by elaborate Parmenidean dialectic (if indeed he could have lived long enough to be aware of Parmenides), and not by Pythagorean mathematical fiat, but by a kind of statement where contradictions are by-passed, in the very process of making the statement. Such a statement would not be either an answer (like the myths of his predecessors) nor a question-with-hidden answer (like the riddles of his folk contemporaries), but a *logos*, a mere statement.

There would be a sort of looseness, of course, in the way such a statement would critically apply to itself. A similar looseness obtains even of the much more fully developed *elenchos* in Plato, which exhibits a variety of logical functions as Robinson presents them. The very openness of possibility for Plato, as earlier for Heraclitus and Parmenides, would allow the *elenchos* to develop. And we may apply to Heraclitus what Robinson says (p. 15), commenting on Plato's use of *logos*, "the assumption that there are no extra premises is made easier by the ambiguity of the phrase 'according to your logos,' which Socrates frequently uses in refutation, especially in drawing the conclusion."[20]

By the time of Heraclitus *logos* means more than a single word (the Greek word *logos* implies a statement, as against *epos* or *onoma*). Where Heraclitus speaks of a single word, he connects it with the process of an utterance which, in syntactic analysis, would be predicative:

$$\text{ἓν τὸ σοφὸν μοῦνον λέγεσθαι}$$
$$\text{οὐκ ἐθέλει καὶ ἐθέλει Ζηνὸς ὄνομα.}$$

> The wise, one, alone does not wish and wishes to be called the name of Zeus.   (B 32)

The signifier *onoma* for a single word connects immediately to a unitary signifier, *hen*, which implies a further prediction of skill/wisdom, *to sophon*, which nests a distinction: "one" taken globally as *hen* and one taken severally as *mounon*. That the question of identity or difference between *hen* and *mounon* may be pressed to yield some of the theoretical foundations of modern number theory would be incidental here. Nor is such theory entirely absent in a philosophical context where the one-many problem was already a live issue, or in a tradition that had produced Pythagoras and would very shortly produce Zeno, Melissus, and Eudoxus. In B 32, however, the quasi-resolved contradiction between *hen* and *mounon* is itself nested in a syntactic contradiction on which it depends, *ouk ethelei kai ethelei*, "does not wish and wishes." This contradiction reverses normal Greek syntax; we would usually get the negative *ouk* second in order, not first. This phrase *ouk ethelei* also stretches the subcategorization rules (to use modern linguistic terms) by which the verb *ethelo* is restricted to animate human or superhuman nouns for its subject. "The one" cannot "wish"—unless "the one" is somehow animate, which would be the case of the god Zeus. Other aphorisms of Heraclitus about the difference between human and divine perception allow us to include in the sense of B 32 a special, intensive sense of the verb *ethelo* when it takes a divine subject. "Not wishing in some human sense I mean, but wishing *par excellence* it is, when the one wishes to be called the name of Zeus." This slant to the reading would also assign a strong semantic function to the abnormal prior position of the negative *ouk*.

There are, I have been saying, several slants to the reading of this aphorism. The slants interlock, to produce not what one normally thinks of as ambiguity, a puzzled suspension between one or more mutually exclusive readings or even the rich harnessing of these for "poetic" effect. Rather, the several slants come sharp and clear. Their coexistence acts not so much for enrichment, though Heraclitus is incidentally "poetic" in this sense, as many poets are. He is also sternly propositional, as poets tend not to be. The effect of the several slants is elenchic and dialectical. They themselves constitute a *logos* in the sense of a chain of reasoning (sense IV, 1, Liddell and Scott) as well as a *logos* in the sense of a voiced statement (sense VI) and a *logos* in the sense of an ordered explanation (sense III). *Legesthai* in B 32 means primarily the second of these, but the other two senses cannot be ruled out, particularly in view of the implied quasi-resolved contradiction with *onoma* (contrasted with *logos* as "locution" with "statement" in earlier usage), and particularly in view of the centrality of the term *logos* for Heraclitus.

6.

The vast complexity of this term works even more forcefully as an indicated process describing the aphorisms, *logoi* in an intensively summarizing sense, than it does for the rich plurisignificance of the inclusive term.[21] The elenchic procedure by which one verbal statement tests another (or with Heraclitus tests itself) may be traced in the counter-Homeric act of questioning, an act explicit in Xenophanes and implicit already in Hesiod's defining separation of truth from falsehood. One final result of such intellectual definition would be a holistic doctrine, like those of Pythagoras and Empedocles. Or the procedure of definition itself can be made the center of speculative activity, at the service of a holistic doctrine. Heraclitus, who may well possess a holistic doctrine like most of his contemporaries, is remarkable and unique for making the elenchic procedure itself become a sort of metalinguistic demonstration: *Logos* as proposition, *logos* as gathering-together, *logos* as affirmation, and *logos* as mere utterance, become one act.

Take, for example, the two "initial" statements which have often been taken as the axiomatic groundwork of Heraclitus' doctrine:

τοῦ
δὲ λόγου τοῦδ' ἐόντος ἀεὶ ἀξύνετοι γίνονται ἄνθρωποι καὶ πρόσθεν ἢ ἀκοῦσαι καὶ ἀκούσαντες τὸ πρῶ-
τον· γινομένων γὰρ πάντων κατὰ τὸν λόγον τόνδε
ἀπείροισιν ἐοίκασι, πειρώμενοι καὶ ἐπέων καὶ ἔργων
τοιούτων, ὁκοίων ἐγὼ διηγεῦμαι κατὰ φύσιν διαι-
ρέων ἕκαστον καὶ φράζων ὅκως ἔχει. τοὺς δὲ ἄλλους
ἀνθρώπους λανθάνει ὁκόσα ἐγερθέντες ποιοῦσιν,
ὅκωσπερ ὁκόσα εὕδοντες ἐπιλανθάνονται.

> The *logos* being this always men are without understanding both
> before they hear and when they first hear. For when all things do
> come to be according to this *logos*, they are like the untried, trying
> these words and deeds, such as I search out according to nature
> distinguishing each and telling how it is. What they do when awake
> escapes other men just as what they forget when they are asleep.
> (B 1)

διὸ δεῖ ἕπεσθαι τῶι
⟨ξυνῶι, τουτέστι τῶι⟩ κοινῶι· ξυνὸς γὰρ ὁ κοινός. τοῦ λόγου δ' ἐόντος ξυνοῦ ζώουσιν οἱ πολλοὶ ὡς ἰδίαν
ἔχοντες φρόνησιν.

> The *logos* being common, the many live as if they had private
> thought.   (B 2)

In B 2 a distinction between speaking (*logos*) and thinking (*phronesis*)
—a distinction still very much alive in philosophy—is superseded by
the distinction between "common" and "private," because the first distinction disappears when the second one is perceived. If men realized
that the *logos* is common they would also then have a common *phronesis*
rather than a private one, a state of affairs which the aphorism presents
as philosophically correct. Still, it is an unattained goal rather than a
mere fact, very much along the lines of B 18, where one must hope for
something to see something:

$$\text{ἐὰν μὴ ἔλπηται, ἀνέλπιστον οὐκ}$$
$$\text{ἐξευρήσει, ἀνεξερεύνητον ἐὸν καὶ ἄπορον.}$$

> If he does not hope for it, he will not find the unhoped-for, it being
> uninvestigated and unapproachable.   (B 18)

What does "the *logos* being common" mean? It surely must refer, as has
nearly always been assumed, to Heraclitus' holistic and unitary doctrine.
That is the strong sense of *logos*. But there is also a weak and casual
sense, where "the *logos* being common" would mean "speech is a shared
activity among men" or "we must share speech to understand one another; so in that sense at least our thought is not private." This casual
observation about language, the weak sense, can be made to produce
the strong sense, again by the elenchic and metalinguistic operation of
the aphorism upon itself.

In B 1 men are always (if *aei* may be said to carry through the
clause)[22] trying individual words (*epeon*) rather than *logoi*, and particularly this *logos* (the weak sense) of Heraclitus, which they fail to
understand both before they hear it and after. They remain in the
semblance of the untried or inexperienced; the *peiromenoi* resemble
a-peiroisin, the latter word usually referring to deeds (*ergon*) not words,
but *epeon* and *ergon* are on a par here as the objects of "trying." Moreover, the words and deeds they are trying are no different from the ones
that Heraclitus sets out. They are "just such (*toiouton hokoion*) as I
am setting out according to the way things are (*kata phusin*)." All this
process takes place, again, "when all things come into being according
to this *logos*"—with the strong and weak senses of B 1 again repeated
for *logos*. There is a permanent situation (*aei*) with an implicit possible
contrast (*ginomenon* could mean "coming into being" or "existing")
and an actual contrast, the permanence of *aei* set against the punctual

moment-by-moment of the aorists in *akousai* and *akousantes*, not likely
to be gnomic in so long a passage.

The final statement here serves both as a conclusion and as a transposition to the category waking-sleeping, which functions in other statements of Heraclitus. That category is here adduced to remove the distinction, strangely, between waking and sleeping, by a logical inference
based on a casual observation. If men "let escape from their memory"
(*epilanthanomai* is causative) what they do when asleep, then the things
they do when they are awake, if those things escape them, have the same
status (*hokosa, hokosper*). In that case their activity (*poiousin*) and
their passivity (*akousai*, "hear" or "obey") have the same character,
and sleeping cannot yet for them be distinguished from waking when
they permanently lack understanding (*aei axunetoi*). The last statement
may also include an acute observation about the sleeper; he tends to
forget his own role in dreams more quickly than the actions of those
around him.

In this process to misunderstand (*a-xunetoi*) the *logos* may carry the
pun, as Bollack remarks, of a divorce from the "common," (*xunos*, B 2,
etc.). Speech is there accessible to all, but it must be understood in a
"deep" sense and it is called deep in B 45:

$$\psi\upsilon\chi\tilde{\eta}\varsigma\ \pi\epsilon\acute{\iota}\rho\alpha\tau\alpha\ \acute{\iota}\grave{\omega}\nu\ o\grave{\upsilon}\kappa\ \grave{\alpha}\nu\ \grave{\epsilon}\xi\epsilon\acute{\upsilon}\rho o\iota o,\ \pi\tilde{\alpha}\sigma\alpha\nu$$
$$\grave{\epsilon}\pi\iota\pi o\rho\epsilon\upsilon\acute{o}\mu\epsilon\nu o\varsigma\ \grave{o}\delta\acute{o}\nu\cdot\ o\check{\upsilon}\tau\omega\ \beta\alpha\theta\grave{\upsilon}\nu\ \lambda\acute{o}\gamma o\nu\ \check{\epsilon}\chi\epsilon\iota.$$

The bounds of the soul you would not find out as you go, traversing the whole way; so deep a *logos* does it have.   (B 45)

Full humanity is here seen as an unending process, to which one would
not have discovered the boundaries even after "traversing the whole
way." They are the boundaries of the soul, in another aphorism, where
the *logos* increases and exalts (both are senses of *auxon*) when it is
perceived as linked to the soul:

$$\psi\upsilon\chi\tilde{\eta}\varsigma\ \grave{\epsilon}\sigma\tau\iota\ \lambda\acute{o}\gamma o\varsigma\ \grave{\epsilon}\alpha\upsilon\tau\grave{o}\nu\ \alpha\check{\upsilon}\xi\omega\nu.$$

Of the soul is a *logos* increasing itself.   (B 115)

Here the predication insists on itself, since we have a copula and it is a
stylistic peculiarity of Heraclitus' shorter statements to omit the copula (B 3, B 33, B 48, B 54, B 60, B 62, B 67, B 96, B 101a, B 103,
B 107, B 119). And the predication is strong: "It is the property of the

soul to be a *logos* that increases itself" and also "it is the *logos* in the soul that is the element that exalts it." *Psyche* retains the weak sense "breath of life," but he has also given to *psyche*, according to Martha Nussbaum, a new, strong sense as that in a man which organizes all his faculties. This statement can also be made a version of one reading of B 1 and B 2: "Human life is properly seen as an increment (*auxon*) of speech-acts." When human life is not so seen, the possibility of the Heraclitean utterance, in its elenchic dynamism (and so, according to Heraclitus, the possibility of any self-conscious utterance) will have disappeared. "It is *itself* (*heauton*) that the *logos* increases."

So Heraclitus, who tends anyway to the third person in Bollack's reading (pp. 11–15), erases himself from the very *logos* which of course he is making at every point, as well as "carrying through" (*diegeumai*, B 1). So he says auditors must go through the logical step of detaching the speaker from the speech in order to perceive the underlying unity:

'οὐκ ἐμοῦ, ἀλλὰ τοῦ λόγου ἀκού-
σαντας ὁμολογεῖν σοφόν ἐστιν ἓν πάντα εἶναι' ὁ Ἡ. φησι.

> Hearing not me but the *logos* it is wise for them to agree they know the one is all.   (B 50)

(For *einai* Bollack reads the manuscript *eidenai*, and this *difficilior lectio* gives a stronger sense.) The act of wisdom (*sophon*) is the act of simple accord or agreement (*homologein*), and going through the process is equivalent to knowing that "one" is "all"—that, among other senses, one *logos* can be taken for all. The stupid man, by contrast, will not face a statement: he flutters in fright before any; and it is part of his stupidity that he is actually fond (*philei*) of doing so. It is a habit or wont (a sense of *philei*) which he enjoys too much to break:

βλὰξ ἄνθρωπος ἐπὶ παντὶ λόγωι
ἐπτοῆσθαι φιλεῖ.

> The stupid man loves to flutter before every *logos*.   (B 87)

More important, as always, than the doctrine *hen panta* is the process of wakeful attention in which it is perceived—but the separation cannot be made between process and doctrine, as Heidegger (1, p. 18) reminds us of B 50: "Heraclitus teaches neither [pantheism] nor any teaching. As a thinker he offers only thinking." Actually, Heraclitus' elenchic process is so comprehensive as not to permit even this restriction. When he induces a thought, the resultant process of thinking provides a center of affirmation as well as a means of restrictive denial.

The variety of emphases and the possible contradictions in the senses of the word *logos* exemplify the actual process of setting contradiction into coordinated statement. The implied affirmation that contradictions are meaningful, and the process by which they are found so—taken together—form the single subject we can confidently locate as central to Heraclitus' thought.

Seen in the light of such an elenchic procedure, a doctrine of Heraclitus, the resolution of contradictions, is inseparable from a constant linguistic technique, the metalinguistic thrust of his utterances. "Does not wish and wishes" (B 32), by being referred to a linguistic procedure (and in this case further explicitly to an act of saying, *legesthai* as used in B 32), is qualified in the contradiction it nests. The same is true for the contradiction between horizontal (*peirata*, bounds) and vertical (*bathus*, deep), resolved by being stated as unachieved in B 45 ("You would not find out"). So that even the possibility of a plain reading leads to an elenchic series for B 60:

$$\text{ὁδὸς ἄνω κάτω μία καὶ ὡυτή.}$$

The road up/down is one and the same.   (B 60)

The double affirmation claims, as it were, the necessity of duplication, of saying "one" and "the same," just because if there must be some sense to linguistic signification, the law of contradiction would seem to be violated in this statement. If the road up and the road down are not in some sense distinguishable then the words *ano* and *kato* would have no meaning. One can read B 60 as saying that for a man whose house is on top of a hill the same road is the road down when he is leaving home and the road up when he is returning. Or in the "life is a road" metaphor that seems to underlie B 32 (and is found in the later reported form of the Oedipus riddle), one can say that it would be possible to attribute life to the beginning of a man's existence and to the end. Any road is "one and the same," from whatever standpoint. One could go on to produce other plain readings of B 60, and these would tend not to exclude one another. They would merely have in common a resolution of the seeming contradiction (up/down) which the predicate of the aphorism itself ("one and the same") would seem to resolve.

Aristotle himself, who formulated the law of contradiction, seems to
pause over Heraclitus as a puzzling case when stating the law: he has
just summarized the law in. the *Metaphysics* and called it the firmest
(*bebaiotate*) of principles. He then states it again:

$$\text{ἀδύνατον γὰρ}$$
ὁντινῦν ταὐτὸν ὑπολαμβάνειν εἶναι καὶ μὴ εἶναι, καθάπερ
τινὲς οἴονται λέγειν Ἡράκλειτον· οὐκ ἔςι γὰρ ἀναγκαῖον,
ἅ τις λέγει, ταῦτα καὶ ὑπολαμβάνειν.

> For it is impossible to suppose that anything whatever that is the
> same can be and not be, as some men think Heraclitus says. For it
> is not necessary, as to what one says, also to suppose those things.
> (*Metaphysics* 1005 b 23)

Does Aristotle agree or disagree with the men who think this about
Heraclitus? As he often does in his historical statements, Aristotle has
stopped just at the point where we would consider the question to be
crucial. The very fact that he has done so ought to put us on our guard
about separating the manner in which Heraclitus states the reconciliation
of opposites from the doctrine that they are to be reconciled. It is fair
to say that Aristotle seems here unwilling either to affirm or to deny that
Heraclitus contradicted the law of contradiction.

The principle of disambiguation (applied by *panton kekhorismenon*,
B 108), which would allow for the contradictions to be sorted out, or
even to be asserted as reconciled, cannot for Heraclitus be detached from
the context in which the statement about anything, including disambiguation, would be made. Contradictions tend to nest other contradictions,
or at least distinctions, as *ano/kato* above nests a more colloquial distinction, *mia/heaute*. In B 32 there is a whole series of such nestings:
*hen/sophon, hen/mounon, ouk ethelei/ethelei, legesthai/onoma, Zenos
onoma/hen*, and combinations of these. But all the nested contradictions and distinctions can be caught up, as the very multiplicity of the
nestings implies, in the elenchic thrust of an utterance: "ethos anthropo
daimon" (B 119), "habit for man, god," has only three words. It is
stripped of its copula for maximum economy (though gnomic sayings
are the one place where the copula may be omitted without wrenching
the Greek language). And it nests as many distinctions as it has words:
ethos/anthropo, ethos/daimon, anthropo/daimon, without reference to

interaction between the potential contradictions, which I shall discuss below.

Heraclitus' aphorism about disambiguation, sets up a context and an experience, itself based on a negation:

ὀκόσων λόγους
ἤκουσα, οὐδεὶς ἀφικνεῖται ἐς τοῦτο, ὥστε γινώσκειν
ὅτι σοφόν ἐστι πάντων κεχωρισμένον.

> Of as many as I have heard *logoi*, no one [either *"person"* or *"logos"* but not both] attains to the point of knowing that wisdom is separated from all things.   (B 108)

This startlingly proto-Aristotelian act of radical definition[23] exemplifies what it asserts, since it is realizing this one principle that separates Heraclitus from everything else that he has heard, all of that (*hokoson*) being defined negatively—being separated (*kekhorismenon*)—by its not attaining to the point of realizing just this principle.

In a similar aphorism (B 72) it is the *logos* that is personified (*dioikeo* normally takes a human subject) as administering such wholes (*hola*) where people incessantly (*dienekos*) traffic, thereby entailing differentiation:

ὧι μάλιστα διηνεκῶς ὁμιλοῦσι λόγωι τῶι τὰ
ὅλα διοικοῦντι, τούτωι διαφέρονται, καὶ οἷς καθ' ἡμέραν
ἐγκυροῦσι, ταῦτα αὐτοῖς ξένα φαίνεται.

> With what they most continually consort, the *logos* managing the wholes, with that do they differentiate themselves; and what they happen upon in the day, those things appear strange to them.
> (B 72)

There is a superlative at the outset here, *malista*, which certainly goes with "continually," and may carry on through the clause. The whole process of "consorting" in any case further entails, and also exemplifies, another process, that of finding alien to themselves or strange (*xena*) whatever they happen upon. Here, though the process may be haphazard, the principle is carried through, however unaware of it the agents might be. Elsewhere, where the same verb for "happen upon" is used, their imperception is the subject in view:

οὐ γὰρ φρονέουσι τοιαῦ-
τα πολλοί, ὁκόσοι ἐγκυρεῦσιν, οὐδὲ μαθόντες γινώ-
σκουσιν, ἑωυτοῖσι δὲ δοκέουσι.

Many do not understand such things, all the persons that happen
upon them, and they do not know them when they have learned
them, but they appear to themselves to do so.   (B 17)

The final reflexive pronoun, *heautoisi de dokeousi*, is odd, as Bollack points out. There is an identity which is circular (*heautoisi*, to
themselves) and so only apparent (*dokeousi*). In this case the same
principle of disambiguation is asserted by the intentionality of an opposite case, where the lack of understanding even after things have been
learned produces a condition where disambiguation is impossible. The
state that Heraclitus is here rejecting would seem, from the point of
view of modern logic, very close to his own notion of the identity of
opposites. But he is clearly stating it here to be an impossible state
of affairs when looked at negatively, even though when looked at positively, the same process of "happening on" (*enkurousi*, B 72) can activate a situation that allows for the *logos* to manage wholes (*hola*) and
for a strangeness (*xena*) to be perceived instead of a mere seeming
identity (*heautousi de dokeousi*).

Such a process is a necessary prior condition to the conscious realization of any fact whatever, Heraclitus asserts, since any fact must be
accompanied by an act of attention, defined as an act of expectation or
hope. Without this there is no approach (*aporon*, B 18) to the fact.

Giving a contextual and metalinguistic twist to his expression of the
unity of opposites keeps Heraclitus from being a mere stater of para-
doxes, a writer of *Dissoi Logoi* (Diels 90; II, pp. 405–16). Even without regard for the elenchic process, the unity of opposites is often qualified in his aphorisms by the explicit statement of measure or proportion
(B 30, B 31, B 94), and by its linguistic equivalent of the simile.[24]

I leave aside what is, if not Heraclitus' all-encompassing doctrine,
one of his most frequent subjects, the unity of opposites as it applies to
the notions of flux and measure. Not only have these questions been
discussed so exhaustively that I have nothing to add to them; I feel that
we are not able, given the statements we have, to adjudicate, for example, between the case for a constant flux (Guthrie) and the case for
a spasmodic one (Kirk). Moreover, the much-discussed river proposi-

tion, which Plato sees as a simile (*apeikazon*),[25] is uncertain in its application, beyond the fact that it was understood in antiquity to indicate flux.

What is uncertain is just how far a general principle can be deduced from the specific assertion, and consequently how the explicitly physical statements relate to those that may or may not be physical. "The road up and the road down" has been related to the river-fragments rather unconvincingly, and even more unconvincingly to the fire-process.

The fire of Heraclitus may well have something to do with the notion of *logos*, but we do not have the verbal evidence to decide just what. *Logos* can mean proportion, which can imply *measure*, and measure (*metra*) as an adverb is applied to both the kindling and the quenching of the fire which is once identified with *kosmos*:

κόσμον τόνδε, τὸν αὐτὸν ἀπάντων, οὔτε τις θεῶν
οὔτε ἀνθρώπων ἐποίησεν, ἀλλ' ἦν ἀεὶ καὶ ἔστιν καὶ
ἔσται πῦρ ἀείζωον, ἀπτόμενον μέτρα καὶ ἀποσβεννύ-
μενον μέτρα.

> This *kosmos*, the same for all, neither one of the gods made nor a man, but it always was and will be an always-living fire kindled in measure and quenched in measure.   (B 30)

Does this allow us to make a much closer connection between *logos* and the fire-process than we could make, given all the *logos* aphorisms, if there were no fire aphorisms at all? For that matter, is there evidence here by which we can confidently say that "kindling" and "quenching" are successive rather than simultaneous acts? (A case could be made for perspectival simultaneity, as with "the road up/down is one and the same.")

7.

"Measure" applied to a linguistic utterance takes for Heraclitus the form of a proportion. A proportion stated in proverbial form in itself contains an elenchic thrust; we are meant to ask what it can mean. Such a proportion or ratio, in the form A:B as C:D, is a thought pattern common in Heraclitus, as Hermann Fränkel (1938) tells us:

ἀνὴρ νήπιος ἤκουσε πρὸς δαίμονος
ὅκωσπερ παῖς πρὸς ἀνδρός.

A man is called childish with regard to a god as a child is with
regard to a man.   (B 79)

The form of the proportion here is almost as bare as it can be, but not
quite. "*Ekouse*," strictly "hears," is used in its sense of "has the reputation of," but taken together with "childish" or "foolish" which literally
means "wordless," (*nepios*) there is a nested contradiction between
"hear" and "not speak" which is superseded by the main proportion.
If the *daimon* may be defined as a god whose presence is perceived but
whose identity is not yet established, then the term already names the
side of the man-god relation which makes man as foolish as a child is
in the *child-man* relation. That is what another aphorism says:

Ἡ. παίδων ἀθύρματα νενόμικεν εἶναι τὰ ἀνθρώπινα
δοξάσματα.

So Heraclitus considered the formed opinions of men to be the
pastimes of children.   (B 70)

This reverses the ratio of B 79 while simplifying it. The aphorism about
the boys who tell Homer the riddle about the fleas, on the other hand,
gives a more complicated ratio:

ἐξηπάτηνται, φησίν, οἱ ἄνθρωποι πρὸς
τὴν γνῶσιν τῶν φανερῶν παραπλησίως Ὁμήρωι, ὃς
ἐγένετο τῶν Ἑλλήνων σοφώτερος πάντων. ἐκεῖνόν τε
γὰρ παῖδες φθεῖρας κατακτείνοντες ἐξηπάτησαν εἰ-
πόντες· ὅσα εἴδομεν καὶ ἐλάβομεν, ταῦτα ἀπολείπομεν,
ὅσα δὲ οὔτε εἴδομεν οὔτ' ἐλάβομεν, ταῦτα φέρομεν.

Men are deceived in knowledge of things visible similarly to Homer, who was the wisest of all the Hellenes. The boys deceived him
killing fleas, saying "All we have seen and caught, we have left behind; all we have not seen and not caught, we carry."   (B 56)

Homer/Men-Men/boys is what we would expect, given the fact that
Homer is "wiser than all the Hellenes." However, when Homer is equal
to other men rather than greater, the men who "are deceived in knowl-

edge of things visible similarly to Homer"; then mere boys can deceive him with the riddle about the fleas. In the strange (but epistemologically central) case when wise Homer is equal to all men: then mere boys, normally inferior to men, can be superior not only to men but to Homer himself. The boys do have the sense Heraclitus exalts: sight [*opsis*, B 55], while Homer is proverbially blind. The subversion of the first part of the ratio (Homer's superiority to other men is mentioned first) entails the subversion of any part. Again, B 56 can be taken as asserting either this metalinguistic principle or else as asserting the epistemological priority of "the knowledge of things visible." In fact it asserts both, and asserts them in conjunction with one another. The Homer-men-boys ratio provides an elenchic context for the epistemological desideratum. The desideratum provides a hard test case for even the wisest of the Hellenes, though a simple one if his blindness is considered.

Subversion of normal proportion is often used by Heraclitus to show the revelatory nature of an extreme case: "If all existent things were smoke, noses would perceive" (B 7). "The *sea* is the purest and most polluted water, drinkable and sustaining for fish, undrinkable and deadly for men" (B 61). "Physicians cutting, burning in all ways, testing the sick badly, ask to take pay from the sick they do not deserve, working so as to make good things and illnesses the same" (B 58). "Corpses should be thrown away sooner than dung" (B 96). "Asses would rather eat sweepings than gold; their food is sweeter to asses than gold" (B 9). "Time (*aion*) sporting, is a boy playing checkers; the kingdom is a boy's" (B 52). "The most beautiful cosmos is like a heap of things poured together" (B 124). "War is father of all and king of all; he has shown some as gods, others as men; he has made some slaves, others free" (B 53).

In all of these the proportion is confounded at an extreme point so as to indicate its reach as a cognitive tool. These proportion-subverting aphorisms, seen in this light, in no way contradict (even in a unity of opposites) the aphorisms which assert that proportion is to be maintained at all costs: "It is necessary to quench excess even more than a conflagration" (B 43). "It is necessary for the city to fight for regulatory law (*nomos*) as for a wall" (B 44a). "The sun will not exceed measure. Otherwise the Furies, allies of Justice (*Dike*), will find it out" (B 94).

Justice, *Dike*, implies a proportion, a logic of counterbalances, in Homer; and also in Anaximander's abstract application of the term to cosmological processes. This last aphorism is cosmological, of course, but Heraclitus elsewhere offers the term in an "existential" and also a metalinguistic sense: "They would not know the name of *Dike* if these things did not exist" (B 23). And again, another use of *Dike* is at once epistemological and social: "For the most believable man knows, guards the believable; and indeed even *Dike* will seize the fashioners and witnesses of lies" (B 28).

The thought pattern in B 90 takes the form of a normal ratio, A:B as C:D.

πυρός τε ἀνταμοιβὴ τὰ πάντα
καὶ πῦρ ἀπάντων ὅκωσπερ χρυσοῦ χρήματα καὶ χρη-
μάτων χρυσός.

> All things are exchanged for fire and fire for all things, just as goods are exchanged for gold and gold for goods.   (B 90)

The naked eye can always tell the clear difference between gold and goods. The point is that they are equivalent and reversible only when the exchange process is activated that allows C to be replaced by D or D by C indifferently.

Gold and goods, C and D, are in the subordinate clause. The main clause deals with "fire" and "all things," whose less perceptible exchange process it explains by a perceptible one. The thought-process, as always, is elenchic, a fact emphasized by the co-existence of three meanings for *antameibetai*: "exchange," "repay," (a notion assimilable to *dike*), and "answer" (a metalinguistic touch). The act of forming ratios lies under the caveat of another aphorism, "Let us not make connections or accords (*sumballometha*) at random about the greatest matters" (B 47). And another can be taken either as a caveat or else as a second-order contradiction about contradictions: "That which changes (*metaballon*) comes to rest" (B 84a), "rest" being the final (and inclusive?) term in a series of contradictory pairs—"Sickness makes health sweet and good, hunger satiety, toil rest" (B 111). The term paired with "rest," *kamatos* ("toil, weariness"), also finds definition elsewhere: "It is toil for the same persons to struggle and to be ruled (*archesthai*)" (B 84b, where the slightly commoner contemporary sense "begin" cannot be ruled out for *archesthai*).

In these paired contradictions there is a focus on naming things properly. Finally, of course, Heraclitus is coming to terms with, and solving, problems that are not just verbal. He would seem to be interested in "sickness," for example, a topic to which he returns for its own sake.

"The wisest man with respect to a god appears as an ape in wisdom and beauty and all other ways" (B 83). The formula "Man is to god as ape (is to man)" does not solve any questions about man and god, a relation that is a major preoccupation for Heraclitus. In fact, his tendency is to refer one major preoccupation to another, as the question about the relation of man to god is not only defined by the term *ape* but also referred to another question he often discusses, that of appearances and perceptions ("appear," *phaneitai*). "An invisible (*aphanes*) harmony is better than a visible (*phaneres*) one" (B 54) rings changes on the same verb root as "appears." The aphorism about Homer's failure to guess the boys' riddle about fleas turns on the same root ("the visible," *ton phaneron*, B 56). But the area of perception is not a firm one, even in its problems, if one sets "Eyes are sharper witnesses than the ears" (B 101a), where the eyes get priority, against "Of as many things as there is sight, hearing, knowledge; these I prefer" (B 55), where ears and eyes are not only put on a par, but these two witnesses of the perceptible are themselves put on a par with the technique for thought, *mathesis*; then again, "Eyes and ears are bad witnesses for those who have barbarian souls" (B 107) and "Sight lies" (B 46).

The pre-Socratics did not clearly distinguish between physical and mental phenomena, and yet some unstable form of that distinction is present here, as it must underlie rejection of Hesiod (and everyman) "who did not know day and night; for they are one" (B 57), where day and night certainly do not appear as "one" to the senses. Their identity is an "invisible" harmony (and so preferable by the standards of B 54) rather than a visible one.[26]

Man may be defined by his perceptions. His perceptions, in turn, are influenced by another distinction important for Heraclitus, the distinction between life and death, one that often involves for him a third term like sleep, or water, or immortality. He defines misunderstanding and imperception of the *logos* in the last clause of B 1, in terms of a spurious identity between sleeping and waking. "All the things they do when waking escape other men just as they forget such things when sleeping." "Death is what we see when awake; what we see when asleep, sleep" (B 21). "Man kindles himself a light in the night having quenched his eyes for himself; living he touches the dead when asleep, waking he touches a sleeper" (B 26). "There await men when they die what they do not expect or conjecture" (B 27). "For souls water is death, for water it is death to become earth, but water comes from the earth and the soul from water" (B 36). Whatever physical process is established here with the help of the fire-earth-water series of B 31, there is a logical process which makes the agent or the element or the means of death the same as the cause of coming into being (*genesthai*). To call "psyche" merely "the breath of life" is to rule out a main distinction; "soul" is radically different from "water" and "earth," though at the same time subject here to the process of coming-to-be and passing-away, to use the Aristotelian terms which are only a later development of this distinction. On the spiritual side, the connection of souls with water is an old Indo-European notion and a Babylonian one as well. Thales, like Heraclitus an Asiatic, echoes this connection in his notions "All things are full of gods" (Diels 11A 22) and "All is water" (Diels 11A 14), notions that here Heraclitus transposes in B 36 by putting them through a logical process. (He may also be refuting the metempsychosis of that contemporary he mentions most scathingly, Pythagoras.) "Sickness" and "souls" themselves come into conjunction in B 68, where the mysteries serve as a remedy from the circumstances "inherent in coming-to-be" (*en te genesei*), and perhaps also in B 67a, where the soul acts like a spider to repair lesions in the body.

The principle of contradiction can apply even to such comprehensive terms: "The same thing are living and having died, and having waked and being asleep and young and old; for the latter change into the former and the former change back again into the latter" (B 88). "The god is day night (*euphrone*), winter summer, war peace, satiety hunger (all things are the opposite; this is mind), and it alters itself just as (fire) when it mixes with incenses, is called according to the pleasure of each" (B 67).

In this last statement the metalinguistic arbitrariness of nomenclatures (*onomazetai*) refers not to bewilderment, but to the most comprehensive term, god. As the god here subsumes the pairs of opposites, so he serves in B 102 as a vantage from which human judgments have less than finality, "To the god all things are beautiful and good and just, but men suppose that some things are unjust and others just." Here the term of distinction begins as three (beautiful and good and just) and ends as one, the just (*dikaios*), a term which includes the *dike* of still other aphorisms.

"Human habit does not have knowledges, but the divine does" (B 78). Heraclitus also provides a deliberate paradox in the first clause, since the word for "knowledges" is the same as for "proverbs" (*gnomas*) and it is precisely "habit" or character or custom (*ethos*) that proverbs express. And by another aphorism, the definition of *ethos* for man is precisely the divine (B 119, *daimon*, however, rather than *theion*).

Moreover, in another statement the distinction between life and death is lifted in order to lift another distinction, that between men and gods, a distinction itself made in the language as between the mortal (*thnetoi*) and the immortal (*athanatoi*):

ἀθάνατοι θνητοί, θνητοὶ ἀθάνατοι, ζῶντες
τὸν ἐκείνων θάνατον, τὸν δὲ ἐκείνων βίον τεθνεῶτες.

Immortals are mortal and mortals immortal, living the death of
the former and dying the life of the former.   (B 62)

Heraclitus here wrenches the normal Greek of "the former" (*ekeinos*) and "the latter" (*houtos*) by omitting the second term and repeating the first instead. *Ekeinon*, "those," repeated when it should be complemented, is suspended in the meaning "the former" and might be taken to mean only "those." The pairing of *ekeinon* in reference implies the distinction "former-latter," but when the paired term is the same term, as seldom or never elsewhere in Greek, the grammar of the pronouns emphasizes the arbitrariness of identifications which in any case in the very first clause, with its emphatic suppression of copula, is equally arbitrary in its application. In what sense are immortals mortal? Surely, not finally in the sense of Xenophanes' cultural relativism. The hardest clause is first; it is more difficult to understand how gods die than how there is an afterlife for human beings, because if gods die in Xenophanes' sense, they cannot really be called "immortal"—or have attributed to them the powerful comprehensive function of the other statements quoted above.

And whether we read "*ekeinon*" as "the former" or "those," we are equally uncertain as to how far back we are to go in the clauses to pick up the pronominal reference. Does "the former" include both members of the first clause (as opposed to both members of the second) "immortals-mortal?" Does it include only the first member of the second clause, "mortals (as immortal)?" In that case should I have added that last parenthesis? Does it include the first member of the first clause and the first member of the second, "immortals (as mortal) and mortals (as immortal)?" Should the parentheses be retained in both instances? Or, when read as "*those*," does *ekeinon* include both members of both clauses in their identifications as in their distinctions? The failure to balance *ekeinon* with *touton* opens all these possibilities and turns the simplest form of flat predication, when it identifies men and gods in the charged area of their central distinction and relationship, into a meta-linguistic maze.

8.

As for Heraclitus' direct treatment of the myths of gods, there is a split between his theological aphorisms and his religious ones. When he talks about theology he tends towards an abstract monotheism that is distinctly post-Olympian; his god sounds like the *nous* of Anaxagoras or the holistically perceiving God of Xenophanes (Diels 21, B 24). But when he speaks of religious observance, he is distinctly pre-Olympian. He mentions the mystery cults of chthonic revival most often, identifying Hades with Dionysus, who has a strong chthonic character.[27] The Thracians, legendary for their savagery, are said by Herodotus (5.7) to worship only three gods—Ares, Dionysus, and Artemis—all three of whom are mentioned by Heraclitus, if we may call "*Polemos*" (B 53, B 67, B 80) a non-Olympian version of Ares. Diogenes does not recognize the distinction when saying (Diels A 1) that Heraclitus wrote three books, "On the All, Politics, and Theology," since the term *theology*[28] in the sense contemporary with Diogenes could equally be applied to Heraclitus' statement about "the all," and to his statements about individual figures, the Erinyes, Dike, Dionysus, and the Artemis of common cult at Ephesus on whose altar he is reputed to have lain his book (Diels 22.A1). Empedocles gives his elements the names of gods, but when Heraclitus mentions the chief of the Olympians, Zeus,[29] he says that "the one . . . does not wish and wishes to be called the name of Zeus" (B 31), and "name" (*onoma*) cannot entirely be separated from one of its senses (sense III in Liddell and Scott), "a name and nothing else; a false name." Even such a seemingly cosmological statement as "The sun is new every day" (B 6) also echoes an ancient Indo-European myth.[30] The pigs of B 13 ("Pigs like mud better than pure water") since the paradox turns on "pure," are not perhaps to be distinguished from the purification rites of the Eleusinia, where they were used for sacrifice.[31] This could bear on the point of "pigs bathe in dung" (B 37). The *kukeon*, the barley mixture which could only be drunk off after being swirled around so its elements were separate, "the *kukeon* separates when mixed" (B 125), was also used in the service of Demeter, the chthonic deity of the Eleusinia, as Guthrie points out (p. 200).[32] In this aphorism, the Heraclitean unity of opposites is itself applied to something which is neither questioned nor defined, a ritual drink in a chthonic mystery cult.

Plato neutralizes the chthonic element of the Cave in the *Republic* while utilizing the primitivism of its social circumstances. Heraclitus, on the other hand, centers on the utterances of a priestess in circumstances associable to caves and chthonic cults. The serpent is a chthonic deity, and it is after killing the serpent, Pytho, that Apollo settled on Delphi as the shrine where his priestess would speak oracles from the cave. Heraclitus is the first person in literature to mention the Sibyl, and he does so in order to praise the unvarnished character of her utterance, as distinct, if we are to trust Plutarch, from the charming songs of Sappho:

> Οὐχ ὁρᾶις . ., ὅσην χάριν ἔχει
> τὰ Σαπφικὰ μέλη, κηλοῦντα καὶ καταθέλγοντα τοὺς ἀκροωμένους;
> Σίβυλλα δὲ μαινομένωι στόματι καθ' Ἡράκλειτον ἀγέλα-
> στα καὶ ἀκαλλώπιστα καὶ ἀμύριστα φθεγγομένη χι-
> λίων ἐτῶν ἐξικνεῖται τῆι φωνῆι διὰ τὸν θεόν.

The Sibyl with mad (*mainomeno*) mouth uttering what is unlaugh-able and unadorned and without incense attains to a thousand years with her voice through the god. (B 92)

It is the unexpected side of the god, the awe-filled *daimon*, to which he attributes the essence of humanity, or else the mere habit of humanity, "habit for man: god," "ethos anthropo daimon," (B 119). This statement at once theologizes and demythologizes itself ("Not a *daimon* but character leads a man"). It has three nested contradictions, and they do not really overlap: the known (*ethos*) versus the unknown (*daimon*); man (*anthropo*) versus either his habit or his lair (a Homeric sense of *ethos*); man versus god.[33] In each case we have a logical transfer, "A to B via X," rather than a true ratio or proportion. The transfer dynamically names, and names as dynamic, the relationship between man and god, who as a *daimon* keeps alive and revives the chthonic setting at the same moment that it is getting a post-Olympian definition.

B 92 refers to the *legomena* of a rite where the *dromena* issue in *legomena*. In the *dromena* of the Dionysian rite, the pre-Olympian phallic procession, resides a comparable quickening of definition. And it is to them that Heraclitus speaks, according to Clement: so he defines his audience:

τίσι δὴ μαντεύεται
Ἡ. ὁ Ἐφέσιος; νυκτιπόλοις, μάγοις, βάκχοις, λήναις,
μύσταις· τὰ γὰρ νομιζόμενα κατ' ἀνθρώπους μυστήρια
ἀνιερωστὶ μυεῦνται.

> Night-wanderers, magi, Bacchants, revellers, mystic initiates; for the mysteries men hold in regard (*nomizomena*, also "keep") they celebrate (*mueuntai*, also "keep secret") in an unholy way.
> (B 14)

This list confounds Persian and Greek, surely deliberately, by including magi in the list, and the fact that they were interpreters of dreams (Herodotus 7.37) may correlate with the first item in the list, "night-wanderers," a term more vaguely inclusive than the others and so perhaps applicable to all of them.

These names suggest both praise and blame, as does his statement about the procession:

εἰ μὴ γὰρ Διονύσωι πομπὴν ἐποι-
οῦντο καὶ ὕμνεον ἆισμα αἰδοίοισιν, ἀναιδέστατα
εἴργαστ' ἄν· ὡυτὸς δὲ Ἅιδης καὶ Διόνυσος, ὅτεωι
μαίνονται καὶ ληναΐζουσιν.

> If it were not to Dionysus that they performed the procession and sang a hymn to the shameful parts, most shameful things would have been done. Hades and Dionysus are the same, to whichever (*hoteo*) they rave and revel.[34]   (B 15)

The connection of shame with the act of worship induces, it would seem, not Xenophanes' question but a renewed and enlivened worship, or otherwise it would not be to bacchants and other night wanderers that Heraclitus would be prophesying. The sacrifices that bring a wholly inward purity ("apokekatharmenōn pantapasin"), as distinguished from the "material" ones (*enula*), are those of "few-well-numbered men"

(B 69). The purification with which such mysteries are properly carried out is inseparable from the awareness of its conditions, as he also says:

καθαίρονται δ' ἄλλωι αἵματι μιαινό-
μενοι οἷον εἴ τις εἰς πηλὸν ἐμβὰς πηλῶι ἀπονίζοιτο.
μαίνεσθαι δ' ἂν δοκοίη, εἴ τις αὐτὸν ἀνθρώπων ἐπι-
φράσαιτο οὕτω ποιέοντα. καὶ τοῖς ἀγάλμασι δὲ του-
τέοισιν εὔχονται, ὁκοῖον εἴ τις δόμοισι λεσχηνεύοιτο,
οὔ τι γινώσκων θεοὺς οὐδ' ἥρωας οἵτινές εἰσι.

> They are purified, polluted with another blood as though one step-
> ping into mud would wash off with mud. He would seem to be mad
> if someone took notice of him doing this; and they also pray to
> these images as if someone should converse with buildings, not
> knowing gods and heroes for what they are.   (B 5)

"The gods and heroes" to whom statues stood in the Greek cities of Heraclitus' time were largely Olympian ones, and the mysteries of purification were largely chthonic. Here it is claimed that purification and images are ineffectual if they are not accompanied by awareness. The split in Heraclitus between abstract theology and formal pre-Olympian secret cults does not abrogate the latter in favor of the former. For this very reason he does not have to mount Xenophanes' attack on the Olympians. If "immortals are mortal and mortals immortal" there is a continuity between gods and man, questionable but ineluctable, perceived in the very use of the senses by the soul, "souls smell in Hades/ according to Hades" (*kath'Haiden*, B 98).

9.

The split in Heraclitus' presentation of religious phenomena is paralleled by the split between himself and the society in which he lived. Unlike the bard of oral culture, who summarizes what are simply the views of the tribe, even if he does so as consummately as Homer, Heraclitus questions the values of the tribe. His goal, he says in an aphorism, was himself, "I inquired after myself" (B 101).

The binary patterns of his statements, as I have said above, are reminiscent of the binary patterns that Whitman finds in the organization of incident in the *Iliad*. If mythic thought, the Olympian system or another, is understood as organized into series of binary oppositions, then the contradiction-system of Heraclitus would reproduce the functional procedure of mythology without having recourse to mythic figures or even, except rarely, to mythic tales.

This does not happen without stress between the thinker and his society. One of the few tales Heraclitus tells is that of Hermodorus, who we know from other sources to have engaged in an activity also characteristic of newly literate societies; he was a lawgiver. The Ephesians cast out Hermodorus because he was "most useful" (*onestos*) among them. For doing so they were "fit to be hanged, all but those who had not attained puberty" (B 121). So starkly does Heraclitus view the situation of someone like himself who separates himself from the multitude. And yet such a separation is what he insists on as a prior condition not only of proper religious observance, as above, but of wakeful thought itself.

The transition to literacy brings about such a self-conscious separation, an orientation towards the eye that can read seriatim words in a book that one person writes and one person reads, away from the ear that intimately and instantaneously hears a common metered message sung aloud to the accompaniment of music. Heraclitus, indeed, does stress the superiority of the eye to the ear explicitly, ("Eyes are sharper witnesses than ears," B 101a) and the term visible or perceptible, *phaneros*, also stresses the eye. At the same time in his own role he has not lost the marked status that adheres to the scribe in societies where literacy is not yet common. He often uses the word "hear," *akouein*, in the sense of "understand a doctrine."[35]

The very fact that legends accrued to him, whether or not they were historical, attests to Heraclitus' "tribal" status. He ate grass on the mountains like Nebuchadnezzar, he died of dropsy lying on a dung heap because of taking his own maxims too seriously, he played knucklebone with children rather than participate in political deliberation. These tales are reminiscent of those told about Pythagoras: that a fold in his garment at Olympia revealed his thigh to be made of ivory; and about Empedocles, that he plunged at night into the flaming crater of Etna but left his sandal on the rim.

At the same time, Heraclitus is sensitized towards the definition of social role, not only in the grim aphorism about Hermodorus. One of his three books according to Diogenes Laertius was *politicon*. The isolation of mental disposition (B 14) or mental perception (B 5) as the criterion for distinguishing pure sacrifices from impure amounts to an ethical one. And Gigon says, with some plausibility, "His central thought is ethical." Heraclitus is already beyond the hieratic literacy of such tribal figures as Epimenides, who, according to the legend, slept in a cave fifty-seven years and had letters written all over his body at death.[36]

Lyric poetry already redirects the Homeric practice to the sensibility of the private consciousness. Heraclitus retains the centered act of consciousness when he strips his utterance of meter. And he goes further than the Xenophanes he criticizes for *polymathie* when he gets his acts of demythologizing and his acts of abstract theologizing into a single frame. That frame, however, itself includes, and talks about, a relation to society that the Milesians and Xenophanes, whatever their experience, did not discuss. Where they are inescapably but silently contextual, Heraclitus refers dialectically to his context. And further, he contains a reference to context in some of his most comprehensive utterances, as he does in B 1.

Sometimes he merely establishes the context by indicating what characterizes the imperceptive (B 19, B 20, B 29, B 34, B 71, B 73, B 74, B 86, B 87, B 89, B 97, B 110, B 116, B 117). He can, however, establish the context graphically and forcefully, as in the aphorisms about exiled Hermodorus and the Ephesian adults (B 121) or Homer and the flea riddle (B 56). "One is ten thousands to me, if he be best" (B 49a). *Aristos* could also mean "possessed of *arete*," and the absence of the definite article before *aristos* allows it to be read in more than an exclusive sense. It could refer to an entire aristocratic class. Heraclitus' own definition of *arete* links it to wisdom, "sound thought (*sophronein*) is the greatest *arete*, and it is wisdom (*sophia*) for those who understand (*epainontos*) to speak the truth and act it according to nature" (B 112). "Best" would then involve a Heraclitean philosophical perception, and so it might be said to anticipate the philosopher-kings of Plato's *Republic*; though, unlike Plato, Heraclitus says nothing in this aphorism to indicate that the qualification would not remain open. Any one could conceivably be worth ten thousands.

There is a tension between the common and the private here, which must be maintained for either aspect to be perceived. On the one hand, *hoi polloi* deludedly suppose that they have private knowledge when the *logos* is common (B 2). On the other hand, *hoi polloi* have a tendency to sink back into the common, and that, too, is to be avoided:

τίς γὰρ αὐτῶν
νόος ἢ φρήν; δήμων ἀοιδοῖσι πείθονται καὶ διδασκά-
λωι χρείωνται ὁμίλωι οὐκ εἰδότες ὅτι 'οἱ πολλοὶ
κακοί, ὀλίγοι δὲ ἀγαθοί'

> What is their mind (*noos*) or their sense (*phren*)? They hearken to
> the singers of the people and they employ the crowd (*homilo*) as
> a teacher, not knowing that the many (*hoi polloi*) are bad and the
> few are good.   (B 104)

Here is the Homeric context of ear-oriented transmission in a nut-
shell. It would not matter that in one sense a preeminent bard might be
one of the few rather than the many. By not comprising the tension
between the many and the few, or between private consciousness and
common language, his songs could not lead to "mind" or to "sense." In
such a state they could only "seem to themselves" (B 17). Yet "Those
who sleep are performers and co-workers of what comes about in the
kosmos" (B 75).

In focussing on this tension between the consciousness of the aphorist
and the society where he finds himself, Heraclitus still falls back on its
conventional emblems. "They do not understand that what is borne
apart is borne together with itself: a back-turning harmony-fit, as of a
bow or a lyre" (B 51). What they do not understand is what they find
as common social objects around them. The bow here gets the name
toxos rather than the name he puns with the same name for life in B 48.
"The name (*onoma*) of the *toxos* is *bios*, but its work is death" (B 48).
In the Homeric poems the bow is a chief instrument for performance
(*ergon*, "work"); the lyre is a chief instrument for unifying the act of
using words (*onoma*). The bow and the lyre serve as emblems to make
clear the distinction between *onoma* and *ergon*, as the word *bios* in
Homer does not. The bow and the lyre also serve as emblems for the
Homeric society from which at the same time they are abstracted. To
see them as "back-turning,"[37] itself a revision of the Homeric epithet
"back-sounding" (*palintonos*), reconceives the conditions of the Homeric society and ultimately transposes them,[38] without performing
Plato's act of rejection upon them.

In this verbal act of Heraclitus', we are not yet able to separate
"poetry" from "philosophy" even though his statement itself constitutes
a comparable act of separating them. At the same time, this verbal act
remains applicable for us in its striking conflation of poetry and philos-

ophy, where Heraclitus' notions about fire, should we have correctly disentangled them, belong at best to the early history of science, and his aphorisms about flux express what is by now a truism. The doctrine of flux, as a principle of change, however, became a truism only after it had been subjected to elaborate analysis at the hands of both Plato and Aristotle, who would seem to have got very largely from Heraclitus a focus on the principle of change which is central to the epistemology and the ontology of both philosophers. If they departed from the powerful verbal technique in which he had couched it, that technique remained, to be revived perhaps accidentally by Pascal, by Blake, by Nietzsche, and Wittgenstein.[39] Its force is a permanent resource.

4.

PINDAR: *"Great Deeds of Prowess Are Always Many-Mythed"*

Pouring hunger through the heart to feed desire in intravenous
*   ways*
like the ways of gods with humans in the innocent combination
*   of light*
and flesh or as the legends ride their heroes through the dark
*   to found*
great cities where all life is possible to maintain as long as time.
    —FRANK O'HARA,
      "Ode to Joy"

As life goes on we discover that certain thoughts sustain us
in defeat, or give us victory, whether over ourselves or others,
and it is these thoughts, tested by passion, that we call convic-
tions. Among subjective men (in all those, that is, who must
spin a web out of their own bowels) the victory is an intellec-
tual daily re-creation of all that exterior fate snatches away,
and so that fate's antithesis; while what I have called "the
Mask" is an emotional antithesis to all that comes out of their
internal nature.
    —WILLIAM BUTLER YEATS,
      "The Trembling of the Veil"

1.

"BEST is water, but gold is a flashing fire" (ariston men hudor, ho de chrusos aithomenon pur, O.1.1).[1] Pindar begins and ends this opening aphorism with the two elements, water and fire, that according to Lévi-Strauss may be taken to sum up and close the "vast system" of myth. But in Pindar the system of myth has lost any primary systemization; in Pindar's work the Olympian myths are already undergoing a transmutation comparable to that in Heraclitus, though Pindar reworks and readapts the system of myth while Heraclitus leaves it behind.

Heraclitus, indeed, also offers us all four of these terms—water in his notion of flux, fire in whatever his doctrine of physical process may mean, "best" in his social oppositions, and gold in some pointed state-

108

ments (B 9, B 22, B 90). He notably connects gold and fire in B 90, while fire and water are connected as interchangeable elements in the cyclic process that B 31 describes.

There is, further, a schematism in Pindar's statement which is logically as well as syntactically analogous to the Heraclitean proportion:

$$\text{Water} \quad : \quad \text{best} \quad :: \quad \text{gold} \quad : \quad \text{fire}$$

Here we have three visible elements and one invisible, a fact which makes Pindar's statement correspond even more closely to B 90, where we are again given three visible elements (fire, gold, goods) and one which is ambivalently visible or invisible (all things):

$$\text{Fire} \quad : \quad \text{all things} \quad :: \quad \text{gold} \quad : \quad \text{goods}$$

Heraclitus' statement, of course, is a proposition. Pindar's is at once more elaborate, more homely, and more casual. It is a passing apophthegm, meant, it would seem, not to alert the thought of a new class of thinkers but rather to evoke what a communal group of victory celebrants may take for granted.

Transitory though it is, Pindar's statement will soon lead up to some myths: it is a "priamel," to use the term Bundy adopts, an introductory statement that will soon serve as a comparison and "foil" for a new, more central subject, but also drop away before it. A little priamel occurs within the statement itself; water itself drops away before gold in this aphorism. Water and gold are both complementary and contrasting entities.

Gold here gets something more than a descriptive term; it gets a metaphoric ornamentation; it is a "blazing fire." The Homeric simile is condensed, while remaining poetic. The poet not only invents the statement but also exhibits the process of invention, publicly. Part of the *Programm* of the epinician ode, to adapt Schadewalt's term, is the poet's obligatory reference to his own skill at composition. An athletic victory crowns a prowess of a sort that the *Iliad* celebrates, a set order of known events. In Pindar's poem, however, the order of events is unknown. The events themselves are unknown, though it is known in the *Programm* that the poet will apply an unforeseeable series of myths and aphorisms in an unforeseeable order to a specific present event, a particular victory in a particular contest, centering on a single victor.

A rapid, self-conscious, and somewhat abstract redeployment of Homeric values is made in the first strophe of this poem, where the excel-

lence of the compared elements, extended by the imagination into their
striking natural setting, is linked to the contest and also to the skill of
the poet:

"Αριστον μὲν ὕδωρ, ὁ δὲ χρυσὸς αἰθόμενον πῦρ
ἅτε διαπρέπει νυκτὶ μεγάνορος ἔξοχα πλούτου·
εἰ δ᾽ἄεθλα γαρύεν
ἔλδεαι, φίλον ἦτορ,
μηκέτ᾽ ἀελίου σκόπει
ἄλλο θαλπνότερον ἐν ἀμέρᾳ φαεν-
νὸν ἄστρον ἐρήμας δι᾽ αἰθέρος,
μηδ᾽ Ὀλυμπίας ἀγῶνα φέρτερον αὐδάσομεν·
ὅθεν ὁ πολύφατος ὕμνος ἀμφιβάλλεται
σοφῶν μητίεσσι κελαδεῖν
Κρόνου παῖδ᾽ ἐς ἀφνεὰν ἱκομένους
μάκαιραν Ἱέρωνος ἑστίαν,

Best is water but gold is a flashing fire
In that it shines out in the night supreme over lordly wealth.
If prizes you wish
To sing, dear heart,
Look for no hotter
Bright star in the day than the sun
Through the desert ether,
And let us proclaim no finer contest than Olympia
Whence the many-speeched hymn is cast round
With the counsels of the skilled, to proclaim
The son of Kronos when they come to the rich,
Blest hearth of Hieron.

Water, gold, the sun, the Olympian contest—these are called up for
their superlative qualities in the poet's sounding voice (*audasomen*, 7).

We are still in the world of Homer, where the elements and values,
the mythic forces, are taken for granted. But Pindar's act of linking
them is so strenuous that it constitutes a redefinition. Hieron's victory
(through a jockey) and his success at rule draw to him the superlatives
that in the song associate him to the "son of Kronos" (*Kronou paid*,
10). The association is emphasized by the poem's opening superlative.
Celebrating this victory at Olympia, praising Zeus, following the counsels of the wise, (*sophon metiessi*, 9), enjoying Hieron's hospitality—
these acts are multiple (*polyphatos*, 8) and comprehensively (*amphi-
balletai*, 8) included in the song (*hymnos*). In the 'hymn' itself Pindar

transfers attention and praise from gods to men, according to Jaeger (1965, p. 208). Hieron's hearth is described as "blest" (*makairan*, 11), a word usually associated with the gods, as it is later (52) in this very poem, where it means "gods." Both parties to the interchange between singer and victor are comprehended (*amphi*, 17) in the clustering (*thama*, 17) around his table; the victor "culling the crests from all virtues" is glorified in "the flower of music":

> Who tends the lawful sceptre in Sicily
> Rich in sheep, culling the crests from all virtues,
> And is glorified
> In the flower of music
> As we men sport
> Clustering round his dear table.   (12–17)

The song declares that song is necessary to effectuate the transition from the praise of Hieron's victory to that myth which at once illuminates the victory and directs its meaning, the myth of Pelops and Tantalus. In Homer, of course, the teller does not appear, and the narration stays with a sequence in the story, making it seem present as it is told. In Pindar's epinicians the myth is necessarily drawn from a past remote enough to be legendary, and it is referred to in a way that makes it seem so within the poem. It is the poet who makes the connection, who "takes the Dorian lyre from its peg" (17); and the glory that "shines" (23) does not automatically reach admiring eyes. The poet can distort, as Pindar accuses precisely Homer of doing; and "the greater throng of men has a blind heart" (*N*.7.23–24)—a phrase that echoes, and as it were assimilates, Heraclitus B 1, B 2, B 19, B 34, B 56, and B 104.

In *Olympian* 1 Pindar is concerned to correct a slanderous version of the Pelops story. Pelops did not lose his shoulder at a cannibalistic banquet given by his father Tantalus, who also stole nectar and ambrosia to serve the gods. It was Clotho, rather, who took him from the "pure vessel," his shoulder already "fashioned illustrious with ivory" (27). Poseidon fell in love with Pelops, as Zeus had with Ganymede "at another time" (*deutero chrono*, 43), and transferred him (*metabasai*, 42) to the dwelling of Zeus, invisible to mortals. Tantalus too was much honored by the gods, "but he could not digest/ Great bliss and in satiety seized/ Overweening madness" (55–57), and incurred the permanent torment of a boulder hanging over his head. But his son Pelops, when "down covered his black cheek in flowered youth" (67–68), married

Hippodameia with the supernatural aid of his divine lover, and she "bore six leaders, sons striving in prowesses" (89). At the very moment of Pindar's poem (*nun d'*, 90), Pelops shares in the glories of sacrifice and possesses a much-visited tomb on the spot of the games he founded, in which he excelled.

The poem emphasizes, first of all, the appealing youth of Pelops, which matches the athletic games won; and then the banquet his father held for the gods, which matches the victory feast; and then his own victory at the foundation of these same games; and then his patriarchal fertility, which establishes a flattering analogy between the legendary, vast foundations of Olympia in the Pelop-onnesus and Hieron's vigorous recent efforts to colonize within Sicily. The transformations over long time, from Pelops to Hieron, already are at work in the movement from Pelops' boyhood to his youth, and then to his manhood, when his erotic appeal for Poseidon becomes the basis for his getting the god's aid to marry Hippodameia.

The central comparison, persistently offered but left reverently unstated, is between Pelops, a mythical figure, and Hieron, a present ruler. As Finley says (pp. 74–75), there is a "tacit and incomplete metaphor underlying the odes. There is something godlike in men." Here the proleptic foreshortening of all other references hints at the further applicability of this myth. Preterition, Bundy explains (p. 19), is a major device in Pindar. It becomes a vehicle for dealing with the ineffable by suggesting through omission there might be more to say.[2]

A relation between men and gods is here recommended that would follow the model of the comparison between Hieron and Pelops. Poseidon loved Pelops and aided him, but Tantalus, even though he did not chop his son up, as envious slanderers have maintained (49–51), did aspire too high and stole from the gods.

Though men and gods are said elsewhere to have a common descent and a common mother (*N*.6.1–3), "a wholly differentiated power/ Constrains us apart, as the one is nothing while for the other the safe bronze seat,/ Heaven, abides always" (3–5).[3] There is a contradiction here that must be managed, and in *Olympian* 1 Pindar buoys up his interpretation of Pelops and Tantalus with a whole series of aphorisms.

The aphorisms come first and last: they predominate in such a way that they serve as summaries of the myths, except that the success of legendary beings, like the success of Hieron to which it is implicitly compared, offers a whole if transitory glory of which the aphorism can catch only one aspect: hence the need for swirling series of aphorisms. "There are many marvels, and as for the speaking (*phatis*)/ Among mortals beyond a true saying (*logos*)/ Do tales (*mythoi*) deceive, decked out with variegated lies" (28–29); "Grace (*charis*), fashions all things honeyed for mortals/ Bringing honor, has made even the unbelievable believed/ Many times" (30–31); "Days coming after/ Are the wisest witnesses" (33–34); "It is seemly for a man to say good things about gods; there is less guilt (*aitia*)" (35). This is all one series, which mingles the terms *logos* and *mythos*, focusing them on the "grace" which is a key term in the ode (18, 75).

"Lack of gain is the frequent lot of slanderers" (53); "If a man hopes as he acts to escape the god, he errs" (64); "Great risk does not take a valorless man" (81); "For those who must die, why should one sit and digest/ An anonymous old age in darkness vainly?" (83–84). "Nobility day by day afresh/ Comes highest for every mortal" (99–100); "Some are great in one thing, some in another; the summit is crowned/ For kings. Peer no longer too far." (113–114).

The time included in "no longer" (*meketi*) suggests that the function of the myth in the act of celebration is to set limits at the same time that it is extending horizons. The myth illustrates the aphorism, the aphorism explains the myth; the interaction between myth and aphorism carries the celebrants safely beyond the kind of questions Xenophanes and Heraclitus would raise about myths and aphorisms.

All the time there is a kind of strain put upon the myth here; its aspects must be presented as flashing facets of a known series of events, rather than presented squarely, as in Homer or even later in the centralizing foci of Greek tragedy. Pindar has, so to speak, totally transformed Homer's verse form by conflating the fixed formula type and the flexible formula pattern: the distinctions discerned by Parry and Hainsworth no longer apply. And even the known series requires a careful tact of presentation. It is wrong to say anything less than good of the gods (or the heroes, one may conclude from the central subject here). And, at the same time, the processes of envy exact a constant sifting of false from true. Pindar's poem sets the record straight; eschewing envy and celebrating glory become aspects of a single act, at once moral and aesthetic: it is the function of the poet to accomplish this complex act. The myth he invokes will have the effect of assessing by comparison, and also preserving, the difficult excellence of the victor by fending off possible errors. And errors consist of exceeding limits, "peering too far"

towards the gods, either by slighting the possibility of persisting through
difficulties to glory; or by slighting the very fact of glory as it emerges
from such difficulties as Pelops had to overcome in order to found the
Olympic games. Here, as elsewhere, notably in the praise of Neoptolemos' comeback in *Nemean* 7, a rhetorical preterition in the form "I will
not say ill of *x*" works both to face and to skirt the unpalatable.

The myth is under enough strain to require management, in short;
the poem emphasizes and exemplifies this again and again.[4] A distinction is made between deed and thought, though both serve the same
ideal. "Strength acts by deed (*ergo*),/ But mind by deliberations (*bou-
lais*)" (*N*.1.26–27). Mortals, at once gloriously like the gods and tran-
siently different from them, must somehow perform strenuous acts of
mind, must attend to this kind of poem, in order to endow the strenuous
acts of body with a grace that in Homeric society would, for all the
gloom of the *Iliad*, have been accorded them automatically.

Time also needs management. The remoteness of Pelops from the
event of *Olympian* 1 has two aspects: it can close the gap of time by
reminding those celebrating one victory at Olympia of the games' foundation; and it can also unify moments in a time no longer cyclic. The
"nobility" of the aphorism quoted above is seen as coming in series, day
after day (*parameron*), and it is the sequent (*epiloipoi*, 33) days that
are the "wisest witnesses." The very phrasing of these commonplaces
contains an energetic assumption of linear time to be managed, rather
than of a cyclic time to be confidently assumed. About the afterlife
Pindar offers not a vague terrain, as Homer does, but two somewhat
opposed ideas; on the one hand man is not to aspire to an "immortal
life" (*P*.3.61); but on the other hand, a quasi-Orphic land of the blest
stands ready for the virtuous (*Olympian* 2). Most vividly seen is a
transience linked to an unreality of perception:

> From Zeus for men there follows no clear
> Token. But still we embark on great endeavors
> Striving after many deeds. By a shameless
> Hope the limbs are bound. The streams of forethought lie afar.
>   (*N*.11.43–46)

Here forethought (*promatheia*) is triumphantly named and linked to a
keen sense of transience somewhat reminiscent of the river aphorisms
of Heraclitus. This is late Pindar, and so is another expression of transience:

> Of a day! What is one? What not? A dream of a shadow is
> Man, but when the Zeus-given gleam comes
> There is a shining light for mortals and a honeyed age.
>
> (*P.*8.95–97)

"Age" (*aion*, also "life") is a time-word, here coordinated with two perceptions in space, one markedly transient, "gleam" (*aigle*) and the other steady, "light" (*phengos*). *Olympian* 1 also ends with a mingling of space and time:

> May it be for you to tread this time on high,
> And for me just as long to consort
> With victors, being eminent for wisdom among Hellenes everywhere.
>
> (115–116)

One person is to be active, in the powerful mixed metaphor of treading time; the other is visibly eminent (*prophanton*). The water, the fire, and the sun of this poem's opening have been displaced by the act of celebration. The sense of limits verges on an acute mastery of time in the very submission to it, and in a subversion of its very features, whereby time can become a very space, like a mountain ("on high," *hypsou*) where one may "tread" (*patein*).

The time here manipulated has become abstract enough to lose its given Homeric periodicity. That heroic time is accepted and at the same time deeply questioned, taking on an abstract character. While Vernant (p. 199) cites Jeanmaire as noting that Hesiod only once mentions the Hours, the notion of time, along with related notions like *acros*, *kairos*, and *akme*, pervades Pindar, bringing a series of myths constantly to bear on one ground and precondition of mythic thought, the awareness of time, which is also dramatized in the composition and the momentary public performance of the epinician ode.

2.

Greek tragedy tests the myth still more profoundly than Pindar does, as I have said elsewhere (Cook, 1971). And the concluding aphorisms of a Greek tragedy are even more general in their application. Homer, too, is finally general: the application of the stories to present cases is left up in the air. Pindar, however, resolves and tests the sense of the myth by giving it a special application, linking it to a single living figure whom the poem is celebrating, linking Pelops to Hieron. If the myth served simply to illustrate the aphorisms, Pindar would not keep thrusting new myths forward. And he can, on occasion, either do mostly without the myth (*P.8, O.8, O.12*), or conclude with the example of the myth rather than that of the victor, as *Nemean* 1 concludes with the marriage of Heracles. And yet, if the myth itself were not needed Pindar could have followed the practice of "Theognis" and given us simply aphorisms, or some other, flatter version of Archilochus' *kallinikos*.

The yield of the myth is a wisdom that conquers the transience in time by accepting it, thus balancing a fame throughout all Greece: space is coordinated with time; and I have been summarizing the last lines of *Olympian* 1. But the thought can be found throughout Pindar's work. It persists, though at the same time it provides the unity of an individual ode, a lead notion so distinct that it might be called a *Grundgedanke* after Dissen, a basic thought or leading idea underlying each ode. Yet each ode's *Grundgedanke* is so perfectly merged into the linkage of myth with victor that it seems inward—as in Schadewalt's definition (p. 3), "The subjective unity of the poem, which is necessarily a unity of thought."

The "thought" of Pindar's longest poem, *Pythian* 4, seems curiously simple and tangential to its myth, which is the founding of Cyrene by an Argonaut's descendant. The thought involves a proposal about the future rather than just a meditation on Arkesilas' chariot victory: in the interests of peace and healing a certain Demophilus should be recalled to Cyrene from exile. This thought is arrived at after an extraordinary series of movements in myth that involve dispersions of persons in space and in time, a complexity unusual even for Pindar. The thought itself, however, remains relatively simple; its *connections* with the mythic material remain the more hidden, and so the more emphatic in the assumed force of its mere presentation. In this Pindar radically expands and transforms the ring composition he may be said to have got from Homer.[5] What Schadewalt (pp. 43–44) says of the enchainment of thoughts is only true here if one allows that enchainment to include both the myths and the particular order of their presentation along with the thoughts: "To compose the 'coherence' according to its many-sidedness is a basic movement in Pindar's way of disposing his thought." That is, in fact, not the solution but the problem.

As for space, the beginning of *Pythian* 4 harks back to an act of colonization, from the island of Thera to the city of Cyrene. Cyrene is the site of the victory being celebrated in this recited ode and *Pythian* 5, the processional ode that follows (though it may have been first in the actual presentation). This theme of movement between two spaces is expanded in the poem, which includes a host of locations. The poet brings in Lake Tritonis (20) and the Nile some distance along the North African shore from Cyrene (6); Cape Taenarus (44, 174), from which Euphamus might have set out (43–53); other locations in the Peloponnesus, such as Argos (49), Messene (126), Pylos (174), and Mycenae (49); Attica, through the Cephisus river (47); Thebes, whence Pindar has travelled to deliver this ode (299); Pherae (125) and Iolcus in Thessaly (188), where Jason lands, about to depart for Colchis at the extreme eastern end of the Black Sea; Lemnos in the northern Aegean, where the remote ancestor of Cyrene's founder was sired (252); Naxos, an island in the Cyclades (88); Delphi, "central navel of the well-treed mother" (74), where the race was won and where the oracle founding these games was delivered. In this poem Pindar touches on every major area of the eastern Mediterranean except Ionia.

The poem is made to recreate, as it were, the new trans-tribal conditions under which Pindar of Thebes receives invitations from all over the Panhellenic world to celebrate the spatial and temporal focus of a single victory. Alone among peoples, to begin with, the Greeks were able to expand their hegemony without radiating from a single capital, though Athens' supremacy for nearly half a century has obscured this point. Indeed, from Archilochus and perhaps even Homer on down, it seems that no writer lived in the birthplace for which he was named, with the possible exceptions of Empedocles of Acragas and Heraclitus of Ephesus. The necessity for alliances in the Persian wars, and the medizing of Pindar's native city, added tension to the internationalism that his commissions formalize and also spiritually assert. The pro-Persian Thebans and the pro-Greek cities all took part in the Olympian games of 480, immediately before Salamis.

The *Iliad* offers a complete, Panhellenic space, elaborately and precisely mappable, as Simpson and Lazenby have shown. The *Odyssey* supplements this with descriptions of miraculous peoples, dimly apprehended, who live on the margins of the known world, margins reclaimed and brought into focus by Herodotus as the result of patient inquiry. Pindar's sense that the legendary world lay open to profound movement and countermovement reinvents a space that in Homer was taken for granted. Homer was confident of his answers. Pindar is obliged to find the locus even of his questions. The space of the victory and its relation to the home territory of the victor is only a starting point, a sort of wavering compass needle around which Pindar builds the compass of his ode.

Except for Cyrene, the locations in *Pythian* 4 are not presented at all as stable settlements in space. Every single one of them exists on what might be called a vector; each is a point from which or towards which someone is moving. Jason, the main mythical person of the poem, has arrived in Iolcos (literally with one sandal on and one sandal off), poised to depart in search of the Golden Fleece as he gathers the famous comrades, among them Heracles and the Dioskouri and Orpheus. These Argonauts are themselves coming on their own journeys from various locations in Greece. Medea is moving, and in her speech (earlier in the poem) she describes Euphamus as moving, in the journey of the Argo and also in the other journey that will ultimately found Cyrene. Jason is moving through Lemnos. Lake Tritonis is seen not as a stable inland body of water but, contrary to geography, as having an outlet into the sea, which washes the magic clod away. Euphamus is moving, and Pindar is moving, and he finally recommends that another person be re-called to Cyrene from an enforced journey away.

So much for space. As for time, the end of all this spatial movement is to have founded the city of Cyrene and to maintain the dynasty whose latest representative is embodied in the victor Arkesilas. The sweep of time back to the founder is seventeen generations long (10), while "Arkesilas among these sons blooms as the eighth in the succession" (*meros*, share, 65). Euphamus is, so to speak, displaced from the central myth; Jason and the more famous Argonauts dominate the poem; but Euphamus is the founder of the line and of the city. Each landing in space is motivated by a series of events in time. Jason himself, confronting Pelias, is in a complex line of his own. He will repair the wrong done to Phrixus (160), son of his great uncle, Athamas, who fled with Helle on the ram of the golden fleece because of ill treatment at the hands of his stepmother Melikerte (162). Athamas is the son of Aiolos and Enarea (108, 142), and the brother of the Salmoneus (143) who was punished for challenging Zeus. Athamas' daughter Tyro (136) had by Poseidon (138) the very Pelias (71 and *passim*) who has caused Jason all the trouble. Pelias' brother Neleus fathered Periklumenos (175) and Nestor, which brings us just within range of the whole Trojan legend, nowhere explicitly mentioned in *Pythian* 4.

Aiolos' third son Kretheus (142) was the father of Aison (118), who fathered Jason; of Pheres (126), who fathered the Admetus (126) of another legend; and of Amythaon (125), who fathered the Melampus of still another. These four remote generations are all woven into the time-references of the poem, and the references to Phrixus and Ino touch on the Theban legend of Pindar's home city. Epaphus, son of Zeus and Io, is mentioned as the father of Libya (14). Europa is brought into the poem (46), and Apollo and Artemis (4), and Boreas (183) and Hera (184) and Tityos (90), and Atlas (289) and the Titans (291), Chiron (102–116) and Oedipus (263).

Jason, throughout many of the lines allotted him, is poised in readiness for his possibilities. To be timely requires timing; "the ripe moment (*kairos*) for men has a short measure" (285). By letting the fateful, symbolic clod of earth be swept away at the wrong moment, then wash ashore on the Thera that Medea is telling about, Euphamus has acted "before its time." So, although he has found the actual fulfillment here being celebrated, he has missed a whole vast empire that Pindar envisions dimly as a might-have-been of escaped prophecy:

> And now the deathless seed of Libya the broad-for-dancing
> Has been poured in this island before its time. For if at home he
>   had cast it to the earth-
> Mouth of Hades, come to holy Taenarus, Euphamus,
> The son of horse-ruling Poseidon and lord,
> Whom once Europa the daughter of Tityos
> Bore by the banks of Cephisus;
> Then the blood of the fourth generation of his children come
>   into being
> Would have taken with the Danaans that broad mainland.
> And in that time from great
> Lacedemon, look, they are rising up and away, [*exanistantai,*
>   "prophetic present"]
> And from the Gulf of Argos and from Mycenae.   (43–49)

The contrary-to-fact statement about the descendants of Euphamus cannot be made without including an intricate genealogical situation both past and future to the failed moment under consideration. The epithet given to Poseidon, "horse-ruling," applying to both land and water, includes past and future by recalling the extended tropes with which Medea has, for these voyagers, characterized the later voyage of settlement, "they shall change fast horses for swift winged dolphins/ Reins for oars . . ." (15–25).[6]

Time is a "servant (*therapon*), but not a slave (*drastas*)" (287); and this aphorism is being brought to bear on Damophilus, who is praised for managing his knowledge of proper timing. Still, even knowledge does not spare some, and Pindar immediately adduces the contrasting cases of the imprisoned Atlas and the freed Titans who benefited from the "changes in time" (292). Here time is a puzzle whose solution does not necessarily bring a prosperous success. In Pindar time is not the complex but manageable seasonal cycle of tribal perception that is taken for granted in Homer.

Action in time tends to encompass space, as in the voyage of the Argo here, and in what Pindar says of the sons of Aeacus in *Isthmian* 6. Their fame—seen, interestingly, as a kind of extension-in-space—exceeds extreme south and extreme north:

> Myriads of roads, hundred-footed in their breadth, are cleft for
>   good deeds
> And beyond the springs of the Nile
> And through the Hyperboreans.
>
>   (*Isthmian* 6.22–23)

Such distances are here conceived of as heroic: Heracles goes through thunder to the Hyperboreans in *Olympian* 3, to bring back the olive-shade of the Olympian crown. Perseus went to the Hyperboreans, but men cannot get there any more "by foot or by ship" (*Pythian* 10.28–35). In *Pythian* 4 we are given circular journeys, all inside the encompassing journey of a Pindar come from Thebes to Cyrene, who speaks of his host's countrymen as "guest-friended at Thebes" (299) in the last words of this longest of his poems. Medea's speech describes one circular journey, that of Euphamus back to Thera. Jason is involved in two circular journeys, the first beginning in his infancy. He is sent from Iolcos, under cover of his pretended funeral procession (110–115), to be reared by Cheiron. When grown he returns to Iolcos. The second, longer journey is the voyage of the Argo out from Iolcos to Colchis, and back again to Iolcos via Egypt and the islands. That these journeys of the myth are analogous to the journey of Arkesilas is stressed by the rhetorical organization of the poem. As Gildersleeve notes (p. 280), "the story of the Argonauts makes the same returning sweep to Arkesilas and Apollo as the Prophecy of Medeia."

Moreover, time is inverted in the sort of vast *hysteron proteron* into which the main presentation of the myth is organized. In the poem

Medea's speech (13–58) comes before the much longer account of Jason's arrival and voyage (67–256), but in time her speech comes after his acts. The occasion of her speech is a future to these events. The voyage of the Argo is shown first as a project and then as a series of past events. Triton's gift of the prophetic sod to Epaphus, with which Medea's speech concludes, is quickly balanced by the account of the oracle's prophecy to Battus (59–63). The first word of the entire poem is "today" (*sameron*), and Pindar "hurries" himself as he comes to the end of the story about Jason to make way for the concluding aphorisms.

These aphorisms reach a crescendo (to use another of Bundy's terms) in the "wisdom" (*sophia*, 212) of Oedipus. Such "wisdom," unclear in its effect, may include the condition of a sort of prophetic function for poetry, since *sophia* is a word Pindar frequently uses to describe his own poetry.[7] Just as it is not clear whether Oedipus' "wisdom" lies in the act of guessing a riddle, the riddle itself, or the existence of the suffering figure himself (as the parable here suggests); so there is not a point where we can assign subsidiary or introductory or merely poetic roles to any of the events presented here, the real ones or the legendary ones. We cannot isolate any of the contrasting elements as the culminating one, though the Oedipus parable of the lopped oak might be conceived of as the last item because of its late position. Still later, however, in the poem comes the contrast of Atlas and the Titans, and still later the injunction to let Damophilus live out his life at home in peace.

The simple and sweeping reversals of time and inclusions of space keep any event problematic in relation to others, and yet susceptible to coordination by the sets of maxims about the meaning and progress of life. The events, the present real ones and the past legendary ones, are nodes; nonsense would quickly result if the analogy between Damophilus or Arkesilas on the one hand and Jason or Oedipus on the other were either pressed too far or not taken into consideration at all.[8] The myths and the present events, like the myths and the aphorisms, are poised in a relation to one another that is not dialectical, because at any point a single aphorism can do the summing up, or a single subenigmatic parable:

> Know now the wisdom of Oedipus. For if one with a sharp-
>   cutting axe
> Were to hew down the branches of a great oak and shame its
>   wondrous form
> Though it be failing of fruit, it would give a vote about itself

> If ever at last it come to the wintry fire
> Or propping with upright pillars in a master's house
> It perform a painful toil in the walls of others,
> Having deserted its own place.   (262–269)

The oak, through the passage of time, would have lost its seasonal function, its function in time, of bearing fruit; and it would have lost its
place. Still it would give a kind of testimony (*psephos*, "vote") about
persistence in time and in spite of space. On the other hand, the application of the Oedipus parable cannot easily be extended to the Cyrene
which immediately precedes in the poem or the healing Apollo who
immediately follows.

A comparable dissociation of statement may be attributed to the
shorter processional poem, *Pythian* 5, which is paired with this recita-
tive ode. And it contains a ritual where echoes of the lopped oak may
be traced. Instead of a lopped oak, which may be a symbol for the recommended Damophilus, we are given a primitive wooden statue with
ritual connections to the Pythian festivals and to an ancient Greek
people, the Cretans:

> The shrine of cypress holds them
> Close to the statue
> Which the bow-bearing Cretans under the roof on Parnassus
> Set up, from a plant single-hewn.   (*P.5.39–42*)

This is even more mysterious in its connections than the lopped oak,
though its ritual context is given. And since this ode celebrates the same
victory as *Pythian* 4, there may be some connection between the hewn
block and the lopped oak themselves. Here the Cretan hewn-block
statue is merely mentioned as standing beside the gifts that the charioteer
Karrhotos has brought to the shrine. The atavistic reminders it may
carry seem simply to be passed over, with a sense of both reminder and
relief, since this particular ode concentrates on wealth (*olbos*), repeating the word again and again.[9]

Karrhotos' success at saving himself from the chariot disasters of the
race where others were killed (49–50) is also passed over quickly, and
the incident where a lion frightened Battus out of his stammer (57–62)
is seen only in the light of its success. Battus is seen not as daring his
way out of the future-laden risks of *Pythian* 4 but as a founder of sea-
routes (81) and a builder of temples (83–87) to Apollo, whose be-
stowals of health, peace, and harmony the ode also celebrates. In this

ode the prophecy is seen not as a dangerous future but as something long fulfilled (55–62).

The constituents of *Pythian* 4 (and of Pindar's work generally) are here reshuffled, with a difference of emphasis that raises the question of how these differences are applied to the same victorious occasion. While "No one is or will be free of the lot of struggles" (50), this maxim merely names Battus' struggles without entering into them for description. He is seen instead as a fixed monument, "a tower for the city and a most shining eye for strangers" (56–57), whose "ancient prosperity (*olbos*) manages this and that" (55). The genealogical and spatial mazes have been provisionally sorted out. Heracles is here a sponsor (71), and Pindar himself is connected, in one tradition (73–81), to Thera through his forefathers, the Aigeidae, who went there via Sparta and thence to Thebes. A guest-friendship also connects the Trojan descendants of Antenor to Cyrene, "who came there with Helen/ When they had seen their fatherland burned up/ In war" (83–85). The peoples are gathered, and the ode brings into equipoise a vision of a firm space and an ordered time. Such is a fit vision for the orderly gathering of this choral procession as against the dark strivings of the trans-Homeric single reciter of *Pythian* 4, who quotes Homer about the welcome messenger (*P*.4.277), while restructuring the Homeric cyclic universe into an expansive space and a much fragmented time. Now Arkesilas is shown to have blessings in the face of such powerful cross-currents—or perhaps to have them, and the other possibility for time is touched on in the penultimate sentence of the second ode:

> And for the rest may the blest sons of Kronos
> Give him that he have the like in deeds and counsels
> Unless fruit-ruining wintry blasts
> Of winds make havoc of time.   (*P*.5.117–121)

Here the progress of the seasons, a cyclic time, is seen as undermining time. The Homeric commonplace that "like to the generation of leaves is the race of mortal men" (*Iliad* 6.140) has been transmuted into a risk at once certain and contingent. This is stated so powerfully that the word "time" (*chronos*) has disturbed commentators. They have glossed *chronos* as "life," sapping some of the energetic questioning in the word by assimilating it to a sense sometimes used of *aion*, "age."[10] Here the energetic questioning is passed over; the ode emphasizes success, but in Pindar the questioning does not pass from view.

3.

Our terms *secular* and *religious* cannot be stretched so as to offer, in contrast with each other, a definition of the complex, transitional situation in which Pindar finds himself with respect to the cults in whose context his epinicians, and perhaps his other kinds of poems too, were delivered. The prediction of Medea in *Pythian* 4 is a sort of secular oracle, somewhat outside of a divine context, though not wholly, since as a witch (implied by *zamenes*, "raging," *Pythian* 4, 11) Medea would have had powers of the same kind a prophetess possessed. To say, as Jaeger does (1965, pp. 205–222), that Pindar has transferred the choral ode from religious cult uses to secular ones is only a half-truth. If the victor is secular and the myth is religious, then the whole point of his activity would be at once to attribute a quasi-religious aura to the victor and at the same time not to fuse him into legend.[11] Did Pindar believe Hieron or Arkesilas to be the same sort of persons the originals of Heracles or Pelops or Jason or Battus once were? Would his victors merge into legendary heroes after the passage of time? There is no way to answer these questions, and there is no way not to ask them. The occasion of the epinician ode bears on these questions, and the occasion itself involves several foregrounded elements, whereas in lyric poetry from Alcaeus on, the only elements in the foreground are a single poet writing and his imagined auditors.

First, there is the athletic contest, at Olympia or Delphi or Nemea or the Isthmus or elsewhere, dedicated to Zeus or Apollo or Poseidon. This contest has a ritual side, but the epinician, which may be recited after the return of the victor to his home, which may be as far away as Sicily or North Africa, is only presumptively a part of that ritual. It may, indeed, at the same time partake of another; *Pythian* 5 may well have been recited during the *Karneia* at Cyrene. At whatever remove, the epinician includes the god to whom the athletic festival is dedicated, and the references are usually explicit and prolonged, like those to Zeus in *Olympian* 1 and to Apollo in *Pythian* 1.

Pindar's epinicians, scored for public performance, include music, and the poet chooses (as a lyric poet also would have done) a preponderant meter, Aeolic or Doric. Though he is, in Thomson's reading, free to vary and blend his meters, the particular mode chosen raises certain expectations, Doric being rather sterner than others, Aeolic rather more high-flown. In the myths themselves, as Ingomar Weiler points out, contests involving music and athletic contests are both distinguished from and associated with each other in many ways. This aspect of the myths finds an echo in Pindar's free but conditioned handling of musical modes to celebrate athletic contests.

The occasion also includes dance, which the poems sometimes refer to, for example, in *Pythian* 2, ("lyre . . . that the footstep hearkens to" 1–2). The particular victory in the contest, chariot race or pentathlon, must also be mentioned, and along with it the home city of the victor. Odes sometimes celebrate even more than one victory, as Hamilton points out (pp. 103–105).

As a focus for the occasion a myth is chosen, and freely chosen: the myth may be that of the founding of the games themselves, as in *Olympian* 1, or the founding of the victor's city, as in *Pythian* 4 and 5, or it may be one deemed appropriate to this particular victory, as the myth about Ajax is seen to be somehow appropriate for the boy Sogenes in *Nemean* 7. The myth chosen may combine all these stipulations: Jason is somehow appropriate to Arkesilas and also linked to him in the past of his city as providing the occasion whereby Euphamus would be on the move enough to have mysteriously begun its foundation.

And the home city of the poet, Thebes, may enter, as it does at the very end of *Pythian* 4. If a Theban myth has been chosen for a particular ode, that cannot be dissociated from the reciting poet. It becomes part of an elaborate compliment to the victor, diplomatic in that it implies that the victor is worthy of evoking from the poet a reference to the myths associated with his own native city.

All these elements are brought together by the act of praise and, finally, unified by it, as Segal's (3) summary of Thummer's categories points up: "(1) praise of the victory; (2) praise of the victor; (3) praise of the victor's family; (4) praise of the victor's city; (5) praise of the happiness connected with the victory; (6) praise of the poet and his art; (7) prayers; (8) main decorative components of the odes (proems and myths); (9) interconnection of the motifs of praise; (10) stylistic means of intensifying the praise."

While, on the face of it, these are not all correlative, the unity of tone tends to make them so. They are bound also in the forceful connection between contest and victor which, for Pindar and Bacchylides alike, defines the occasion of the epinician ode. One could not refer to these motifs of praise in the context of the contest without interconnecting them. Pindar may vivify his own verbal acts of connection more impressively than Bacchylides does, but both poets are called on to perform the connection, in an act of recitation that is at once individual and public, that celebrates the commonalty of myth while at the same time resisting an unconsidered fusion into a cyclic, tribal world.

This yoking of the legendary and the momentary, the private act and the public celebration, keeps in dynamic suspension the connection between the myth and the poem's moment, rather than simply transmitting the myth, as Homer may be said to do. So the connection between the aroused individual celebrant and his tribal myth is loosened.[12]

Where Heraclitus sets up a crux of definition between the individual and the crowd, the many and the few, Pindar dramatizes their poised reciprocity. Heraclitus allows the crowd to be sleepers but the *logos* to be common. Pindar does not wake them from the Homeric sleep other than to redefine the Homeric universe. The community of *logos* that he offers is not a philosophical questioning but a shared act of poetic redefinition passive on their part and active on his, but common nonetheless. It is with reference to Homer's audience that he says, "the greater throng of men has a blind heart" (*N*.7.23–24). The groups of heroes in flower are connected with the gathering of peoples in space, implicitly in the emotional equivalent between the collective expedition of the Argo and the impetus of celebration in Cyrene, explicitly in the act of praise:

> Without a shout did the flowers of heroes dwelling round about
> Desire and willingly yield to his leadership,
> Those who marshalled the host in craggy Athens
> And the descendants of Pelops round Sparta.
> A suppliant to the holy knees of Aeacus for his dear city
> And for those citizens I seize and bear
> A Lydian mitre ringingly bedecked,
> A Nemean ornament for Deinias in the double stade and his
>   father Megas.
>
> (*Nemean* 8.9–14)

Pindar is free not to use the formulaic verse-staples of the Homeric traditions, as were the poets who preceded him. The private lyric expression they developed is available to him, and the given conditions of the epinician occasion themselves offer a substitute for formulaic verses, since they amount to a sort of repertoire of thought-formulas.

And myths, too, are thought-formulas, in that they carry their connections along with them when chosen whole. To choose Aeacus or

Pelops or Heracles is to choose congeries of story-units or mythemes from which some or all may be selected for presentation.

To contrast these mythemes, and their consequent gnomic concomitants, and to set them into prelude-like "priamels" and "foils," performs a dynamic testing of the formulas. This testing does not undermine them; it revitalizes them. The glory Glaucus invokes when encouraging Sarpedon in the *Iliad* on the eve of battle is what all heroes may be said to assume. All victors assume the glory that the contest gives, but they are themselves powerless to express it, as silent as statues before the sounding articulation of the epinician ode itself.

4.

Pindar, as it happens, abjures the identification of his epinicians with the cult statues of heroes, which had notably proliferated in the "severe" style of the archaic sculpture just before him:

> I am not a statue-maker to fashion images
> Reposing on their very pedestal
> To stand; but upon every towed boat and in a skiff,
> Sweet song, speed from Aigina, announcing
> (*Nemean* 5.1–3)

This very denial establishes a closeness of function between the statue and the poem, while insisting on the distinction between them. He substitutes for such static images an image of movement.

The epinician ode does have one kind of monumental repose; it doubles back upon itself in the threefold repeated colometry of strophe, antistrophe, and epode. There is in Pindar what Schadewalt calls a "horror . . . before the hiatus" (p. 40). Still, the very breaks between the stanzaic sections or *cola* of these triads produce a disjunction that is alien to the seamless and uninterrupted circularity of Homeric ring composition. That form is continued, as Illig and Finley (p. 71) have argued, in the rhetorical structure as well as in the rhythmic repetitions of the Pindaric ode. Schadewalt (p. 75) points out that *Pythian* 3 so composes the relation between Asklepios and Hieron. Here in his form, as in other respects, Pindar continues Homer, but with a signal difference.[13]

Homer moves unbrokenly, line by line, from a perceived item through its associations and back again to the perceived item. It is possible in-

deed, as Whitman has shown us, to map the whole presentational pattern of the *Iliad* as a set of geometric correspondences, an overall ring
composition that eventually circles back on itself.

In Pindar, however, there are abrupt rhythmic breaks from stanza to
stanza, and also abrupt interruptions of subject matter. Moreover, he is
constantly circling back because in a sense he is always saying the same
thing: that the heroic victor deserves godlike praise in the very brevity
of life.

Pindar moves freely into his subject. The constant counterpoise of
"foil," "priamel," and "cap" maintains the elevation while in fact permitting this associative freedom. And the complexity of the ode's *Programm* guarantees that no element freely taken up in a given line will
be unrelated to some aspect of what the poet's commission obliges him
to say. Pindar makes the *tria* of Stesichorus and Simonides sustain a
digressive pressure which calls attention to both the manifest mainte-
nance of the form and its ostensive subservience to a flow of constantly
renewed myth-recall and axiom-testing.

By bringing an elaborated fixed form to bear upon a freely varied
staple of statements Pindar highlights both the balance of the one form
and the fluidity of the statements. His very freedom to turn where he
will in his verse obliges him to make the fluidity work so as to bear up
the staples of an ode's *Programm*. In terms of words or verses (*epeon*)
he speaks of their marshalled ranks (*stiches*, P.4.57) and of their placement (*thesin*, O.3.8). The second strophe of *Olympian* 3, a rather even
passage, may be taken to illustrate his strenuously careful attention to
the placement, or ordonnance, of his words, item by item, in their effect
at sustaining both the myth and the aphorism:

> δᾶμον ῾Υπερβορέων πείσαις ᾿Απόλ-
>   λωνος θεράποντα λόγῳ·
> πιστὰ φρονέων Διὸς αἴτει πανδόκῳ
> ἄλσει σκιαρόν τε φύτευμα
>   ξύνον ἀνθρώποις στέφανόν τ᾿ ἀρετᾶν.
> ἤδη γὰρ αὐτῷ πατρὶ μὲν βωμῶν ἁγι-
>   σθέντων, διχόμηνας ὅλον χρυσάρματος
> ἑσπέρας ὀφθαλμὸν ἀντέφλεξε Μήνα,

Having persuaded the people of the Hyperboreans, Apollo's
      servant, by a statement,
Thinking loyal thoughts for the all-taking grove of Zeus
      he besought

A shadowy growth common for men and a crown of prowesses.
Already for him, the altars to his father consecrated,
A split-month moon had shone forth its whole
Eye of the golden-charioted evening.   (16–20)

So far from formulaic is each of these words in turn that no one can be expected after the other. In that sense this poetry is already "modern," emphasizing its liberation from its own conventions as well as from those of ordinary discourse. Yet in this instance there are no surprises of conjunction beyond the surprise of freedom. *Pista* does go with *phroneon* ordinarily enough, that thought with *Dios* whom one associates with *aitei* and with *alsei*, which in turn is expected to be *pandoko*, a subformulaic adjective, like *skiaron*, and *chrysarmatos. Stephanon* is conventional for *aretan* as well as literal—there will be a crown for the Olympic victor. The poetry of the last line resides not so much in invention of image as in the verbal conjunction which has suspended the subject of a sentence to the very end, linking each of the three nouns to an adjective from which it is separated by the strongly marked rhythmic phrasing of the dactylo-epitritic cluster: "hesperas opthalmon antephlexe mena."

The effect is one of a constant elevation which, in its very suspension, calls attention to the mythic units being offered for glorious inspection. It is, as it were, correct but misleading to call this a "symbolic" effect. As Schadewalt says (p. 58), "Images have a far greater concrete valorization than we may feel in the 'poetic image'." Pindar is not a symbolic thinker in the sense that he offers, as the body of myth may be said to do, a single figure from whom a rich and somewhat contradictory set of statable inferences may be drawn. Rather, he takes that "symbolic" function over from the given body of Greek myth, precisely as a given. His poetic work consists in making it yield inferences, creating a balance thereby between the myths and the inferences. The "poetry" resides in the connections brought dexterously about between them. Pindar's act of poetry is to make the myth yield inferences: he is less dark, and at the same time less to be taken for granted, than the myth-system on which he draws. In this sense he is, like Heraclitus, a wise man, a *sophos* as he repeatedly calls himself in a term that surely calls attention to more than the disjunct metrical and compositional skills of the *aoidos* ("singer"). "It is often impossible to define Pindar's exact implication . . . The difficulty of understanding him is not in his boldness of language or use of myth or cult, but in the weight of meaning which his

mythic figures carry." (Finley, p. 6). If this is true, it is true globally
of Pindar, rather than in an individual ode, where our very sureness that
Pelops is being applied to Hieron or Jason and Euphamos to Arkesilas,
acts as a guide to establishing the connections. Then, in the ode's
achieved system of connections, we have left the fixed Homeric-Olympian cosmos of assumptions. Thus to reaffirm this cosmos is to establish
it in a freedom of utterance that radically qualifies it.

The consequent freedom of poetic statement is not just a personal
achievement of Pindar's; Bacchylides enjoys a similar freedom, though
he chooses a linear clarity of deliberate presentation for his myths. Pindar in his freedom gives a richness of designative function to the individual metaphor, a richness independent of the myth if correlative with
it. So when Jason is made to say of Pelias (P.4.109) that he was "obey-
ing white thoughts" (leukais pithesanta phrasin), white, probably a
hieratic color in early Greek and pre-Greek religion, probably has no
hieratic function here, whether it refers to envy or simply to "the opposite of Homer's black" and so "clear" rather than "deep" as the scholia
say (Drachmann, II, 125, ad loc). The same may be said of the water
and gold of Olympian 1 and Olympian 6 and elsewhere. J. Duchemin
(p. 279) sees gold as "luminous burst or a color first of all, a visual
notion." The very isolation of the common words for light and its effects
that Duchemin goes on (p. 282) to list amounts to a disjunct naming
of mere qualities without reference to hieratic system: phaneros, phaidi-
mos, aglaos, phengos, phaos, auge, phlegein, lampein.

Terms like these are in their nature hyperbolic. They accord extravagant praise to their object. If Zeus, "god of the bright sky" in A.B.
Cook's designation, is the source of light, then these terms of light carry
with them an animism that becomes residual once the features of light
are attributed to an object assigned but arbitrary, things associated to a
winner in athletic games. The religious aura of the terms partakes of
and evokes the religious aura of the games; but at the same time it
releases that aura for uses which are also secular in their very freedom
from the fixities of ritual utterances, to say nothing of ritual acts. Pindar
never reminds us, as Burkert does (1972), that the Olympian and Pythian festivals have their origin in a sacrifice. The connection with cosmological magic is now vestigial; yet the sanctified air of that connection is
deliberately called into play.

As J.A. Symonds (I, p. 349) says of Pindar, "splendor became his
vital atmosphere." Pindar's hyperbole, a marked and constant feature

of his poetic practice, cannot be divorced from the function he is performing. It is not just a stylistic option, chosen as an eighteenth-century poet or a modern poet might opt for the sublime. It resides already, at the very least, as a powerful tendency, both in the mythic situs of the games and the application of myth to a victor. To call hyperbole constantly into play is to evoke that situation and at the same time to master it by controlling it in a new poetic order. The whole mythic universe has been rendered available to personal but public manipulation: we are on our way to Greek tragedy (and in one sense at least, Pindar is more secular than Greek tragedy, which transposed but did not forget sacrifice).

The very meters of the poems have a hyperbolic ring. The especially long lines may be taken to suggest elevation, as may the elaborate variation from line to line and of metrical figures within the given line. A particular phrase attributed to the sons of Hermes in the list of Argonauts (*P*.4.179), *kachladontes Heba*, "ringing out with youth" not only sustains the elevation of the catalogue with an extravagant metaphor, it would seem to underscore the hyperbole with a particular swelling of long syllables.

"Flying" and "bold transgression" (*Übergang*) are the terms Hermann Fränkel (1927, p. 233) uses to characterize Pindar's style. Hyperbole also characterizes his diction, not only in his fondness for terms about light, and not only in the use of superlatives, as David Young finds superlatives placed strategically first at the beginning and then at the end of *Olympian* 1. His diction generally tends towards hyperbole; he constantly uses religious terms: *hieros, hagnos, hagnizo, katharos, semnos, sebizo, daimonios, deinos, terpnos.* (This particular list is Rudberg's, p. 265.) Verbs like *thambein*, "to wonder," or the very frequent *thallo*, "to blossom," have a hyperbolic cast, as do many other verbs he uses.[14] The key terms *aotos* and *kairos* themselves are hyperbolic in conception: they denote a supreme moment in time, as *acme* does in space (and time). Many of Pindar's most frequent adjectives too, carry a hyperbolic effect.[15] And since the subjects he dwells on partake of the superlatives that are accorded them, his nouns frequently add to the hyperbole as well, nouns for sun, gold, eagle, renown, surge, crown, king, might, master, *omphalos, hybris*, grief, festival, bronze, garland, hymn of praise, hero, victor, splendor (*charis*), prophet, happiness, delight, wealth, desire, satiety, bliss, danger, lightning, peace, youth, effort, heart, herald, gain, thunderbolt, portent, fruit, perhaps even horse, and peak. To these, of course, the names of gods and heroes carry a superadded hyperbolic force.

The "counter-flash" (*antephlex*) of the Moon in the strophe quoted above from *Olympian* 3 breaks into a particular hyperbolic emphasis close to the end of a sentence whose final slowed rhythms suggest control. The immediately following antistrophe rhythmically matches and continues the elevated expression with a string of all but constantly hyperbolic words:

> And a holy judgment of the great contests and along with it
>   the fifth-year festival
> He established on the hallowed banks of the Alpheus;
> But the ground of Pelops did not blossom then with beautiful trees
>   in the vales of Kronos' son.
> The garden bare of these seemed to him to be subdued to the
>   sun's sharp rays
> Then his spirit urged him to journey to the land.   (21–25)

Moreover, the whole passage gets a further hyperbolic force from the fact that all of these events are being recounted about a hero *par excellence*, Heracles.

The hypotactic syntax, of which Bacchylides did not avail himself so flexibly, helps to keep the sublime at its hyperbolic pitch, and also to display the inventive talent of the poet, whereas the hyperboles of ritual utterance in many cultures are characteristically paratactic and merely cumulative in their effect. At no point can one find in liturgical texts the constant effort at inventive variation that Pindar offers.

Pindar puts himself in a position where the hyperbole constantly lifts the assertion into acts of praise that in a primitive style would be more automatic. Blame is not a possible use of poetry for Pindar, and he is conscious, as he keeps telling us, that pessimism is to be avoided. Even "at a distance" he says he has seen the straits to which the practice of calumny had reduced Archilochus (*Pythian* 2.55), and yet it is significant for his sense of his own inventions that he thus singles out this particularly inventive poet as a predecessor.

The meter, too, at every step makes us aware of the poet's necessity to invent, because the length of a strophic line is not fixed till it is produced, nor is the length that of the next line. The hexameter itself, in Nagy's reading, is a composite of underlying Indo-European meters, an expansion from the base of the pherecratics which are still a resource for Pindar. In that sense his usage takes advantage of primitive patterns in this and other comparably staple lyric measures, when he would choose an Aeolic measure for part or all of a poem. But the hexameter is fixed, whereas Pindar, in Thomson's reading, can change the meter in mid-line, or even change the mode through devices of protraction, overlap, resolution, link, anacrusis, echo, and even concurrence, when two meters are arguably present. And by Pindar's time, in A.M. Dale's deduction, the metrical patterns had become an abstract, partially interchangeable repertory. Certainly we must allow some version of Thomson's and Dale's theses, indeed, when the same scansions produce somewhat different, and equally plausible assignment of metrical combinations to, say, *Olympian* 1, from Thomson, Snell, and Gildersleeve. The dactylo-epitrites of *Pythian* 4 and other poems often flow along almost like dactylic hexameters, but the poet is always free to shorten or lengthen his line. This freedom, in concert with hyperbolic diction and the eulogistic occasion, makes it seem that Pindar, unlike the Homeridae he mentions in *Nemean* 2.1, is not drawing the means of praise from hoary tradition, but strenuously creating it anew with every foot of his meter.

Doric, Aeolic, Ionic, and Paeonic are each still more composite as meters than is the hexameter or even the Sapphic and Alcaic stanzas. The Homeric hexameter moves from more variables at the beginning of a line (Russo) to fewer at the end—towards a poetic closure in the line itself—while Pindar's meter stays open to the end. Pindar goes further and blends the modal measures so that their already composite figures are made to blend into further compositions with each other. This produces the significant overtones of combining the mood-associations of the individual modes. *Pythian* 12, written for a victory in a flute-playing contest, speaks of Athene's inventing the art of flute-playing as a death dirge for Medusa, and the myth of the many-headed monster and the much-varied music are linked in the description, "finding it for mortals to have/ She called it the mode of many heads" (*kephalan pollan nomon*, 22–23). The statement converges with the poetry, the act of those who use statement with that of the singers (*logiois kai aiodidois, Pythian* 1.93, where *logiois* in its combination must mean something like "unaccompanied and unmetrical statement-makers"—a term which might well include others than Farnell's 'historians' [sub voc] among the *logioi*).

To begin with, poetry of celebration occurs, according to the typology of the Chadwicks (III, 706ff.), at the earliest stage of oral literature. Their type D comprises appeals, exhortations, hymns, elegies, and panegyrics. It would therefore include all the kinds of poetry Pindar wrote —epinicians, dithyrambs, hymns, *parthenia, enkomia, hyporchemata, prosodia*, and paeans. This poetry of celebration is prior to all other types, except for the other 'primary' type E, poems of personal diversion (of which the Pindaric epinicians might also be considered an expansion). Narrative poetry, both heroic (war) and nonheroic (religion and law), their type A, tends to be derived in primitive cultures from the poetry of celebration, as are type B, "speeches of dialogues in character," and type C, "didactic poetry or saga."

Whether or not this typology is wholly or partly adopted, the early productions which it is classifying highlight by comparison Pindar's act of reversion to what is a kind of primary poetic mode. The sense in which he elaborates his predecessors is triumphantly apparent in the very hyperbolic character of his work. What is less apparent is that the substratum of hyperbole itself amounts to a recovery, as well as an invention, of a direct state of mind that wills a union of distant god and present leader-hero under the aegis of ritual praise. In this, as in other respects, Pindar's poetic practice parallels the chthonic revivals of pre-Olympian religion contemporary with him. And the very elaborateness of his invention, at the same time, brings to bear upon that act of praise a kind of purified mind, which parallels the purity that Heraclitus enjoins upon those who would celebrate sacrifices without pollution (B 69).

5.

Certain of Pindar's hyperbolic nouns, like *kairos, aotos*, and *charis*, have the force of philosophical abstractions. They define the special qualities of the area where myth is predominant but are not themselves susceptible of being combined in philosophical propositions, beyond the after-the-fact of a gnomic apophthegm. They are, however, susceptible to remythologizing. The "truth" which is "laid bare" (*a-letheia*, in Heidegger's emphasis) is itself derived, improvisationally and thus unstably, from this or that combination of mythic figures: "O mother of gold-crowned contest, Olympia,/ Mistress of Truth" (*O*.8.1–2); "Truth, daughter of Zeus" (*O*.10.4); "O mistress Truth, beginning of great virtue" (Fgt. 205).

In each of these cases truth is a product equally of the outcome of the victory and of the poet's utterance—an abstract product, managed beyond the function of the poet to confect credible lies. This ability to tell charming lies, which Hesiod claims as the validation of his poet's function, Pindar explicitly avoids. And yet his "truth" has not yet become what it will be for the philosopher.[16] It could be rendered simply as "veracity" in each of these passages.

The very improvisational character of these phrases forbids our taking them allegorically, while their myth-oriented genealogy at the same time would easily lend them to such a function. They are freer and quicker, we may conjecture, than, for example, Alcman's attempts in this: "Chance, sister of Good-order and Persuasion/ And sister of Forethought" Fgt. 62, (45). Pindar's combinations provide a comparable phrasing—"Who did not bring Pretext,/ Daughter of late-born Afterthought" (*P.*5.26–27)—but this is parenthetical, as is another comparable phrase, "the streams of forethought lie afar" (*N.*11.46).

Here the identification of abstractions and the possibility of myth-combinations flow into one another in a sensitized but open state of expression. Before long a more rigid meter, the hexameter, will be used to cast such faintly allegorized abstractions in the role of rigid and powerful quasi-mythic figures, the Aletheia of Parmenides, the Philotes and Neikos of Empedocles. The last of Pindar's phrases quoted is a thread in a tissue of maxims:

> Trees are not wont in all circuits of years
> To bear a sweet-smelling flower equal in wealth,
> But in a change. And thus does fate conduct
> The mortal race. From Zeus for men a clear sign [*tekmar*, "goal"]
> Does not follow. But still we embark on great endeavors
> Striving after many deeds. By a shameless hope
> The limbs are bound. The streams of forethought lie afar.
> It is necessary to hunt for a measure of gains.
> The rages are too keen of unattainable desires.   (*N.*11.40–48)

Characteristically, the pressure of the ode at its conclusion leaves only gnomic abstractions to sustain a summary. The tale of the myths alone will not do, except sometimes at the very end, and then sketchily. Here the power of the myth is rendered in the metered deliberations of conventional thought. That power is still present, but it stands in need of constant linguistic resuscitation.

The very arbitrariness of combination permits "cap" after "cap" of statement (to expand Bundy's term somewhat), derived from and at the same time brought to bear on the legendary figures Heracles (27), Orestes (34), and Melanippus (37), as well as on the faintly abstract divinities Hestia (1) and Themis (9). Such recombination is in fact characteristic of the odes, which often offer series of mythic figures in quick succession, as in the beginning of *Nemean* 10 and *Isthmian* 7 or the end of *Pythian* 8 and *Pythian* 11. The last, like *Nemean* 10, presents Castor and Polydeuces as surviving among the gods after complex attainment, whereas in the *Iliad* they are held by the "life-giving earth" (3.243), examples of a seasonal circularity. The old system of Homeric virtues and rewards—*timé, areté, euchos, aidos, alké, kleos,* etc.—is still present in Pindar, as Podlecki notes. But it is made to undergo a circuit of recombination and revivification of which the athletic contest itself—a contest is not, after all, a war—may be taken to be a symbolic expression.

"Great deeds of prowess are always many-mythed" (*aretai d'aiei megalai polymuthoi,* P.9.76), and the *arete* of a heroic performance leads up to and away from a myth in both directions, a process Pindar defines by the act of bringing *arete* and *muthos* into a perpetual, and arbitrary conjunction.

The unity of the poem and also the main thrust of its impetus must be located in this constant mediation. As Schadewalt says (p. 18), "It is, however, also the force of substantive thinking and discovery that operates in the manifold inflections of the nuclear motifs under consideration in the song's beginning." Pindar keeps emphasizing the need for the poet to accord honor, quoting Homer in this connection (P.4.277 ff, a version of *Iliad* 15.207). For him, the act of according honor is one with the act of bringing it into interpretive relation to the myth. "For the all there is want/of interpreters" (*es de to pan hermaneon chatizei,* O.2.85–86). He *thinks over* his mythic material and draws conclusions from it, in a manner not wholly different from Herodotus', and with a specific occasion before him calling for associative explanation, as Herodotus' larger occasion also does.

6.

Without effectuating Heraclitus' problematic fusion between men and gods, Pindar holds himself back before the possibility of transfers of identification among them, through the agency of myth. Myth, which organizes the realm of the gods, may be made through poetry to yield a gnomic wisdom that is the property of men. And part of that wisdom is to know human limits, "Peer no further" (*O*.1.114). The assignment of myth to the gods and proverbs to men is not stable, however, because it is precisely the myths that can be made to yield the proverbial utterances, and from one vantage there is "one descent of men, one of gods; we both breathe from one mother." (*N*.6.1–2). Even if one were to peer further, the wisdom of men falls short of that of the gods:

> What do you hope wisdom (*sophia*)
> To be, in which but a little
> Man holds over man?
> For there is no way the gods'
> Counsels can be tracked out for a mortal mind.   (Fgt. 61)

Having a god present, traditionally, lengthens bliss (*olbos*): "for planted with the god/ Does bliss linger more for men" (*N*.8.16–17).

Philip Slater discerns a whole quasi-Freudian family dynamic in the mythic system of Greece, wherein terror at the power of strong female figures produces the counter-reaction of emphasizing powerfully heroic males and cultivating, both athletically and erotically, younger men. Pindar, who is supposed to have died in the arms of an ephebe-lover, and who celebrated the living athletes by associating them with legendary heroes, not only inherits but vivifies this dynamic; and it is suggestively appropriate that he both mentions the mother goddess and is supposed to have had a shrine dedicated to her before his house. His dwelling on mother goddesses energizes the same constellation of features that underlay the chthonic revivals in the Demeter and Persephone cults, the mysteries and so on.[17] But this whole, special dynamic is not exactly affirmed (or denied) by Pindar. Rather, it is a framework for another dynamic, that of envisioning, and articulating, and also evoking, the power of the myth in such a way as to provide a focus for both men and gods. "Life (*aion*) with rolling days changes one way and another; but unscathed are the sons of gods" (*I*.3.19). This conclusion to a poem so short that it has no myth just evades making absolute the main man-god separation of its basic contrast by referring not to gods but to the "*sons* of gods," leaving open the possibility of the divine parentage for mortals, in Aeacus and Peleus and Amphitryon and Coronis and others, that enters so often into the myths he does recount.

The heroic act or athletic victory itself moves up to, and is contained by, the at once analogous and inseminating mythic power. As Paolo Vivante says (p. 130) "the action grows out of the vision." And this is equally true of the poet, a *sophos* who possesses his *sophia* by nature, "Wise he knowing many things by nature" (*O*.2.86). The beginning of *Olympian* 2 affects to ask "what god, what hero, what man shall we proclaim?". It answers its own question by naming one of each: Zeus, Heracles, and Theron. Their points of similarity are kept at once provisional and vividly present as an impetus for the particular poetic act being carried out:

> The god achieves every goal [*tekmar*, "sign"] for hopes,
> The god who found even the winged eagle and changed
> The dolphin in the sea and bent one of high-thinking mortals
> And gave ageless glory to others. I must
> Flee the violent bite of slanders   (*P*.2.49–53)

Here, too, the act of granting glory to some mortals and denying it to others is coordinated with the power of managing the hieratic figures of air and sea, and not only of inspiring the poet but also of obliging him to avoid the practice, and hence the fate, of the Archilochus whom Pindar here goes on to name.

The heightened seasonal world of cyclic time glimpsed in these lines, and expressed by Pindar generally in his sense of peak-moment (*kairos*) and flower (*aotos*), both includes and transcends a tribal sense of the relation between men and gods. After the beginning of literacy, some such vision of permanence in the transitory tends to qualify a merely cyclic and tribal sense of seasons and generations. Such a notion transmutes the Homeric notion about the good seasonal life of peacetime; it performs a reflective act thereupon, and it is Pindar, first and foremost, who formulates the transmuted notion about the seasons, in such a way that even hoariness and youth can be associated with one another fruitfully but unseasonably (*para ton halikias eoikota chronon*, *O*.4.31), a notion with which he concludes a short poem. The island of Rhodes fuses with the rose (*rhodos*) plucked by the sun in *Olympian* 7. Kings, wise men, and heroes recover from the cycle of Persephone's punishment (Fgt. 133), and the land of the blest in *Olympian* 2 is a heightened version of seasonal enjoyments here on this earth. In fragment 131b a distinction is made between the body and the persistent life, an "image of age" (*aionos eidolon*) "which alone is from the gods."

Beyond the seasons is the momentary but successful presence of a human life for which the victor's splendor stands. All the presences in Pindar's victory odes illustrate what the athlete or his sponsor is supposed to glimpse, some kind of transcendence of momentary glory. They participate in celebration while being taken formally just as occasions for deduction and recommendation; the latter function is one not to be found in tribal rituals at all. And the earliest festivals had been celebrated each time simply with the "*kallinikos*" poem of Archilochus (*Olympian* 9.1). Pindar, by centering on deduction and recommendation about his victors, has displaced and somewhat suppressed the dominance of the sacred in the act of celebration, thereby rendering it at once more questionable and more powerful. The act of poetic deduction is a bridge of evocation across the abyss that separates gods from men.

In *Olympian* 2 such a state clarifies the vision of the afterlife, itself only partially resolved into a recommendation for virtue. In *Olympian* 14 the Graces are its sources and its guarantors: "Heirs of Cephisian waters who inhabit a lovely-colted seat, mistresses of song," say the opening lines of that poem. Not only "is all this pleasing and/ sweet achieved with you for mortals,/ if a man be wise, if handsome, if glorious" (5–7) but "not even the gods without the holy Graces/ Can proclaim dances or feasts." The effect is to evoke a state so primal that both men and gods, from this momentary viewpoint, stand identically disposed towards it. The gods accord bliss, but in the conclusion of another poem so short as to be mythless, *Pythian* 7, men even in the face of envy enjoy a "steadfast . . . blessedness" (*parmoniman . . . eudaimonian*), "For they say/ Thus for a man steadfast/ Blossoming bliss/ Brings this and that" (15–18). Here the contrast between the bliss and the envy is not resolved nor does it need to be. The many victories of Megacles and his kin here (10–14) persist in such a state, under the sponsorships, indistinguishably blinded, of Apollo (8), the city of Athens (1–7), and the poet (3, 14).

The bliss of contact between men and gods can be sexual, as in *Pythian* 9's poetically savored union between Apollo and the nymph Cyrene. And if the sexual bliss is illusory, it will be fatal: on a cloud he believes to be Hera Ixion fathers a creature who, in the next generation (*Pythian* 2), mates to produce the race of centaurs, dangerous but benevolent. Still, the benevolence can be itself dangerous, and Asklepius is punished for trying to bring back the dead, a limit we are reminded of in a poem (*Pythian* 3) whose overreaching rhetorical thrust is to express the somewhat contrary wish that Asklepius' sire, the centaur Cheiron, were still alive to cure the sick Hieron.

That a limit exists between men and gods is a *topos* so recurrent in Pindar that its very presence as a negation makes it linger as an aspiration:

If one peers to the far
He is short to reach the gods' bronze-floored seat   (*I.*7.43–44)

The bronze heaven will not ever be approachable to him   (*P.*10–26)

Do not, dear soul, aspire to immortal life.   (*P.*3.61)

Do not seek to become a god.   (*O.*5.27)

The limit governs the expressed closeness, and the more rarely expressed distance, between heroes of legend and victors of the real present. The "wondrous road" that Perseus travelled to the Hyperboreans long ago "you would not find going by ship or on foot" (*P.*10.29–30). Happiness may come if the second generation persists, as Amphiaraus' son Alcmeon does in *Pythian* 8, or for the descendants of Ixion; or unhappiness can come, as it does to the seemingly wholly blissful Cadmus and Peleus, "who they say held the highest bliss of mortals" (*P.*3.88–89).

To this day in Africa in oral, tribal cultures the lines of ancestors are recited by rote. Something like such a recitation persists in the formula-fixed patronymics of the *Iliad*. In exploring dynastic origins, Pindar piously preserves them and at the same time boldly questions them for their aphoristic yield of possible connection to the descendants of the present day. It is in such a connection that *Isthmian* 5 offers (20–53) a long list of Aeacids. Usually they are not left in their series; the series is shaken up. And Pindar is remarkable, in contrast with Homer before him or the tragedians after, for dwelling on the earliest state of his dynasties, on the foundation of the Olympian games by Pelops; on Aeacus and the Aeacids; on Cadmus and Peleus rather than on Oedipus and Achilles. The birth of Heracles in *Nemean* 1 is an "ancient statement" (*archaion logon*, 34), as Méautis emphasizes (p. 174). But then Pindar gives us the successors too, Adrastus and Amphiaraus of the *Seven Against Thebes,* and the son of Achilles, together with his role in establishing the Pythian games, Neoptolemos, at greater length than Achilles himself.

Amphiaraus prophesies for his son in *Pythian* 8 as Medea is made to prophesy for Euphamus in *Pythian* 4: the dynastic past is rendered as a hopeful future. And the figures carry their own weight, as a kind of present, rather than in the simple past ancestor-series so familiar from oral cultures around the world. So the very end of *Pythian* 8, coupling extreme and illusory transience with a bright Zeus-given glory, concludes with the bare near-litany of heroic names: Zeus; Aeacus, the founder of a dynasty; and Telamon, the father of a Trojan warrior who built the walls of Troy. After all these comes the legendary hero himself. His connection with the Aeginetan boy wrestler of immediate celebration is left hanging, the poem having worked up to a conclusion that it can totally take for granted:

> Of a day! What is one? What not? A dream of a shadow is
> Man. But when the Zeus-given gleam comes
> There is a shining light for mortals and a honeyed age.
> Aegina, dear mother, on a free voyage
> Conduct this city with Zeus and with ruling Aeacus,
> Peleus and good Telamon and with Achilles.
>
> (P.8.95–100)

7.

If there is anything asserted at the center of Pindar's epinician odes, it is an attitude, which is recommended to both the winner and, by social inclusion, the reciting poet and his auditors. The attitude would seem to cry out for recommendation, and to require the definition that the ode provides. The attitude does not begin as a staple, even if it ends as one. It must be tested, by the realms of the gods and the heroes of the legendary past, and by the facts, perceptual and emotional, of the recited present.

The quasi-permanent bliss of the victor is, as always, cursorily envisioned in *Olympian* 1:

> The victor for the rest of his life
> Has a honeying calm
> Because of his prizes. Nobility ever day by day afresh [*aiei*]
> Comes highest for all of mortals.   (97–100)

Yet the contradiction is not resolved just by this perception, and not just by the corresponding awareness of transience and mortality. As Charles

Segal says of this poem (1964, p. 228), "though the First *Olympian* ends in triumph, it is a triumph gained only through the fullest acceptance of the negative implications of mortality. The joy and radiance of Pelops' fame do not cancel fully the darkness and suffering of his prayer."

The equilibrium is dynamic that obtains between the radiance and the darkness. The poem, in its progression, calls into play what seems a single force welling up, a powerful pressure that channels all the fluidity of the contradictions. In visual terms these can be tabulated not only into "radiance" and "darkness," but into the near (human) and the far (divine), as Young (pp. 49, 116–120) has impressively done. But the far is always envisioned by the near, and the near always stands in need of a prospect on the far that the elevation of the poem provides.

Pindar's key words, into which his gnomic language can be resolved, and his key myths, which are at the center of most of the individual odes, are alike in providing this elevation. Not only can the myth be translated into the key word, and vice versa, myth into language and language back again into myth. This very process is not simply a technique of explanation offered to the auditor, something the *Theogony* may be said to present before Pindar and the poems of Empedocles and Parmenides after him. Rather, it is an act of participative realization. The dark side and the bright side of the myth are not offered for completeness, but rather for a hortatory relationship to the very side of life which both the athletics and the mythology are seen to bring into coherent focus. Nearly every epinician ode turns a celebration of past triumph into an exhortation for a future whose guiding light will be an informed, and aroused, realization of what the triumph has implied. This notion can be pressed to seem a Xenophanic side of Pindar, and "Do not, dear soul, strive for life immortal" can imply an injunction to stress the bright side of life rather than the hidden side of the gods.

The complex reminders of *Nemean* 7 amount to an encouragement to thread through such difficulties as time may present to mortal life, for, after all, legendary times presented comparable ones to the founding heroes. Though the goddess of birth provides light (*phaos*, 3), "we do not all breathe to equal ends" (5). Even "the glorious songs of verses with Memory of the shining diadem" (15–16) may require some such act of realization as Pindar provides to resolve the contradiction between the beauty of celebratory verse and the facts. Pindar asserts that the fountainhead of "verses" (*epeon*, 16), Homer, has through the sweetness of his verse (*dia ton haduepe*, 21) given a too preponderant, and in fact a false (23), reputation to Odysseus over Ajax. "Skill (*sophia*) steals, leading astray with myths" (23). This maxim is not a caveat about himself, but the announcement of a way resolutely to transcend Homeric practice, as Heraclitus has transcended it, by weighing properly what the myth may yield. "Skills (*sophiai*) are difficult" (*O.*9.107–108).

The Neoptolemos of the ode's central myth is factored down from various lies about him to a base of joy-after-suffering. He is buried at Delphi after sacking Troy (35–36), since the "wave of Hades weighs on the famous and the fameless alike" (31). The contradictions here are sorted out between the desirability and the inconsequentiality of fame-bestowing song, not by logical resolution but by the plain circumstances of the case. Pindar reminds the audience it is common knowledge that "sacking Neoptolemos came to an honored rest; the witness is not false" (49), "rest is sweet in every deed" (52), and "even honey and the pleasant flowers of Aphrodite have satiety" (52–53).

However difficult it may be to interpret just what Neoptolemos did, it is clear this is meant to be overcome by the act of heartening that the ode achieves, for the audience, and explicitly for the victor, Sogenes; for his father, Thearion, to whom maxims are also addressed (58); and for Pindar, who himself resembles Neoptolemos in being a voyager whom no one should blame (64–65), since he observed his limit (*terma*, 71) like the very athlete of the pentathlon whom he pointedly readdresses (70). "If there was toil, delight comes along the greater" (74), and this can be applied to Aeacus and giant-taming (90) Heracles too (83–105). As Charles Segal shows us (1967), the complications are themselves a kind of intellectual foil pointing to their own resolution, through the myth and the carefully managed interpretation of myth.

The result of awareness is a state of mind "weaving together a bliss for gentle youth and old age" (*N.*8.98–99), a state addressed as "Loving-minded Peace, great-cited daughter of Justice" in *Pythian* 8 (1–2). The late ode places in the foreground a resolution of moods, against "unhoneyed grudge" (8) and "*hybris*" (11). The hero may have strength, but mere strength is not enough without awareness and control, "force deceives even the great-boaster in time" (15), and the mythic exemplum is again the Typhon of *Pythian* 2. Aegina is located in space as "not far from the Graces" (21), the trope of litotes evoking both nearness and distance as it links the gnomic and the mythic, the actual and the legendary, the human island with its tutelary gods. What

Amphiaraus riddled (*ainixato*, 40) is now increased (*auxon*, 38) by the victor, and by the poet who is responding from his own debt or need (*chreos*) to the boy (33). This victor, having actualized the circuit of myths around the Seven against Thebes, has been granted by Apollo "the greatest of delight" (64). He is welcomed home by feasts after his victory, and there is the string of victories won by various members of his family at various contests (70–84). For the losers there was no such "grace (*charis*) of sweet laughter roused round their mother as they come home." They "cowered, bitten by chance" (85). This contrast leads into the concluding contrast between the brevity of life and its glory, achieved by the ode in such a way that another series of mythic figures need only be named.

The structure here is constantly mobile and self-defining. But the end effect is a poise that Finley (p. 23) compares to architecture. Pindar frequently borrows metaphors from architecture to designate his poems, as Burton (p. 17) points out.[18] The contrastive inspection of myth tends to freeze not the cult figure but the whole, balanced contemplation of victory and related myths and poetry into one apprehended object, rather like a temple.

Pindar's handling of myth is complete. He differs from Plato, who either receives his myths without any question or subjects them to mere allegorization, as he does with the myth of Prometheus, or invents wholly new ones. The myth of Er in the Tenth Book of *The Republic* translates a pre-Socratic cosmology into an eschatological myth. Plato, who quotes Pindar off and on in *The Republic*, does not mention him in this vision of the afterlife. Pindar's afterlife in *Olympian* 2 is too fully absorbed in the poetic ascertainment of conditions and possibilities for bliss to alter what he has been given. He merely translates it, by a strenuous act of forcing the conditions of the epinician art to yield a self-definition.

5.
INQUIRY:
Herodotus

*On the European Continent incomplete conquests fell into
two patterns. The main stream of migrations, which had over-
run Europe from East to West, was reversed about the eighth
century: from West to East the French pressed against the
Flemings and Germans, the Germans against the Lithuanians
and Slavs, the Lithuanians and Poles against the Russians, and
the Russians against the Finnish tribes, and ultimately also
against the Mongols; each nation was yielding ground in the
West, and gaining much more at the expense of its Eastern
neighbours; in the East were wide spaces and a reduced capacity for resisting pressure. Similarly the Swedes spread across
the Baltic, and the Italians across the Adriatic. The Flemish-
Walloon problem in Belgium and the Franco-German problem
in Alsace, the numerous problems of Germany's ragged Eastern border, Poland's problems both on her Western and on
her Eastern flank, and the conflict between the Yugoslavs
and the Italians, all originate in that great West to East shift
on the linguistic map of Europe. The other pattern of conquests whose consequences were formative of nineteenth-century European history, goes back to the continued Asiatic incursions, of the Avars, the Magyars, and Turks into South-Eastern
Europe. The Germans met them at the gate of the Danube,
between the Bohemian quadrilateral and the Alps: this is the
origin of Austria whose core was the Ostmark round Vienna,
with its flanking mountain bastions and its access to the Adriatic. Germans and Magyars in their head-on collision split off
the Northern from the Southern Slavs and established their
dominion over that middle zone; and next the subjection of the
Southern Slavs and the Rumans was completed by the Turkish
conquest of the Balkans.*
LEWIS NAMIER,
Vanished Supremacies

1.

LOOKED at the way we must inevitably see him, backward, Herodotus
offers a flat linearity of presentation that is almost impossible not to see
as somewhat naive. Looked at ahead, however, from the imagined vantage of his own immense task, his very linearity is a triumph. Herodotus

145

breaks the hold of the circular and cyclic view, which Homer maintains over his events; he does so by expanding a single large event, one he designates as culminating in the "largest expedition of which we have knowledge." He expands it all the way back to one before the Trojan War (7.20). He traces this Persian War as far as he can in the known world of space and what can be properly researched in time. This act of inquiry (*historie*) is cast in a new form, divorced from verse, the standard vehicle used by the earlier society for conveying societal reflections and meanings. Herodotus writes in what is not yet called prose, and he does so without recourse to the *isocola* of balanced utterance wherein Gorgias and Heraclitus had retained a ghost of the parallelism of balances accompanying early verse.[1] Herodotus casts off not only verse but also the persistent verselike element in prose.[2]

Prose in earlier societies is used only for bare record. Even the standard liturgies of cult are conveyed in formulaic repetitions. In an early oral society language free of such rhythms is a language of almost pure matter-of-fact recorded link of word to object, almost a simple "reference," in Frege's use of that term. The connection between signifier and signified is made too sharply, too univocally, to confirm or conflict with the systems of myth and cult, which are confined to rhythmed utterance for their expression. The language of the Linear B tablets is a language of inventory, a language not far from mere count-scratchings on a tally stick. Such a record is not easily distinguishable, as a verbal usage, from such a nonverbal point of reference as the standard meter measure now preserved at Paris. The owner tallies up his sheep so that he can check his count at a later time, just as last year's mark of a child's height on the wall, compared with this year's mark, shows how much the child has grown, without reference to feet and inches or meters and centimeters. Writing, in Greece or Babylon or Israel, is first used to codify laws, which are similar points of record, put down in the form of their exact framing for a later checking, as one might check the sheep-count by a tally or a board measure by a yardstick. The "eye for an eye" of the codes of Hammurabi or Leviticus preserves this principle of simple correspondence.[3] Of course law and its linguistic expression grow more complex in Greece, notably after Solon, who figures prominently in Herodotus' opening book, and notably in the period of Herodotus' lifetime. It has often been pointed out, most elaborately by Benardete, that the events in Herodotus are presented as though they were cases at law.

In Homeric usage the word *histor*, which never appears in Herodotus, means one who judges or discriminates, presumably after inquiry into the circumstances, in a specific law case. *Historie* appears in the first sentence of Herodotus' account, right after his name ("Hērodotu Halikarnēsseos historiēs apodexis hēde"); it is in the genitive and modifies *apodexis*, which means "indication," "showing forth," "exposition." It would be hard to find a better lead-word than *apodexis* to cover the primitive use of prose in the oral societies Herodotus is helping to transcend by redefining them. A standard meter, an inventory, a codified law—all are *apodexeis*: they merely point out and set forth plainly what is conceived to be, in our language, a fact.

But one fact stands in connected relation to another. The first problem of the historian, once he has taken the epochal step of searching out verifiable facts, is the concatenation of those facts. Facts have "causes" (to use a terminology much questioned since Hume), and "cause" (*aitie*) is the next term, of major and concluding emphasis, in Herodotus' prologue. All three terms, *historie, apodexis,* and *aitie,* are relative neologisms, though *aitie* has a Homeric history as an adjective and some corresponding usage in the pre-Socratics.[4] All three terms are bound up together in ways it would take a whole examination of Herodotus to account for. Gentile and Cerri find the question of "cause" animating Herodotus also in the related terms *arche* ("beginning," "occasion") and *prophasis* ("pretext").

Briefly, an inquiry can result in a showing forth only if somehow a cause is presented. *Historie* can only be formulated in language if it becomes an *apodexis,* the sort of linear presentation that is possible in Homer without either inquiry or argued assignation of cause. And *historie* as inquiry cannot be carried through without assignment of cause, *aitie.* Herodotus, who also uses *aitie* of the cause of a single event, here seems to use it of the whole complex Persian war, and in the singular. *Historie* exemplifies its success by making *apodexis* and *aitie* versions of one another. *Historie* is *apodexis* plus *aitie,* facts ascertained and then the principle ascertained that will link them.

In Homer the Trojan War is preordained and preconcluded by a divine action, "a plan of Zeus brought it about" ("Dios d'eteleieto boulē" *Iliad,* 1.5.). This near-formula is echoed in the *Theogony,* "the thought of great Zeus was fulfilled" ("megalou de Dios noos exeteleieto" 1002). Herodotus, as though to de-mythologize (but not to de-theologize) his undertaking, presents two possible mythic accounts of Europe against Asia as conflicting accounts. He offers the Persian, Greek, and

Phoenician versions of the rape of Io on the side of Asian injury to Greeks, and the rape of Helen on the same side. He passes by these conflicting accounts not to go to the root of a single cause for his great war, a topic to which he never returns. Rather, he singles out a historical individual, one who might be recalled by a series of living memories. He singles out Croesus, who was "first to begin unjust deeds," a fact Herodotus says he "knows himself" and can therefore "point out" ("having pointed out him I know to have begun unjust deeds against the Greeks, I shall proceed further in my account" 1.5.3). Herodotus declares that he will proceed (*probesomai*) from this certain knowledge (*oida*) of unjust actions that are "against the Greeks," but will not do so until he has concluded the whole story of Lydia and Croesus. Later, however, Herodotus will point out that the Lydians are effectually midway in custom, as they are in space, between the Greeks and the Persians (1.94). They differ from the Greeks most notably in the custom of prostituting their daughters, and an inversion of this custom begins the dynasty which Croesus concludes. His progenitor Gyges helplessly but guiltily murdered Candaules after being forced to this impasse by the queen whom he has seen naked and who gave him the choice of usurpation or death.

This beginning is not only explicitly declared to be later than other contingent but inextricable happenings; it is designated by a word that includes the notion of contingency by referring to existence as well as to inception (*hyparxanta*). And Croesus' attack, more simply than any other attacks, is designated as "unjust deeds " (though finally, I believe, Herodotus may be said to take the pacifist position that all attacks against alien peoples are ill-advised—see 1.87.3ff and 7.139ff). The complex of events is subject to a verdict, as in law. Herodotus is "proceeding" by an act of simple verbal "pointing out" (*semenas*).

Collingwood (p. 11) distinguishes the kind of record that an official inscription, or an inventory, provides from the kind of question Herodotus asks—the data of history, as we would say, from the writing of history. But this distinction, which is not to be found in Homer, is also not to be found in Herodotus, and if we make it we are in danger of separating elements which it is his achievement to keep together even while he is radically redefining them. In his *apodexis* Herodotus manages to include an *aitie* without separating it off. Like the most sophisticated modern fiction, a story for Herodotus both records an actual state of past happenings and contains a message, while retaining the noteworthy flatness of a bare inscriptional record. Dionysius of Halicarnassus (*De Thucydide* 5, as quoted by Bury, p. 25) says that the earliest historians gave just traditions and records "without adding or subtracting anything." Now this is demonstrably the practice to which Herodotus confines himself, while at the same time he attempts to preserve the Homeric comprehensiveness, as Hecataeus did not do for history and Pherecydes of Syros would seem not to have done for myth. Starting from a prose record, he reinvents a noncyclic view of a single, large event whose exemplary character must be visualized in its interconnections to be perceived as exemplary. It cannot be taken for granted, and it cannot be said to rest on merely gnomic or culture-bound formulations. In the sense of this comprehensiveness Herodotus goes behind Hecataeus to Homer and repeats him, remaining "most Homeric" (*homerikotatos*), as Longinus called him (*On the Sublime*, 13.4), linking him in this trait with Stesichorus, Archilochus, and Plato.

Our easy distinction between fact and fiction is itself perhaps too easy, since ultimately we judge the stories of fiction by their complex correspondence to facts unstatable in other terms. Homer comprises both "fact" and "fiction" as he comprises both the category "myth" and the category "history," since the *Iliad* is at once a record of what happened in the past and a formulation of events in the lives of the Olympian deities. Although Herodotus has redefined his subject of inquiry as the materials of history in our sense, thus shifting the emphasis markedly away from myth, it should not be assumed that he is thereby invoking the other distinction between fact and fiction or can be judged as failing this or that canon for the transmission of fact.

An early distinction between fact and fiction can be found at the beginning of the *Theogony*:

Ποιμένες ἄγραυλοι, κάκ' ἐλέγχεα, γαστέρες οἶον,
ἴδμεν ψεύδεα πολλὰ λέγειν ἐτύμοισιν ὁμοῖα,
ἴδμεν δ', εὖτ' ἐθέλωμεν, ἀληθέα γηρύσασθαι.

Rustic shepherds, evil reproaches, mere bellies,
We know how to speak many falsehoods that are like genuine things,
And we know how, whenever we wish, to utter true things.

The terms here echo those used in the *Odyssey* (19.559–569) to distinguish the dreams that come through the gates of horn from those that come through the gates of ivory. We have here not two categories, but three: *pseudea* ("false"), *etumoisi* ("similar"), and *alethea* ("true"), with connections between them of other than opposition, since the lies the Muses tell are "like the genuine" (thus, it could be argued, invoking a fourth category, that of resemblance); and the "genuine," the *etuma* which are always tied to words in Homer, have to be distinguished in the main opposition here from the "true things" with which in loose attribution they are identified. Pietro Pucci has shown some of the complexity that may be derived from this triad of terms. He points out, too, that *homoios* may mean either "similar" or "identical."

Moreover, the root meaning of "lay bare" for *alethes* is present in these circumstances. The utterance of "truths" depends on the caprice of the Muses, who, Hesiod here tells us, revealed these words to him in a vision on Helicon. This particular utterance, which can be applied to itself and considered an utterance of true things, is cast in the formal and interactive context of a ritualistic verbal castigation.[5]

The favor of the Muses is further accorded here to kings, in a passage that sets forth succinctly the condition of instantaneous communication and command in an oral society. This kind of speaking cuts across the old Indo-European distinction between the function of the king and the function of a priest-poet:

> She [Calliope] serves kings at the same time who have respect,
> Whomever the maidens of great Zeus do honor
> And look on as he is born, of Zeus-nourished kings.
> They pour a sweet dew upon his tongue
> And the honeyed words flow from his mouth. The people
> All look to him to distinguish the ordinances
> With straight judgments. He, speaking securely,
> Would in his knowing bring even a great strife to cease.
>
>   (80–87)

Herodotus' detachment from this posture, wherein Hesiod identifies his own source with a ruler's, is radical. His kings or tyrants, who are wholly dependent on advice, calculation, oracle, and divine favor, maintain a preeminence precarious enough to prohibit any of these kinds of messages from converging into such a Homeric-Hesiodic tribal unity. Herodotus is as detached towards his subject matter as the Ionian philosophers who preceded him were towards theirs. He approaches human events with a spirit of inquiry very like that applied by Thales to cosmological events and by Pherecydes of Syros to mythological ones. His limited field is large enough to include both the general principle of Anaximander, a "justice" (*dike*) which contains more than a hint of legal judgment, and such a specific act of Anaximander as his reputed invention of the first map. Herodotus offers us the sorts of maps complex enough, as Myres argues of his "square" geography, to be formed on two principles, an Ionian (4.36; 5.49; p. 26) and a Persian (4.37; p. 37). These maps are appended to ethnographic data included in the general account.

Such data are presented in a version of the literary technique Shklovski derives from Tolstoi, "estrangement" (*ostranyenye*), each fact given as if for the first time and afresh. So in Herodotus it is all told as if he were starting from scratch, even when it deals with what must have been generally known (for instance, the climate and geography of Ionia in 1.142), whereas the Homeric catalogue of the ships makes the opposite assumption: that the tribes of whom a count is offered are known to the auditor by virtue of his understanding Greek.

In Hecataeus the genealogies would seem to have been separated from the geography. Herodotus, through the careful and painstakingly linear procedure of his presentation, keeps the two inseparably connected. Nor does he pay exact attention at all times (for example, in 2.145) to genealogical succession, attending to it, even for the gods, only insofar as it bears on the train of his discourse. A map itself is used in 5.48 by Aristagoras to make a strategic point to Cleomenes.

2.

In Herodotus when linguistic communication fails there is the sign language which corresponds to his bare record: the Ethiopians give a bow to the invading Persians, communicating its meaning through interpreters, the "Fish-eaters" who understand the Ethiopians' language (3.22). And when the Samians have not succeeded in making their need understood to the Spartans, they pass them an empty sack (3.47)— which is still not understood.

The Persians always request of a people not yet subject to them that they send "earth and water" as symbols of submission (4.26; 7.32, and elsewhere). The Scythians, who are simply devoted to "signs" (*eikasia*) in Benardete's interpretation (p. 164), give Darius, instead of earth and water, a mouse, a bird, a frog, and five arrows, which it takes two inter-

preters (4.131–132) to decipher as meaning that even if Darius were at
home under the ground, in the air, or in the water, he could not escape
the arrows of the enemy. This complex sign, in Cohen's reading, presents a sort of connected syntax among its particulars. It also responds
metonymically with a mouse instead of the requested earth and a frog
instead of water.

Herodotus in his own vast linear presentation recognizably adopts a
comparable framework with his sign-system, a system whose particulars
require that the reader do some of the work of making connections.
Thrasyboulos gives a lesson to the fledgling tyrant Periander by knock-
ing the tallest ears of wheat and "adding no word" ("*hypothemenos
epos ouden*," 5.92). The chains still hanging in the Acropolis after the
Persians have burned its walls (5.77) are a different sort of silent communication, from past to present, of a complex set of events, the freeing
of Chalcidians who have been bound in punishment for collaborating
with a Spartan attack on Athens (5.77). But four lines of hexameter
about the chains are included to explain them in a different mode than
the prose narrative of Herodotus himself. The lines of verse are themselves a fact, a datum, in his prose narrative, like the fact of the chains
and the fact of their duration.

The language of Herodotus, in its matter-of-fact linearity, keeps every
gesture at once totally detached as it is brought to ascertainment and
totally culture-bound, so that both its singularity and its function in
series are dependent on a whole complex of events yet at the same time
perceptible, as properly presented, in a simple *apodexis*. In myth the
gnomic exists as a kernel at the center of a known story; Pindar strips
off the husk and presents the kernel separately. In the stories of Herodotus' "inquiry," the events are at once submythic and postgnomic. The
association between story and proverbial proposition has become problematic.

3.

Herodotus has, so to speak, arrived at the point Ranke describes, that
of setting himself the task of ascertaining and presenting "*wie es eigent-
lich gewesen ist*," "the way it really happened." To arrive at this formulation requires a number of prior decisions, and the formulation itself
almost begs the many questions it conceals.

How meaning gets coded into a story is a question central not only

to the practice of historiography but to any literary presentation whatever. Words come inescapably in sequence; if the words are bound in
rhythm above and beyond the sound patterns germane to the language
—if they are verse—then to that degree the words are insisting on something that lies below the sequence and determines it. In an oral society
this something involves the cyclic pattern which the rituals of the society
celebrate and to which they refer. This year's fertility festival, coming
in sequence after last year's, is made invariant. It is cast in patterns of
repetition, verbal ones and rhythmic ones, as well as in patterns of
gesture.

It does not matter in which particular year the ritual happens. In that
sense ritual, like myth, conforms to the half-truth of Lévi-Strauss's assertion that it does not matter in what order the events of a myth are told.
It does not matter because in structural analysis the underlying structure
is all, and the order wherein the binary elements are presented in no
way determines the coded interrelation of these elements.

But a myth is also a process. It occurs in time and it must be told in
time. It is the young Oedipus who bests the Sphinx, the middle-aged
Oedipus who launches a fatal inquiry into the past, the old Oedipus who
fades away in the grove at Colonus. At a certain point, the point of
literary formulation, it is not enough just to retell the myth. A meaning
must be coded into it that further subjects it to temporal strategies of
order and inclusion. Inclusion involves exclusion; it is only late mythog-
raphers, intent on the particular goal of completeness, who give all the
details they have ever heard, most of which we may presume to have
existed early. We learn from Apollodorus what Sophocles knew but
chose to exclude from his particular presentation.

Homer is already literary in this sense. He chooses to include only
material that bears on the wrath of Achilles or the events in the home-
coming of Odysseus. Thus in his encyclopedic task he can concentrate
mythographic purposes upon particular individuals without questioning
larger group actions. These are simply labelled with the formulaic-typify-
ing epithets, as, "bronze-greaved Achaians" or "long-gowned Trojans."
The social picture of the Homeric world we infer from a host of details;
and Homer's vision of human destiny we infer from the presentation of
the events, as in most literary works. Group action in Homer provides
his typifications, givens that do not question the congruence of group
action with individual human destinies. I have discussed elsewhere the
complexity of Priam's embassy to Achilles (Cook, 1966; pp. 114–116);

at no point does this complexity rest on other than the situation of an old enemy father begging his son's body from the victorious supreme warrior.

In Herodotus, group actions do converge with individual human destinies, and yet there is no attempt either to depend wholly on staples of typification or to make this particular series yield a Thucydidean exemplum of universal applicability. The human, the ethnic (Lydian), and the personal (Croesus) are already in unstable relation to one another. The Persians are characterized by a host of tiny stories and customs, as are individual groups among the Greeks, though the Spartans and the Athenians and the Ionians all display characteristics globally Greek which would be known to his readers. Any invasion presents practically and, as Herodotus demonstrates, also theoretically, the problem of unforeseen intricacies of cross-cultural differences.

This process is involved when it brings in the most remote peoples in space, the Ethiopians and the Scythians, the Babylonians and the Egyptians and the Indians. Herodotus builds up the characteristics Homer takes for granted, producing a known world by exact ethnographic construction. And while Homer is writing about a world at some distance in time from his own, Herodotus implies at the outset that he must confine himself to what he himself knows (*autos oida*, 5.3); his is that history of recent events that Latte indicates to be the common mode of ancient historiography.

We know that Hecataeus, like Herodotus, was encyclopedic. And we know that he also exercised a critical and corrective scrutiny on particular traditions coming to him through Hesiod (Fgt. 19. Jacoby). But Hecataeus, we may presume, was "flat" not only in presentation but in final meaning. Nothing lurked under the story, or so we may again presume. Herodotus takes the techniques of Hecataeus and rebuilds a world as coherent as Homer's, though it leaves behind the cyclic Homeric universe without even following the philosophers of Herodotus' youth in criticizing the Olympian gods. In this sense, too, Longinus' ascription "most Homeric" retains its aptness.

Herodotus presents us in an exacting form with the question of what lurks under the story. The rigorously sequential linearity of his inquiry is rarely broken for the presentation of a moral; and yet, as Benardete keeps reminding us, the moral is everywhere. The story is thinned out as expansively as in a nineteenth-century novel, without many of the telltale stylistic gestures beyond the faintly rhetorical ones noticed in

him by Demetrius and Longinus by which we might guess the sort of
meaning in the story lurking underneath.[6]

How can something lurk under a story? Something always does, if
the story commands attention. *Anna Karenina* and even *Finnegans
Wake* are cautionary tales no less than is "the fall of Croesus." All such
stories are expanded "ostensive" definitions, or definitions by example.
As Balzac understood (Cook 1960), and as Borges somewhat differently understands, this condition of utterance for expanded stories under-
cuts the easy distinction between "history" and "fiction."

In all verbal formulations of myth, including literary ones, something
related to the force of the unknown that the myth is devised to name
remains and lurks under the story or other sequence. Historiography,
in its initial conception as radically devised by Herodotus, takes this
force away from the sequence of the story and substitutes something for
which the large sequence is itself a pattern, one not susceptible of such
cybernetic remapping as Lévi-Strauss's, and yet still more sequential
than any presentation of myth can be. Nor could such a linearity of
historiographic presentation yield even to such a summary as might be
given for Apollo's career, for example, in a lexical entry under Apollo.
What would be lost in such a lexical entry would be precisely the force
of Apollo, by definition an unknown. What would be lost from a lexical
entry under Croesus would be the pattern that Herodotus has presented
lurking under his story, something defined as known rather than unknown, a result of inquiry into cause and not an unknown cause that
can only be propitiated and sung about.

It is in fact natural for the novel, as well as written history, to include
large collective social events, not only in popular works but in *War and
Peace* and *Finnegans Wake*. Morton White's deliberate characterization
of historiographic writing would apply equally to the novel (p. 372),
"much of historical explanation takes the form of what Hempel calls an
'explanation sketch'—something which falls short of an explanation
through a failure to express all the generalizations involved."

What White calls "failure" is of course a necessary condition, as
Hexter has pointed out. The *apodexis* is never complete. And if what a
historiographic text presents is to carry a special meaning, something
must lurk under the story.

Herodotus clearly does get behind the events he lays out. There is an
aitie lurking under his *apodexis*; if there were not, his data would seem
jumbled. The presentation itself is linear, and it proceeds forward in

time, first demarcating a time separated from the remote past when it is possible to produce the causal enchainment. He jumps from Io and Helen to Croesus, a figure who enables him to get behind the Persian War, his announced subject.

From then on he moves forward through his events to the very end of the Persian War. But this main forward movement, from past to its future—the *apodexis*—entails a counter-movement, from past to what preceded the past, to *aitie*. Croesus' invasion gathers momentum until he is countered by Cyrus, whose accession must be explained (1.95–129), just as Croesus' was (1.5–27). "The Lydians then were enslaved under the Persians" (1.94.7) brings the whole first sequence to a natural term, a succinct *apodexis* which calls for the *aitie* lurking under it. "Our account seeks out next in order about that Cyrus, who he was who brought down the dominion of Croesus; and about the Persians, in what fashion they became the rulers of Asia" (1.95.1).

So Herodotus proceeds in general. The Milesian deputy Aristagoras, after a series of complications engendered by a difference of ethnic styles as well as a divergence of interest between Persian and Greek, decides to foment the Ionian revolt (5.24–38); he goes to Sparta and then to Athens to seek aid. This movement forward in time entails a movement backward, to explain what the situation is in Sparta (5.38–48) and in Athens (5.55–75), and also the complicated relations, likewise engendered by a divergence of interest and a difference of ethnic styles, between Sparta and Athens themselves (5.79–92). Moreover, Aristagoras is here repeating the pattern of Croesus, who similarly decided to seek out, in a different style and a different order, the help of Athens. The end of Aristagoras' campaign is similarly disastrous, but he dies as a result and Croesus does not.

This constant procedure produces a broken and loosely open form of ring composition, as Myres' outline and table of correspondences (pp. 118–134) show graphically. But it is ring composition with a difference. The flat fact held in view keeps the ring open. The search for a momentary cause loops back, and then the narrative itself proceeds forward in its more direct sequence, that sequence itself constituting a somewhat wider loop. The much-mooted "*logoi*," the separate accounts of the Egyptians and the Scythians to which nearly all of the second book and most of the fourth are devoted, constitute such loops, their presentation so flattened out that the lurking *aitie* ("Who were the Egyptians anyway?") takes on the character of *apodexis*. The ethnographic data tend to be either aftermath (6.119f; 1.88–94) or prelude (Egypt, Scythia).

And this is really always the case. Herodotus throughout is making the technique of Hecataeus, the flat prose record, produce the effect of something like Homer, a global explanation.

Herodotus' investigation involves time, and the Lydians can only be defined as the end product of a series of linear events in time, which can only be conveyed in sentences like "The Lydians, then, were enslaved under the Persians" (1.94.7). Anaximander makes a map in space. And he also defines *dike* or justice as a supervening principle in all events, physical and other, "according to the ordering of time" (*kata tou chronou taxin*, Diels 12.B1). Herodotus fuses these two sides of Anaximander's thought and makes the map in space coordinately dependent on a series of events in time. While he is willing to ascribe non-justice, *a-dikia*, to individual acts, he is at all points seeking a cause, an *aitie*, wherein the enslavement of the Lydians is a constituent factor as well as a discrete event.

The prospective condition of inquiry, *historie*, announces a search for, or a seeking out of, something not obvious as the goal of the sentences of the work that then stretches ahead. This procedure revolutionizes the procedure of Homer, who assumes he can take for granted that his auditors already know, at least in rough outline, what he reinvokes. He does not have to seek it out, to "*historein*." He need only be a mouthpiece of the goddess, and command that she "sing the wrath of Achilles, son of Peleus" or "tell" him "about the man of many turns." For Herodotus the connections have become radically problematic, and the truth-value, instead of being assumed, has to be constituted from scratch, sentence by sentence. The atoll of *aitie* that rises above the sea of imperception is built up like a coral reef from myriads of integers of reference and verification.

Independent of the gods, something complex and unique lurks in the events. The story, properly presented, reveals what lurks in the events, as for example in the final marshalling of forces by Croesus:

> Croesus marched against Cappadocia for these reasons: from a desire to gain land, wishing to add more to his own share, and being especially trusting in the oracle, and wishing to punish Cyrus for Astyages. Astyages, son of Kyaxares, who was both the brother-in-law of Croesus and the king of the Medes, Cyrus, son of

Cambyses, had subdued and was holding, him who had become son-in-law to Croesus as follows: a band of nomad Scythians had revolted and got out to the land of the Medes. Kyaxares son of Phraortes son of Deioces was tyrant of the Medes at this time, who treated them well since they were suppliants, so that he held them in high regard and entrusted boys to them to learn the language and skill with the bow. As time went on, when the Scythians were always roving and always bringing something back, once it happened that they caught nothing. When they returned empty-handed, Kyaxares (for he was, as it had appeared, quick to anger) treated them roughly and injuriously.   (1.73.1–4)

The Scythians then who "judged that they had suffered unworthily (*anaxia*)" took one of the Median boys, killed him and dressed him like game, delivered the corpse to Kyaxares and fled to the Lydian capital, where, once again, they "became suppliants" (*hiketai*, the word repeated from the Median occasion a few sentences before). The Medes asked the Lydians to hand over the Scythians. The Lydians' refusal occasioned a war between Lydians and Medes that lasted five years, till the sudden occasion of an eclipse (which had been predicted by Thales) made both sides "eager for there to be peace between them."

> Those reconciling them were these: Syennesis the Cilician and Labynetos the Babylonian. These men were eager that there should be a compact and brought about an interchange of marriage: they came to the conclusion that Alyattes should give his daughter Aryenis to Astyages the son of Kyaxares. For without a strong necessity strong reconciliations do not wish to persist. These nations make the sort of compacts that the Greeks do, on which occasion they cut their arms on the surface of the flesh and lick each other's blood.   (1.74.3–75.1)

Hesiod is already a historian in the several senses that Rosenmeyer explores, resting on the distinctions among the five ages of man in the *Works and Days* (109–201) made by Eduard Meyer, and between *Sagengeschichte* and *Geschichte*. On this large scale, even with its verifiable counterparts of the change from bronze to iron technology, Herodotus sees either a legend which at times (2.23) can disappear "to the vanishing point" (*es to aphanes*), or else, simply and neutrally, small cities becoming great and great cities becoming small (1.2). Where Hesiod's five ages are devoid of personal names, either historical or divine, as Rosenmeyer points out (p. 279), Herodotus embodies his enchained events in distinct and particular individuals like Croesus and Cyrus, who have a tempo which is at once personal, ethnic, and human, all three intertwined. Like Hesiod, he will offer for small events an alternate explanation (*heteron logon, Erga,* 106–107); and like Hesiod he is implicitly offering an "explanation sketch," hitting the high points as Hesiod does in the verb Rosenmeyer stresses from this passage, *ekkoruphoso* ("touch the main points"). Herodotus never uses this verb, though he does once use a related compound, *apokoruphou* ("give a summary answer," 5.73), and something might be made of the difference between the selection Hesiod makes in the *ek,* "out," of his prefix and the mere contingency suggested by the one Herodotus here applies, *apo,* "from." Herodotus, in any case, is of course more detailed than Hesiod at every point. But he has his eye no less on what lurks under the story, and in avoiding such predecessors he is avoiding the large periodizations of the five ages along with the meters in which they are cast.

Here the linear presentation is all a carefully managed backward loop of explanation, since Croesus is already at the point of invading Cappadocia, and this story explains why. Folk motifs like the Scythian banquet-of-Thyestes described above are not exploited for their submythic overtones of relation to the celestial and psychological universe of theogonies. The connection of the motif with Ouranos in Hesiod or Atreus in legend has nothing to do with the meaning Herodotus gives to the motif. It is repeated with variation: Kyaxares' son Astyages, to punish Harpagus for saving Cyrus, has Harpagus's son killed and served up to Harpagus for dinner; Astyages then stays around for the result (1.118–119), later fatally forgetting enough to put Harpagus in charge of an army (1.127). But this repetition, like all those in Herodotus, is part of the patient, gradual buildup of case-histories, which reknit the combinations of the personal, the ethnic, and the supervening human. Civilized peoples tend to receive suppliants. The Greeks do, and it is pointed out here that interethnic complications can result when both the Medes and the Lydians receive as suppliants a kind of people, the Scythians, who themselves will receive none. A suppliant comes for a reason—either political, as here, or personal, as in the case of the Phrygian Adrastus whom Croesus unwarily receives in his court—thereby ensuring the predicted death of his son Atys, whose whole upbringing has been framed to avoid that oracle (1.34–43). On the merely personal level, Kyaxares' predisposition to anger triggers a series that leads to a five-year war, broken up not by a macropolitical resolution between the Medes and the Lydians, but first by the skill of an Ionian wise man, Thales, consulted earlier by Croesus (1.74).

This truce is sealed by the intervention of advisers who may be said to be bringing their own ethnic customs to bear on the question, since this is the only marriage of state carried through in all of Herodotus. A failed one, to be sure, is proposed to Amasis of Egypt by Cambyses (3.1–3). The Cilicians, we have heard (1.28), are one of the only two peoples west of the Halys that are free of Croesus' rule. They have a good political reason, transcending ethnic style, for wishing these powerful neighbors to make a truce. So do the Babylonians; but, alas, this sort of peace leaves them free to be captured by Cyrus (1.188–191), after having gone into allegiance with Croesus in his expedition, under the very same Labynetos (1.77). Here, earlier on in time, we are given what is also the very first mention of Babylon in Herodotus, a small beginning dovetailed into another story.

The linear story is thus a tissue of analogies which build up case precedent for a law which exists only as its meaning—for an *aitie*. Kyaxares is prone to anger; that is the defect of the quality of courage attributed to him in the only other expanded mention in the text, coming ironically after this in sequence: "He is said to have been still more valiant than his forebears" and he conquered Assyria (1.103).

We are given three reasons here for Croesus' aggression. They are not coordinate in presentation: the last requires this expansive explanation. Though given on the same flat, linear plane, their lack of coordination keeps the analogies they inevitably pick up from being coordinate in meaning as well. If any overriding general rule of politics may be deduced from Herodotus, it is this: ethnic groups exist within natural boundaries roughly defined in space. It is always bad policy to drive across such boundaries, no matter what the provocation. And it proves to be, in the biggest and most disastrous expedition of all, the last battles of the Persian wars against Greece, a bad policy for the Persians too, even though they, unlike Croesus, have been provoked. Croesus' whole expedition stands in implied antithesis to their later ones. But his desire to expand his territory is a natural human desire that the Persians, in less justified activities than their expedition against the Greeks, have also exemplified: in their incursions against the Egyptians and the Scythians and the Massagetae, against the Libyans and the Assyrians and the Babylonians and the Ethiopians—in all directions, actually, except towards Greece, which they do finally attack after they put down the revolt of those closer land-neighbor Greeks, the Ionians, who once formed part of Croesus' own empire.

Desire for conquest is Croesus' first reason. His second is reliance on divine hints, hints which Herodotus presents as being at once necessary and untrustworthy. Oracles must be sought, but they should be managed with respect to other considerations. They give clues, not solutions. Croesus is in the process, touched on here, of misreading the biggest clue of all. A great empire will indeed be destroyed if he attacks the Persians, but not theirs; his own.

The oracle is only one of three from Delphi, and only one of the many Croesus has solicited—from Libya, Abae, Dodona, Amphiaraus, Trophonias, and Miletus (1.46). Part of the danger lurking in the prosperity for which Croesus was proverbial even in Herodotus' own day is that he will overspend in some area. He is shown trying to bribe Delphi with gifts (1.50–41) and covering the map of Greece with his search for divine indications. He has received an oracle that corresponds to a version of his inmost desires, a circumstance which tends to accompany oracles anyway, as Saul Levin has noted. But he had to sift to get that one, and then he misinterpreted it by jumping to conclusions.

The other reason, the third, is on a still different plane, not that of politics or religion but of family. It is a family situation, however, that can be traced right back to politics, since his sister only married the Mede Astyages two generations earlier because of a state marriage brought about through an interethnic tangle involving six peoples (Medes, Persians, Lydians, Scythians, Cilicians, Babylonians). Croesus had been gathering his forces, before this in the narrative but after this in time, by trying to knit together a corresponding ethnic tangle, marching finally with help promised but not fully forthcoming from the Spartans, the Ionians, the Egyptians, and the Babylonians (1.77).

Croesus' marshalling of forces is doomed to failure, since the Persian empire is so vast it would not need such complicated alliances in order to field an army; or later, as we learn in the Ionian arguments (6.8–9), to float a navy. As the warning advice of Sandanis has just held (1.71), Croesus' expedition can do no more than effectuate an ethnic transfer whereby the powerful but simple Persians will take over the wealth of the high-living Lydians, assimilating this trait which had become proverbial for Persians rather than Lydians by Herodotus' own time.

The earlier reason given for Croesus' marshalling was not ambition,

oracle, or family pride, but a partially defensive and preemptive one
superior in political canniness to any of those that have superseded it as
actual war is approaching. This political reason also includes the prior
mention of Astyages, not here designated (since that is not here an
aitie) as Croesus' brother-in-law:

> Afterwards the fact that the sovereignty of Astyages son of Kyax-
> ares was seized by Cyrus son of Cambyses and that the affairs of
> the Persians were on the wax put a stop to Croesus' grief, and he
> took on the intent, if he somehow could do it, before the Persians
> became great, to take over their waxing power (1.46.1).

This is a more sophisticated motive than the blind group self-defense
which even animals share.

Astyages, we later learn, had himself tried to be preemptive against
the "mule" Cyrus. Cyrus was a half-breed precisely because of the state
marriage between Astyages and Aryenis; Astyages had married his own
daughter off to the Persian Cambyses in order to forestall the predicted
conquest by allying her to someone then of a lower class (1.107–130).
Upper has, however, now become lower: Persian, in fidelity to the
oracle, becomes dominant over Mede. Astyages, as Herodotus postpones
telling us till the general subject "Who was Cyrus," lives in an only
moderate disgrace at the court of Cyrus, not enough, surely, to trigger
the revenge of Croesus. It is characteristic of Persians to be in some
ways more generous with those they defeat than are the Medes, or the
Lydians (unless the particular Persian is personally insane, as is Cambyses); we learn that the last political act of Croesus' reign was the
murder of Pantaleon, his rival for the Lydian throne, by the torture of
dragging a carding-comb across his back.

Croesus is to be put to death on a funeral pyre, but the Persian is
always prone to magnanimity; one portent and a whispered bit of wisdom are enough to save Croesus. He then plays out as a captive what
he had entertained as a ruler with Thales, with Syennesis, and with
Labynetos: the motif of the wise stranger. He becomes an adviser to the
Persian court, this being a Persian ethnic tendency in other cases (His-
tiaeus, 5.23–25; Demaratus 8.234–237; Democedes, 3.125). Croesus
goes on to outlive Cyrus himself.

Successions, indeed, tend to activate interethnic complications. Another whole tangle, on the Persian side, surrounds the family and political relations of Cyrus. Here the tangles are narrated on the Lydian side

from the viewpoint of the captive Astyages, who is an occasion for vengeful attack. Cyrus, like the two sons of Croesus (but also unlike them—they die young), again exemplifies the motif of the boy in the shadow of an oracle.

At the end of the passage quoted above (1.74.3–75.1) a general maxim "strong necessity must bind strong accords" is countered and complemented by an ethnological datum, the licking of blood, a custom primitive enough to be useless from a Greek point of view, but superseded here after all by the marriage compact.

This is the middle of the Lydian history, the normalizing sexual resolution of a state marriage. As it happens we have possibly analogous sexual conjunctions at both the beginning and the end of the Lydian history. At the end we are told, as last and longest in the narrative of Lydian customs, that they have the "shameful" habit of prostituting their daughters. This custom can be seen as an extreme, an acting out of an attitude polar in the area of shame, to the custom that Lydians "and most other foreigners" (*barbaroi*) do not look at each other naked (1.10), male or female. At the beginning, Gyges himself wisely adduces a maxim that Herodotus surely would not confine just to Lydia: "A woman casts off shame (*aidos*) in casting off her clothing" (1.8), using for the only time in all of Herodotus the word *aidos*, which is common in Homer and the shame culture he depicts. It is in the iron framework of this custom that Gyges kills Candaules, beginning the Lydian dynasty and also initiating the curse that it will end in five generations, a curse cited at the defeat of Croesus (1.91). In the pattern of such extremes, even a normative human act like a state marriage is subject to the larger oracular condition that it must contribute to the downfall of a ruler who has inherited his kingdom after such a double violation of the particular Lydian rules of modesty and the general human rule against murder. State marriages are dangerous anyway because the inter-ethnic is inherently unstable.

The verified, small progressions of event here link up, by both temporal progress and logical analogy, with other events in the sequence. The inquiry builds these up step by step. The single passage, as here, and the single story carried along—the Scythians' banquet-of-Thyestes which I have summarized—has its own flat existence as a fact. It is as such that it enters the tissue of explanation, through a kind of spiralling ring composition. We are given Croesus and Astyages, and much later Cyrus and Croesus, and then Cyrus and Astyages and Croesus. Having

Lydians fighting Medes over Scythians in this anecdote, we will soon have (since this is retrospect) the main, final battle of Lydians and Persians, on which follows, as explanation, the ascendancy of the Persians over the Medes. This splinter group of nomad Scythians is never heard of again, but the course of explaining Median domination entails accounting for a period of Scythian domination (1.103–106). Later on, (after Cyrus has met his death by following the advice of Croesus that he should preemptively invade the land of the Massagetae, the Scythians' neighbors and fellow savages [1.201–214]) there will be a subsequent, abortive expedition against all the Scythians as a people who, at the point we are inspecting, have failed to give Croesus aid.

As for the Babylonians, the Labynetos in this passage, who is better known to history as Nebuchadnezzar, drops out of the story for the time being. His son and namesake, however, will be defeated by Cyrus, son of the daughter who resulted from the union here sponsored by Labynetos. This Babylonian stalemate-conquest, accompanied by the standard ethnographic digression (1.178–200), is surpassed by the severer and more complete later conquest of Babylon by Darius (3.150–160).

4.

Logos in Herodotus means both bare narrative account (*apodexis*) and explanation of the bare facts (*aitie*). It is this verbal result which the inquiry, *historie*, is aimed at achieving. These two meanings, tale and explanation of tale, are inseparable in the word *logos*, and they are the two meanings that prevail. *Logos* here takes over from the earlier word for story, *muthos*, which is used only twice in all of Herodotus, and then with the modern pejorative sense, "false legend." Just as *muthos* slowly accrues the full meaning it will have in Plato, a myth in the honorific or descriptive sense, *logos* will accrue an abstract meaning increasingly divergent from it. Here, though, in Herodotus' usage as it confirms the theoretical foundations of his practice, *logos* unifies the presentation of the facts with their explanation, the story with its reason. These two senses, in their union, stand as far simpler than the spectrum of twelve senses with their subsenses that Guthrie reads into Heraclitus' context.[7]

We only make sense of Heraclitus if all these senses are operative. And we only make sense of Herodotus if his two senses are seen in the force of their union. It violates his unity of purpose, then, and first of all his verbal uses, if we extrapolate his promised *Assyrioi logoi*, along with the ethnographic accounts we do have, and separate them as a distinct kind of writing from the flow of political events, presented in a "pediment" composition of story frieze after story frieze. Myres' division into *logoi* and pediment units, handy for preliminary structural grouping, cannot be followed in its exclusive separation, though there is a recognizable similarity of digression and expansiveness in the accounts of the Babylonians (1.195–198), the Egyptians (all of 2), the Scythians (most of 4), the Thracians (5.3–8), the Libyans (4.181–190), and even the Persians (1.133–140), as Myres tabulates them (p. 73). And there are still other such accounts.

They function, however, in the same two-edged way that the "straight" narrative portions do, themselves a network of the sort of interrelated analogies analyzed above. The items in the "pediment friezes" of this narrative work are never distinct. They can flow without break—and without mythic intervention—into the gnomic, and then into the ethnological, as they do at the end of the passage analyzed above:

> Those reconciling them were these: Syennis the Cilician and Labynetos the Babylonian. These men were eager that there should be a compact and brought about an interchange of marriage; they came to the conclusion that Alyattes should give his daughter Aryenis to Astyages the son of Kyaxares. For without a strong necessity strong reconciliations do not wish to persist. These nations make the sort of compacts that the Greeks do, on which occasion they cut their arms on the surface of the flesh and lick each other's blood.

The names of the mediators give way to the names of both sponsors and principals (itself a full ethnological kinship complement) in the mediated marriage, which gives way to the political maxim, which gives way to the ethnological datum about blood-licking. This datum has to be somewhat ominous; it is a "barbarian" custom, though at no point is an unexamined opposition between barbarian and Greek allowed to operate. The oaths are after all like the ones the Greeks make.

The maxim would hold for all peoples whatever. Even where an ethnological contrast is activated—and the activation of such contrasts occupies all of Herodotus—the unexamined contrast is dangerous, unless an underlying similarity is also posited, as it is here. The question of similarity and contrast between civilized and primitive (our modern version of Greek and barbarian) is a puzzling one, still not resolved just by asserting for it a kind of uneasy identity. Herodotus generally shows us both similarity and contrast, as he does specifically here. As Benardete argues, the point of the separated "*logoi*," Egyptian and Scythian and other, is to produce a network of similarities and contrasts. This is clearly true here. It is not, after all, the Scythians, the silent, wild occasion of all this battle and negotiation, who have the custom of blood-licking, but presumably the more civilized Babylonians, Cilicians, Lydians, and Medes, all of them barbarians if set in unexamined contrast to the Greeks. Later the Arabians will have blood-smearing with oaths attributed to them (3.8.1). This is in the context of their giving friendly passage to Cambyses. And still later, on the occasion of the invasion of Scythia, the Scythians themselves are reported as drinking blood mixed with wine to ratify an oath (4.70). Meanwhile there is nothing so subsidiary or incidental about this ethnographic sentence that would permit it, to use a modern format, to be reduced to the level of a footnote. Were this to happen, the "blood-licking" footnote would have an ironic relation to the text. We cannot be sure that Herodotus is not being ironic here, as he certainly is in some instances. But we can be sure that the targets of the irony would not be exclusively the Babylonians, the Cilicians, the Lydians, and the Medes.

Thirty-one times Herodotus uses the word *logos*[8] to refer to his own book comprehensively. And he also refers to the explanation which the book constitutes. The *logos* is story plus explanation. Other accounts are also *logoi*, both stories and explanations. When they are in accord, they are "common," a *xunos logos* between Greek and barbarian (4.12). The possibility of such additions as the datum about blood-licking, or the whole account of Egypt in Book Two, is posited by the comparative method of letting one account act as an explanation for another. As Herodotus says when he brings Elis in as a third, and Greek, group to explain the customs of two barbarian groups, the Libyans and the Scythians, "For my *logos* has sought additions from the beginning." (4.30.1. The word for "additions," *prosthekas*, could also be rendered "insertions.")

Fact, for which another word is *ergon*, "deed," is often contrasted with *logos*, explanation or narrative of facts either in their difference (as 4.8) or their similarity (as 8.107). At the point of Darius' accession he makes such a distinction to Otanes, "There are many things which it is not possible to show in a *logos*, but in *ergon*; and there are others that are possible in *logos* and no clear *ergon* comes from them" (3.72). To speak in error, as Herodotus accuses Hecataeus of doing (6.137), is to speak "unjustly." Hecataeus is three times called a *logopoios*, a statement-maker, but the same word is also used of Aesop, a teller of tales that are both exemplary and cautionary, like those of Herodotus himself (2.134). All the senses of *logos* in Herodotus that mean not the bare thing said or the story but a systematic view of the bare thing said may be subsumed under "explanation"—"theory" (2.15, *touto to logo chromenoi*), "condition" (7.158), "purpose" (3.48), and even "truth," where *logos* is coupled with the word "true" (1.20; 5.41) or "right," *orthos*, (217; 6.68; 6.53) or "most just," *dikaiotatos* (7.108).

Reportage on the hearsay of others' statements underlies his own big statement at every point. "In all my *logos* it is established that I write the things said to my hearing by everyone" (2.123). But he distinguishes this process from believing an individual fact. A *logos* is thus an explanation designed to set out the facts, neutral as to their individual credibility, "I am obliged to say the things said, but I am not obliged to *believe* them wholly" [Italics—"*ge*"—are Herodotus'] and let this word hold for my whole account" (7.152).

The accumulations of data in the first four books around Persia, and in the fifth book around those Greeks who are on the Persian doorstep, the Ionians, leads into the account of the close and prolonged engagement between the two peoples in the last four books. As Benardete says (p. 154), "The Persian Wars will prove to be a surface phenomenon that has its basis in the principles and elements he has discovered in the first four books. They will show, as it were, his own *logos* in action." The action becomes more purely temporal, in a shorter span but in a closer focus, in the last four books. The shift from a long view of time to a short one in the two halves of the *History* overrides the uniform linear presentation. "The first part does turn on *logoi* as the second on *erga*."

The *History* is an explanation of the Persian Wars, and a massive gloss on "Persian" precedes the account of the actual wars themselves. The gloss, however, is presumed to bear on the battle, and the complex of ethnic styles subsumed in the campaigns of Books Six through Nine carries into *ergon* the *logoi* of the earlier books. Finally the customs have the same status as the events that illustrate them, which they in turn give an explanation for—"Custom is king of all," a phrase that Herodotus borrows from a highly privileged informant, Pindar (3.38; Pindar Fgt. 169).

5.

"Custom is king of all," Pindar's phrase, is introduced by Herodotus as an *ex post facto* conclusion to the cautionary tale of Darius' staged experiment (3.38). Darius first showed that the Greeks at his court would not eat their ancestors at any price (as the Calliatae among the Indians do); then he tried unsuccessfully to get the Calliatae to burn their dead (as the Greeks do). For both peoples, "a pattern or a custom is established," this whole phrase rendering the one Greek verb *nenomistai.*

Herodotus himself is establishing a pattern that differs from, and yet includes, the patterns, the *nomoi*, which he here says the poet Pindar rightly (*orthos*) said was king of all. This tale of cultural relativism, and its appended motto from Pindar, is inserted between a set of Persian events, the outrages occasioned by the madness of Cambyses, and a set of Greek events, the career of Polycrates of Samos.

The gnomic and the mythic here exist in separation, and the gnomic is not a conclusion but rather a stepping-stone. As Benardete notes, Herodotus manages to mention six of the Seven Wise Men in the traditional list. They traditionally produce gnomic sayings, and Herodotus says the *gnome*, the proverbially phrased opinion, of Bias is in one instance "most useful," *chresimotate* (1.170). Bias advised the Ionians to abandon their territory and colonize in the West, while Thales, at the same point of the narrative, has given them the equally good advice that they federate around their geographical mid-point, Teos.

Herodotus records such advice, himself offering not advice but the result of an enquiry. Custom presumably kept the Ionians from taking either set of good advice, as custom at an earlier point had kept Croesus from drawing the full conclusion from Solon's advice. Yet he is saved by whispering Solon's name on what was to have been his funeral pyre.

Solon's wisdom is partly occasioned by a mission not unlike Herodotus' own. He is travelling for *theoria*, observation—but this is a "pretext," *prophasin* (1.29). His real purpose is to give ten years of his absence to the laws, the *nomoi* or pattern observances, that he has promulgated "so that he should not be compelled to loose any of the laws he had established." Had he stayed in Athens, the earlier *nomos* would have undone his *nomoi*; he would have been heeded, finally, no more than Bias or Thales.

Croesus asks Solon if he has "seen any man more blest than all others" (30). Solon first names the Athenian Tellus, and he gives three reasons for Tellus' happiness: his wealth, his satisfaction as a parent of noble sons, and his heroic death in battle. On further inquiry, Solon ranks after Tellus the brothers Cleobis and Biton, who, replacing the usual oxen, drew their mother's cart to the temple of Hera and died of heartstrain.[9] But when pressed further, Solon simply puts the days of man into a linear succession (32): 26,250 days. And "In all is man circumstance" ("pan esti anthropos sumphorē"). After some reasoning he gives what is a proverbial conclusion: "we should wait till a man is dead and call him not yet blest but fortunate."

Of course Solon offers the example of Tellus out of a fund of common Greek, and human, proverbial wisdom. And yet if he had followed just this he would never have promulgated the laws of Athens. He can say this much and still be on safe ground—except that it angers Croesus, who as a Lydian and a king would like more to be made of earthly prosperity. It is a set of tales meant to be cautionary to Croesus, as Croesus's whole story, in which it is embedded, is cautionary for the progress of the Persian empire.

Thucydides, who never mentions Herodotus by name, is understood to be criticizing him particularly when he taxes the *logographoi* for "putting things together" (*xunethesan*) in such a way that, "more persuasive than true," these things remain unexamined (*anexelenkta*) and "win out" towards the "mythy" (*muthodes*) (1.21). *Muthodes* means both "story-dominated," as Herodotus surpasses his contemporaries in being, and "false," a usage which in fact is Herodotus' own sense for the word *muthos*. As for the actually verifiable facts taken one by one, Herodotus, in the several cases where his account conflicts with Thucydides', tends to surpass him in accuracy, as Myres points out (pp. 17–18).

Thucydides, who uses *muthodes* in the sense of "storytelling" in Gomme's gloss, has already distinguished the *logographoi* from the poets. He goes on to characterize his own work as the opposite, as "non-mythy" (*me muthodes*, 1.22.4), a phrase which must include something more than storytelling, since he does also tell stories. His own work entails "accuracy" (*akribeia*) thereby, or a "precision" which makes the particular that sort of tight fit with the general that Herodotus neither achieves nor, we may imagine, could achieve. In Herodotus' time, thirty years or more before Thucydides, philosophical discussion about the relation of the particular to the general had not yet definitely developed into the nearly Platonic point we find in Thucydides' writing.

The cautionary tale in Herodotus—and all tales in Herodotus have a cautionary side—relates fact to explanation, and thus the particular to the general, in a looser way than the tight pattern of Thucydides would permit. Herodotus gets some of the aura of persisting question from divine myth out of his story by not attaining the strict and austere pattern that Thucydides imposes. Thucydides has one story to tell, a totally exemplary one. Herodotus' stories hover between the one and the many, and the uncertain or certain presence of mediation between divine favor, human intelligence, and ethnic proclivity keeps the single exemplum from having a universal application. Thucydides returns the analytic intelligence to the method of Homer; it is free to penetrate events and see them once more as cyclic.

Herodotus inserts his reference to the fact that "there is a cycle of human events" ("kuklos tōn anthrōpēōn esti prēgmatōn," 1.207) in a story. Croesus uses it to counter the advice of the Persian counselors who would have Cyrus defend himself rather than attack the queen of the Massagetae. Croesus, having adduced this principle of the wheel of fortune (the cyclic view become gnomic, and drawn from Croesus' own bitter experience of ups and downs), goes on to the military principle that attack is the best defense. The advice is qualified by the actual result: Cyrus loses his life on this campaign. Later Croesus almost loses his, too, from Cambyses' delayed resentment over this very advice (3.36).

Herodotus has taken simple prudence and applied it to the whole course of world history in his time, displacing mythic explanations while putting together an equivalent for the force of finality in myth. Thus the motifs of repetition, "wise alien counsellor" or "misinterpreted oracle," are not sufficient in themselves to do his work. Still less so are those motifs that we might catalogue in our own indices as repeating patterns from various cultures: the motif of the son marked for death on the hunt (Atys), or the motif of the humble child rescued from a death sentence delivered to avoid an oracle, who then becomes a king (Moses, Christ, Oedipus, Cyrus). Motifs map the recursive, where Herodotus is so fully preoccupied with the successive that he will include the recursive only randomly.

A persistent change underlies these patterns, but it is not really an overriding principle of change. It is "custom," rather, that is "king of all." As Collingwood remarks, the Greek commonplace about the necessary variability of fortune is not deterministic (p. 23). The divine power, on its incursion, is said to be "destructive and disturbing" (*phthoneron kai tarachodes*, 1.32). But the incidence of incursion is itself uncertain, and there is such a thing as divine favor: Cyrus' survival is such a providential happenstance, and Croesus' preservation occurs at the hands of Apollo, on whose shrine he had heaped offerings; the last mention of Croesus tells how Croesus saved Miltiades (6.37). What Vernant argues (p. 124) of the *dynameis* in Hesiod, and what is deducible from two key terms in Anaximander, applies even more forcefully to Herodotus, that in these powers there is a relation between justice (*dike*) and chaos or the unbounded (*apeiron*). The instability between particular and general in Herodotus is thus uncertain enough to make a possible irony play over his text.

If we look, with Bury (pp. 69–70) and others, for Herodotus' governing criteria of inquiry, we find ourselves applying the historian's passing remarks to individual facts. We may say, with Bury, that Herodotus suspects miraculous occurrences, keeps an open mind before conflicting accounts, and prefers a firsthand account. But all these principles come down to the same thing, really, and none bears on the principle of organization. Homer's Trojan War is itself a mythic past; if the present is to be measured by a legendary past—as it is occasionally in tragedy from *Oedipus Rex* to the *Ion*, as well as in the Trojan plays of Euripides—then different principles are called for.

Advice is often given by agents in Herodotus; and the principles on which it is given are gnomic or analytic. The advice only has a divine cast if it has a divine source, the oracle. Candaules does not heed Gyges' advice, and he suffers—at the hands of Gyges. Croesus does not heed Adrastus' advice, and he suffers—at the hands of Adrastus. This is a motif. But Cyrus heeds the advice of Croesus, and still he suffers. It is a divine portent, a dream, that leads him to change his mind. The dream repeats itself; then it comes a third time, to Artabanus; Xerxes heeds the complex of advice, human and divine, and suffers. This too is a motif (as in Mimnermus, 2.15–16, Solon 13.5–6 West, etc.). When

Artabanus advises Xerxes not to carry through his intent of dressing Artabanus up as Xerxes and putting him on Xerxes' throne so that Artabanus can have the same dream, Xerxes does not heed his advice, repeating the first motif. Artabanus does dream the same dream and changes his advice, combining the first motif with the second.

The human is here not sorted out from the divine, and Herodotus is not offering advice himself. He is weaving advice, as a general view of the particular, into his own general view of several particulars. Gods, legend, historical events, and reports, are all presented on the same linear plane. Herodotus' subject is "deeds great and also wondrous" *erga megala te kai thomasta* (1.1), and deeds of men will therefore necessarily prevail. He will later say of Homer and Okeanos, it "carried the myth to its vanishing point" ("es aphaneston muthon aneneikas," 2.23), and this is in the long ethnographic account of Egypt, which offers both a neutral ground and a point of origin as yet undiscovered for the Greek gods. In his account of the founding of Cyrene he covers some of the same ground as *Pythian* 4 (4.144–180), of course without any of Pindar's afflatus of numinous partiality. His neutrality serves not only for Greece, but for the myths of other peoples, for the Persians with their retained Median magi whose presence, as West persuasively argues (though of Heraclitus rather than Herodotus) was pervasive in the Asia Minor where Herodotus grew up.

A neutral openness towards the operation of myth, without recourse at any point to the whole circular relation between general and particular posited by a myth-bound view of events, gives Herodotus' stark linearity and his proto-ethnography room to come into relation, as law to case and general to particular. To say that law or custom (*nomos*) is king of all is to be at one remove from *nomos*, a remove with a power that can be made to cover all of recent history in the known universe.

6.

The distinction made by the Greeks between those who spoke their language and all others—between "barbarians" and Greeks—would seem to have become usual in the Greek language with Herodotus. Homer does use the expression *barbarophonoi*, "br-br-speaking," of the Carians (*Iliad* 2.867), but in a way that may not indicate a foreign language. Pindar's one use of *barbaros* (*Isthmian* 6.24) also refers purely to speech. Heraclitus' inclusion of the magi among those to whom he preaches (Diels 22.B14) already posits the sort of ethnic equivalence to be found in Xenophanes' view of the relativism of tribal gods, the Ethiopians making their gods snub-nosed and black, the Thracians making theirs blue-eyed and red-headed (Diels 21.B 16). And Heraclitus' attribution of "barbarian souls" (Diels 22. B 107, "*barbarous psuchas*") to those whose eyes and ears are bad witnesses goes even further than this in changing the term from a social description to a psychological one (Nussbaum). Still, the word *barbaros* does not occur very often before Herodotus; he uses it more than two hundred times. Framing the distinction between Greeks and *barbaroi* as a regular part of his discourse, Herodotus removes it to a plane of ethnographic neutrality, saying of the Egyptians that they called those who did not speak their language *barbaroi* (2.158).

The Egyptians are more neatly opposite the Greeks than those other *barbaroi*, the Persians. And the xenophobia of the Scythians—Herodotus tells of the "penalties they exact from anyone adding a foreign custom" to Scythian, as the half-Greek Scyles was beheaded for doing (4.80)—makes them, in this regard, hyper-Greek. To introduce a lengthy ethnographic account right after the death of Cyrus at the hands of the more savage Massagetae in the North allows Herodotus to kill two birds with one stone, and to do so before the Persians muster for all the complications leading up to the Greek expeditions. He can define both Persians and Greeks by reference to the Scythians who, differing from both, more clearly resemble the Greeks at certain points.

The Egyptians generally resemble the Greeks in being civilized. They also resemble the Persians in this, as Cambyses seems not to recognize, perhaps because he is blinded by the very ethnological differences which Herodotus unfolds before he returns to the conquests of Cambyses, with which he begins Book Two (2.1).

The Egyptians are not only counterparts in Herodotus' time to the Greeks, a mirror sometimes reversing and sometimes merely reflecting;[10] they are also in their dim past a solution to Hesiod's questions about origins. The Greek gods originated not in a theogonic series, but by distant acculturative borrowing; they originated in Egypt (2.49–52). And yet the Egyptians are not the oldest people on earth. They are the oldest people but one. They themselves wished to inquire who the earliest people were,[11] resembling in their curiosity both the Ionian philosophers and Herodotus himself. This is the first thing we are told about them, that Psammetichus located the inquiry in the sphere of—language

(2.2). Infants were isolated from birth and carefully watched to discover what their first word would be. Their babble finally produced the
word *bekos*, the Phrygian word for bread. The Egyptians, who stand as
an origin for the Greeks in time, themselves have comparable predecessors, the Phrygians. This story sets up the ethnographic relativism on
all sides, in time as well as space, through an almost Heraclitean proportion: the Phrygians are to the Egyptians as the Egyptians are to the
Greeks. But the Egyptians like the Greeks are endowed in that present,
as the Phrygians presumably were not, with the means to inquire into
the fact. And that the distinction hinges on language closes the circle on
the term *barbaroi*, underlying which is a vast temporal dispersion. Later
the Scythians ("youngest" of peoples, 4.7) stand as counterparts to
their predecessors, the Cimmerians (Cimmerian: Scythian as Egyptian:
Greek), and as opposites to somewhat older peoples like the Greeks
and the Persians.

Herodotus begins the story of the Egyptian campaign with a long
ethnographic essay; he has just ended his account of the campaign
among the Massagetae with a short one, itself balancing not only the
Egyptian account that follows but the Babylonian that precedes (1.192–
200); to be balanced itself by the more expanded account in Book Four
—which mainly balances that of the Southern Egyptians—of those main
Northerners, the Scythians, with whom the Massagetae, their neighbors,
are confused, as Herodotus here notes. This account of the Massagetae
touches on most of the topics still of concern to the ethnological in-
vestigator:

> The customs [*nomoi*] they use are the following: Each man marries
> a wife, but they use them in common. The Greeks say the Scyth-
> ians do this; it is not the Scythians who are doing it but the Massa-
> getae. When a Massagete man desires a woman he hangs his quiver
> before her wagon and has intercourse with her freely [*adeos*; liter-
> ally, "without fear"]. No particular boundary of the lifecourse is
> set down for them. But at the point when a man becomes old,
> those who belong to him gather together and sacrifice him, and
> some domestic animals along with him. Then they boil the flesh
> and have a feast. This is accounted the most blessed condition
> among them; a man who dies from sickness they do not eat but
> bury in the earth, considering it a [bad] happenstance that he did
> not get to the point of being sacrificed. They sow nothing, but they
> live from livestock and fishes, which come unstintingly for them
> from the river Araxes. They are milk-drinkers. They worship the

> sun alone among gods, to whom they sacrifice horses. This is the
> rationale [*noos*] of the sacrifice: on the swiftest of all the gods they
> bestow the swiftest of things mortal.

Here we are given the marriage-customs, and even the relation between
the incest taboo and the marriage classes (*adeos*) is touched on, as is a
neutral expression for clan organization ("those who belong to him,"
hoi prosekontes, a term whose ethnological neutrality is obscured if we
render it "kin"). While we do not have here the age-grouping traditional in primitive societies, there is a major discrimination about when
one becomes old. This is tied in with funeral customs, a theory of what
constitutes a life well lived, diet, source of food supply, economic organization, religion, and even a bit of theology. The modern field inves-
tigator could not add much to the list except detail under these headings
and analysis. But of course Herodotus' narrative presentation already
constitutes analysis of an important kind. The anthropological insight
of seeing people in the relief of their contrasts of mores is fed into the
historical insight of seeing a particular sequence of events that interacts
with mores.

Herodotus' succinct list of the customs and ways (*ethea kai nomoi*,
2.35) in which the Egyptians are diametrically opposed to other nations
is preceded by the explanation of this divergence, that their climate is
other (*ourano heteroio*) and their river has a different nature (*phusin
alloien*). Through this principle of mediation, geography has the same
status as history in his inquiry, though of course at the point of the
inventive link between them both are also transformed. The link of
geography to custom, preceding the link of custom to historical event
at this point of his account, gives one reason why the geographical
account of Egypt largely precedes his ethnographic survey, and also
why the question of the exact boundaries of Egypt geographically are
partially defined by, and define, the moral properties of this people, as
of others. Boundary disputes are partially settled by questions of ethnographic discrimination, and vice versa. The Libyans who do not wish to
eat cows' flesh get a geographical-boundary reply when they ask the
oracle at Ammon their dietary question (2.18), and Lévi-Straussian
correlations between the map and the sources of diet, as in *L'Homme
Nu*, only serve to put this connection in potentially algorithmic terms.

At the point of geographical remoteness the resemblances between
peoples get more remote and the contrasts sharper, as with the Arimas-

pians who have just one eye (4.14; 27) or the Amazons (4.110–117) or those Indians who have intercourse openly "like animals" and whose sperm is black to match the color of their skin (3.107). Most elaborately examined of the remote peoples are the Scythians of Book Four, where Herodotus is aware that he is actually dealing with various peoples who cover an indefinite but vast space. The accuracy of his account has been confirmed by modern archaeology, which has discovered that the Scyths are the "youngest" of peoples by tracing their arrival north of the Black Sea to about the seventh century B.C., when presumably the Second Millennium kingdom of Urartu (the Cimmerians?) would have fallen. Upon the Scyths there fell from heaven a gold yoke, a plow, a sword (*sagaris*, possibly "axe"), and a flask (4.5), which would account for the transition from nomadic to agricultural life, both ways of life being represented by Herodotus. The other peoples he surveys in this book may take us, with the Cimmerians and the Hyperboreans, all the way to the Baltic in the north, and across the vast Central Asian plain, whose extent and characteristics he faithfully sketches, to the forebears of the Tibetans, the Mongols, and the Huns. It is by his attention to customs (the Tibetans) and to appearance (the Mongols) that we are still able to ascribe an identification to the tribes he lists.

Egypt itself has an intrinsic interest, with a multitude of marvels (*pleista thomasia*) and, compared to other lands, more works of account (*erga logou*), which explains why Herodotus is lengthening his own account (*mekuneon ton logon*).[12]

Herodotus thus pursues ethnological inquiry both for its own sake and as an exploratory tool. The union of these two purposes keeps the general harnessed to the particular without either the philosophical abstractness of his immediate Ionian predecessors or the empirical disjunction of Hecataeus. The Egyptians explain the Greeks and the Greeks explain the Egyptians; explaining the Egyptians explains why the Persians were moderately unsuccessful at taking them over, as they were later to be unsuccessful at taking over the Greeks. Among the Greeks and the Persians, a dietary practice leads to decisions, though the Persians make their deliberations when drunk (1.13e), the Greeks when sober. Describing their attempts at conquest locates the Persians in a temporal sequence; they are defined by the unique course of their recent history rather than by recursive attributes of the label "alien" (*barbaros*) or submission, in their fashion, to an equivalent of the Homeric king-oriented society. For Darius is presented as choosing kingship from among the alternatives of tyranny, oligarchy, and democracy (3.80–83). Such a choice is inconceivable in Homeric society, and even, we may say, in Persian. Darius is, so to speak, imagined as pervaded by a Herodotean consciousness in choosing to go with custom and be a king.

Ethnological relativism gives perspective not only to the historian Herodotus, but to the participants themselves, in the events he narrates. The Greeks have had all sorts of earlier interactions with Egypt (2.112–121 and *passim*). The Milesian Thales and the Athenian Solon advise Croesus, and this Lydian in turn over a long span advises two Persian kings. By the very nature of rule in the internationalism of the sixth century and, according to Herodotus' account, for long before as well as after, any dominant people is caught in the cross-currents of neighbors with like territorial aspirations but different social styles and customs. Croesus' marshalling of forces is accompanied by appeals, of predictably varying degrees of success, to varied nations. Only a state as large as Persia in the culmination of his account is free of pressure from cross-currents, and even Persia has overreached in other directions before overreaching towards Greece.

The presence of alien advisers in the Persian court is in fact a mark of the sort of sophistication Mardonius evidences when he deplores the Greek practice of slaughtering their enemies on the battlefield instead of negotiating terms (7.9). We measure the Greeks, then, by the Persians, as earlier by the Egyptians; but the Persians are also measured against the complex international standard of Herodotus' *History*. There is no explicit comment on their custom of burying transgressors alive (7.14). Mere sophistication and mere syncretic tolerance of Lydian advice or Greek medicine will not protect the Persians from the inevitable consequences of their drive to power (even though the principle of accepting advice from former or prospective enemies accords implicitly with Machiavelli's recommendation in *The Prince* about coopting former enemies).

Benardete sees the unfolding complex of international confrontation as a tool of logical contrast. It is also perhaps Herodotus' most persistent temporal theme; time's progression elaborately tests hard cases as the interweaving of events both binds in all the varied ethnic threads and also twists the fabric in unexpected directions. Always there are, for a given people, and presumably for the Greeks of at least a generation after the Persian Wars who are Herodotus' audience and contemporaries, the customs to fall back on. Darius gives the *nomoi* as the crowning reason (3.82) why the Persians should choose monarchy, staying with the custom of their fathers, rather than democracy or oligarchy. At the same time Herodotus shows, with possible irony, forms of both democracy and oligarchy prevailing as the choice is made; the *isonomia* of democracy operates because the seven conspirators vote by a bare majority for monarchy; oligarchy, because there are only seven. And the unexpected does supervene as always. The king is to be chosen by a test: the man whose horse neighs first will be king. Darius becomes king through trickery—he has a groom surreptitiously bring the scent of a mare within reach of his own horse's nostrils.

7.

The true historiographer, in Hexter's analysis, tends to tell a story. In doing so he must include in his story other data than those that would seem to be logically necessary to subsume the particular fact under the heading of a general law. On the side of the general, a logical argument does not constitute historiography. Gorgias' "defense of Helen" is, rather, an imaginary legal brief, as are all the arguments of his rhetorical successors. There are, after all, legal briefs that are narrative in character and considerably longer than Herodotus. They are still not historiography, for they are dominated by the exclusive principle of subsumption to a legal code, even though we are given both general and particular in a narrative form. The psychological case history, too, is usually dominated by the exclusive subsumption of its data under the general principle of psychoanalytic causality, and the sociological study, pace Morton White, must be prevailingly synchronic and demographic in character rather than historical. It analyzes the characteristics of particular groups according to particular principles at a particular point in time. It is, in fact, endemically rather than exotically ethnological. Such studies, ethnological or sociological, as Oscar Lewis's *La Vida*, subsume even verbatim narrative tapes to the general synchronic analysis of social groups.

Farther towards the generalizing extreme of the general-particular spectrum in verbal accounts of human behavior we have nothing so expansive as legal briefs and sociological studies and psychological case histories. We have legal codes, model summaries, statistics—and gnomic aphorisms. These are all generalizing-classifactory aids that can be borrowed by the historian: where the modern historian uses statistics, the ancient one uses the gnomic aphorism, bending it to a historiographic usage, and thereby showing, when compared with a tribal aphorist, an originality and a sophistication as great as those of the statistician compared with a primitive tallier of herds and goods. Herodotus dots his own account with aphorisms, and Tacitus is even more liberal with them.

Toward the general end of the spectrum for verbal discourse about human behavior, then, we can distinguish at least two classes of organized statement that are too dominated by generality to classify as historiography: case histories or briefs, and statistics or codes or aphorisms. In the narrative of history itself there is a sort of visionary point of connecting particular to general which the historian aims at through his vastly detailed cautionary narrative. However fully the data in modern academic historiography may be organized to present a brief, some indirection to the presentation will still remain to lurk under the case— whether presented narratively as a story or not—, some discontinuity between the cumulative answer and the implied question. A recent statistical study of slavery was probably taken correctly to be aimed, indirectly, at the adjustment of complex questions around the coming to a head of the American Civil War. Mere statistics on a social institution, however elegantly framed, would not have this force; there would be nothing lurking under them.

Herodotus has in mind, so to speak, a law that has not yet been encoded and could not be encoded. He then allows data to enter the linear narrative on a principle beyond that of the sort of coherence a brief would have. The historian is expansive by nature. He tells us that these tribes licked blood to confirm an oath. Or that Cambyses was depressed. Or that Mardonius made an offhand remark about the Greeks. Or that the wife of the false Smerdis was very frightened when she was feeling his head to see if he was an earless Mede.

In an individual story, "the accession of Darius" (3.60–86), the historian adds to those data whose particulars are easily subsumable under the general law of an imagined brief, a number of other particulars that are contributing to his vision. These constitute a sort of "visionary filler" above and beyond the account, and the reasons for including them are as hard to uncover as are the reasons why a novelist who sticks to his story about an adulterous union tells us what the menu was at the banquet where Emma Bovary and Rodolphe first struck up their ac-

quaintance. And to code the constituents of this menu for their significations, along the lines of Roland Barthes's elaborate scheme (1970),
would still not account for the logical necessity of their presence in the
stream of the story. The historian, too, uses visionary filler, and every
detail of it is tested on the new principle Herodotus invents, by the criteria of *historie*. These criteria would include not only, we may presume,
the necessary condition that it be ascertainable as not false, but also the
sufficient condition of contributing to what lurks under the story. This
would be so for the oral and eyewitness reports of the first half of the
Egyptioi logoi or the document-sources he says he is following for the
last half (2.99). Herodotus is so magisterially linear that it is hard to
isolate data and call them "visionary filler" as distinct from the "causal
core" of his narrative. It is both his achievement and the condition he
sets, in fact, to suspend our judgment of what exactly the causal core is,
whereas in Thucydides and Tacitus it is much easier to tell.

Herodotus was seen a hundred years ago as naive, as lying very close
to the particular end of the spectrum. At that end of the spectrum, too,
are works that deal with human behavior in the past but do not constitute true historiography—works like the Domesday book, Villani, Geoffrey of Monmouth, Holinshed, Charon of Lampsacus, Selden—the list
would include, possibly, every supposed historian who wrote, every
"historical document" we have, between Einhard and Vico. These chroniclers fall so near the particular end of the general-particular spectrum
because their data is sorted along lines no more complex than those of
random successiveness, or else in too simple a conformity to the Christian principle of divine will (Eusebius, Bede). Here the looseness between general and particular has an unformed character, communicating
nothing of the visionary.

Of course even chroniclers have willy-nilly subjected their data to two
principles of exclusion. The first, that of Whitehead's "misplaced concreteness," is the forever unknowable. As I sit writing, there are millions
of data, including all the particulars of the momentary chemical consti-
tution of my body, which arguably have at least some bearing on my
behavior, and so on my participation in lived history. But these are
forever unknowable. My temperature is not being taken, nor are my
blood pressure, blood sugar, and hemoglobin being measured. The second principle of exclusion is that of "displaced concreteness." The
chronicler of the city where I live might know who I am and still not
list me by name in the annals of the city.

The true historian, as Hexter tells us, works on a principle of still more discriminating exclusion. He not only counts oxen but not people, as the Domesday Book does; he also decides to exclude the complete Congressional Record debate on the Civil Rights Act of 1964 as mysteriously not bearing on the special general-particular weave he has in mind.

Still more telling is the historian's principle of inclusion, the visionary filler he chooses to include, and Herodotus here resembles the modern historian in the principle of relating particular to general. The quotation from Namier that is the epigraph for this chapter could be taken for an implied summary of Herodotus.

In the case of Herodotus there is a large accumulation of particulars in time to define and classify an entity, "Persia." Seeking in the dimmest past for the first incursion of Europe into Asia, which incited Persia to a delayed counterattack, he singles out and "indicates this one man" (*touton semenas*, 1.5), a particular person, Croesus. We classify Croesus with reference to other aggressors, and there is a typically Lydian form of aggression, which differs from the typically Persian. Lydian is midway between Persian and Greek, both geographically and psychologically. The conquest of some larger entity, Egypt, succeeds upon the conquest of Lydia. Elaborate comparisons, the drawing of some kind of general law from particular cases of aggression, are being built up, as Benardete revealingly argues. The Egyptians are like the Greeks in space—one of a series of projected Persian victims. The Egyptians also resemble the Greeks in time: they stand as the true origin for what is most intimately Greek, the Olympian pantheon and its cult practices. After narrating the partial conquest of Egypt, Herodotus passes to a Greek principality midway between Persia and Egypt, Samos (3.39–59).

Many changes are rung on the motif of aggression, all leading up to the culminating act of aggression: the long, disjunct attack of Persia upon mainland Greece. Particular cases are building up a sense of what is peculiarly Persian and what is universally human in these aggressions. And to wage war there must be a leader, who may have come to power through a power struggle analogous to war. Consequently we are given many story "pediments" of accession.

Accessions, like aggressions and most other things in Herodotus, tend to take on an international cast. The Medes and, at an earlier generation, the Lydians, are complexly involved in the accession of Cyrus. And accessions also have an ethnic flavor. There is a "Persian" style of accession: it usually involves some form of the introjection (rather than suppression: conflict is the defect of this quality of assimilation) that the Persians have performed on the Medians they conquered and left among themselves as dream-interpreters and counselors. The Mede Astyages gives his grandson Cyrus trouble, and four generations later the false Median Smerdis tries to carry off the trick of his Median forebear Deioces and act as the Persian Smerdis through the mechanism of bureaucratic invisibility.[13]

Four Persian accessions are described, those of Cyrus, Cambyses, Darius, and Xerxes (not counting a fifth interregnum, that of the false Smerdis). To fail to compare these is to assume that Herodotus just plunges randomly ahead. If compared, they may all be seen to conform to a Persian type of accession, a palace intrigue. Thus they differ from changes of power among the Athenians, which conform to a type of democratic power-group struggle; and among the Spartans, which involve interaction between the unstably balanced dual kings; and among the Egyptians, which in a long succession tend to exhibit the Egyptian style of smooth uniformity, here as in other aspects of their national life.

There are particular differences in the Persian accessions, a slackness of conformity between particular and general that allows for the visionary yield of Herodotus' visionary filler. Darius' is the longest, and it is also the most crucial. Cambyses' is the shortest, a sudden happenstance occasioned by Cyrus' absence on the ill-fated expedition against the Massagetae.

If we look at Darius' accession, moreover (3.61–87), we find that the linear details each belong to a different sphere, though each belongs to a sphere where there are other Herodotean motifs. Cambyses, to begin with, dies because he is "struck" (*etupse*) with vexation (3.64), being insane anyway, that killing his brother Smerdis has not defused the dream prediction that he will be succeeded by Smerdis. He is thus preoccupied enough to leave his sword uncapped, and so receives a mortal wound in his thigh while mounting his horse. He is out on horseback because he has been ill-advisedly pursuing military campaigns so far afield that the false Smerdis could get a foothold at home.

Here we have the motif "conquest-obsession" in an especially virulent form, accompanied by the further motif of the indeflectibility of an oracle. Croesus and Astyages and Cyrus had experienced the latter (and so it is still further motif that oracles tend to apply to certain kinds of cases, to conquest-projects and to succession-conditions). Part of the indeflectibility-motif is the ironic feature that trying to prevent an oracle helps bring it about. Astyages' special version of this feature is that any of his descendants is bound to be the "mule" the oracle says will succeed him, since he is a Mede married to a Lydian (for reasons involving still other motifs). So it in fact changes nothing for Astyages to marry his daughter into the lower classes, to a Persian, an act that anyway perpetuates the "mule" form.

Smerdis' takeover conforms to another motif: the effort at total bureaucratic control. His exposure involves still another: loyalty and betrayal in the unstable condition of the interracial marriage. The motif of conspiracy on alertly marshalled power-principles is still another; that of the debate-at-the-power-crossroads is a distinguishably different one with different conditions.

Each of the motifs in itself is a principle classifying particular instances under its general heading. But each of the separate motif-spheres in "the accession of Darius" differs enough from the others—oracles from seclusions and seclusions from conspiracies and conspiracies from discussions—to resist global classification. They must then, so to speak, be referred to the next higher level of englobing motif, that of "succession" which in this instance includes all these disparate others. A succession is at once a unique instance, and an ethnic type, "Persian accession," and a general motif in human affairs; and each one includes in its composition events which are "tinier" motifs.

The divine generally dominates all the motifs in Homer, who is also a historiographer insofar as he enunciates a special relation between particular and general, but not in the uncritical way he admits his data without testing them or their sources, and also not in the principle of motive, which is usually just psychological (the wrath of Achilles) or theological (the plan of Zeus). Herodotus puts the theological on the same plane as the psychological and the social and the ethnic, in a way that allows them to be differentiated only provisionally. The linear equivalence into which he organizes them motif by motif and event by event substitutes his own vision of the relation between general and particular (without the philosophizing of his Ionian contemporaries) for that relation between general and particular which is the communicative function of myth in all preliterate societies. Herodotus is a pioneer assimilator. His typical word for conjecture is "putting together" fact and fact, *sumballo*, a sense found earliest in him and in Heraclitus (B47).

8.

"The godly in its existence is all destructive and also disruptive." ("to theion pan eon phthoneron kai tarachōdes," 1.32). This summary statement puts the source of myth in the position of a permanent source of the unexpected, an account of what is otherwise unaccountable. Such a view, which is not far from one modern anthropological explanation of religion in society, allows Herodotus to include the unaccountable in his own account without bending the whole account in its direction. Skepticism, taken by itself in his work, is incidental as it is applied to this or that specific datum, Oceanus or earthquakes at Delos. His belief, on the other hand, is more thoroughgoing in its effect on the narrative. Standing on a par with other accounts of events, it bends the whole narrative away from even a denial of the Homeric-Olympian view. The Olympian gods are accepted, and so are the chthonic mysteries, along with the oracles, which had proliferated in Greece since the time of Homer (who mentions only the one at Dodona). Their effect remains the same, while their relation to other factors in the mix of general and particular has undergone radical alteration. If its "existence is all destructive and disruptive," the godly may not always be isolated as a factor in some unexpected event; it gets no mention in the sudden death of Aristagoras (5.126), though it does bear on the death of Cambyses (3.64).

Herodotus, in other words, is far more remarkable in his radical alteration of the relation of myth to language, of the gods to narrated time, than he is for his particular attitudes to the gods, where it is the old belief and not the new skepticism which determines the presentation of his inquiry, the *apodexis* of *aitie*. On the one hand the gods are always destructive and disruptive. On the other hand Herodotus performs a fantasy derivation upon the word *theos*; he derives it from the verb *tithemi*, to put in order, in the Pelasgian language, "They called them gods from the fact that they put all things in order and possessed all laws" (2.52). The power of fantasy for Herodotus in this attribution is shown in the fact that this is one of the few places where he contradicts himself in the text, for he had earlier said that the Pelasgians had an unintelligible tongue (*barbaron glossan hientes,* 1.57).

The gods as establishers of order, of both *kosmos* and *nomoi,* and the godly as a disruptive influence, have contradictory effects that together make up the antinomic power that myth tends to address in the first place. Herodotus turns this power, so to speak, into an intellectual principle, for in Herodotus' history we have an account where disruptive particulars are loosely referred to a general order without being abstracted. Once the godly is on the same plane as all other happenings, differing only in its hidden, omnipotent source and its unpredictable effect, it can be seen either as disruptive or as ordering, depending on whether we take the short view of an episode in one place or the long view of a century in the known world, a long view it is Herodotus' fundamental concern to establish, as he clearly says in his prologue reference to the rise and fall of cities.

"The godly in its existence is all destructive and also disruptive" is said by Solon as something he knows (*epistamenon*) to Croesus' whom he is trying to warn. The giver of *nomoi* might well see the gods not as establishers of *nomoi* of their own but rather as a disruptive force. In saying this, of course, Solon is only acting in a way typical of the wise man. The gnomic saying is a version of what he goes on to say differently, "call no man happy till he is dead." He says it in response to Croesus' question about why Solon seems to be taking so little notice of Croesus' own royal prosperity (*eudaimonie*). Solon replies, in effect, that *daimon* is ominously buried in *eudaimonie*, even if the less dynamic term *to theion* be applied to it. He is implicitly correcting Croesus' language while explicitly correcting his idea, by removing it to that other plane, which the example of Cleobis and Biton illustrated, since they died unexpectedly and yet are to be accounted blest.

Here, as generally in Herodotus, the gods are seen only as they bear on a context, except when they are detached for ethnological inspection; and then the whole inspection is contextual in another sense. If the Greek gods were originally Egyptian in origin though Pelasgian in name (2.51–53), this tells us something about all three peoples, about their relations to the gods, and about their relations to each other. In another context the god delivers a distinct but cryptic message, the oracle.

It is congruent with his historical circumstances as well as with his incorporation of the divine in his historical narrative that oracles flourished particularly in the Greece where Herodotus was born. If he has from time to time what Eduard Meyer (p. 15) calls "*grosse Scheu vor allen göttlichen Dingen,*" he would seem to be scrupulous in his report of oracle-consultations and to be careful not to discredit their "truth" (8.77); oracles never fall within the purview of "displaced concreteness"—they are not something he would ever choose to omit, even though in some respects he is "not desirous of narrating such accounts as I have heard of godly things" (2.3). In this passage he goes on to adduce his crucial principle of human relevance for including them, "I consider that all men know about them equally; the ones I mention specifically, I shall mention when constrained by my account. They [the priests of Heliopolis] all agreed as follows . . ." (2.3.4). (I have rendered the aorist subjunctive by adding the adverb "specifically.")

The oracles in Herodotus operate in a tension to the political events on which they provide either a window that a Cleisthenes (5.72) refuses to look through or a mirror that a Croesus takes for a window. If they are fulfilled, the fulfillment is not personal and not episodic: rather it tends to involve a significant and pregnant event, such as the fall of Lydia. Oracles surround Croesus at every point, and they crop up on the Greek side of the final long defense against the Persians. Dreams figure more prominently in Persian affairs than oracles do. The Persians, like the Greeks, are at once subject to, and heedless of, divination; but they have dreams and the Magi instead of the oracle and a priestess.

Among the Greeks the oracle serves as just another factor in the three-cornered struggle between Athens, Aegina, and Thebes (itself acted upon by Athens' relations with Sparta, and involving Chalcis and Boeotia). What Namier says of nineteenth-century Europe (p. 170) could apply with equal force to the Greece of just before the Persian Wars— and for nearly a century after: "The game of power politics, in whatever terms it was played, normally made a neighbor into an enemy, and therefore the neighbor's neighbor on the opposite flank into an ally." Still another bribed oracle (5.63) is involved here, and the complications around the oracle tend to mirror, ominously, the complications of these struggles among Greeks (Kirchberg).

When the oracle stands fully on the ground of the supernatural, it tends to be simple, and just to fill in an ethnographic picture, as when the Italian Metapontines are told by the oracle at Delphi to believe in the reality of the ghost of Aristeas of Proconnesus, who appeared among them as he had appeared among those on his side of the known world (4.15). Referring the oracles largely to the crucial events in the activities of the *polis* points already to the desacralization that Vernant (p. 151) claims the *polis* to sponsor in general, as happens with astronomy in its growth away from the sacral Babylonian matrix. It is perhaps significant that seldom or never are Herodotus' magi shown consulting the stars, and that the invention of the calendar by the Egyptians is pre-

sented in wholly secular terms, when for them it was intricately covered
by religious significances and a sacred nomenclature (2.4).

The handling of the oracle by Herodotus instances in its political
effect another version of his treating the sacred exactly as he does the
secular. Arion (1.23–24) has the same status as Croesus and Xerxes,
Darius and Cleomenes. And the same would seem to be true of Heracles
(4.6; 2.45) and Perseus (7.61, 150), who exemplify what Ranke calls
a "fusion of saga and history" in Herodotus ("*Verbindung des Sagen-
haften und Historischen*," quoted by Schadewalt, p. 198).

The gods are "material for what happens in poems" (*hoi en poiesi
genomenoi*, 2.82), but Herodotus describes this function, at a hard and
neutral remove from it, as he credits Homer and Hesiod with giving
a theogony to the Greeks (2.53.2). Ascribing the Greek gods to the
Egyptians allows him at once to de-theogonize them, to typify them
beyond their names and some accidental functions, to relativize their
ethnic individuality, and to place them firmly in the linear time line of
his sequential account.

Herodotus' judgment on events, as Myres (p. 46) and Heinrich
Bischoff (p. 310) show, appears in the text indirectly, typically as a
warning given by one person in the narrative to another. This approach
when it is brought to bear on the traditional source and cause of events,
the gods, keeps them massively in place as a sort of constant while
Herodotus deliberately and at great length organizes the variables of his
inquiry in time.

9.

To become "the father of history," Herodotus had to invent a sense
of time beyond the "arrangement" (*taxin*) of Anaximander. Later Plato
would go a step further, replace Hesiod's stages of culture on his "great
year" version of Herodotus' millennial time span, and define time as the
moving image of eternity (*Timaeus*, 38).

It is significant that Herodotus gives his longest spans of time among
the Egyptians, who are "most adept at accounting" (*logiotatoi*) for the
memory of human events (2.77). The change from eight gods to twelve
was made "seventeen thousand years" before the reign of the sixth-
century monarch Amasis (2.43), whereas Homer and Hesiod lived no
more than four hundred years before Herodotus himself (2.53). It is in

Egypt that the Phoenix occurs every five hundred years (2.72), a phenomenon linked with a transcendence of seasonal time in the mythology Detienne (1971) analyzes. Herodotus, like an Ionian physiologist, sees an archaeological range of time, ten or twenty thousand years, in the silting up of a river bed (2.11). Like Xenophanes, whom he perhaps follows in this, Herodotus supposes a primeval sea on the evidence of the seashells he has observed on mountaintops.

Otherwise he rarely gives time designations, except to coordinate events, the eclipse Thales predicted or the mention of Gyges in the poem of Archilochus. Inaros and Amyrtaeus (460–455 B.C.) are inserted into events of seventy years earlier, "flatly," without any comparative time-marking, a practice Herodotus tends to follow when referring to events after the Persian Wars (3.15).

"In long time" (*en to makro chrono*), Solon says to Croesus, "there are many things to see that one would not wish, and many things to suffer" (1.32). The simple undifferentiated progress of time allows Herodotus sometimes to make his moral judgments implicit, as when he simply describes without any comment the un-Greek cruelty of the Persian practice of impalement or the caprice of Darius, who kills all the sons of Oiobazus because that old man had asked that at least one of them be spared the Scythian expedition (4.84). Xerxes goes Darius one better, cutting the body of Pythias' eldest son in half in response to a similar request (7.39). The entire army is marched through with half this body on either side. To be sure, the Athenians do crucify the Persian Artayctes for violating women in a temple (7.33).

At other times he can also make the moral judgments explicit, as Pohlenz notes (p. 92). As Herodotus says of Pheretime at the very end of the Libyan campaign (4.205), "while alive she festered with worms, so that indeed for men whose vengeances are too violent, these become occasions for grudge (*epiphthonoi*) with the gods." An evenness of time allows him to be indifferently implicit or explicit in his moral judgment, and also indifferently specific or general in the inferences drawn; the paratactic style here permits a "so that indeed," or "as therefore" (*hos ara*) to keep the relation between the instance and the gnomic maxim from being rigorously tight. The possibility of either stating or implying a sense to the event allows Herodotus that play of consciousness we call irony, which enters significantly in the same verbal set as his objectivity. It will undergo a rich development in Plato's tonal definition of Socrates.

His judgments tend to be inconclusive; but then inconclusiveness is a feature of the loose fit between particular and general that characterizes the handling of time by *historie.* Herodotus' whole work is inconclusive in a sense other than that it is unfinished, as Hermann Fränkel describes this aspect of Herodotus' paratactic style (p. 85), following Aristotle's hints (*ouden echei telos, Rhetoric* 1409a). A linear range permits all possibilities, as Herodotus says, using the phrase "*makro chrono*" somewhat differently (5.9), "Anything might happen in the long span of time" ("genoito d'an pan en tō makrō chronō," 5.9).

Paula Phillipson finds in Hesiod an "immense tension between the powers of Being and Becoming," (*diesen ungeheuren Spannungen zwischen den Mächten des Seins und des Werdens*). The same tension between becoming and being is observable in two philosophers who are close contemporaries of Herodotus, Parmenides and Empedocles. Herodotus does not set up an abstract and terminological inquiry as they do. Rather, he patiently unravels all the complications of a single large event, thereby single-mindedly resolving such "tensions" in thought. On the plane of his events we are at the point of "becoming" till after the battle of Salamis, and even then there are a few particulars to recount, themselves of a highly interwoven complexity. And we are also, point for point, at the point of "being." Structure and function, type and process, have been identified. The gnomic and the mythic have neither parted company nor been forced into a new union; they are simply utilized, along with every other datum, for a view of data in which what is to be analyzed and the mode of analysis have been identified with each other; *historie* makes the *apodexis* an *aitie.*

6.
OVID:
The Dialectics of
Recovery from Atavism

1.

IN a complex bureaucratic civilization, that of Augustan Rome or our own, a ritual system incorporates elements of myth to which credence is assigned; and this kind of religion coexists with verbal manipulations of myth and investigations of the nature of myth. In Rome these manipulations and investigations included quasi-positivistic rejections of religion and theology; the treatise of Lucretius was a notable early example. While at the midpoint of Ovid's career one extreme of the Empire served as the location for a radical transformation of religion and theology, and so of history, the process of conversion on which the Christian revelation had to begin found in the Roman Empire only parallel social forms (Nock). A religion more primitive in some aspects of its practices than anything in Homeric Greece still flourished in Rome, systematically resuscitated in the institutional revivals of Julius Caesar and Augustus.

A poet like Vergil or Horace or Ovid was expected, by both his audience and himself, to reconcile his thick array of somewhat atavistic cults with the elaborate repository of Greek myth, itself somewhat differently belief-charged, and also with the tradition of intricate theological discussions that ran from Hesiod through the Roman Stoics. In Ovid's library Cicero's *De Natura Deorum* would have lain side-by-side on the shelf with Varro's encyclopedic *Antiquitates Rerum Humanarum et Divinarum*. This compendium would have been amply supplemented by the broad spectrum of Greek writers from Homer and Aeschylus to Theocritus and Callimachus who, over a period longer than the significant history of Rome, had already put into poised form treatments of nearly all the myths Ovid would himself rephrase.

Pre-Roman Italy was inhabited by a congeries of disparate peoples and their cults. The range was broad: from the cults of the pre-Roman Aborigines (Cato, cited by Servius on *Aeneid*, 1.6), the Ligurians, the

190

Umbrians, the Sabines, the Etruscans, the Falerians, and the cremating Celts, all the way to those of the sophisticated Greek cities of Magna Graecia and Sicily where Pythagoras, Empedocles, and Zeno had been systematizing some elements of the religion into philosophy. The development in Rome itself, from the various primitive rituals of these peoples to philosophy, was unprecedentedly rapid. Ovid was the heir of this development. The Romans, once they became politically dominant, acknowledged the syncretic, layered character of their cults, distinguishing the *Di novensiles* from the *Di indigites*. From the latter they derived such preliterate ghost worship as the cult of the Manes and Lares (*Fasti* II, 411; II, 616; V, 147) and the animism of Jupiter Feretrius (*Fasti* II, 69; III, 383), etc. There were also such adopted gods as the Magna Mater of the Near East, whose introduction into Rome was a historic event (204 B.C., *Fasti* IV, 182–349). The Roman religion, in fact, underwent a pervasive acculturative process; it was Hellenized in general (Wissowa, pp. 63ff).

As Ovid has the vaguely known indigenous goddess Carmentis say to the early legendary king Evander:

> "Di" que "petitorum" dixit, "salvete locorum
> tuque novos caelo terra datura deos"

> Hail to the gods of the sought-for lands,
> And you, earth, who will give the sky new gods.
> (*Fasti* I, 509–10)

Ovid says of his own eclecticism, "add, my Muse, Latin causes to the foreign ones," "Adde peregrinis causas, mea Musa, Latinas" (*Fasti* II, 359).

In the poeticized religious calendar of Ovid's *Fasti* these gods derived from various stages of social development are put on a par with different stages or aspects of the same god compressed into one. Janus, with whom Ovid opens the *Fasti*, is a rudimentary god as primitive as Terminus (I, 95–101) and, at the same time, a comprehensive, quasi-monotheistic, quasi-pantheistic deity identifiable with almost any force or thing in nature (I, 103–14).

Vesta is one of those moderately rudimentary; perhaps correspondingly, her temple has no statue (*Fasti* VI, 245–60). In the second book of the *Fasti*, for example, the rudimentary Terminus exists side-by-side with the personified earth spirit Faunus (540ff); the ghostly Manes (535), and the Lares (616). The eponymous founder Romulus becomes

Quirinus, Dumézil's god of the third agricultural-management function. Here, too, are the ruling god Jupiter himself (509); the deified Augustus (*passim*); the personified Tacita, Iuturna, and Fornax
(525); and Juno-Lucina, a general goddess specified into a function
(436). Each of these gods has an ontological status distinct from that of
any other, and so do the persons with whom they occasionally identify
or interact: Romulus, Augustus, the miraculously surviving legendary
Arion (83ff), Callisto who becomes a constellation (156–188), and
finally the type of the Virtuous Matron, Lucretia, whose rape by the
legendary king Tarquin provided the occasion for the founding of the
Roman Republic (741–852). This rape culminates the book not only
by introducing a political focus but also by performing what may be
called a simplification. Its earlier parallel in the book, Faunus' failure
to rape a Hercules dressed in the clothes of Omphale as he sleeps beside "her" (335–44), puts an earthly spirit into interaction with a deified hero and a legendary woman-earth sun goddess. Broad humor and
strong piety mingle strangely here. The acts Ovid describes we may identify as the vestiges of rites: the legendary queen is shaded from the sun
by an umbrella (311–12) and honored by a combination of transvestism
and Holy Marriage (319–34). Faunus, transfixed while groping for the
groin of the recumbent, skirt-clad Hercules, may be taken to travesty
all this, but Ovid is serious about Faunus at the same time.

2.

Ovid's two supreme and contrasting works, the *Metamorphoses* and
the *Fasti*, take two different, complementary approaches to the syncretic
and historically layered Roman awareness of mythic beings. The *Fasti*,
more complex in material and simpler in organization, sets itself the
task of accounting at varied length for the diachronic multiplicity of
Roman religious practice on a synchronic plan; it treats the festivals of
the Roman religious calendar taken day by day. The *Metamorphoses*,
climaxing in the apotheosis of Julius Caesar (XV, 745–870), centers
on myth rather than religion, and literature rather than cult, coordinating the stories that the poets and tragedians had re-elaborated over many
centuries, and with a predominantly Greek focus that is almost exclusive until the last two books. Even there, in Book XIV, Ovid emphasizes a Greek connection to Circe for the Roman Picus (XIV, 320ff;
Haupt II, 389). While he does give an account of the Roman version
of the Muses, the *Camenae* (XIV, 430–34), his prevailing reference is

to the nine Muses of Greek, and literary, association. The Greek Muses themselves were systematized as to their functions only in Roman times. Ennius, on the other hand, had already fused the Camenae with the Greek Muses two centuries before in order to exalt the native and the local (Badian).[1]

Ovid's own relation to the past, worked out in this implied, clean opposition of his culminating twenty years, was sensitized and ambivalent, befitting someone whose modality to the past's central mythic inheritance remained problematic and quasi-ironic. His own ambivalence of belief appears in his very attitude towards the primal past from which the myths came. On the one hand he revels in his modernity:

> Prisca iuvent alios, ego me nunc denique natum
> gratulor: haec aetas moribus apta meis.
>
> Let the atavistic please others, I congratulate myself
> For being born now so late; this age suits my ways.
>   (*Ars Amatoria* II, 121)

(I have taken the liberty of emphasizing one aspect of *priscus* and underplaying its connotation of venerability.) On the other hand Ovid has Janus use the word *priscus* to describe his godhead, and in a sense that cannot be other than laudatory: "sum res prisca," "I am an atavistic thing," (*Fasti* I, 103). The whole of the *Fasti* glories in the old, and as early as the *Amores* Ovid saw an access to the past as a solution even in love: "Tolle tuos, tecum, pauper amator, avos!" "Carry your grandfathers with you, poor lover!" (*Amores* I, viii, 66). The balance between these two attitudes, however, is clearly stated in the *Fasti*:

> Laudamus veteres, sed nostris utimur annis;
>   mos tamen est aeque dignus uterque coli
>
> We praise the old but use our own years;
>   Each custom is equally worthy to be fostered.
>   (*Fasti* I, 225–26)

Ovid has Janus, himself, seen fictively enough to stand in some ironic light, declare Ovid to be in error with his times:

> risit et "o quam te fallunt tua saecula," dixit,
>   "qui stipe mel sumpta dulcius esse putes!"
> he laughed, "O how your age deceives you," he said,
>   "If you think honey is sweeter than money in hand."
>   (*Fasti* 191–92)

And Janus is made to go on to say how even in Saturn's time money was sweet, when the love for it kept growing. However, Ovid preserves the ambivalence by having Janus somewhat reverse this picture of the golden age, and he paints (197–214) a picture of modern Rome in which Rome has a glory that "has touched at its crest the topmost gods" ("tetigit summos vertice Roma deos," 210), blending in the positive side of his negative assertion about greed. The positive, indeed, can be felt as ambiguously underlying the negative in his opening statement. "Pluris opes nunc sunt quam prisci temporis annis," "Wealth is of more account now than in the years of atavistic time" (197); the same word, *priscus*, is here repeated.

It is old usage that vindicates the identification of Juno with the moon in Rome, "Vindicat Ausonias Iunonis cura kalendas," "The cult of Juno vindicates [also "claims"] the Ausonian kalends" (I, 55). Ovid participates, personally but at some diminished distance, in the rites at the grove of Nemi, speaking of the stream that flows there, "saepe sed exiguis haustibus, inde bibi," "Often, but in scanty draughts, have I drunk therefrom" (*Fasti* III, 274).

Ovid, then, qualifies a contrast between past and present that is already encompassing and insistent in Lucretius, who uses the very cult of Venus to assert atomic analysis against the fear-ridden *religio* of old Rome.

The Thucydidean consciousness about history, explicitly adapted and paraphrased in Lucretius' analysis of the plague (VI, 1120–1286), is freed from its cyclic implications for humanity and given a one-way direction by Lucretius, who insists on the ultimate dissolution of all things living and dead. This Roman attitude towards direction in history, implied also by Sallust, makes possible the unique assimilation of non-Romans into the legal status of Roman citizenship, and it may be seen to inform the whole abstract system of Roman laws and imperial administration—providing more detachment from the tribal and the mythic than Greece ever knew. The very syncretism of the *Fasti* allows for an equivalence of mythic beings, without their being qualified out of existence, and without their being accorded the dominance of maximum credence. The *Metamorphoses*, too, offers a one-way movement from past into present, since rarely is anyone transformed back from bear into woman or from corpse into person—Tiresias (III, 316–38) is a case whose re-metamorphosis makes him share something of the objectivity of the poet of the *Metamorphoses* himself. Proteus, who might have been given one of the longest episodes in a poem dwelling on Meta-morphosis, is handled quite briefly (VIII, 728–37). Just as the atoms in Lucretius recombine but people die, so strange and terrible meta-morphoses take place while the principle of metamorphosis remains constant.

Pythagoras is made to transmit to the Roman king Numa a doctrine of metempsychosis (XV, 60–479) that would virtualize the multiple procedures of change we have been shown; taken schematically rather than narratively, they place the past and the present on a par, just as the *Metamorphoses* set an idealized Greek permanent present against the layered Roman past of the *Fasti.*

The aetiological myths of the *Fasti,* too, as Ovid handles them poeti-cally, are at once proto-anthropological and sub-satiric, since Ovid does not take the alternate "scholarly" accounts of origins which he offers as seriously as, say, Herodotus does his. In this respect, too, Ovid may be said neither to believe in his myths nor to disbelieve them, but rather to modulate their elements for his purposes.

3.

A story is admitted to the *Metamorphoses* only if it involves a trans-formation of its central subject or can be construed, often quite arbi-trarily, as involving such a transformation. All of the other multiple points of analogy between one myth and another are arbitrarily subor-dinated to this principle of metamorphosis, yet once the metamorphosis has been dealt with, the whole attention of the writer can be directed to the other items of the story and their structured presentation.

Transformation in myth, and its lingering literary manifestations, evokes awe at the crossing of so seemingly impassable a barrier as that of the kinds of living things (Massey), an awe akin to that before hu-man mortality itself. This awe clings to metamorphoses in the myths of primitive peoples all over the world. Taken more philosophically, the idea of transformation serves for Empedocles or Lucretius as a profound principle, the basic one, in the scientific explanation of the universe. And since almost any tale has a point that could make it qualify, while the length of treatment given a particular tale can be arbitrarily lengthened just because the metamorphosis need not be given major emphasis, the principle may serve as a simple rhetorical one for both sorting and amplifying stories in any order at all; it advertises its arbitrariness. It can be a *carmen perpetuum*, as Ovid calls it in his first lines, echoing and exceeding the phrase of Callimachus, *aeisma dienekes*, an "unbroken song." The blend of myth-awe and scientific abstraction with the fictiveness of an arbitrary rhetorical-presentational strategy corresponds to, and expresses, Ovid's own problematic state of belief in the myths which he both easily manipulates and treats as sources of a shared religion. He saves till the end, and for the subordinating dramatization of an opinion delivered from Pythagoras to Numa, the exposition of the largely Lucretian doctrines that expand the poem without really serving to inform or explain it:

> omnia mutantur, nihil interit: errat et illinc
> huc venit, hinc illuc, et quoslibet occupat artus
> spiritus eque feris humana in corpora transit
> inque feras noster, nec tempore deperit ullo,
> utque novis facilis signatur cera figuris
>
> All things change, nothing perishes: the spirit wanders,
> Comes here thence, hence there, and takes up any frames
> It pleases, and goes from beasts into human bodies
> And ours into beasts', equally, and at no time loses,
> As with new figures wax is easily stamped.
>
> (XV, 165–69)

This does not describe any of the changes that have happened in the poem, exactly, but rather it presents a metempsychosis which would be a new, and much less violent, version of metamorphosis. The doctrine it presents would be of no help to the suffering Io or the melting Narcissus, nor does the even more Lucretian doctrine into which Pythagoras is imagined as swelling serve as other than a sort of virtual qualification for the poem's events: "cuncta fluunt, omnisque vagans formatur imago;" "All things flow, and every image is formed while in transit" (XV, 178).

The first clause is also Heraclitean,[2] though Lucretius in other respects refutes Heraclitus; but in no case is any figure in the *Metamorphoses* an *imago* in this sense. What Michel Serres characterizes as Lucretius' revision into an *eidolon* of the Platonic *eidos* is here allowed only a kind of faint analogy to the tone of the poem, rather than a defining force over its figures.

Consequently, Otis's assertion (p. viii) about metamorphosis as a principle of order must be qualified. "Not the linking, but the *order* or

succession of episodes, motifs and ideas . . . constitutes the real unity
of the poem." Actually, order in the sense of succession, and order in
the sense of linking, are equally operative in the poem. Its achievement
is to take the principle of linkage, at once arbitrary and profound, and
make it work to equalize the events whose elaborate structure of analogy
Otis has so amply demonstrated. Arbitrariness holds sway over Ovid's
showily casual transitions. And the arbitrariness enters the tone of Ovid's
initial invocation of his quasi-philosophic principle:

> In nova fert animus mutatas dicere formas
> corpora; di, coeptis (nam vos mutastis et illas)
> adspirate meis primaque ab origine mundi
> ad mea perpetuum deducite tempora carmen!

> My spirit is born to speak of forms changed into new
> bodies; gods, on what I have begun (for you
> changed even those forms) breathe, and from the start
>   of the world,
> lead a perpetual song down to my times.
>   (I, 1–4)

It is notably the masculine "gods" rather than the feminine Muses
(sometimes, *deae*, as *Fasti*, V, 9), whom he invokes. While both continuity and variety are brought in by this expression, as Otis notes (p.
45), the question of unity seems to be left hanging. It is precisely the
shift between what may be called the high philosophic or Pythagorean
sense of "forms" here, and the low or narrative sense of blind bodies
caught in a plot that is lightly retold, which makes this invocation hyperbolic rather than sublime. Between unity and variety, between philosophy and rhetoric, between credence and fiction, the poet weaves his
web of words.[3]

The *Aitia* of Callimachus differed in its tonal range from the *Metamorphoses*, so far as we can judge from its fragments and from Catullus'
translation of one of its episodes (Catullus LXVI, Callimachus Fgt. 110
Pfeiffer). It simply expounded the origins of its myth, being encyclo-
pedic-euphuistic without any hint of philosophical qualification or abstraction. The *Fasti*, too, abounds in raw data of diverse origins, and it
celebrates that diversity, whereas the *Aitia* would seem to have assumed
a parity of origin and a common Greek past for its myths. The *Hete-
roieumena* of Nicander, which may have suggested the topic of metamorphosis to Ovid by its title and to some degree by its procedures,

seems to have combined the procedures of both the *Fasti* and *Metamorphoses*, and so to lack the unifying conception of either.

In the *Metamorphoses* the connection between episodes is accidental, not only theoretically but also in the mode of their transition. To take but one example, Ovid introduces the Orpheus story tangentially through the seemingly less important Iphis (X, 5ff). The contingency of connection reinforces the contingency of choice of episodes and even the contingency of the form a metamorphosis may take. All these contingencies become an undogmatic equivalent for the philosophy of the Epicureans about the gods and of the Stoics about the progression of events; though Ovid, again, does not enunciate, or refuse, a particular doctrine. If he follows Lucretius in the culminating doctrine he assigns to Pythagoras, he does not do so by assigning the gods to an Epicurean limbo detached from human events—except by providing an equivalent for the Epicurean *ataraxia* in his tone.

Ovid occasionally offers some smaller-scale chronological and topographical organizations, but he also has an overall chronological organization from the origin of the world to the presently ruling deified emperor, and an implied topographical one from early Greece to present Rome. Still, this sequential principle undergoes abstraction and qualification in the systematic similarity of the episodes: all involve metamorphosis. The likeness-in-difference of episodes, indeed, provides another principle, parallel to and derived from metamorphosis, which leads logically as well as temporally from one into another, as the sacrilege against the tree of Ceres of the devouring Erysichthon corresponds to, and leads into, the visage of the famished Fames. This in turn corresponds to, and before long leads into, the fate of the too violent Meleager, expiring because the flames devour a piece of wood in which his life is magically tied up (VIII, 338–525). Or to follow one of Otis' multiple correspondences (p. 226), Byblis who was changed into a fountain, as punishment for her guilty, incestuous love (IX, 453ff) offers a contrast with the innocent unnatural love of Iphis (IX, 668ff), who is rewarded by being changed into a man. These are both set in analogous contrast to the loves, themselves both alike and different, of Ganymede (X, 155), Orpheus (X, 72ff), Hyacinthus (X, 162ff), and Cyparissus (X, 106ff). As a beloved of Apollo changed into a cypress tree, Cyparissus is also analogous to Daphne (I, 452ff). All these human figures whose unnatural loves involving gods are partially justified by metamorphosis find further analogues in the Propoetides,

who were turned into prostitutes out of vengeance for their scorn of
Venus, and then into stones (X, 221, 238; they are analogous to any
other petrified figure in the poem). These are analogous to Pygmalion
(X, 243), whose innocent, unnatural love for an ivory sculpture was
rewarded by its metamorphosis into a woman; and to Myrrha (X, 312f),
whose guilty incestuous love for her father is punished, as Byblis' for
her brother was, by metamorphosis into a tree. Still, there is a different
benign issue in her birth of Adonis (X, 524ff)—himself loved by a goddess (unlike Ganymede, etc.), but with the fatal consequences of dying
under attack from a boar; his blood itself, however, metamorphoses into
a flower.

Another set of analogies in the third book—any of which could be
correlated to this set—would establish correspondences among Actaeon,
torn to pieces by hounds for glimpsing the naked Diana; Semele, giving
birth to Bacchus after being consumed by Jupiter's thunderbolt on un-
wisely following the advice of the disguised Juno; Tiresias, turned into
a woman for separating snakes; Narcissus, pining away at his own image;
and Pentheus, torn to pieces by his mother for spurning Bacchus.

Ovid does not juxtapose these episodes schematically, and the analogies may be seen to stand out in even stronger relief. With artful casualness the narratives are intertwined and framed, as in the fourth book a
daughter of Minyas unnamed in the text (38ff) tells several stories:
Pyramus and Thisbe, Mars and Venus, and Leucothoe and Salmacis-
Hermaphrodite; all of which could in turn be coordinated with the two
sets of stories discussed so far.

Such correspondences, of course, pervade the poem. But they operate
at a level both of complexity of difference and simplicity of likeness
which keeps them just below the possibility of Lévi-Straussian factoring.
If this were applied to the *myths*, it would detach them from *Ovid's text*,
which always verbalizes its elements without either deducing conclusions
or subjecting a given mythic pattern to the profound examination which
Aeschylus accords Prometheus or Sophocles Oedipus. The mythemes
Ovid presents receive the constant, abstracting mediation of his verbal
manipulation. He also, in effect, juxtaposes them in the sort of arbitrary
equivalences I have discussed above. Both procedures would render
merely subliminal any other mediations which might be performed upon
them.

There is, further, a large-scale pattern; and, because the analogies
among single episodes are themselves multiplex, possibly more than one

large-scale pattern. Otis offers one (pp. 84–85), with a first section mostly involving divine amours (I–II), a second section of love episodes framed by episodes of divine vengeance (III–VI, 400), a broad third section wholly occupied with amatory pathos (VI, 401–XI), and a final fourth section balancing the exemplary history of Troy with the cresting history of Rome (XII–XV).

Given the arbitrariness of analogy by which Ovid presents the myths in both the *Metamorphoses* and the *Fasti*, the idealized pastoral land-scape of *loca amoena*, while constant in its attributes as Segal (4) main-tains, still does not have imposed on it a closed order of significations. Theocritus is not possible as a final equivalent for either long poem, though both poems adapt Theocritan procedures and refrain from di-rectly transcending Theocritus in a Vergilian direction.[4]

4.

Instead of trying for Vergil's depth, Ovid in his very diction (Bömer and Kenney) turns Vergil's practices into a common, standardized for-mal resource. The subjectivity in landscape and elsewhere that Vergil discovered is, it would seem, taken for granted by Ovid, who combines it with a narrative that runs at a faster and simpler pace than Vergil's.[5]

The corresponding lightness of his bearing towards mythical mate-rials gives Ovid a freedom far greater than Vergil had, to transpose the special qualities of Callimachus which Capovila delineates (II, 404–54): the *lepton* ("subtlety"), *poikilia* ("delicate variation"), and *drosos prokios* ("fine freshness," literally "early dew"). But these qualities are made adaptive to the tensile implications of the central conception. Or as La Faye puts it (p. 95) there is a "general . . . contrast" between the "ease (*aisance*) of the style and the studied irregularity of the compo-sition." All this fine manipulation is put at the service of an ironized suspension of devotion to the area for which the myths stand. Ovid drops personages from, or adds them to, the *Metamorphoses* with a deliberate abruptness, as though insisting on his power to name or keep silent, as he chooses. As Bernbeck says (pp. 40–41), "Juno and Tisi-phone, marginal figures from the viewpoint of the original saga, possess greater weight than the chief figures Athamas and Io." Bernbeck con-trasts this procedure with the normal one in epic, when in Ovid's poem "there is lacking the usual information on the provenance and destination of personages. And the scenic background is often only sketchily delineated, so that the presentation often appears to run off into empty space." There are, further, missing conclusions to scenes (pp. 64–67) and missing intervals in the known sequence of events for the myth (pp. 68–69). All these procedures extend the arbitrariness of the writer into the constantly worked-over foreshortening or expansion of episodes: he seems never to be leaving them alone.

In both the *Fasti* and the *Metamorphoses* Ovid's tone ranges all the way from jocosity approaching frivolity to dead earnest.[6] This range makes accidental Heinze's derivation of the former's tone from the elegy of its elegiacs and the latter's from the epic meter of its hexameters. Indeed, one could reverse his equation and find awe in the *Fasti*, tenderness in the *Metamorphoses*. In both poems the super-Callimachean surface acts to neutralize in tone and to modulate in idea whatever is presented; one need only contrast the dramatized Lucretian matter, relatively earnest in tone, of *Metamorphoses* XV with the dire urgency of Lucretius himself, to catch the highlight of the Ovidian fictiveness. Ovid himself plays with the idea that the *Fasti* changes tone from his other elegies (*Fasti* II, 3–16). Comparing the presentation of Cacus in the *Fasti* to that in Propertius and Vergil, Otis (p. 34) finds in Ovid "a reduction of the epic scale and tone," which I would rather characterize as a transposition of mythic force, or as a virtualization, present in the pointed playfulness of the style. A line from the slightly earlier *Ars Amatoria* will illustrate the ironization of a dire myth. The Minotaur, born to Pasiphae after she has intercourse with a bull, is described as "semibovemque virum semivirumque bovem," "a half-ox man, a half-man ox" (*Ars Amatoria* II, 24).

These words, alternate additions of the same monstrous figure, seem to cancel each other out by balancing exactly; they mock their own attempt to apply, as it were, some syntactic equivalent of Lévi-Strauss's binary categories to the Minotaur. Ovid invokes Thalia, who is said to move with the "uneven wheels" of the elegiac couplet, in touching on the comic side of the *Ars Amatoria*:

Hactenus, unde legas quod ames, ubi retia ponas,
  Praecipit imparibus vecta Thalia rotis

Thus far, whence you would choose what you love, where you put nets
  Thalia teaches, carried on unequal wheels

                                        (*Ars Amatoria* I, 263–64)

Here, too, we are given a version of what Marouzeau calls Ovid's characteristic stylistic procedure of interweaving verbs, which applies even
more flamboyantly when he is quoting, as in a passage cited above
(*Fasti* I, 509–10).[7]

As Albrecht well says (p. 419), Ovid's *dicacitas* or sprightly ver-
bosity "appears directly to *destroy* the reality of the gods" (italics Albrecht's). In diction Ovid adheres to the middle-range selection classes
of normative nouns and verbs along the lines I have defined elsewhere
as characterizing "the refined style" (Cook, 1966). But his syntax is
not normative; it performs an excess of manipulation upon this style,
diverting it from its balancing view of a delimited universe. Narrative,
calling for linear presentation, resists such embroidery. But he uses it
notably in the flow of the narrative to which he turned in both the *Metamorphoses* and the *Fasti* after the set-piece letters of the *Amores* and the
Heroides, and the versified treatise of the *Ars Amatoria*. Take this passage from late in the *Metamorphoses*, rendering Glaucus' arrival at the
courts of Circe:

> inde manu magna Tyrrhena per aequora vectus
> herbiferos adiit colles atque atria Glaucus
> Sole satae Circes vanarum plena ferarum.
>
> thence with a great hand coursing through Tyrrhene seas
> Glaucus arrived at the grass-bearing hills and courts
> of sun-born Circe, full of vacuous beasts.
>
> (XIV, 8–10)

The words are general ones, *vectus* and *aequora* being conventional, and
Sole satae itself part of a standard epic repertoire. "*Manu magna*" however combines metaphor (one is normally *vectus* in a ship), metonymy
(the hand is attached to the arm, which does the swimming), and double
synecdoche (hand for hand-plus-arm-plus-body; one hand for two).
Two strong genitive phrases entirely make up the six words of the last
line here, of which the first, *Sole satae Circes*, is not attached to what
we are waiting for, the modifier of *atria*, but the second is, *vanarum
plena ferarum*. The word *vanarum* is logically climactic as well; it implies what threatens Glaucus, and it anticipates a failed version of the
metempsychosis Pythagoras will expound, as well as a striking version
of his doctrine that forms are vain and changing anyway. *Vanarum* can
also be said to condense the whole plot of Circe's treatment of those
she seduces.

Amplification and condensation, indeed, are the constant resource of these large poems of Ovid. For example, this couplet:

> dicite, quae fontes Aganippidos Hippocrene,
>   grata Medusaei signa tenetis equi

> Speak, you who hold the fountains of Aganippe's Hippocrene,
>   the pleasing marks of the Medusean horse.
>   (*Fasti* V, 8–9)

Here there is a relatively low incidence of syntactic manipulation. But the first line is quite amplified, since Aganippe and Hippocrene are nearly synonymous as fountains on Mount Helicon, and they mean no more than instances of reference to what the general word *"fontes"* already names, associated with the very activity which *"dicite,"* addressed to the Muses, implies; the line has the amplification of high redundancy. The second line, however, is quite condensed. It refers to one story, the striking of the springs on the mountain under the hooves of Pegasus, through still another, the release of Pegasus from the blood of the neck of Medusa as Perseus was slaying her ("Medusean" in that sense). And the phrase also includes the birth of Pegasus through a secret amour with Poseidon ("Medusean" in that sense too). The trope "Medusean horse" would normally imply a genitive of possession, as "Herculean strength." Here it is grammatically double, a genitive of origin and also a sort of metonymy.

What these two words condense the *Metamorphoses* in turn amplifies —one of the many correspondences of myth between it and the *Fasti*— where the whole Perseus story is told at great length (IV, 476–V, 279).

5.

Myths, insofar as they reflect kinship systems, emphasize woman, on Lévi-Strauss's showing, because women are mediators between nature and culture. Women are at once the sources of reproduction and the key commodities of social exchange within and between the generations. Myths, insofar as they reflect the Freudian unconscious, deploy a sexual force into the kinship pattern of the nuclear family.

A tribal society needs no more than its myths for the categorization of the sexual life. But in more complex societies the sexual life, along with the reflections that accompany highly developed sublimations, requires acts of more strategic understanding: a further transposition of myth into literature. Sophocles and Euripides plumbed the sexual life more deeply than did Aeschylus, for whom the Suppliants and Io were largely victims, and Clytemnestra largely a scandal. By Hellenistic times pastoral poetry and New Comedy confined themselves to a generally demythicized universe of staple interactions that focussed on the delicate problems the sexual life might present. The Ovid of the *Amores* and the *Heroides* stayed pretty much within those conventions, and the mythical figures in those works function as *exempla*, types for contemplation. The sharp discriminations of Propertius and the soft subjectivity of Vergil are still beyond Ovid, as is the modulated, personalized savagery of Catullus. But none of these poets catches so much of the myth-mystery in the nets of his verse.

Ovid takes as his ground in the *Ars Amatoria* the sophisticated code of the erotic intrigue, leaving behind the whole piety-charged and tradition-defined family basis to the Roman *gens*, built around the Roman *matrona*. Thus he produces a principle which retains extremer versions of myths as *exempla*, Pasiphae or Mars and Venus. He orders this material on the time-line of the gestures that might lead to a consummation detached from past and future. He deals with the sexes "psychologically" as detached individuals engaged in an enterprise of mutual but temporary interest. In his objectivity he resembles Lucretius and echoes him in drawing the effect of infatuation on the lover, though Lucretius had gone much further in identifying love and death as processes that deeply revealed the principle of the flow of atoms (since the sight that leads to infatuation is dependent on such movements).

In Lucretius, too, there is an overriding ambivalence (Schrijvers) that Ovid has so far found no way to approximate. Venus is an urgent force —at the origin of Rome—and a source of delight for men and gods, as the first line of *De Rerum Natura* declares, "Aeneadum genetrix, hominum divomque voluptas." And yet the religion of which Venus might be a prime example is to be shunned as a savage terror; human sacrifice, like that of Iphigenia, is a direct result thereof: "tantum religio potuit suadere malorum," "So much of evil did superstition induce" (*De Rerum Natura*, I. 100). Still, Mother Earth and Cybele, too, come in for a kind of awe (*De Rerum Natura*, II, 575–600).

Lucretius' Venus is an impulse, a general force, an idea, and at the same time something like an allegorized figure (*De Rerum Natura*, IV, 105ff).[8] "Pursue," "celebrate," "cause to abound," and "publish abroad" are all relevant senses of the first verb he gives the fostering Venus whom he invokes at the beginning of the poem, *concelebras,*[9] an action she performs on ship-bearing seas and fruit-bearing earth (nature and culture thus coupled) under the gliding signs of the sky:

> alma Venus, caeli subter labentia signa
> quae mare navigerum, quae terras frugiferentis
> concelebras
>
> (I, 2–4)

In his longer poems Ovid finally approaches the Lucretian ambivalence by fusing the effects of love and of death in the myths he narrates. He re-renders the inexplicability of the myth as the awe therein, not as a special posture but as a common denominator to mythic events. The *Metamorphoses* shows that a common action typically underlies and causes the mystery of the miraculous transformations it takes as its announced subject. Often involved therein is the treacherous uncontrollability of the erotic impulse and its strange drift, phrased by legend, towards boundary-crossing. A sexual involvement that gets phrased into a myth tends to have crossed natural lines (incest, self-love, hermaphroditism, human and divine, even patriotism in the case of Scylla). A recursion of atavistic horror here takes over from the sophistication of the *Ars Amatoria.* What crops up regularly in the *Metamorphoses* is a random risk in the *Fasti.* Characteristically, it may either be left unmentioned (the fact that Aristaeus is in trouble because he attacked Eurydice) or given extended treatment (the crucial change of Roman government occasioned by Tarquin's rape of Lucretia). The almost daily presence of atavistic figures for worship in the Roman calendar can robustly accommodate, we may infer, what evidently obsesses the abstracted network of the mythology that serves as the raw material for literature. The rawness of the material is tamed not by being diluted or redirected, but by the overcontrol of a literary manipulation that holds it in check by magnificent means and by an arbitrary leading idea.

As Segal says (4, p. 8), there is, for the very landscape of the poems, "erotic coloring even of metamorphoses which are presented as *successful escapes* from love." Even in this escape, as always in this chief activity, there remains a psychologized but impersonally presented version of the Lucretian ambivalence, "a polarity of urbanity and violence" (p. 1). Even in the *Fasti* Castor and Pollux are seen in the role of tragic suitors (V, 699–719). Love involves what Bernbeck calls a pervasive paradox (p. 111). Daphne's wish and her body are at odds: "votoque tuo tua forma repugnat," "your form fights against your prayer" (I, 488). The *maiestas* of the gods, declared to be their central quality in Book V of the *Fasti*, is also declared to be incongruous with the love which the gods also obsessively pursue:

> non bene conveniunt nec in una sede morantur
> maiestas et amor

> they do not go together nor dwell long in one site,
> majesty and love
> > (*Metamorphoses* II, 846–47).

It is as a patron of prostitutes that Flora urges women to gather ye rosebuds while ye may (*Fasti* V, 353–54). Even at the crescendo of the Roman sections that conclude the *Metamorphoses* the deeply pervading erotic troubles have not been banished. Vertumnus woos Pomona in a sort of idyll. Still, to induce in her "greater fear" (*magis timeas* XIV, 694) for Venus and Nemesis—significantly coupled!—he disguises himself as an old woman and tells her the tale wherein Iphis died of love for Anaxarete, who then turned to stone.

The very inception of the love is described in terms that suggest the strangeness and pain that will later befall them both:

> viderat et totis perceperat ossibus aestum
> luctatusque diu, postquam ratione furorem
> vincere non potuit, supplex ad limina venit
> et modo nutrici miserum confessus amorem

> He saw her and perceived a burning in all his bones,
> and long strivings, and after he could not conquer
> the furor with reason came suppliant to her door,
> and now confessing his sad love to the nurse
> > (XIV, 700–704).

The act of poetic perception puts us, through Ovid, in the position of Vertumnus and Pomona, between whom this tale is exchanged. We are presumptive sharers in the mastery that a Roman citizen has access to, which includes mastery over those very forces in the myth that the disguised Vertumnus tells Pomona. Ovid codes all this into the poem as a means for dealing with what in myth is essentially uncontrollable.

Ovid's triumph is a tour-de-force of suggestiveness, wherein a lightness of touch and a total control of literary means, by suspending credence without mocking it, bring the phases of myth into overlay, without either Vergil's engulfing fusion or Dante's distinct levels.

PART THREE

ELEMENTARY FORMS

We have tended to see such forms as the riddle, the parable, and the proverb systematically, as permanent resources for simple expression. These forms, if they are looked at historically, show traces of a kind of backward-looking battle against the total dominance of myth. The kernel story, the framed question, the simple expression of social wisdom, stand free of mythic beings by notably not naming them. Their content only feebly echoes any mythic story, and their language offers a low phenomenological incidence of mythic elements. More than this, the very form of the riddle, the proverb, or the parable tends in each case to replace, or at least to transpose, the concerns of myth. As for the metaphors which we persistently feel to be essential for poetry—even though poems can exist without them—our feeling attests to their very power, which is akin to that of myth. As poets from the Romantics on have said in various ways, metaphor is an access to that charged area on which myths draw. And of course metaphors do strongly parallel myths, offering a high phenomenological incidence of mythic elements.

These elementary forms tend to take firm shape just at the time in history when literary forms generally are coming into being. And this is also the large moment when religions, as Bellah represents them, in various places all over the world develop doctrines of "transcendence," which often seem to entail a rejection of the world. Literature then, we may say, restores the world, sometimes to religion but never directly to myth. The literary forms perhaps secularize but certainly redefine myth. As Bellah summarizes the situation, (pp. 38, 43):

> in the first millennium B.C. all across the Old World, at least in centers of high culture, the phenomenon of religious rejection of the world [is] characterized by an extremely negative evaluation of

209

> man and society and the exaltation of another realm of reality as
> alone true—Plato's classic formulation . . . that the body is the
> tomb or prison of the soul. . . . in Israel the world is profoundly
> devalued in the face of the transcendent God. . . . In India we find
> perhaps the most radical of all versions of world rejection . . . in
> the Buddha's [image that] the world is a burning house. . . . In
> China, Taoist ascetics urged . . . withdrawal. . . . [later] the Qu'ran
> compares this present world to vegetation after rain.

And the same phenomenon repeats itself in another phase as during the
early middle ages Christianity replaces paganism while at the same time
the literary forms of our era take on characteristic shape.

Generally, then, the period of "transcendence" also produces the rise
of literacy, and of literature itself, in nearly all the forms we know. In
dialectical interaction with a transcendent rejection of the world there
emerges the possibility of an independent, personal, articulated re-
representation of the world, those literary works of unparalleled richness and supreme value which include scriptural documents promul-
gating that transcendence. Along with these, and heralding them, come
those humble forms of strong persistence, the proverb, the riddle, and
the parable. Meanwhile, the metaphors that are notably scanty in the
earliest epic poetry now come magnificently, and protractedly, into
their own.

7.

BETWEEN PROSE AND POETRY: *The Speech and Silence of the Proverb*

1.

THE proverb, which seems to be the simplest sort of literary form, a felicitously phrased commonplace preserved often in a single sentence, actually embodies a number of presuppositions and emerges from a fairly complex set of social conditions. On the positive side, the proverb implies a normative situation which it phrases and applies; on the negative side, it has detached itself at least provisionally from what may be called the universe of myth, because on the historical evidence proverbs only appear when the universe of myth begins to undergo qualification.

Any utterance in natural language, as linguists have recently shown us,[1] must in certain situations enlist presuppositions, as distinct from lexical entries, phonological principles, and syntactic rules. To take a simple example, Robin Lakoff (p. 148) demonstrates of *and* and other conjunctions that "For all conjunction a common topic is necessary." An utterance like "John likes Vivaldi and the Pentagon has an oversize budget" is ill-formed for other than lexical, syntactic, or phonological reasons: because there is no plausible common topic, *and* cannot be used.

The presuppositions governing such utterances bear on just the competence of a native speaker. When we move to performance, the question of context, as well as of presupposition, bears on the utterance. A proverb is a speech act. Even an utterance so simple and seemingly detached from a specific context as a proverb may reflect nothing less than the whole social matrix that uses it. This was already something like Bacon's view, "The genius, wit and spirit of a nation are discovered in its proverbs."

Yet the pragmatic test for utterances in natural language usually resolves to a single instance in a single context. For example, the puzzle about the metaphoric statement "this old man is a baby," where the status of each noun phrase as tenor or vehicle can only be resolved by pointing either at an infantile white-haired oldster—making "this old man" the tenor—or at a wizened baby in a high chair—making "this old man" the vehicle. In ordinary language this is a single instance; if the instances begin to converge towards a rule that applies past norms to future situations, then the utterance approaches the condition of the proverb.

Wherever the proverb occurs, and under whatever specific conditions, it constitutes both an appeal to old experience and a formulation to be used for new experience. It offers a normative rule as a guide. We may assume that the coordinates of the experience would have to be drawn in specifically for a location in space and time, and all the more when, as often happens, the proverb is widely distributed in space and time. The proverbs about courtship and marriage in the Bible cannot have had the same use in Jewish society of the fourth century B.C. as they might in twentieth-century American society, even that part of it for which the Bible is still a sacred book and its proverbs therefore canonical. However, the very abstractness of the proverb's normative substratum of both presupposition and context allows it to drift in space and in time. Flies, for example, despite local differences in species or habit (they are more seasonally confined in Russia and Germany than in Spain, Italy, or Ancient Sumeria), are everywhere undesirable. *Into a shut mouth flies fly not* (Gluski, p. 198). The English version of the proverb has a shade more rhetoric than the Russian, *V zakr'it'ii rot mukha ne vletit*, to which the Spanish version adds the playful touch of a rhyme and a terminal climax, *En boca cerrada, ni moscas ni nada*. Italian is emphatic about time, *In bocca chiusa non entra mai mosca*, while French gives a logical emphasis, *Dans une bouche close, il n'entre point de mouche*. German alone in this group puts the proverb in the form of a blunt command, using a pejorative for the mouth, *Halt's Maul, so fliegt dir keine Mücke hinein*. Who could have guessed, without the evidence, that this proverb also occurs on Sumerian tablets from the beginning of the Second Millennium B.C. (Pritchard, p. 425): *Into an open mouth a fly will enter*.

Language can easily accommodate and preserve proverbs. These, in turn, are also easily assimilated to become idioms like "carry coals to Newcastle," which has lost its character as a separable sentence and become something like an expanded verb.[2] Indeed many Chinese ideograms, at least to one who knows no Chinese, have the air of assimilated proverbs.[3]

In its full form as a separate sentence, the proverb not only implies a situation facing the hearer which is recursive enough to be normative; it may also imply a series. *Many a mickle makes a muckle* is a riddle involving series either easily solvable or completely unsolvable. Unapplied, it is redundant nonsense, "Many is many is many." Applied, it suggests a Protestant-ethic or savings-bank psychology, and indirectly offers a warning, as the German form of the fly-mouth proverb directly does. In its indirectness it implies that the imagined hearer has already internalized the advice. *Verbum sapienti*, "A word to the wise," is itself sufficient, and there is an equality between speaker and hearer assumed of such a sort that the "mathematical" rule *Many a mickle makes a muckle* need only be stated for the hearer to infer, as the speaker has, that a long-range view might recommend keeping the object in question, say a dollar, rather than using it up. Even the more direct Biblical version of the idea, *Go to the ant, thou sluggard; consider her ways, and be wise* (Proverbs 6:6), states not only the principle but a necessary process of reflection to apply it. And yet there is a kind of inequality between speaker and hearer, or the hearer would not be presumed to need the advice. In the Wisdom of Ptah-hotep and in Proverbs this takes the form of advice from father to son, an inequality which will become an equality if the son listens. The advice of "Theognis," too, is cast rhetorically as from elder to younger. Societies where a code is completely internalized—societies in which the initiated stand on a completely equal footing —would seem not to have produced proverbs, or not in the profusion of more complex, self-questioning societies.

Many a mickle makes a muckle, however, implies a stability of conditions, material conditions in this instance. On the day before the end of the world, or close to the death of the hearer, or in a war-torn society, it would cease to apply; its utterance would even be an insult. Proverbs in general imply a stability of conditions, and even *A word to the wise* implies that the hearer and the speaker will continue their relationship under the same conditions long enough for both hearer and speaker to cash in on the hearer's agreement with the proverb. The proverb would lose its felicity conditions if spoken by a traveller to a customs inspector on a border he was crossing once in his lifetime.

When the conditions disappear, the proverb may lose enough of its anchorage in reference for its sense to be altered. It is said that in a modern American university half the entering freshmen interpreted *A rolling stone gathers no moss* as a warning against staying put and accumulating moss rather than as a warning to stay put and put on sub-stance. The proverb tends to lose its meaning with its effect in a society where 20% of the population moves annually and a high premium is put on mobility and on oral gratification. The implicit anality of *Many a mickle makes a muckle* comes to seem undesirable, and *muckle* to accrue associations with *muck*, when a general prosperity induces an inatten-tion to accumulation. Indeed, proverbs generally, which come as a mer-cantile society is on the rise, both in their attention to acquisition and in their implied function as mechanisms of social control, correlate well with the anal traits that are characteristic of mercantile societies.

The implication that a specific context must be at hand to trigger the felicity of the proverb is substantiated by the existence of antithetical proverbs. *Haste makes waste* ceases to contradict *Seize the day* if they are seen as applying to different situations; the first proverb fits a situa-tion in which there is a temptation to take unwarranted shortcuts in fin-ishing a task that requires deliberation; the second one fits a situation in which there is a temptation to unwarranted delay.

Seize the day recommends a prudent abandonment of caution; in doing so, it formulates a rule based on the fact that situations can change: *Here today, gone tomorrow,* a stable principle for instability. This condition could be generalized to cover the future envisioned by the proverb, which is unstable enough to need the proverb as a tricky verbal arm against instability. This feature of the proverb's warning-system could also be applied metalinguistically to itself; the proverb often does so, and warns against infelicitous speech (*A soft answer turneth away wrath*) and against speaking generally (*Into a shut mouth flies fly not*).

While proverbs have finally settled into their status as folklore and would seem to imply a homely and homogeneous agricultural proletar-iat as their natural locus, even taken synchronically they may involve a complex context and a number of presuppositions as both constraints on their meaning and extensions of it. Taken diachronically, in most if not all social instances they arise from a society more complex by far than a simple post-Neolithic agricultural or pastoral one. The earliest proverbs, those of the Wisdom of Ptah-hotep, datable to as early as 2450 B.C., already rest on the elaborate organization of the Egyptian Old Kingdom. The Sumerian proverbs of the early second millennium refer to catamite temple priests (Gordon 2.97–106; pp. 246–55) and to a variety of occupations including commerce and transport (292–94).

Those codified in the Analects of Confucius come after at least a millennium of royal dynasties. The book of Proverbs is attributed to Solomon in the first words of the collection,[4] which means either that some of his utterances are incorporated into the book or at the very least that the book was compiled well after his reign, which was late and somewhat bureaucratic in comparison with those of other Israelite rulers. These proverbs say, over and over again, that they will lead one to become *chakham*, "wise," a condition which is social as well as intellectual. The *chokhemim* were a somewhat secularized version of a priestly caste. In Greece it is well after the period of kingship and as tyranny was breaking up, that we first get separable proverbs, some of the statements of Archilochus, the long proverb series of "Theognis" (which may just be a collection of proverbs), and very soon thereafter the adoption of what amounts to the proverb form for strong philosophical assertion by Heraclitus.[5] We have six possible utterances of Heraclitus (Diels 22 B 130–35) which would be lost if they had not been included in an ancient proverb collection, and others seem to have been quoted for their point as proverbs.

At this time, too, we get the beginnings of an assignment of the proverb form to the proletariat as its natural locus; Aesop is first mentioned in the 6th century B.C., a traditional source of proverbs as well as of fables. He will come to seem a simple black slave, but Herodotus calls him a *logopoios*, a statement-maker or prose writer, the term which he applies also to his great predecessor in historiography, Hecataeus. This process of assignment downwards, from a secularizing intellectual class to an egalitarian rural proletariat, may be observed in America too, where perhaps the most famous codifier of proverbs is Benjamin Franklin, an urbane secular intellectual of the Enlightenment who at once imagined and foretold the social destiny of his aphorisms in farmers' almanacs and the like by casting them in just that form, *Poor Richard's Almanac*. The almanac itself as a form derives not from a nascent agricultural society; it is an adaptation as literacy developed of the Neolithic attention to the calendar, and even the *Works and Days* of Hesiod, which incorporates some proverbs, incorporates other material than just weather saws. We see the process accelerated as the sayings of a military intellectual, Chairman Mao, are force-fed to a urban and rural proletariat.

It is significant that the very proverb which expresses an almost theological justification for egalitarianism, *Vox Populi Vox Dei*, occurs first in a letter of 798 A.D. from an intellectual (Alcuin) to a bureaucratic-imperial king (Charlemagne).[6]

Characteristically, the proverb, at its origin, redirects wisdom in an increasingly secular direction. The Wisdom of Ptah-hotep is much less god-centered than typical Old Kingdom hieroglyphic texts, and the same is true of the Sumerian proverbs. Confucius has virtually no theological references, and "Theognis" tends to replace gods with abstractions. The *Analects* recommend *Chung Hsing*, "Middle conduct." As Pound renders it, (p. 163) "The master man's axis does not wobble. The man of true breed finds this center in season." Even Proverbs, though deeply pious, mentions the divine name somewhat less often than other parts of the Old Testament. For Heraclitus the proverb was an instrument for prying human thought away from a total dependence on myth. During the Renaissance an efflorescence of collecting and employing proverbs accompanied a questioning and redefinition of the religious orientation. We have the *Adagia* of Erasmus, the proverb-adaptation of Montaigne and Rabelais, such documents as Heywood's *Dialogue of Proverbs*, and the very elaborate use of the proverb by Shakespeare, Nashe, and many others in the sixteenth and seventeenth centuries as catalogued in Tilley's large collection. I have quoted Bacon's appreciation of the proverb. In this light Chaucer's penchant for the proverb can be connected to his skepticism more easily than to pseudo-folksiness on his part. The same may be said of another late medieval intellectual, François Villon, and his work, particularly the *Ballade des Proverbes*. And indeed the popular locus imagined for the proverb may be taken as a social projection of this impulse to secularization rather than as the actual history of the form. It is significant that the Spanish Jesuit Gracian, who wrote proverblike aphoristic texts, was in constant and grave trouble with his superiors. Scorn and irony (*melitsah*) are coupled with proverbs in the Bible. The impulse to satiric redefinition in the formulation of the proverb is still recognizable, though mutated, in Flaubert's *Dictionnaire des idées reçus*, as of course it is in the aesthetic aphorisms of La Rochefoucauld, Vauvenargues, Chamfort, and Joubert.

2.

This process of increasing secularization, which the emergence of the proverb as a genre exemplifies, does not betoken social abandonment of that irreducible unknown which myth renders in coordinated story form. Rather it involves a transposition of the force of that unknown into other areas. Proverbs come characteristically late in a scriptural tradition, the Wisdom literature being the latest part of the Old Testament canon and "Theognis" markedly later than Homer.

Since our picture of the oral cultures of remote antiquity is necessarily only a conjectural reconstruction, it is distinctly possible that the proverb form did originate in a lower class, to be taken up and adapted by a Homer, then detached for more demarcated attention, and finally reassimilated into the mainstream of spoken language where we now find it. Whatever historical sequence we assign to these steps, the function of the proverb, with its emphasis on the individual's calculation of prudential behavior, finally makes accessible to the folk a kind of leverage in this literary form that carries some of the force of more complex literary artifacts. The impulse underlying the proverb may result in works of a more elaborate sort. The odes of Horace are an amplification of *Ne quid nimis*, "Nothing to excess." The attention can be directed to secular areas without any detachment from the transcendent or abstracted religion of the culture, as in "Theognis." Indeed, the proverb can be taken to substantiate a religious orientation, as it does in Proverbs and the Analects of Confucius.

Proverbs tend to be as free of metaphor as they are of myths (Taylor, p. 69). The metaphor in a proverb retains none of the force, the quasi-mythic force, which our Romantic-participative theories account it the most powerful function of metaphor to convey. *A stitch in times saves nine* merely classifies activities as being prudential. *All is not gold that glitters* includes pinchbeck as well as the con man, *Fish or cut bait* can also apply to fishing. "Stitch," in other words, can serve as instantiating tenor while it is mainly a classifying vehicle, the homely side of the proverb. It enjoins upon the statesman taking precautions, say, a wisdom not different from that of the housewife mending a seam. The force of the comparison works as a classifying leveller, and also perhaps as a kind of reassurance: at no level of complexity in the decision process are the principles not reducible to those on which a seamstress might operate. There is, in this light, a strong emphasis on the adequacy of natural logic, which the proverb's reduction of even Homer's use of figurative language may be taken negatively to reinforce. Overtones are not needed for the metaphor in proverbs, where they serve only as a logical tool. Differences resolve into possible identities sorted out by natural logic; the seamstress operates as does the statesman even though a general relativism obtains: *One man's meat is another man's poison* (a proverb which also finds a parallel as early as the Sumerian).[7]

The proverb is literary, however, in form as well as in the time of its historical origins. Figurative language is found in proverbs as early as the Sumerian (Gordon, p. 187), and as the Wisdom of Ptah-hotep, *Good speech is more hidden than the emerald, but it may be found with maidservants at the grindstones.* This saying, attributed to a courtier, announces as its principle the double function that the proverb embodies, homely in its social focus while serving as a powerful and inobvious formulation of principle. As Erasmus said (Phillips, p. 6), *Proverbia est sermo manifestam obscuritate tegens.* "A proverb is a saying that covers the obvious with an obscurity."

The proverb of Ptah-hotep is literary not only in its use of figurative language, a simile in this instance, but also in its antithetical form, a form Driver finds characteristic of proverbs and Taylor of the folk tradition generally. Antithesis is both a logical tool, applying the law of contradiction, and a rhetorical one, balancing the members of an utterance: *All is not gold that glitters, Fish or cut bait. Street angel, house devil,* in the most rudimentary possible form for its double antithesis, uses otherworldly categories, without either affirming or denying them, merely to link the social and the psychological in a coordination that enunciates a type without asking about the ambivalence behind the type. *Young saint, old devil* deploys the psychological and the social on the time-line of a type of life course.

The proverb, even in Sumerian,[8] tends to harness the most rudimentary of literary forms, the sound-recursions of poetry. It deploys the axis of selection upon the axis of combination, to use Jakobson's terms, so that our category *prose* cannot apply to it; nor will our category *poetry* work in all instances either. The form is so elementary as to resist the subordination of such classification. *All is not gold that glitters* transposes across its one noun and its terminal verb, a recursion of $g + l +$ the dental. At the same time it suggests, in its phonetic differences, a logical difference underlying a seeming similarity, between *gold* and *glitters*. The same process happens in *Many a mickle makes a muckle,* *muckle* performing a kind of phantom or nonce-ablaut change upon *mickle*, creating a mock grammar in which *muckle* serves as a sort of intensive for *mickle*. Thus we are given three words for "many," beginning with the word in natural language, *many*, shifting to the homely-archaic *mickle* and then to the ablaut variant *muckle*. Echoing the m + vowel + k series, the one verb, *makes*, transposes and preserves the similarity. As it happens, this proverb eroded into its present form; the 1599 version listed in the NED is *Many a pickle makes a mickle*. It is as though the individual proverb sought out a form of maximum expressive economy in its evolution.[9]

This simplest of literary forms, typifying social experience without recourse to myth or elaborate sequences, raises few of the linguistic problems that fuller forms do: the utterance need not be deviant, and its metaphors tend to be not only reductive in force but kept carefully within the selection classes for natural language. *He is a lion* crosses +human and —human, but *Better a living dog than a dead lion* violates no selection classes in its grammar, even though in logic it makes the same comparison. If dogs and lions are logically included in the assertion that this utterance makes, they would not be included in its illocutionary aim, which is wholly at human beings. The metaphoric framing of the proverb draws on the subsidiary differences between the items compared (cowardice of man to dog, courage of man to lion) only for rhetorical force: the hearer's effort to spell out the analogy and the likeness exhausts this force, whereas in poetic metaphors the differences between the items of likeness induce the hearer to dwell on the myth-suggestive, charged ground that the differences and the likenesses taken together activate. Pindar's "gold is a blazing fire," or Keats's addressing an urn as "Thou still unravished bride of quietness," by naming these disjunct objects, create a ground on which they may interact, in thought. A pale, precious substance that is a stable metal and a flashing, unstable, ravaging source of heat, or a timeless, shapely art object and a human sexuality envisioned in time—these somehow coexist and have their contradictions interact.

In a proverb the contradictions are assigned to the illocutionary force, and they do not operate at all on the level of proposition or assertion of a proposition, though the whole proverb must offer both of these. Even if the logic of *Once a thief always a thief* may be figured differently from that of *A leopard cannot change his spots*, the illocutionary application would be the same to a thief in the dock, and the kind of experience being classified is the same. The analogy to the leopard is only a mode of coordinating the human experience, and the superior force of the metaphoric formulation over the unmetaphoric one here does not extend to include leopards in its range of sense as Pindar's extends gold to include fire and Keats the urn to include sexuality. In the proverb the metaphor serves merely as a trenchant inducement to apply the rule it phrases.

The proverb gains force from the use of such elementary literary strategies, which it superadds to the normal rules of language. Another of these strategies is that of detachment or abruptness: wisdom propounded in a normal, running discourse ceases to be proverbial. The proverb's very succinctness, as well as its tendency to typify experience, gives it the force of rule. The early laws of many civilizations can be distinguished from proverbs only by their specificity. Solon and Solomon, legendary repositories of wisdom, are sources of good laws, good judgments, and good proverbs, all at the same time. There is a large body of legal proverbs (Taylor, pp. 86ff, with bibliography); some of these still have moral validity, *Two wrongs don't make a right*, or legal validity itself, *Finders keepers, Ignorance of the law is no excuse, Testis unus, testis nullus.*

This last proverb, that one witness is no witness, comes into use in the New Testament, where the context of the proverb is enlarged. For the proverb has a kind of roughness that makes it mainly useful only as a rule of thumb, a roughness derivable from the open-endedness and complexity of the experience it addresses. Law deals with the past, with deeds actually performed, whereas the proverb typifies the past in order to apply it to the future.[10] The proverb is purposive and potentially illocutionary; it does not make a promise but indicates something of the condition under which a promise to the self might be fulfilled: *Many a mickle makes a muckle, A stitch in time saves nine.* Its illocutionary locus lies between promise and warning. In this light the proverb, detached from the mythical formulations of the spiritual life as its first dialectical step, in a second dialectical step reassimilates the spiritual life in many aspects.

The multiplicity of aspect appears in the many terms attributed to proverbs in the first four verses of Proverbs: *chokmah* (wisdom), *musar* (discipline, chastisement), *binah* (sight, perception), *tsedek* (righteousness), *mishpat* (judgment), *mesharim* (straightness, equity), *daat* (knowledge), *mizmah* (plan, purpose), *tahbuloth* (guidance, steering). Theognis vaguely recommends the prideful (*orgen*) adaptability of the octopus (West 215–16), but at the same time he is constantly urging a discrimination between good and bad, in a social world where property is a factor, *Many a mickle makes a muckle.* His term *chremata*, meaning "goods" or "money" indifferently, operates in an instability between concrete and abstract that evokes the alertness of the prudence for which the aphorisms stand (186, 189, 226–35, and *passim*). The stance is not so different in its essential typification of experience, caution against unawareness, and future orientation, from that of the Nietzsche (1867) who early in his career commented on Theognis. Plato also quotes Theognis, and both Plato and Aristotle tend to use poetry generally as a kind of proverb-mine. Aristotle (*Rhetoric* 3.17, 1418a 21) characterizes Epimenides as one who "did not prophesy about things to come but about things that had already happened and were inobvious." The proverb, according to the aphorism of Ptah-hotep quoted above, offers emeralds that are hidden. The proverb is cryptic, too, according to Proverbs: "to understand a proverb and the interpretation" (1:6), "*le havin mashal u melitsah*," "to perceive at once a likeness (*mashal*) and its obliquity" (*melitsah*, from a root *layits*, to scorn, to turn aside, or to be ironic).

The very discreteness of the proverb lends it power, a discreteness from any validating numinous source, though it may stand loosely, and generally, under the sanction of canonicity. *Know thyself* and *Nothing to excess* are only incidentally, so to speak, derived from Apollo, since the content remains without that divine sanction. And so does the other discreteness, the curtness of the proverb, its access from a neutral context of staple wisdom into another context of linguistic interchange free and clear of other connections than those the hearer will make. Its discreteness from a flow of discourse constitutes a challenge to interpret and apply it properly. *Faint heart never won fair maiden* would not be said to a eunuch. The proverb envisages not any specific situation but the specific situation *sui generis*, a staple form whose applicability to a staple situation is an implicit invitation to act upon the situation. *Many a mickle makes a muckle* would be an infelicitous remark to make to a Rockefeller, whose situation needs no change in that regard. *House angel, street devil* is a warning not to be deceived by a particular kind of person.

Since the proverb summarizes the past in order to apply it to the immediate future, while itself detached from the temporal flow of other discourse, it embodies attitudes towards social time, attitudes often expressed in proverbs: *Seize the day, Festina lente, Haste makes waste, Don't put off till tomorrow what you can do today, Time brings all things to light.*

The view of time in such proverbs is non-cyclic, though if weather saws be reckoned proverbs, the genre does include calculations about cyclic time. Proverbs that refer to nature, in Gottschalk's vast and richly detailed classification, almost all rest on individual observations of wind and water and cloud, earth, tree and bird, without combination into seasonal patterns. Even *One swallow does not make a spring* (p. 222), often given a social direction, is more cautionary than it is coordinating. The social proverb itself, however, bases its calculations on a recursive but single pattern of events: the proverb stipulates the underlying pattern. So its aim is awareness, not propitiation: philosophy, not ritual, even in weather saws.

The awareness in proverbs easily becomes metalinguistic, language about language. So, again, the "good speech is more hidden than the emerald" of Ptah-hotep. *Pro-verb*, *Sprichwort*, and *Poslovitsa*, all name a verbal element in the term for the form. *He that refraineth his lips is wise* (Proverbs 10:19). *The words of a man's mouth are as deep waters* (18:4). *Speech is silver, silence is golden. Actions speak louder than words. A soft answer turneth away wrath. A word spoken is past recalling. Many a truth is spoken in jest. Into a shut mouth flies fly not. Children and fools speak the truth.*

These last two proverbs set out felicity conditions for utterance, or rather they imply a principle for felicity conditions.[11] The speaker should know when to speak, or even a sharp utterance, a proverb, will lose its point. *As a thorn goeth up into the hand of a drunkard, so is a proverb* [*mashal*, KJ "parable"] *in the mouth of fools* (Proverbs 26:9).

The sufficient conditions for the production of a proverb would include some detachment from the stipulations and explanations of myth, as well as an attention to patterns in experience. This is already close to enough linguistic leverage to produce philosophy as a form, and Heraclitus turned the form to just that usage. Wittgenstein's "Of that whereof man cannot speak, thereof he must be silent" differs only in the specificity of its application from the prescriptions of the speech proverbs quoted above. Blake's *One law for the lion and the Ox is oppression* and *Energy is eternal delight* retain the proverbial form, and delight in it. They are in fact called proverbs by their author, though they tip the balance towards the future and away from the past rather more heavily than proverbs that become anonymous do.

In its implied reformulation of old experience and its illocutionary call for application to new experience, the proverb provides for a recreation of social matrices. It thereby serves as a sort of sub-Hegelian agent to use the old forms of society in order to move them into new paths. Proverbs are lying ready to hand, so to speak, in the flow of Homer's narrative, ready to be detached in the separate form that will help transform the society that produced the Homeric poems. Indeed, poetry when it appears in society as a form contains the power to generate proverbs as part of its recreation of experience. Bartlett's quotations became familiar by being read, then passed by word of mouth, then reprinted. There is no way of telling if the proverblike expressions in Homer differ from the other expressions in their relation to his tradition. In this distich from the *Songs of the South* (Hawkes, p. 78) to evoke the distant early Chinese culture, who could tell whether the poet has invented or inherited a proverblike contrast? "Fish by their thatch of scales are told apart;/But the dragon hides in the dark his patterned brightness." Proverbs can even pass among a people wordlessly, as they do among the Ashanti in the form of traders' weights. A bird caught in a trap signifies "It is the trapped bird who sings sweetly," and just a figure of a porcupine indicates "Do not rub bottoms with a porcupine." If proverbs are not detached, they lie along the flow of a narrative or are buried in the categories of a code, like all the many Indian proverbs collected by Böthlingk. Indian philosophy never detached the proverb, and was also never able to detach itself from myth.

Once detached, the proverb can reenter the stream, as an element for dramatic interchange: Sophocles and Shakespeare are both full of proverbs. Heywood's *A Dialogue of Proverbs* orders strings of them into a narrative illustrating two unhappy marriages. Cervantes creates and sets loose a kind of proverb-machine, Sancho Panza, to test appearances in experience, including the seeming contradictions in proverbs that are antithetical to one another. Gracian expands the proverb into a short discourse somewhat more pointed than the *Epistulae* of Seneca. The *Pensées* of Pascal are suspended as both fragments of an unfinished treatise and whole proverblike utterances.

A non-mythic story may be devised to illustrate a proverb, thus producing a parable, which in turn can generate new proverbs. This is a process observable in fiction as the genre develops: Proust contains many more maxims than Stendhal. Verga, a conscious imitator of Flaubert, buoys up the *erlebte Rede* or *style indirect libre* of his narrative by proverblike utterances that on inspection often turn out to be quasi-proverbs rather than common saws. Indeed, in one sense fiction never gets beyond a vast amplification of the proverb: *Plus ça change plus ç'est la même chose* summarizes *Finnegans Wake*. In line with the proverb's attention to time, the operation of involuntary memory in *A la Recherche du temps perdu* can be taken as an expanded illustration of *Festina lente*.

The writer of fiction, however, has not just amplified the proverb with illustration. He has countered it with a large, internal access to an emotional world; that is, he has reimported into the deduction of behavioral norms something beneath or beyond those norms: the myth. Proust philosophically extends the depth-nuances of behavior: Joyce, setting up a typifying pattern for behavior at the border between waking and sleeping, life and death, radically destructures language ("the abnihilisation of the etym").[12] In fiction the proverb, which had begun by separating from myth, reunites with it, once the concerns of myth had been transposed into other modalities of language.

8.
THE SELF-ENCLOSURE
OF THE RIDDLE

1.

MYTH is an answer to a question we do not have, riddle a question to which we do not have the answer. This opposition of Jolles' gives the key to the relationship between the large form of narrative or thought, myth, and the concise form of posed problem, riddle. In the myth there lurks an unresolvable unknown. A riddle takes an unknown to which there is usually a lexical answer and foregrounds the fact that it is an unknown by phrasing it in such a way that the answer must be deciphered. The answer, in other words, has been removed quite far from the reference of the scrambled lexical items, in the question: a hearer must attend to the sense of the individual words and from them piece together a reference, the answer.

The riddle presupposes linguistic interchange, an effort on the part of the hearer to run these integers of sense into a sum of reference. Once solved, it stands like a hurdle for the next hearer.[1] Ordinary language, and the narration of a myth, do nothing like this. They are supposed to smooth a path, not offer hurdles. The solution-machine of the riddle is an implied metalinguistic instrument: it advertises its own temporary insolubility, thereby turning the hearer back to scrutinize its units instead of bringing him on ahead to more language.

The riddle is constructed as a dialogue either actually or in its rephrasable form. In this it is unlike the proverb, which is aimed at a hearer who will take it to heart for prudential application, and which needs no reply. The dialogue of the riddle is self-contained, without any necessary illocutionary force, and without conditions or context derivable from the form of the utterance itself—a freedom from context which itself constitutes a mode of relation to a context. Once a riddle has been solved, its work has been done, and the nature of the work sheds light on the reversal of the solution. The riddle, unlike the weather saw, characteris-

tically does not school anyone in the properties of fire or wind or egg
or needle or horse—to state some common riddle answers. It spends
itself in concealing under diversionary language the known features of
the entities that solve it. As a riddle whose solution is, metalinguistically,
"riddle" says, "When first I appear I seem mysterious/But when I am
explained I am nothing serious." (Taylor, no. 100, p. 40). The riddle
sets up a community of play, between two or among a few people, for
gratuitous linguistic pleasure.

If a riddle has a point, it is then a proverb, like this one from Proverbs:

> There be three things which are too wonderful for me,
> Yea, four which I know not:
> The way of an eagle in the air;
> The way of a serpent upon a rock;
> The way of a ship in the midst of the sea;
> And the way of a man with a maid.
>
> (30:18–19)

As a riddle this conforms to Taylor's tripartite type (pp. 50–54).
Actually this diverges rather widely from the riddle form by naming its
difficulty (*niphl'u*= "are difficult," "too wonderful for me") when riddles usually leave their difficulties unstated, simply building them in.
And the rest of it is not so much a finished riddle as materials for some
alternate riddles on the invisibility of sexual sympathy in its progress.
"The way of a man with a maid" would be the tenor-solution to a riddle whose vehicle could be the moving eagle or serpent or ship.

The riddle element in this utterance is exhausted with the solution.
The element that constitutes a warning about sexual behavior, a recurrent subject for its immediate context, makes it also a proverb, and we
can here neatly separate the proverb function from the riddle function,
though the two forms can either coexist or alternate for the same tenor
and vehicle (Maranda, p. 223).

The mythemes of a myth-story are independent of any particular linguistic formulation; their coordination, according to Lévi-Strauss, functions as what may be called a parallel language, a metalanguage. In
proverbs the actual words and their order are essential; the proverb is
a small, economical literary form. Now the riddle shares features of both
myth and proverb. Like the myth, it accommodates a very wide variety
of possibilities for its vehicle. The answer *fire* will serve as the tenor for
a number of verbal vehicles:

What is it even though it's locked in can get out? (Taylor, no. 112)

What is it that you can feed, but can't give water? (235)

What eats everything? (260–65.7)

What is without bones yet walks? (264.11)

Little cow crummy,
She sits in her stall,
Give her little or much,
She'll eat it up all.
Give her water, she'll die,
Give her butter, she'll fly. (399b)

The person one dresses in the evening and undresses in the morning (587)

What is it that shineth bright all day,
and at night is raked up in its own dirt? (786)

These are not variants of the same riddle, since the vehicle is important for the content. The drama of the riddle is as important as the answer. On the other hand, *Look to the ant, thou sluggard* and *Many a mickle makes a muckle*, convey the same message and have a comparable illocutionary force. But with a riddle one can get many vehicles for the same tenor, as in the fire riddles above; and it is also possible to have many different tenors for the same vehicle: "He eats with his belly and voids through his back," or a similar phrasing, has many solutions in the examples Taylor collects (no. 240): a saw, a plane, an adze, a mill, a chaffcutter, a cotton-jenny, a sieve, a weir, a pot, a pump, a chimney, a bag, a lamp, and a gun.

The answer in the riddle dialogue is always short; it is usually a noun or noun-phrase. The question, however, admits of a range of rhetorical and poetic working, from the bare statement of some of the fire riddles quoted above through the antitheses of most of them to the six-line rhyming poem of one. Early riddles are often poems with the answers sometimes unstated, like the Anglo-Saxon riddle poems or the riddles of T'ien Wen, "The Heavenly Questions," (Hawkes, pp. 45ff).

Between the answer and the question, then, is a formal divergence of stylistic range, as well as the necessary divergence between puzzling vehicles and solving tenor.

In the figure of a myth, or in a poetic symbol, such divergences are packed into the term, the "Apollo" of the Greeks or the "rose" of Blake. It is in this sense that Hegel can say "the genuine symbol is *in itself* a riddle" (*Aesthetik* I, 385, italics Hegel's). In an actual riddle the question-and-answer form breaks up the complexity of the symbol into a divergence that is preserved as a dramatic interchange while it is lost as a significative unit. The fire in the fire riddles above is a simple lexical unit. It has none of the force of Pindar's "gold is a blazing fire," or T.S. Eliot's "consumed by either fire or fire." As Hegel goes on to say, in a riddle the significance is clear and complete for the solver. In Maranda's analysis (p. 229 and *passim*) the divergence between the terms of the vehicle-question and the term of the tenor-answer may express a union of two sets, as in the "metaphor" riddle, or it may express the intersection of two sets, as in the "paradox" riddle.[2] Either way, the divergence is maintained, and clues from the semantic field of the tenor are carefully excluded from the vehicle: "What can engulf a whole forest in its burning?" is a question about fire, but it could not be a riddle. The word *burning* would have first to be taken away.

The function of paradox in a riddle is often not to evoke a deep contradictoriness in existence, as can happen in other poetry, though stretches of poetry turned to riddle-use may possess such overtones, in Brian Caraher's analysis of Anglo-Saxon riddles. Then we would be justified in separating off the "riddle element" from the "poetry element," just as we did for the "riddle element" and the "proverb element" in "the way of a man with a maid" quoted above, or more complexly in the aphorisms of Heraclitus. Antitheses in riddles point up the seeming impossibility of solution. In the vehicle an antithesis is absolute. In the tenor it disappears.

"Big as a barn, light as a feather, and sixty horses can't pull it" (Taylor, no. 1260). "Big" would seem to be the antithesis of "light," and absolutely. There is no visible substance of which a barn-sized piece would weigh no more than a feather. And to reinforce that deduction we are told that "sixty horses can't pull it," which would seem to denote "very heavy." But when the answer, "the shadow of a barn" tells us that we are dealing with shadow, not substance, the antitheses disappear. Checking back on the question of the vehicle, we see that our assumption of "substance," which the reference to size and weight seemed to entail, was not justified. When a riddle is solved, the antitheses disappear; in a poem they remain and resonate hauntingly. "It goes all over the mountain on its head, and it sleeps on its head" (no. 187a) proposes activities that stand in antithesis to our assumptions of the uses of a head. To be on the head is to be inverted, and so unable either to walk or to sleep. Here a lexical trick gives the solution, "a horseshoe nail," and we are at a listing in the lexicon for "head" which reads "—animate," "the top of an object," rather than "+animate," "the top of a person or an animal." The top has indeed been inverted, because usually the head of a nail faces out or up, not down, though a horseshoe nail is one of the less frequent cases where it does face down, like the nail in a boot (188c), also the subject of a few such riddles.

Knowing the answer includes the hearer in the speaker's group. The dialogue structure of the riddle is that of an initiation, but an intellectual initiation. The answer to a riddle is usually a single noun, or a simple combination of nouns. And only rarely is the noun an abstraction. Usually it is an object, a pin or a bell or a clock, or a horse, snow or rain or the sun.

The answers fix and nominalize their objects, constituting an act of simplification upon the question. They not only solve the question, they reduce it to a simpler form. An egg is a favorite answer for riddles, but it rarely occurs in the question (Taylor, p. 5). "A head but no hair" becomes a pin or a bell or a clock (Taylor, p. 10). Riddles of motion also resolve to visible objects—fire (no. 112), shadow (113), river (114), tide (115), the sea. Heraclitus may turn the road antithesis (122a–122b) to philosophical usage; its riddle form simply turns "what goes up and down and never moves" into something you see outside your door and can name with a single noun.

By avoiding cyclic processes and hieratic entities—there are few riddles the answer to which is the name of a god or a mythological being— the riddle, though arising in a religious society and sometimes with the question steeped in religious feeling, as in some Anglo-Saxon riddles, performs an act of desacralization by transferring the complexity of the question to the simplicity of an answer lacking a myth-charge. Using analogy, it escapes the theological problems of analogy which condition a religious language (St. Thomas, Ross).

The very form of the riddle implies that fire is mythless and salt a simple item on the table. The scrambled question takes the awe surrounding Promethean fire or Biblical salt and intellectualizes it by coding it into a doubt that the answer then resolves. Instead of explaining Apollo, so to speak, the riddling process puts the speaker, or the hearer,

in the position of Apollo, as Lucian (*Vita Auct* 14.554) says of Heraclitus and his riddling.[3] Often the direction from question to answer
and vehicle to tenor is from nature to culture, as though to domesticate
the visible universe: a pig is a pipe (Taylor, no. 383) or a needle (386)
or a grist mill (387); a bull is a pot (395) or a forge (401); and a cow
is a mowing machine (400b and c). Even when the direction is from
culture to nature, the two are on a simple par without the complex interaction that myth mediates between nature and culture in Lévi-Strauss's
analyses, as:

> She washed her hands in water
> Which neither fell nor run;
> She dried her hands on a towel
> Which was neither woven nor spun.
>   (Taylor 1104b),

to which the answer is "dew and sun." The same explanatory equality
obtains when the direction is nature to nature, as "Down in the meadows
there was a red heifer, Give her hay she would eat it, Give her water
she would die" (399), to which the answer is "fire," and the zoological
puzzle about dietary habits is reassuringly resolved.

And the same holds true for the fourth possibility, a vehicle-tenor
transfer from culture to culture:

> I have a little house,
> And it wouldn't hold a mouse.
> There's as many windows in it
> As in the king's whole house. (1263b)

The answer, "a thimble," in its particular form and cultural utility offers
an answer already coded into the *langue* for the antithesis between a
tiny house and its many apertures.

A kenning is a sort of one-word riddle. *Hronrad*, "whale-path," is a
kenning for *sea*; the Biblical wonder about whales is certainly not increased by the kenning, nor is the awe about these cold and treacherous northern seas, so different from the Mediterranean. The kenning,
like the riddle, fixes in sub-formulaic stability an analysis that has the
effect of desacralizing what is referred to, whereas we are used to reading back into kenning the contrary procedure, the sacralization of the
charged poetic metaphor.[4] To call the sea a whale-*path* is to say that a

treacherous course upon it has as fixed a direction and as stable a ground as an already beaten track on land, while to call it a *whale*-path is to posit an analogy between man and whale with respect to movement rather than to stand in awe at the difference.

Taken synchronically, the riddle is not charged in its form and does not refer to a charged context. Taken diachronically, it is conceived of as arising in a charged context, the death-test. The fact that Oedipus saved his life by answering the Sphinx's riddle occurs in the tradition much earlier than the quoted forms of the riddle,[5] what the actual riddle was. In the earliest version (Robert, p. 56) the Sphinx was overcome by force, not by a riddle. And as riddles emerge in Greece, they tend to be associated with oracles, urgent but cryptic sayings, which if misapplied may lead to catastrophe. Taken this way, the riddle and the oracle both differ from the proverb by envisioning the future as a unique happening whose problematic relation to the past is unsolvable.

The relation between future and past in the oracle resembles the relation between answer and question in the riddle.

The riddle's emergence as a death-test occurs in other cultures, too, notably in Germanic culture. In the *Vafthruthnismol* Odin and the Giant Vafthruthnir confront each other simply as a test of wisdom about mythological lore, though in the poem the tension is resolved simply by declaring Odin the wiser, and the death of the gods is mentioned in the questions rather than invoked as a penalty. In the *Fafnismol* Sigurth conquers and slays the dragon Fafnir after a contest of questions. The question-and-answer frame is there, ready to be detached for the specific form of the riddle, and then to be separated from its connection, become inessential through the very process of answering, with the domain of myth.

All these developments take place in societies that are sensitized to the appearance of literacy. Most of the Oedipus material can be traced, or is attributed, to the period between 750 and 450 B.C. when the alphabet was taking shape. In Norse culture the alphabet holds a magic charge of myth: it is in the form of runes, and runes are frequent in the Eddas, in the *Sigrdrifumol*, for example. Brynhild when waking speaks runes to Sigurth (*Gripisspo* 17). Probably contemporaneous with the Anglo-Saxon riddles, the Anglo-Saxon rune poem reverses the riddle, giving an amplified description of an object to be appended to each letter, replacing the magic of the rune with a known object at a time when the magic still clung to the runes. For each letter-rune we get two or three lines appended to a word that begins with the letter, as "ice" for "I":

> Is byp ofercealt, ungemettum slidor, glisnap glaeshluttur
> gimmum gelicust, flor florste geworuht, feager ansyne.

> Ice is very cold, immeasurably slick, glistens glass-clear,
> most like to gems, a floor wrought by frost, fair to see.

According to Eberhard (p. 291), Conrady asserts that the *I Ching* originated as a dictionary of the Chou script. If so, it combines the rune, the oracle, and the puzzling lexical staples of the riddle, all in one.

The death-riddle may be said to condense and encapsulate the whole process of human survival into a single verbal exchange. It lingers on as the attribute of a distant or magical past in fairy-tales; only by a trick can Rumpelstiltskin's name be known. The aura of such magic is imported for dramatic use into *Pericles*, with its death-riddle also involving a kinship short-circuited into incest, and into *The Merchant of Venice*, where the woman who is won by solving a series of choices with riddles like clues, herself then solves a legal dilemma by an antithesis between flesh and blood which it would be possible to rephrase as a riddle.

The whole of *Finnegans Wake* may be analyzed as a giant riddle, which has taken the scrambling of the questions in a riddle and applied it back to the answers, atomically. We do not even know if the scrambled words are answers or questions. The separable questions that it does ask, in the "Triv and Quad" chapter, are just intellectual, catechisms in a scholastic context, though they are framed as riddles. It also mentions runes (279, 19; 479, 34) and quotes some Tantric runes (571). In an advanced technological culture like our own the riddle, too, like the myth, becomes ironic, a self-trivializing mechanism for pure play, like the puzzles of Lewis Carroll and even the part of *Scientific American* edited by Martin Gardner, who has annotated Lewis Carroll, the pure play aspect of scientific calculation. A very far cry from myth indeed is the search for words letter by letter—in denatured runes, as it were— to conform to a given but arresting definition, the crossword puzzle.

Emerging from the charged context of a death test, the riddle as a form celebrating explanation easily accommodates to the pure play of a desacralized society—or to the resacralization of an inner quiet where resacralization and desacralization converge. In this sense the aphorisms of Kafka are not proverbs but post-riddle forms, like "What is the sound of one hand clapping?"—a post-riddle Zen question to which there is no answer but the silence of both hearer and answerer, the silence whose desacralization is felt, by hearing the question, to converge with a re-sacralized sound (sound in oral cultures is sacral); sound and silence become one.

9.
PARABLE

Die Sprache selbst auf dem metaphysischen Unterschied des Sinnlichen und Nichtsinnlichen beruht, insofern die Grundelemente Laut und Schrift auf der einen Bedeutung und Sinn auf der anderen Seite den Bau der Sprache tragen.
—Martin Heidegger, *Unterwegs zur Sprache*

(Speech itself rests on the metaphysical distinction between the sensible and the non-sensible, insofar as sound and writing on the one side and sense and significance on the other side carry the structure of speech.)

1.

A PARABLE, first of all, is a story with a message. The message in a parable must be signified in some special way, because any story whatever, parable or not, contains a message at least to the extent that it has some unconscious content, a trace of mythic substratum. This is true even of the "shaggy dog" story, the story with no other decodable message than the unconscious content. We are a story-telling kind, and our stories cannot be detached from references to the unconscious, hence to that for which myth constitutes either a parallel or an explanation. Stories cannot help being like dreams, as dreams can be recovered only in retelling. Indeed, it may be that there is something of the parable in every story, except those that directly recount myths concerning gods. The birth of Apollo or the birth of Dionysus cannot be taken as a parable; the voyage of Jason or the blinding of Oedipus can.

However, the term *parable* is used in the more restricted sense to apply to stories, usually of a single episode, with a message that pretends to be formulable in a single proverblike sentence, while resisting the closed designations of such formulae. Hebrew *mashal* means "parable" as well as "proverb." If we extend the definition of parable to include pointed stories in general, then fables about beasts are parables; and

234

those with a miraculous component, fairy stories, may contain a more or less prominent element of parable. More than once in the New Testament the parable is described as a sort of puzzle deliberately put into code, aligning the parable with the riddle, another meaning of *mashal*. All these simple literary forms—riddle, proverb, parable, fable—are abstract types that may be combined and intermingled in the actual, connected utterance.

In a riddle the separation in the order of an utterance between its components and its signification has been foregrounded. In a proverb it has been stripped to a form of its message. The reference of both is also apparent; they are answers: it is clear that a fire riddle names fire and that *Haste makes waste* recommends caution. A myth, however, is an answer to a question we do not have; its message about the gods may be clear, but its reference is unclear, waiting to be partially decoded by a Frazer or a Lévi-Strauss. It does not obviously refer exclusively even to those weather patterns whose manipulation by ritual magic it explains. Since the reference of a myth is by definition shrouded in mystery, the order of the elements in it is not subject to manipulation, as in a riddle, nor may its references be put into neat order, as in an allegory, nor may a reformulable exclusive message be derived from the myth (pace Lévi-Strauss), not even a message about the unconscious thought processes for which it can be taken as a sort of rebus. In this sense a myth is both free of narrative sequence and bound to its component elements.

A story whose elements are subject to manipulation becomes possible, again, only in a society that has begun to perform questioning operations upon its myths. Aesop begins beast-fable and the *Panchatantra* comes long after the Vedas and the Upanishads. The parables in the New Testament were a relatively new form.[1] The significance in them pretends to be patent but actually lurks under the story. Fairy stories manage a very special reassignment of mythic elements to stories whose handling of their components resembles that in a parable.

While a myth is free of any context more specific than that of the cultural unit where it occurs, the parable tends to refer to some specific context. The parable of the Prodigal Son implies a specific historical situation where the population of the Diaspora is about eight times that of Palestine itself,[2] and the parable of the sower is based on the practice of sowing a field before plowing, because of the rough terrain. The parable of the Laborers in the Vineyard implies both a labor market and the freedom of a charitable employer to redefine its conditions for

the benefit of late-hired unfortunates. As John P. Brown says of Matthew 22:7 (p. 75), "the royal parables are a fund of suppressed political
comment." The new Christians of the New Testament were subject to
three interlocking administrations, all of them problematic for the nascent group: the Roman Empire, the kingdom of Herod, and the Temple
(Sherwin-White). The Sermon on the Mount applies its aphorisms on
the way to becoming parables to a context where Roman law is operative, but also rabbinical law, and the currents of Gnostic, Essene, Phar-
isee, and Sadducee discussion, are very specifically brought into focus
(W.D. Davies).

The parable centers on a single prominent figure, a son or a steward
or a sower or a householder or a bridegroom. The complexity of its
context entails some disjunction in the reference of the allegorical elements, which must be present in the parable for the story to carry a
message. It announces at once hope for its auditors and a reassurance
that the fear underlying the open order of its significations need not be
finally confusing. The order of the story will redeploy the allegorical elements rather than presenting them in simple abstract sequence, as in the
Faerie Queene or the *Roman de la Rose* or even *Moby-Dick* and *The
Castle*. Order of event, message, unconscious content, allegorical correspondence, general social context, and point-by-point signification are
set by the parable into a vivid and interactive, if simple, relationship,
moral exhortations predominating in early parables and metaphysical
perplexities dominating later ones, Zen or Kafka, though both moral and
metaphysical elements are present in all parables, whatever their proportion.

The parables in the New Testament manipulate still more pointedly
than the narrative context in which they occur the significations and what
stands behind the significations. Here is a parable rather fully qualified
in its immediate context:

> And he spake many things unto them in parables, saying, Behold a
> sower went forth to sow; And when he sowed, some *seeds* fell by
> the wayside, and the fowls came and devoured them up: Some fell
> upon stony places, where they had not much earth: and forthwith
> they sprung up, because they had no deepness of earth: And when
> the sun was up, they were scorched; and because they had no root,
> they withered away. And some fell among thorns; and the thorns
> sprung up, and choked them. But other fell into good ground, and
> brought forth fruit, some a hundredfold, some sixtyfold, some
> thirtyfold. Who hath ears to hear, let him hear. And the disciples

came, and said unto him, Why speakest thou unto them in parables? He answered and said unto them, Because it is given unto you
to know the mysteries of the kingdom of heaven, but to them it is
not given. For whosoever hath, to him shall be given, and he shall
have more abundance: but whosoever hath not, from him shall be
taken away even that which he hath. Therefore speak I to them in
parables: because they seeing see not; and hearing they hear not,
neither do they understand. And in them is fulfilled the prophecy
of Esaias, which saith,

> By hearing ye shall hear, and shall not understand;
> And seeing ye shall see, and shall not perceive.

(Matthew 13:3–14)

Here the immediate story is simple; it differs from allegory only in the
literalness of the vehicle. Nor does the tenor share in the properties of
the vehicle: the sower is only following normal Palestinian procedures
of covering the land randomly with seed (Jeremias, p. 11). The vehicle
is natural processes, the fate of seeds in various growth locations. The
tenor is the spiritual destinies of a human life under various growth conditions. That is the tenor to the seed, and while it holds simply point for
point between seeds actually and human beings metaphorically on stony
ground or scorched by sun and rootless or on good ground, its illocutionary inception is not simple. A little later (13:18–23) the tenor is
interpreted as "hearing the word," and so the seed is seen prominently
as referring to what will later include such parables as the Parable of
the Sower—but not yet. The word is not yet the text; the text is, rather,
a historical account of the live presentation of the word. Christ, indeed,
Jeremias points out, himself has the expression "*logos*" attributed to
him only with reference to parables. This is the "middle" or specific
sense of *logos* here, then, "message of a parable." But there is a weak
sense in which *logos* is not much more than a pronoun covering the reference plus the truth-value of the story told. And there is a strong sense
in which all the Greek philosophical history of *logos* and all the Hebrew religious accumulation of *davar* ("word" and "thing") are con-
jointly operative.

Moreover, "word" is only one tenor, although the main one, for the
vehicle "seed." There are others; the act of hearing the word makes the
hearer also the tenor, though he is, at another angle, a tenor for the
vehicle of the ground, the thorns, etc. And what is being recommended
to the auditors? On the one hand, this discourse to a "multitude in the
shore" (13:2), if it have any bearing of exhortation at all, must recom-

mend that they try not to be on stony ground and try to be in good ground. Yet this is precisely what seeds cannot do. Something like the mystery or problem of predestination—in more modern terms, of *Situation* as Jaspers and Sartre use the term—is at issue. On the one hand a man is like a seed. He grows in certain ground, and his development is conditioned by probabilities. But on the other hand he can aspire; there is a sense in which he can choose his ground. Fusing the two senses together in the parable, the speaker leaves his auditor in what has to be an interdependent and inextricable reliance on faith (because he is conditioned) and on good works (because he is somehow free).

What about the Sower? He can only be analogous to God. In this way he may also be analogous to the Son of God, the preacher of the word. But as a human being, the sower is analogous to the auditors, many of whom in Palestine's agricultural villages of this district will have sown seed in just this fashion. The auditors, then, are distributionally, so to speak, like the seeds, but collectively like the sower. The simple tale, in the order of its presentation, turns its narrative sequence to a fusion and multiplication of significations.

As for the force of myth, that has been wholly redeployed into the secrecy of understanding the tale, and into the context surrounding it. The agricultural cycle now does not generate a vast, correlating set of myth. Instead it serves only as random example, good ground, stony ground, thorns, and the like. While there are many correlations between cyclic myth structures and the Christian story (Rahner and Bultmann), those are not being drawn on here; the dimension in solar myth of God the Father and God the Son are not operative, even though the effect of the sun is mentioned in the instance of scorching and implied in the other instances.

The ordering of events in the parable, just because it must be deciphered to be understood, moves the significations of its message outside the area of myth. The parable does not answer questions with a covering name like Apollo. Rather, in its richness it provides an assurance that enough answers are forthcoming for the initiated to be able to manage. The defining condition becomes not only the message of the story but the context of the story, which includes, crucially, the predisposition of the hearers to understand it, even though the seeming transparency of the message contains displacements of signification. By understanding, they are already on good ground; their act of understanding corresponds to the optimal conditions of the parable, making it a reassurance as well as an exhortation.

"Who hath ears to hear, let him hear." The thrust is illocutionary, an explicit command to be attentive. And the subject of attention is also named, "the mysteries of the kingdom of heaven." These mysteries, again, are not myths, but a congruence at once moral and developmental between natural processes and human processes, then between earth and heaven, at once factoring out and embodying the contrast between the expressible and the inexpressible. The parable activates the double antithesis Davies quotes Albertz and Daube as applying to the Sermon on the Mount, an antithesis between the law and its deeper sense, and then an antithesis between the law and its opposite.[3] Here the subject is not the law, which can be formulated in apophthegms like the Beatitudes in the Sermon on the Mount, but rather natural processes that have a deeper sense if attended to, and that can also be supplemental to their opposite (a seed has no choice; a human being in some sense has).

These hearers are energized, and energized along lines prophesied by Isaiah, here quoted. Those who see and hear (13:26) are distinguished from all others. It is the function of the parable's secret formulation to keep these others from the meaning it would be improper for them to assimilate:

> For this people's heart is waxed gross,
> And *their* ears are dull of hearing,
> And their eyes they have closed;
> Lest at any time they should see with *their* eyes
> And hear with their *ears*
> And should understand with *their* heart
> And should be converted, and I should heal them. (13:15)

The prophet has defined the conditions for hearing the parable, and these have also provided the conditions for framing in a simile or side-case (*parabole*). But hearing the parable takes the hearers beyond the prophets, "For verily I say unto you, That many prophets and righteous *men* have desired to see *those things* which ye see, and have not seen *them*; and to hear *those things* which ye hear, and have not heard *them*." (13:17).

All these conditions are laid out before the interpretation is then offered:

> Hear ye therefore the parable of the sower. When any one heareth
> the work of the kingdom, and understandeth *it* not, then cometh
> the wicked one, and catcheth away that which was sown in his
> heart. That is he which received seed by the wayside. But he that
> received the seed into stony places, the same is he that heareth the
> word, and anon with joy receiveth it; Yet hath he not root in him-
> self, but dureth for a while: for when tribulation or persecution
> ariseth because of the word, by and by he is offended. He also that
> received seed among the thorns is he that heareth the word; and the
> care of this world, and the deceitfulness of riches, choke the word,
> and he becometh unfruitful. But he that received seed into the good
> ground is he that heareth the word, and understandeth *it*; which also
> beareth fruit, and bringeth forth, some a hundredfold, some sixty,
> some thirty. (13:18–23)

The interpretation applies the conditions themselves back to the parable, making it metalinguistic. The hearer is ground as well as seed, and
the determinant of how well growth takes place is in what manner he
assimilates the word, including as a salient and culminating example just
such words as this parable. Other details reinforce the eschatological
context, as the identification of the birds who take away the seed with
"the wicked one" (*poneros*, also "useless"; this is still clearer in Mark
4:15, "Satan," and Luke 8:12, "the devil"). The story form makes the
eschatological, the metalinguistic, the natural, and the human adaptively
interactive, without confining them to the system of correspondences that
the initially simple and allegorylike series of alternatives for the seed
would seem to dictate. If in Umberto Eco's analysis art is always an
open structure that makes reference to other structures that are themselves closed, here art, the literary form of the parable, tries to keep
open the other structures, those in which its auditors live, by allowing
its own structures at once a maximum openness and a kind of maximum
simplicity and a very disappointment about closing the meaning, as re-
inforcements of its illocutionary thrust. As for the structures of the world,
the illocutionary injunction is after all not confined just to this parable;
it includes the whole gospel, and it therefore enjoins the hearer to do
nothing less than to save his soul and to convert the world.

The conditions set forth here are meant to define the context of the
aim of other parables, simply told, the Good Samaritan, the Prodigal
Son, the Unjust Steward, and so on. At their most condensed, the parables shade into aphorisms that converge with the proverb form. "Cast
not your pearls before swine" (Matthew 6:6) realigns the prudence of

the proverb in a spiritual direction; it comes at a moment of the Sermon on the Mount.

The actions of Christ are parablelike, too, as in the Raising of Lazarus or the Driving of the Moneychangers from the Temple. The Gospels themselves contain as part of their narrative form not only history, an account of events that actually happened, but also parable, the story with a moral. When just before his utterance of the parables in Matthew, Christ responds to the Pharisees' request for a sign (*semeion*), he replies to them with what he declares to be a defective sign, since they are improper hearers, of the sort he will shortly define with the parable of the sower:

> An evil and adulterous generation seeketh after a sign; and there shall no sign be given to it, but the sign of the prophet Jonas: For as Jonas was three days and three nights in the whale's belly, so shall the Son of man be three days and three nights in the heart of the earth. The men of Nineveh shall rise in judgment with this generation, and shall condemn it: because they repented at the preaching of Jonas; and, behold, a greater than Jonas is here. (Matthew 12:38–40)

The "sign" of Jonas, with all its typological correlatives to the Old Testament and its myth motifs of a descent into darkness, is not quite a parable; it has yet to take on the order of the story here, which it does have in the book of Jonah, where it constitutes something like parable, a story with a mysterious point.

The richness of the context here, the definition of the "generation," and the function of scripture, have still not taken on the pitch of parable. Later that pitch, once it has been reached, will be raised:

> Except a corn of wheat fall into the ground and die, it abideth alone: but if it die it bringeth forth much fruit. He that loveth his life shall lose it, and he that hateth his life in this world shall keep it unto life eternal. (John 12:24–25)

Here the parable of the sower and the seed has been simplified in several directions. The sower is gone, and the seed holds all its options in one. That one now takes paradoxical form, setting earth and heaven into explicit antithesis. This is spoken just before the Passion, itself the culmination of an overarching parable. Likewise condensed are the parables spoken before the Passion in Matthew, beginning with another derived from the agricultural cycle:

> Now learn a parable of the fig tree; When his branch is yet tender, and putteth forth leaves, ye know that summer is nigh: so likewise ye, when ye shall see all these things, know that it is near, *even* at the doors. Verily I say unto you, This generation shall not pass, till all these things be fulfilled. Heaven and earth shall pass away, but my words shall not pass away. (Matthew 24:32–35)

The cycle is used to indicate the transcendence of the cycle, and the words declare their special character of eschatological permanence.

In the overarching parable-narrative of the Gospels, the separate parables come at culminating points: first after much healing and preaching; then just before the Passion.[4] In context they create an emphasis of contrast in mode and similarity in sense to other forms of Christ's speaking and action. And they come in series; the Fig Tree introduces a series that runs through the Wise and Foolish Servant, the Wise and Foolish Virgins, and the Unjust Steward. Parable is defined at one point as the exclusive—which we may interpret as the most characteristic—form of Christ's utterance, at least at these culminating moments, "Without a parable spake he not unto them" (Matthew 13:34).

Heracles is not the subject of a parable, and none of the heroic stories about him has that status, though he might be drawn on as an exemplum. The hero of myth is locked in separation from men and from gods; whereas parable would seem to require a typological union, and transcendent religious leaders, who redefine myth, make use of parable as a verbal instrument for permuting prudential with spiritual meanings on a time line. Sometimes the leader himself is the center of the story, as the Buddha is for the *Jatakas* and saints for saints' lives. Sometimes he disappears entirely, as in the Zen parables or the tales of the Dervishes.

The parable form, like the riddle and the proverb which can enter into combination with it, begins to emerge as an abstract structure for utterance when an anthropocentric figure calls the myth into question. Job is a questioner, and The Book of Job already begins to look like a parable. Judah Halevi's medieval riddle about the grain of wheat that can only live by dying (Taylor, p. 39) puts that parable into riddle form. The dog in the manger is a parable if it is put in story form, the parable where the analogy is animal rather than vegetable; as a locution it is a proverb, and so catalogued by Erasmus (*Canis in praesepi, Adagia*, I, X, xiii). Solomon's act of judgment with the baby (I Kings 3.16–27) is many things at once—a sort of rebus (since it goes through the psycho-drama partly without words), a riddle which only the true mother can decipher, the raw material for a proverb, a parable, and that longer, looser form of the cautionary story which we know as a unit of historiography when it is declared to correspond to past fact. The story of the Lydian dynasty, in Herodotus, which begins with a man who is forced either to kill the husband of the woman he has seen naked or to die himself, offers a piece of history in parable form complete with appended proverb-moral ("A woman puts off her modesty—or loses her respect (*aidos*)—when she puts off her clothes." Hdt. 1.8). It is an exemplum used to further a large sense of something lurking under the story. Rimbaud, when he adopts the Pool at Bethsaida for a prose poem, presumes that act of healing to be something like a parable; his rhetorical acts form themselves on the assumption of such a substratum.

The parable, being so dependent on a dialectical manipulation of context over against figurative signification, tends at once to resist and to suggest closure, as the New Testament parables so abundantly demonstrate. A salient resistance to closure is a requirement of the form of the Zen parable, and perhaps also for the Chasidic tale. Both the resistance to closure and the necessity for closure are enlisted by Kafka as the central paradox of his parable about parables, where the central word, *Gleichnis*, functions back and forth between a strong sense "parable-story" and a weak sense "likeness-comparison":

> Viele beklagen sich, dass die Worte der Weisen immer wieder nur Gleichnisse seien, aber unverwendbar im täglichen Leben, und nur dieses allein haben wir. Wenn der Weise sagt: "Gehe hinüber," so meint er nicht, dass man auf die andere Seite hinübergehen solle, was man immerhin noch leisten könnte, wenn das Ergebnis des Weges wert wäre, sondern er meint irgendein sagenhaftes Drüben, etwas, das wir nicht kennen, das auch von ihm nicht näher zu bezeichnen ist und das uns also hier gar nichts helfen kann. Alle diese Gleichnisse wollen eigentlich nur sagen, dass das Unfassbare unfassbar ist, und das haben wir gewusst. Aber das, womit wir uns jeden Tag abmühen, sind andere Dinge. Darauf sagte einer: Warum wehrt ihr euch: Würdet ihr den Gleichnissen folgen, dann wäret ihr selbst Gleichnisse geworden und damit schon der täglichen Mühe frei. Ein anderer sagte: Ich wette, dass auch das ein Gleichnis ist. Der erste sagte: Du hast gewonnen. Der zweite sagte: Aber leider nur im Gleichnis. Der erste sagte: nein, in Wirklichkeit, im Gleichnis hast du verloren.

Many complain that the words of the wise are perpetually merely parables and inapplicable to life, which is the only life we have. When the wise man says: "Go over," he does not mean that we should cross to the other side, which we could do anyhow if the result of the way were worth it; he means some fabulous yonder, something unknown to us, something too that he cannot designate more closely, and therefore cannot at all help us here. All these parables really set out to say merely that the incomprehensible is incomprehensible, and we know that already. But what we struggle with every day is something else. About this a man once said: Why do you resist? If you only followed the parables you yourselves would have become parables and with that would be free of all daily cares. Another said: I bet that is also a parable. The first said: You have won. The second said: But unfortunately only in parable. The first said: No, in reality: in parable you have lost.

(Based on the Muir translation.)

2.

When the parable approaches closure, it becomes social and quotidian, losing the supernatural side of the doubly open religious parables. It becomes a beast fable, a story about animals with a proverb appended. And all the sophistication of La Fontaine does not change that fundamental metaphysical and ethical bearing. The onus of his fables, like that of Aesop's, lies in the concluding proverb. There, too, the animal has ceased to be totemic in any way, to be invested with Lévi-Straussian networks of mythic mediation. It is merely a vehicle of analogy. In the fairy tale, however, the wonder of myth is reimported into the parable, and the supernatural element reenters for a reasserted prominence.

The fairy tale or *märchen* only becomes possible—like its scientifistic opposite number, the tale of fantasy in Todorov's analysis—at some sort of intersection between the natural and the supernatural worlds. The fairy story depends on the sense that what happens in it is technically miraculous, superhuman if not supernatural. Even when feats of the hero become easily explicable, it is only Puss-in-Boots or the Little Tailor who is privy to the secret behind the exploit. Both face and overcome giants who are real in the story. For a terrain or a being or a series of exploits to be miraculous, there must be a clear counter-definition of the nonmiraculous. In this epic and fairy tale may differ. The dragon whom Beowulf faces is as real as a band of warriors or as Grendel's mother; Hrothgar may be an historical king. The world in which the

Odyssey appeared, where Circe and Calypso coexist with Penelope and Helen, depends on myth, and it does not provide such a counter-definition. Consequently, though Odysseus' exploits resemble those of a fairy-tale hero, their mode of relation to the unknown, to that which the myth explains, remains crucially different.

The air of the miraculous in a fairy tale is imported for a use which does not require explanation, or separable coordination, but only resourceful mastery. If the protagonist fails, as in "The Juniper Tree," the wonder remains, he is resurrected, and the pattern persists for coping with the randomly unexpected out of an alertness and even a deep generosity. Fairy tales, like parables, which are more directly religious, do provide models for action. As Tolkien says, (p. 77) "The Frog King" is "a queer tale with a plain moral."

In the earliest references to what may have been fairy tales, those in Plato and Aristophanes,[5] they are defined, the way they are later in the Middle Ages, as tales told by old women or nurses to children. Some of Grimm's informants were old women. As for New Testament parables, a special kind of auditor, the child, is required. The special development from the late seventeenth century onwards (Ariès) of stories directed exclusively to children only compartmentalizes this audience of the acculturated.

Old women and children appear also as protagonists in the stories, and important ones. The motif of "the youngest daughter" or "the youngest son" can be translated as "the most childlike"; and the trait of unquestioning generosity recurs in the fairy tales as the key to success at impossible exploits more often than does that of mere martial prowess. To face the old woman carries with it not only the Freudian overtones of facing the Disguised Mother; it implies facing Death itself, the Death Mother of Marie von Franz's attribution. Tolkien stresses this aspect, too, of the eucatastrophic structure of the fairy tale, its yield of joy before the seemingly invincible.

Kindness and generosity, traits highly valued in the Christian and other religious traditions, are at the center of the parable-injunction of the fairy tale. And it is important that the kindness and generosity derive from no merely prudential motive; the yield must be unexpected beforehand and even concealed afterwards, preserving its connection with the world of the miraculous. In this sense, the moral dimension of the fairy tale inverts that of the proverb; someone who relies on *Many a mickle makes a muckle* does not suddenly deplete a small store of

food for a little man met on the path of a strange forest: older brothers
and sisters typically do not.

What will define the fairy tale is the intersection of human mastery-
in-innocence and supernaturally shaded tasks. These seem riddlelike
when faced by the protagonist, and indeed that task sometimes takes
the form of solving a riddle. Solving the riddle, however, is not an end
in itself, but rather the means to some other end, one deeply involving
a joy that may include sexual fulfillment as its natural center and employ sexual imagery in its depictions.

The fairy tale differs from the beast fable because, as in *Der alte Sul-
tan*, the talking animals stand on a miraculous par with the human
beings, for whom in beast fable they are figures. In such a universe of
miracle anything is miraculous, including the charitable and childlike
moral gestures by which the persons come through either to success or
to vindication. The mythical unknown surrounds but does not control
the events, and so the miraculous acts of help performed by animals
have a different effect from comparable events in American Indian
myths. There, once the bear has saved someone's life, that figure becomes a remembered tutelary figure for the entire tribe; the achievement is permanent, and ritualized. But in fairy tale these events, evoked
as the quid-pro-quo for kindliness, do not hold outside the sphere of
the benefited person's life. Only as a personal reward and a personal
achievement does the mythlike even yield its force. "They lived happily
ever after."

The protagonist can die, however, and the moral remains very much
the same. While Little Red Riding Hood is not called upon for acts of
kindness in the tale, the first sentence describes her as "sweet" and
"liked by everyone." Her errand to her grandmother consists of taking
cake and wine to the old woman, who is weak and ill. Though in one
version she is devoured, it is while she is on this succoring errand of
mercy, which she herself characterizes as an act of some restoration for
the grandmother. "I want to make everything right," is what she literally
says as she sets out, "Ich will schon alles gut machen," though in colloquial usage she is merely saying she will obey her mother's order.

The parable element that gives coherence to a fairy story is independent of the actual outcome of a life in it, though on balance it tends to
establish joy against odds. For both "Sleeping Beauty" and "The Juniper
Tree," as for either ending of "Little Red Riding Hood," such a relative
independence of outcome differentiates the fairy story from more so-

phisticated literary genres. Nahum Tate's *King Lear*, ending with the marriage of Edgar and Cordelia, is simply ridiculous. *The Tempest* could not be disappointed of its marriage.

In this attribute, too, the fairy story translates hope and fear into general conditions opening out into specifically justifiable reactions to some natural set of circumstances. Facing hopeless terrors, in all their psychoanalytic complexity, may indeed help to fortify hope, as Bruno Bettelheim urges in his praise of fairy tales. He takes them as illocutionary agents for self-realization. Cinderella has no good reason to hope. But she is close enough to childhood, and open enough to the miraculous, for that not to matter. Or in the apophthegm-phrasing of the New Testament, "Except ye be converted and become as little children, ye shall not enter the kingdom of heaven" (Matthew 18:3). The word "converted" means simply "turn" (*strapheite*). The fairy tale is a parable that at once creates an ambience and provides an injunction for turning.

10.
METAPHOR:
Literature's Access to Myth

The problem of double meaning is not peculiar to psychoanalysis. It is also known to the phenomenology of religion in its constant encounter with those great cosmic symbols of earth, heaven, water, life, trees, and stones; and those strange narratives about the origin and end of things which are the myths are also its daily bread. . . . a particular way in which man places himself in relation to fundamental reality, whatever it may be. . . . the expression of a depth which both shows and hides itself. What psychoanalysis encounters primarily as the distortion of elementary meanings connected with wishes or desires, the phenomenology of religion encounters primarily as the manifestation of a depth or, to use the word immediately, . . . the revelation of the sacred.
  —Paul Ricoeur,
    Freud and Philosophy,
    translated by Denis Savage (revised)

1.

FIRE, water, cloud, sky, sea, earth, stone, oak, grass, air, apple, house, rose, sun, moon, star, wind, mountain—the images largely from the natural world, before they enter into a statement of metaphoric combination, and after they have ceased to belong to the codings of a mythic pantheon, remain to pervade the consciousness, sometimes just when they are merely named. Fire has an underlying psychic set, and so does water, in Bachelard's phenomenology. These images, taken by themselves in the naming, cannot wholly shed their dream life and become univocal references in all uses. In many uses they are multivocal, they are charged. And to call their charge "emotive" is to simplify their effect by giving it a direction, itself univocal, thereby neutralizing the special ambience of fire as opposed to water, oak as opposed to stone. And one would also thereby neutralize the inter-associations. By von Franz's Jungian formulation, "in the unconscious all archetypes are contaminated with one another."[1]

248

These image-charges do not belong in the lexicon, and yet they stand ready to hand for such uses, ritual and poetic, as the language may call upon them for. As Ricoeur says (p. 388), "the mechanisms of dreaming manifest the confusion between the infra- and the supra-linguistic." A semiotic account of what happens just in naming must allow for the mechanisms of dream or archetype or primal image, along with other mechanisms that can be disambiguated—the lexical, the syntactic, the phonetic, and the "encyclopedic" (Levin, quoting Carnap), as well as that in the pragmatic or contextual which does not draw on the image-charge.

In societies still encompassed by their mythic system, the charges in the words are not subject to manipulation: fire is always Agni. Prometheus always endowed men with fire, stealing it from the gods. When the myth becomes questioned, the charges can be manipulated, or even abandoned. Heraclitus' fire doctrine, whatever it may mean, strives to perform abstract manipulations upon the concept of fire; it does not simply interpret the Greek myth-context of fire. Pindar rethinks and draws upon the mythic charge of fire, localizing a salient manifestation of it at the base of a volcano managed by a giant who is resistant to such poetry as he may utter; poetry itself is seen also in the mythic light as a sleep-producing charm derived from Apollo.

A proverb uses a term like fire, metaphorically or not, without any semiotic enlistment of the image-charge. Fire is simply a practical entity with discernible, lexical features, in *There is no smoke without fire, The burnt child dreads the fire,* and *Fire and water are good servants but bad masters.* In the riddles whose answer is fire, the act of building a lexical term into a puzzling question, even if it mimes the wonder that charges a mythic entity, does so in a form that neutralizes the mythic force. Again the image-charge is largely absent. In the semiotic framework of the fairy tales that refer to fire, the image-charge of fire simply endows the context of the story with an air of miracle. A fairy story involving fire, like "The Fire Bird," or "*Das junggeglühte Männlein*" (about a youth restored in a fire bath), really rephrases what is essentially a myth. Otherwise fairy stories are never about fire: they have no Prometheuses, no Ragnaroks. Aschenputtel, Cinderella, named for sleeping in ashes, has access to a magic other than that of fire. In "Hansel and Gretel" the witch is simply pushed into the fire she has had Gretel prepare in the oven for Hansel, and this fire is an image and a utilitarian resource without special status in whatever mythic substratum might be assigned to this story or factored out of it. The fairy story keeps all its images on a par; it tends to be unmetaphoric in its investments of the world with wonder.

Indeed, metaphor itself, in natural language, comes readily into use. As Margalit and Cohen point out, the nonce-metaphor arises in natural language at the same time, roughly, as syntax rules are learned.[2]

In natural language "the existence of a metaphor, like that of a sentence, is a *feature* of *langue*, not of *parole*" (Cohen and Margalit, p. 738). All the analyses of metaphor in terms of species and genus, with Aristotle; or in terms of domains of thought and dominant traits, with Brooke-Rose; or in terms of sortal logic, with Van Dijk; and all characterizations of metaphoric processes as acts of substitution or logical interactions of terms, with Max Black; ultimately describe any metaphor as it stands towards the *langue*. An act of *parole*, however, has both a pragmatic context and an illocutionary thrust. Of *That old man is a baby* we would have to know from context whether we were looking at a childish oldster or a wizened infant to understand the reference, and also to analyze the sense, of the metaphoric expression. And we would want to know why the speaker had used such a strong expression. As Dorothy Mack says of metaphor in natural language, "Deletion enhances the power of the hearer; as the speaker is less explicit, the hearer must be more active" (242). The metaphor in her characterization is a "shortcut" (a dead metaphor) or a "freshcut" (a live or nonce-metaphor).

In literary use, or "poetry," the context includes a complex set of conventions governing the production of such an utterance at all. If the *parole* of a poem, in Jakobson's assignment of components to the speech act, does center on the message, there would still remain the crucial question of what kind of message it might be that would communicate itself by calling attention initially to itself.

Even in ordinary language, metaphor and metonymy, as Lacan interprets them, activate a whole circular process of interaction between Self/self and Other/other: speaker and hearer are a model for the dynamics of psychic action as well as for the logic of transmitting information. A tree or a cloud or the sun can be pointed out in a single designative act, but underneath even this act there lies an act of psychic selection. When the charge accompanying this act is foregrounded into the word, the image-charge of the word is increased. And when the image-charge is manipulated, we are already on the ground that literature has appropriated from myth; a power whose source is ultimately unknown has been harnessed. It will not do, of poetic predications in an act of *parole*, even if logically correct for the *langue*, to classify them as references to a private "possible" world that the hearer is invited to accept through the implied dimension of a deleted "I imagine" at the head of all such statements (Levin). It will not do, first because the reference is to the actual world. "The present king of France is bald" refers only to a possible world, since in the actual world there is no king of France. But in the actual world there is some psychic ground within me to which "Ah, Sun-flower! weary of time" refers; its reference draws on, and its truth-value interprets, that ground. This psychic ground is as much a part of my actual world as a flower that grows in my garden, and the meaning as well as the force of the poem by Blake, as against that of trivial statements about a non-existent king of France, derives from that actuality. The image-charge is enlisted, and it is somehow manipulated by the crossing of selection classes (weary implies +animal as an attribute synonym for *tired* and +human as a particular locution. We say men are *weary,* animals *tired.*) Second, the reference to "possible" worlds will not do (though initially correct) because it ignores the crucial difference between the triviality of "the present king of France is bald" and the force, ultimately illocutionary, of "Ah, Sun-flower! weary of time." One could generate the bare statement through "possible world" classifications and "I imagine" deleted head sentences. But one would not generate the expression; and as Austin said, "the total speech act in the total speech situation is the *only actual* phenomenon which, in the last resort, we are engaged in elucidating" (p. 147). The world that the poet "instantaneously construes" (Levin) is an actual one. When Leontes in *The Winter's Tale* says "I have drunk, and seen the spider," (II, i, 45) comparing the apprehension of imagined adultery to taking poison in a drink with a poisoned spider at the bottom, his syntactically simple statement enlists a complex psychic substructure of hysteria before the female genitalia and acts analogous to breast-feeding (Schwartz), and also a Renaissance context of fraudulent methods to do away with rulers, as an item of a fictive situation (there is no adultery here) within a fictive situation (it is a play), as part of a moment of complex interaction whose ultimate reference is an actual world in which we all live, of love, authority, age, generation, marriage, friendship, parenthood, as well as imbibable liquids and dangerous insects.

Blake's "Ah, Sun-flower" performs a number of interrelated metaphorical operations, including the overall one of analogy and antithesis to a corresponding poem in "The Songs of Innocence," "The Blossom":

Ah, Sun-flower! weary of time,
Who countest the steps of the Sun:
Seeking after that sweet golden clime
Where the travellers journey is done.

Where the Youth pined away with desire,
And the pale Virgin shrouded in snow:
Arise from their graves and aspire,
Where my Sun-flower wishes to go.

The Sun-flower is not just the garden plant, but a kind of hybrid, as its hyphenated name indicates. The goal of its desire involves nothing less than something at once comprising full sexuality and death after a full life, and yet beyond them—since the Youth and the Virgin arise from their graves there.

   2.

There are degrees to the amount of symbolization in the use of an image—the largeness of the significative area to which, say, Blake's "Sun-flower" refers. And there are also degrees to the number of selection classes which are crossed to form a metaphoric expression like "weary sunflower"; much of the discussion of metaphor by linguists from Aristotle on has attended to the logic behind the acts of reclassification that a metaphor may carry. And in addition there are degrees to the presence of an image-charge; the charge is strong or weak, or all-but-absent, as in most cases of metaphor in natural language and in such myth-shedding forms as proverb and riddle.

The degree of symbolization and the degree of selection-class violation can be largely accounted for by attention to the lexical and syntactic components of an utterance. But the degree of image-charge derives mostly from pragmatic context and illocutionary thrust. Even though a high degree of symbolization may accompany a high degree of image-charge, one reinforcing the other, the two are not identical. The image-charge of "I have drunk, and seen the spider" is quite high because of the richness of the context; but the degree of symbolization is quite low.

To say of metaphor that it harnesses the likenesses and the differences between tenor and vehicle in order to set up reverberations between them is to allow of metaphoric syntax some of the same effect that the image-charge, taken by itself, may produce. Metaphor reinforces image-charge just as symbolization and image-charge reinforce each other—in poetry.

And distinct from strength and weakness there is a scale of lightness or heaviness for the image-charge. "Ah, Sun-flower! weary of time" or "O Rose, thou art sick," or "Thou still unravished bride of quietness" are moderately heavy, at least in comparison with the image-charge, still strong, in this nursery rhyme:

> How many miles to Babylon?
> Three score miles and ten.
> Can I get there by candle-light?
> Yes, and back again.
> If your heels are nimble and light,
> You may get there by candle-light.

Like many nursery rhymes, this delights in its own seeming nonsense, and it may be, as the Opies suggest (p. 64), that "Babylon" is a corruption of "Babyland." If "Babylon" refers to the archetypally corrupt city of scripture, its range of symbolization is quite wide however—and quite unchildlike. The poem, in its context of playfulness is addressing, even singing to, a child about something a child could know only as a future—and so the imputed hearer of the poem could only know as a future—Babylon as Babyland but also as Babylon.

" 'Can I get there by candle-light' was a common saying in Elizabethan times," (Opie, p. 64) which makes this expression a dead metaphor, brought into live re-use. For the Biblical reference of "three score and ten" is firmly to a human life span. Taken this way, the nursery rhyme has a central underlying metaphor of space (three score miles and ten) for time (three score years and ten), a strongly charged version of the life-as-a-journey metaphor. The terminus of this journey, however, is not Babylon but the implied Biblical opposite of Babylon, the heavenly Jerusalem. To get to Babylon and back again, metaphorically to live one's life, is to open the earthly city out into a heavenly city. This requires a sort of dexterity ("if your heels are nimble and light") where the prudence that the proverb enjoins and the spiritual readiness that the parable implies are fused. Moreover, the puzzle of a riddle is approximated in the mysteriousness of this nursery-rhyme, and the rhyme is, in fact, well on its way to being a riddle, the answer to which is "human life." There are riddles that take the form of nursery rhymes, like the fire-riddle beginning "little cow crummy," quoted on p. 227.[3]

In this nursery-rhyme the act of symbolization is strong, the meta-

phors cross large selection classes, and the image-charge is strong. Yet
all this richness is lightened by the abstract context of this rhyme, adult-
to-child, and by its illocutionary thrust. It enjoins a spiritual salvation
upon the hearer and reassures him that the whole matter, although mysterious, is rather like taking a candle on a long but delimited trip, skip-
ping the whole way. "Jack be nimble, Jack be quick/Jack jump over
the candlestick," has some of the same force, derived as it is from a
form of fortune telling and from a St. Catherine's Day Festival (Opies,
p. 227)—from which, however, the rhyme has been de-ritualized; it
lightens and attenuates whatever myth-references may have informed
this particular ritual, while retaining the image-charge, precisely as in a
fairy tale. "Jack and Jill," which could derive from loaded Scandinavian
or other myths (*pace* the Opies, p. 226), takes what looks like a sudden
death ("broke his crown") and makes it a minor accident ("old Dame
Dob, who patched his nob"). The lightness and disconnectedness of the
references themselves point to the wonder of a world where such easy
resurrections occur in homely circumstances—something that myths
rarely allow without long and painful initiation, though fairy stories do,
as in "The Juniper Tree" and elsewhere.

Thus the figurative language in literary use offers a particularly salient
case of the dialectic activated between a speaker and a hearer. As Ricoeur puts it, there is necessarily a transcendental reflexion (in Husserl's
terminology) in the hermeneutic act, or else it traps itself in the semantic structure of the symbol. The myths in a tribal culture fix this dialectic
in a closed network, even where the network, under Lévi-Strauss's interpretation, provides a principle for the management of discontinuities
along the nodes of the network. The metaphors in a literary work liberate this dialectic, enabling its components to enter into various relationships—even the relationship of automatic cyclic interreference, which
is the status of the symbols in *Finnegans Wake*. As Lacan has suggested
of this novel (1975, p. 2), the technique of the portmanteau word at
once universalizes and foregrounds the psychic substructure, or "symp-
tome" of language.

3.

The modality of the assertions implied in a poem's use of an image or
metaphor is determined by much more than the selection classes it cuts
across, the strength or weakness of the image, and its relative lightness

or heaviness. A woman is already a complex image even in the voices of silence emitted by the Venus of Willendorf. Ovid performs quasi-ironic manipulations upon his muses or upon Persephone, playing fast and loose with the *locus amoenus* and the lovely denizens who are in some senses at home in it and analogous to it. His "lightness" modulates the kind of devotion his acts of virtuosity call up, though he is still less dialectical than, say, Charles Olson:

> mother-spirit to fuck at noumenon, Vierge
> ouvrante
> > (A Prayer to Our Lady of Good Voyage
> > Sunday November 25th
> > 1962

Here we are offered many areas of statement—the sense of anthropological reconstitution; personal psychic history; Jungian archetype; Christian symbolism; art typology (*vierge ouvrante*) and its blasphemous opposite, erotic readiness; Kantian epistemology; an actual church in Gloucester, Massachusetts, which embodies a stated relationship between the economics of a dangerous voyage and less questioning religious devotion; and the precise diary-entry of a speaking *persona*. All these are put into dialectical interaction so as to call up, to cancel, and to set in angled lines of relationship to other historical-geographical complexes of date, the layered image of the virgin for a short utterance that is defined unironically as a qualified prayer.

In Pound's progression from the cancelling of image-charge in imagism to the deliberate dialectical re-evocation of image-charge in *The Cantos*, the woman already emerges as a central figure whose modality does not admit of simple presentation. There is a strategy of image-circling that is psychologically indistinguishable from the strategy of reconstituting a plenary, numinous universe, the "poetry as a substitute for religion" of many commentators. Open form, in fact, may be characterized as a structural technique for trapping the image-charge at an angle so as not to oversimplify its verbal proportions. The nets of language need this extra dimension to trap the myth. The strategy of omission, of pretending to sap the image of its charge, lends dialectical leverage to the prose of Hemingway and Robbe-Grillet, understandable in its modality only if it be apprehended as the result of a sapping rather than as the simple set of declarative structures to be found on the page.

The same is true of surrealism, wherein the positive openness to free combinations of image interacts with the negative exclusion of logical connection between images to produce an illusion of a homogeneous and plenary dream universe:

> Le papillon philosophique
> Se pose sur l'étoile rose
> Et cela fait une fenêtre de l'enfer
> —André Breton, "Hotel des Étincelles," 117.

Butterfly, star, rose, and window are all drawn from the typology of a modern *locus amoenus*, but the metaphorical connections between them are cancelled by being stretched, while singly the images are evocatively presented—except for the hint that butterflies do land on roses, though rose has been displaced from noun to adjective of color. And all these terms stand on a par with the abstract *philosophique* and the theological *enfer* (a lightly suspended antithesis to the paradisal images of the window).

The strategy here of circling the image by levelling linguistic procedures at once parallels and reverses the philosophy that is haunted by metaphor.[4] In this midnight the sun always shines, and a complex strategy of language opens the door to a simple utopia.

Already in the Renaissance a priest set upon by a problematically liberating eros performs a re-demystification upon his images through rich, self-neutralizing metaphors whose own irony dramatizes their own submissiveness to the robustness of their evocation:

> If they be two, they are two so
> As stiffe twin compasses are two . . .

>   . . . were we not wean'd till then?
> But suck'd on countrey pleasures, childishly?
> Or snorted we in the seaven sleepers den?

To simultaneously evoke and suppress the image is to intensify the gravity of the poem's linguistic act of relationship to myth by paradoxically calling it into question. So Montale decharges and re-fuses his Romantic words (Cook, 3, pp. 31–32). So Pound trains poetic images, a torch and the night, along a flat, pseudo-historiographic discourse that mimes Herodotus, as Olson learns to do from him, in order to reconstitute dialectically a usable version of what Herodotus has replaced:

> So that Tien-tan chose bulls, a thousand
> and covered them with great leather masks, making dragons
>   and bound poignard to their horns
> and tied torches, pitch-smeared, to their tails
> and loosed them by night from ten points
>   (*Canto* LIV, 1–5)[5]

So Valéry and Stevens set their images in the brackets of philosophical discourse, re-abstracting them, neutralizing them, and at the same time liberating them for poetic use. Even Blake's Sun-flower carries, along with its earnestness, some tinge of an art-song re-rendering of what the Metaphysicals and others had toned down and out as a way of recapturing it: the "sublime" of Collins has been intensified by being subjected to what on the surface looks like simplification.

4.

Literature has generated a number of figurative techniques not just for individual statements in poems or stories but for their initial fictions. One of the most persistent is pastoral, the implied comparison of nature, abstracted and idealized to harmonize it in the order of the work, with art or the sort of factitious artfulness that makes the language of a poem itself analogous to highly mannered, courtly speech. Shepherd-as-poet-as-lover and green-landscape-as-world ring changes on each other: this whole literary act, taken globally, highlights artfulness and fiction, glorying in its instrumentality for creating an order in the work. The end-product of pastoral is thus nearly always a kind of accomplished delight, and the varied uses of pastoral deepen only in combination with other rhetorical-semiological structures, with the paradisal vision when comedy enters into the combination (McFarland), with encyclopedizing celebration in the potpourri of forms in *Finnegans Wake*: Anna Livia Plurabelle at the stream includes the pastoral as part of its rhetorical framework.

Pastoral can be described as an allegory, in which there is a one-for-one correspondence between ordered verse spoken by a shepherd and any civilized discourse,[6] as also between the benign landscape and any more complex sphere of human activity. The simplification, redundancy, and boundary crossing of semantic classes are all semiological strategies common to formed literary works; in both pastoral and allegory, one initial conception comprises simplification, redundancy, and boundary crossing.

Allegory, by advertising its discontinuities through persistence, at once appeals to and avoids the image-charge. "O Rose, thou art sick" has a strong, heavy image-charge, and "ring-a-ring-a roses, A pocket full of posies" a strong and light image-charge. The rose of the *Roman de la Rose*, persisting through the work, has an image-charge which is held on a tight rein by the advertised sign-reference of its discontinuity between flower and woman. This is the case, too, for the mystic rose of Dante's *Paradiso*. Its elaborate composition, the tiers upon tiers of the blessed, becomes possible as a communicative act because the initial discontinuity between petals and people is maintained; consequently the fourfold senses can at once be distinguishable and converge, in a fusion which the prose allegorical interpretations of Richard of St. Victor, for example, do not permit (Cook 1966, p. 217–18).

Dante, through his converging structures, including those of sound-recursion, does keep the image-charge alive, whereas allegorical interpretations of classical or Biblical myth refer merely to the abstract patterns which in a literary allegory are a mode of manipulating, rather than translating, the image-charges. Since allegory proceeds by a rather stiff set of one-for-one correspondences, the abstract significances are a potential threat to the image-charges; they may take over entirely, and then we would have Boethius' *Philosophia* instead of Dante's Beatrice. Romantic writers were keenly aware of this threat, Melville and Kafka no less than Goethe and Coleridge, and all wrote allegories in spite of (or rather as a counter-assertion to) their awareness of the threat.

In allegory the one-for-one correspondence generalizes in a uniform set the kinds of correspondence between fictive and real that any literary work must initially embody. Consequently allegory, too, enters as a component, an abstract rhetorical form, into the rhetorical structure of many works not exactly classifiable as allegories: the late plays of Shakespeare, *Finnegans Wake*, and those fairy tales that have as their hero a sort of abstract figure (Lüthi, cited by von Franz). In fact, the "monomyth" pattern of heroic self-realization, which may be seen to underlie any story in some form, from awareness to journey to risk to test to purification, is itself phrasable as an allegory. Typological interpretations of scripture, too, provide an allegorical schema as a means of correlating two points on a time-line of overall narrative, Mary as a version of Eve, Christ as a version of Moses when he is also a version of

David and of Jonah, etc. The future and the past, identified semiologi-
cally, become sacramentalized as versions of each other (Daniélou).

For Dante to take such systematizing procedures and use them in
a comprehensive poem, a whole context of discourse must first stand
ready to hand. He must stand in an anthropological situation of all but
totally shared belief, and the belief would have to have undergone the
most rigorous sort of inspection: universal Catholicism and a developed
scholastic philosophy are contextual preconditions as well as semiological areas of reference in his poems. For Dante's trans-allegorical use of
metaphor, as for all other uses, the act, and the possibility of the act,
that manipulates the image-charge in the free construction of a literary
work, at once testify to, and create some mastery over, the unknown
forces to which the denizens of tribal culture were content to be slaves.
Metaphor is no deviance into mistake, but the sign of a richly asserted
relative freedom.

11.
LANGUAGE AND MYTH

*As a matter of fact, it is what philosophers find on the way
that constitutes the body of philosophy for if the end is ap-
pointed in advance neither logic nor the lack of it can afford
their passage. Jean Wahl wrote to me, saying "I am just now
reading the* Méditations Cartésiennes *by* Husserl. Very dry. But
he affirms that there is an enormous (ungeheueres) *a priori in
our minds, an inexhaustible infinity of a priori. He speaks of
the approach to the unapproachable."*

*This enormous a priori is potentially as poetic a concept as
the idea of the infinity of the world. Jean Wahl spoke, also, of
other things in which you might be interested: of Pascal in a
frightened mood saying* "Le silence de ces espaces infinis m'ef-
fraie," *adding appropriately that in Victor Hugo one might find
echoes of that idea.*
—WALLACE STEVENS,
"A Collect of Philosophy"

*In reality there are more meanings than beings. Allegory of-
fers a statement in which the number of beings is made to equal
the number of meanings, whereupon the natural surplus of
meanings hauntingly invades our sense of the allegory.*
—after LIONEL ABEL (remark in conversation)

1.

PHILOSOPHY, poetry, history—the realization of what these distinguishable areas of statement could be empowered to say had to begin with
the possibility of distinguishing between them, of separating Heraclitus
and Pindar and Herodotus off from Homer. And the separation had to
take place with a transfer of power, not with a loss of power, the power
being that which for the Greeks was invested in myth. Already for Hesiod
the distinction between "true" and "false" is not only qualified but also
connected to a transfer of power, from the Muses to a solitary shepherd
on a mountain.

Hesiod is already many millennia from the "Old Europe" described
by Gimbutas (7000–3500 B.C.), which is in turn not the first stage of

260

Neolithic culture. The relation of myth to language has been changing, we may presume, at least from earliest Neolithic times all the way to the present. The attempt in our times to recover the power of myth in sophisticated literature, the attempt to explain myth as a rational structure, and the attempt to define emotional sequences as following patterns already intuitively and complexly laid down in myth—these attempts may all be related to one another as derived from the post-Industrialization factoring of inexplicable patterns into relation with linguistic structures, myth with language, or religion with art.

In some senses Vico is our Herodotus in this enterprise, Mallarmé[1] our Pindar, and Nietzsche our Heraclitus. Perhaps Lévi-Strauss is our Aristotle and Freud our Plato. The possibilities of such parallelisms are themselves a characteristic language-game of our culture, the Spenglerian version of Vico's attempt to account for the spirit of a culture in terms of its developmental stages.

At any stage of culture a speech act brings into focus, and refers to, the entire context of its performance.[2] Part of the context is the deep motivation of the speaker, which itself carries a dialectic of relation to those inner forces of which he is either unaware, his unconscious, or to which he gives the names that codify them as outer forces of an unknown, the myths. The unknown thus bears upon any statement: or, myth bears upon language. In societies where we can trace the process, as David Dirringer points out (p. 157), the alphabet, a crucial development for formulating written language, follows upon and accompanies a development of religion, a formulation of myth.

That the entities of myth, seen from the point of view of systematic reference, are subject to the categories of truth and falsehood—and also transcend them—is a notion to be found not only in Hesiod but characteristically in the myth-systems of many peoples, as Éliade lists them (1963, pp. 18–23). The Muses in their own words Hesiod attributes to them are "perfect," "just," "prepared," "of an exact fit," *artiepeiai* (*Theogony*, 29; *Iliad* 22.281).

At some Neolithic point myth and language may have been fused inseparably; then no single lexical item would have been without its inseparable mythic depth. In this sense Emerson's dictum would apply in other than the trivial, etymological sense, "Language is fossil poetry." The hieroglyphic name for the religious center-city Memphis was Het-ka-Ptah, which means "the temple of Ptah" or "the double of Ptah." As a complement to the other ways of periodizing myth-systems, one could produce a set of periods according to the degree of linkage between myth and language. In such a "relational" periodization the Egyptians of the Middle Kingdom, while at a fairly advanced period of abstract development for their gods, would stand in this respect quite close to the Neolithic point before the separation of myth from language for relative independence and increasingly attenuated interaction.

Cassirer's approach to the problem of the interaction between myth and language is to subcategorize all communicative procedures as symbolic forms. This has the effect of defusing the mythic or emotional side, and it is parallel to the more elaborate *Mythologiques* of Lévi-Strauss, where emotional dynamics get factored out as structures of intellectual explanation. The totalization of the emotional context as a communication system between a psychoanalytic Self/self and an Other/other, Lacan's procedure, would make of myth only a mode for handling the relations between the symbolic, the imaginary, and the real; myth then becomes a sort of metonymy/metaphor machine, it is referred to language.

So far so good. Botany is needed, but if all gardens are in some sense Eden, the force on which they draw cannot be accounted for by enumerating and calculating their special effects. The "use of myth" in a poem cannot just be accounted for by a grammar of metaphor, confusing as Christine Brooke-Rose properly finds honorific accounts of metaphor to be. A linguistic account, her own "grammatical" one, has at least the advantage of accounting for something, whereas theories of metaphor or allegory do tend to be circular: to deal with a cause by accounting for effects.

On the other hand, *Hamlet* does not converge with myth, even if his leap into Ophelia's tomb, for example, does distantly mime the myth motif of Descent into the Underworld. To speak ontogenetically of orality or phylogenetically of such motifs as the swallowing or engulfing act of the Orphic Zeus would only produce a common context and one analytic scheme for the inclusive, the comic, and the high-oral mimetic in such different linguistic performances as those of Rabelais, Joyce, and the stand-up comedian. As always, an account of the message would have to include elements of both myth and language, and also to address their interaction. A crucial dimension of their interaction would be the elaborately determined series of temporal cues within the work (language is temporal, both in its syntactic presentation and in its lexical origins: a word is chosen at one moment of its drift through time, as the date "1605" or "1976" may be assigned to the word). These temporal cues, in turn, themselves both enlist an "expectation horizon" in the hearer-reader and call into play the dialectic of his quasi-Heideggerian self-definition in and through time.

As an instance of what may be involved in such effects, take Yeats's "Leda," a poem which complexly evokes the legendary effect of an encounter between an overriding god and a mortal of divine ancestry in its long-range historical and social impact:

Leda and the Swan

A sudden blow: the great wings beating still
Above the staggering girl, her thighs caressed
By the dark webs, her nape caught in his bill,
He holds her helpless breast upon his breast.

How can those terrified vague fingers push
The feathered glory from her loosening thighs?
And how can body, laid in that white rush,
But feel the strange heart beating where it lies?

A shudder in the loins engenders there
The broken wall, the burning roof and tower
And Agamemnon dead.
               Being so caught up,
So mastered by the brute blood of the air,
Did she put on his knowledge with his power
Before the indifferent beak could let her drop?

The immediate impetus in Yeats' context for this poem was political,[3] and its bearing is certainly macropolitical. But it combines the political, a common motif for the sonnet since Milton, with the amorous, an even commoner one. The macropolitical is seen in its conjunction with the amorous, and the amorous in its conjunction with the divine: the birth of a fatally fascinating woman ("And Helen has all living hearts betrayed," as Yeats says in "The Tower").

These two large spheres of reference, the political and the amorous, which the sonnet as a rhetorical form may be said to expect and accord with, are more specifically complemented by the kinds of sonnet form Yeats has chosen for the octave and the sestet separately. The octave, which describes the love-encounter, conforms to the pattern of the most notable love sonnets in English, those of Shakespeare (*abab, cdcd*). The Petrarchan sonnet, in Milton's adaptation of it, would have had only two rhymes in the octave rather than four; it would have tended to make the octave one rhythmic unit rather than two distinct quatrains.

The Shakespearean sonnet ends with a third quatrain and a couplet. But Yeats, shifting from love to politics, also shifts his form for the sestet from the Shakespearean to the more political Miltonic form; instead of a third quatrain we are given a Miltonic-Petrarchan sestet unit (*fghfgh*), the third line, pivotal for the rhyme, broken by a full stop in the middle and given an enjambment.

These and other metrical peculiarities are made to echo from the form-staples of English poetry, and from the deep emotional-evocative potentialities of the rhythmed language that all poetry calls into being.[4]

These staple emotional effects are here patterned and subordinated in a rhetorical frame that calls the wonderment of the statement into play by reversing the normal order of question and statement. Here we are given first a statement and then a question, and then another question. That is the octave; the sestet repeats and varies the pattern, first a statement, then a question.

The final question leaves open, and leaves hanging, a form of our identification between what language accounts for ("knowledge") and what myth expresses ("power"). Both knowledge and power are declared to be certain attributes of a sort of godhead, problematically transferred together through the erotic act, which certainly transfers one of them, the power. DeQuincey's opposition between "the literature of knowledge" and "the literature of power" has, so to speak, been bypassed. The word *indifferent* applied to Zeus's beak hints at something very like Lévi-Strauss's neutral and objective underlying myth-calculus.

If we try to account for the modality of Yeats' belief here, we are on terrain more complicated than we are with the Zeus in whom Homer believes and the Jove who for Shakespeare is a complicated artifice-reference. Yeats is asking, and answering, a version of Herodotus' question, how divine influence gets into history.

The central systematic account in Yeats' own terms of how this happened involves a psychology of unconscious processes, "will," "mask," "Creative Mind," "Body of Fate"; these "faculties" are in turn transmuted into "principles": "husk," "passionate body," "spirit," "celestial body." The particular modes of interaction among all these reflect the phases of the moon, this whole doctrine having been communicated to

Yeats through his wife's spirit-mediumship. The occult and the erotic are thus put in a kind of relation by Yeats in his own life.

That relation translates the inner of the unconscious into an outer of astrological recursiveness in order to make sense of a much vaster recursion, the Platonic Great Year. Yeats uses "Leda" as an epigraph for the concluding chapter of the treatise in which he expounds all these matters. Thus in *A Vision,* this poem has the further modality of exemplifying a doctrine. Its power, so to speak, is at the service of what purports to be a kind of knowledge.

Staying within Yeats' system will produce complicated correspondences between myth and language. The persistent evasiveness of the system's relation to either myth or language, taken together or separately, leads one far beyond notions of rhetoric or metaphor. Here the speech act somehow posits itself, and somehow this happens just because of the high generality of the doctrine it wishes to propound. As Yeats says in his prose account (*A Vision,* p. 268),

> I imagine the annunciation that founded Greece as made to Leda, remembering that they showed in a Spartan temple, strung up to the roof as a holy relic, an unhatched egg of hers; and that from one of her eggs came Love and from the other War. But all things are from antithesis, and when in my ignorance I try to imagine what older civilization that annunciation rejected I can but see bird and woman blotting out some corner of the Babylonian mathematical starlight.

The two uses of the word *imagine* here are self-qualifying enough for us not to reject the attempt to come to terms with the sort of archaeological evidence that does give us, long before the Mycenean age of Homer's imagining, in Gimbutas's figures from "Old Europe," various fusions of woman and bird. And at the same time the worshipper and the tourist are hopelessly confused in the visit to the Spartan temple that is evoked as some kind of equivalent for proof. Here allegorized abstractions, and the principle of antithesis, and the elements of myth, stand in an uneasy marriage.

The poem itself, however, celebrates the marriage: it somehow brings it off. And the nagging question of how to believe any poem, let alone so teasing a one as this, cannot be handled by an analysis of its language, because the language of a poem has power as well as knowledge: it mediates some access to that which it is also discussing.

2.

This is the case in our time. Myth serves us not as a compendium of belief, and still less as a reservoir of history and convenient fiction, but rather as the modality wherein we consciously mediate between fiction and belief, between language and whatever it is that lies beneath or beyond language.

Literature characteristically finds words, and in poetry it also finds rhythms, for the wordless state of access to a world of perception akin to the states evoked in tribal ritual. A poem has the help of its rhythms, a play has the help of its concentrated actions, and a novel has the help of the indirections whereby it livens that which lurks under the story. With these helps it evokes such states, which are not equivalent to syntactic patterns or lexical entries. Moreover, poems use phonological patterns differently from ordinary language. They can therefore no more be accounted for by seeking out that which can be separately analyzed in an account of syntactic structures than the analysis of the lexical entry "mother" can account for the dynamics of a person's real mother in his or her unconscious.

Longinus put this point in its most reductive terms by calling that which we translate as "the sublime" something that existed (*phu*) on a superior level (*hyper*), the *hyperphua*, which leads not to conviction but to a state of transport ("ou gar eis peitho tous akroōmenous all' eis ekstasin agei ta hyperphua" 1.4). He included Herodotus in this category, as we may too, by virtue of something lurking under his story by means of which it produces effects like those we expect now from fiction, and this at a time when only historiography used the significant prose narrative. For Heraclitus, too, the distinction between poetry and philosophy had not yet come cleanly to pass. Heraclitus stands, to begin with, in the posture of something like a shaman. His *isocola,* stripped of meter and down to the bare bones of the Homeric contrasts, give his aphorisms the air of anti-poems. They are vaguely akin in their ontological self-questioning to the *Poème pulvérisé* of his modern admirer René Char.

Literature, of course, transforms and attenuates the states that might be evoked by a tribal ritual, so that the person reading or hearing is not thereby melted into the tribe, or at least not without a consciousness that enlivens and preserves him in something other than a role. This separation from identity with a mass feeling involves a critical state, and

Hesiod moves into his theogony after being subject to a ritual of mocking at the hands of the Muses. As for the power in mockery, the satirical figure of Archilochus provides the earliest post-Homeric posture, and he remains dominant enough nearly two centuries later to enter the discourse of Heraclitus (B42), of Pindar (*Olympian* 9.1; *Pythian* 2.55), and of Herodotus (1.12), all three. Modern lyric poetry arguably got some of its start in the Goliards' rapturously satiric inversion of medieval values for poetic purposes. The Archpoet is also an anti-poet.

Such simple inversions constitute acts of "estrangement," which Shklovski attributes to all literary expression in some degree. "Nearly everywhere that there is an image there is 'estrangement'" (p. 115; Todorov 2, p. 90), and Shklovski's context is one where the question was being argued around the possibility of defining all literary expression as a management of images. By "estrangement" (*ostranyenie*) he means what results from setting two systems of value in confrontation (as Stendhal does), as well as what results from describing an event as though one had never seen it before (as Tolstoi does). Further, when, in Ohmann's reading, Beckett mixes logical categories and social contexts in his presentation, the result is "estrangement" as much as it is absurdity. It is the result, not the procedure, to which we attend.

The speech act that constitutes a poetic utterance, in its bare context of expectation—what 'poem' means to an auditor—will evoke something like an "estrangement," a procedure that cannot be separated from a sense of the numinous terrain of the mythic. Even weather saws, barely informational verses, transmit with their rhythms more than just an aid to memory. The dedicatory hexameters on the "Nestor cup" or the "Ithaca cup," our earliest specimens of Greek writing, sacralize, in Homer's meter, as well as formalize, in the order of verse, a casual act. Ashanti proverbs are without either meter or words, translated into animals and other beings. The proverb is rendered as an art object, a tiny sculpture. These have at once an exchange use as gold weights and the signification of a tribal wisdom not wholly divorced from the totemic —and myth-structural—function of the animals, even though the proverb encodes the gesture of a partial separation from myth. Aesop, too, associates the gnomic and the animal. The animals, as allegories, are at once reductive (less than men) and yet still intensive (foci of human qualities), though the totemic myth-charge in them has been weakened below the voltage of, say, Heraclitus' pigs.

In La Fontaine, the proverbial use of animals is transmuted by a delicacy of metrical qualification, which suggests discriminations finer than either the barely gnomic or the merely allegorical. The enchantment produced by the metrical delicacy is different in kind, though comparably attenuated, from the remote sacral origins of the animals that enter the fables. The metrical enchantment sophisticates the relation between myth and language, where the animals, taken just as proverbial agents, have left the mythic force largely behind.

Heraclitus sets the gnomic in opposition to the mythic; he makes the gnomic do the work of the mythic while carrying out an act of demythologization. In Pindar the gnomic and the mythic interact, while in Herodotus the gnomic, under the form of the experiential maxims he frequently adduces, will not quite cover all of experience, since on the one hand there are the incursions of the divine to upset the experience such maxims codify; and on the other hand there are the inter-ethnic and temporal complications which it is the business of the *History* to set forth. Isaiah takes up the gnomic, as Proverbs later codifies it, and puts it to the transumptive use of producing a vision about society, not of past experience but of the future, and not of the homely but of the tremendous. These are all "literary" uses, where the language of proverb and the domain of myth are set into fruitful and significative interaction.

Any linguistic act is at once individual and social, an act of *parole* that uses the *langue*. Poetry, seen in Adorno's terms, provides an especially intensified interaction between the individual and society; a Baudelaire, through his "I," gives voice to a general *Weltschmerz* (1958; p. 87). *"Im lyrischen Gedicht negiert, durch Identifikation mit der Sprache, das Subjekt ebenso seinen blossen monadologischen Widerspruch zur Gesellschaft."* ("In the lyric poem, through identification with language, the subject just negates his bare monadological opposition to society.") The act of "negation" (*"negiert"*) is also an act of use, like any linguistic act; and, like any, it posits an intersubjectivity as the condition of communication. Beyond this, the poem turns intersubjectivity into an arousal, a transport in Longinus' terms, which uses the unconscious (Adorno's *"kollektiver Unterstrom,"* p. 89) and to some degree controls it in the very process of arousal.

Theory since the Romantics has viewed the use of symbol or image or even allegory as a means of access to the source of power with which the myth is shaped to deal. But there is a corresponding negative sense, in which all human speech is circumlocutory, the "inexpressibility trope" of Dante and other medieval writers. This may be seen to follow logically, as it follows in time, the scriptural distinction between earthly utterance and heavenly, as in John 16:25, "These things have I spoken unto you in proverbs: but the time cometh, when I shall no more speak unto you in proverbs, but I shall show you plainly [*parrhesia*, "in free speech"] of the Father." The word *proverbs, paroimiai,* is the regular Greek term for what is gnomic; but it is here used for application to a kind of statement normally labelled by another biblical term *parabole,* "parable," which emphasizes the discontinuity of meaning between the story and its signification, the *para* in *parabole* emphasizing juxtaposition.[5]

The single poetic act, in its linkage between language and myth, can be seen either as a continuity, insofar as the myth-domain is evoked and expressed; or as a discontinuity, insofar as the distinction between a statement and a mythic referent cannot be given a lexical account when it involves so complex an evocation.

The riddle as a persistent *"einfache Form"* advertises such a discontinuity, both in its folk manifestations, however elaborated by the riddles of the Exeter Book;[6] and in the enigma-glorying formulations of the medieval skald, of Góngora, and of Mallarmé. *"Tel qu'en lui-même enfin l'éternité le change"* offers a paradox about a dead writer. It translates the topos that a poem lives longer than the poet into a sort of puzzle for solution. The palm of Valéry, the swan of Rilke, are not wholly divorced from the puzzling definitions of the medieval riddle-types, which in fact often dealt with animals. And Irving Ehrenpreis describes even the poems of Swift as subliminal riddles, "How is a cottage like a church?," etc. In this sense poetic practice inherits the riddle's management of myth by a questioning separation from it.

In the programmatic surrealism of Breton, and more loosely in "pure poetry" generally, the element of riddle has been pushed beyond even paradox. The "white-haired revolver" (*"revolver à cheveux blancs"*) couples entities that cannot be resolved even into opposition. These radically dissociated lexical classes are strung together syntactically in order to evoke some other realm, to which Breton, the friend of Freud, would be willing to give the name "unconscious." Indeed the poem, in this program, serves as a mechanism to waken and celebrate this other realm. Seen as a significative structure, the surrealist poem, in Per Aage Brandt's formulation, is a "dialectical text machine," which works by moving up and down the levels of a "poetic text," a "text in sleep," and a "text in dream." Sets of propositions are evinced that connect the aesthetic, the oneiric, and the political. Seen as a poetic act, however, the surrealistic poem declares the poetic function (Brandt's "aesthetic") to be paramount just because it is ancillary to the function of the unconscious: this highest use of language is to renounce language in favor of an equivalent for myth.

A similar function is to be found in the "angel" of Wallace Stevens, and in the modality of all poems that are surrealistic in the looser sense. Indeed the diffusion and unclassifying generality that I have elsewhere (Cook, 1967) argued to be characteristic of modern poetry can be seen as a proto-surrealism, as a strategy for returning the poetic performance in language to the power lying in the source of poetry, in myth.

3.

The power of myth, the power of verse, and the power inherent in the capacity of writing—all tend to move into close association for primitive societies, whose normal use of language would have to have continued this power without fixing or invoking it. As Grimm points out (p. 68), the runes connect with the word for mandragora (*Alraun*: a mandragora as a magic picture), with secret speech (*raunen,* "speak secretly"; *rune,* "secret": in Ulfilas), and with writing (*rista*). Runes are the method by which a priestly caste codifies the religion into formulas, thereby working spells that are supposed to have a power over nature. As Parke points out (p. 63), Greek oracles tended to be associated with human sacrifice. So did riddles, notably in the riddle Oedipus saves his life by solving. In the Old Norse mythology, the *Alvissmol,* and elsewhere, the riddle is used as a death test, while the sequence of riddle-like questions and answers still covers the nomenclature of the known world, of men, gods, elves, giants, and dwarves before it moves on to simple objects like pin, egg, and horseshoe nail.

In the Bible, the proverb (*paroimia*) serves the same function as the parable (*parabole*), as in the passage above. In the Old Testament *mashal* may mean either a story with proverbial force or a proverb. Both stories and proverbs belong to the wisdom literature, Job standing under the same heading as Proverbs, with the interesting classification "Writings" (*khetuvim*). Even inspired scripture, the passage from John, sees an indirectness in proverb and parable which can be contrasted with a "plain" directness of utterance of "freedom of speech," a *parrhesia.* This

word, originating in the distinction of free from slave in Greek democratic life (Kittel, sub voc), transposes that whole political condition
into a distinction between earthly and heavenly, since "freedom of
speech" in the passage from John cannot mean fluency of utterance, ordinary *parole*. It is an imagined heavenly language where the very need
for parable and proverb will have fallen away.

In this context the very movement from ordinary language to the form
of proverb and parable suggests the possibility of such a still further
development. In that sense, the gnomic usage implies the possibility of a
prophetic one, and the desacralization of questioning religion implies the
re-sacralization of dialecticizing it, a possibility which Amos and Isaiah
actualize, and which underlies the typology of scripture. The Bible takes
the pattern of story motifs and renders them apocalyptic. As Bultmann
says (pp. 116–17), the predictive aspect of the New Testament abolishes
the distinctions between the literal, the allegorical, and the typological.
Dante, of course, knew this well and formulated it in the fourfold categories of the *Convivio* and the *Letter to Can Grande,* applying the fusion
to the history of his own time; the past of the gnomic and the future of
the prophetic are made to converge from the vantage of an imagined
eternity. As Daniélou says of the New Testament, and the Old, "la
prophétie est déjà interprétation typologique de l'histoire" (p. 135).
Claudel and Neruda, who were alike in being diplomats by profession
and poets by calling (if at the opposite ends of the political spectrum),
both apply a paratactic-orotund trans-gnomic discourse and an image-
stream to events as a way of rendering the discontinuities of political
event into a kind of exhortation. Prophecy is to them as penitence is to
Dante, at once a means and an end. Their anaphora serves some of the
same use that Meletinskii finds in the anaphora of the Eddas. This means
of heightened language reaches for that to which the realm of myth is
a ground. Perse offers a stream of anaphoric abstractions, floating images. For all these, as for Heraclitus, Pindar, and Herodotus, to alter the
relation between the mythic and the gnomic—for the Greek writer to
transform Homer—is to alter a linguistic set entirely. In literature the
linguistic set is defined by, and defines, a relation to myth.

The folk-motifs classified by Thompson, which pervade the stories of
all earlier literature (or indeed, of all literature), themselves tend to
attract staples of sacral reference and function, as Durand argues. Combinations of these motifs are also classifiable, though they occur in other
contexts than those which simply recount myths, in the binary algorithms

of Lévi-Strauss; the motif is a mytheme elsewhere than in a myth. And the motif serves as a vessel for the civilized psychological states that Bachelard traces for Lévi-Strauss's primitive dominant substances, fire and water. In all these functions the motif, like the proverb which will be appended to it in Aesop or the *Panchatantra,* traces a continuity amid what would otherwise be discontinuities.

Motif is to the continuous as episode is to the discontinuous. Every motif raises the question of the degree of generality we should assume for it (just a disfavored daughter, or a youngest among three daughters, or a disfavored child, or a disfavored younger person generally?). Degree of generality is a central question for the use of Thompson's index, and also of Bachelard (Fire, water, or simply a fluid, lambent substance?).

For motifs as they enter a text there is the further "syntactic" question of the relations between such items, and here Lévi-Strauss is syntactic insofar as he is relational, if not in some other respects. And then there is the still further question of narrative sequence, of the diachronic series of events, unique for a given sequence if typifiable in ways that Propp's practice may be taken to suggest, if not to prove.

Taken together, these three questions would provide a lexicon, a syntax, and the possibility of a context, for motifs—all insofar as they enter into combinations of language. But motifs also urgently draw upon and evoke myths. The whole of Greek tragedy, coming after the pre-Socratic revolution, may be taken to reimport the questions of myth as problems rather than as certitudes into the linguistic area dominated by proverb and motif.

In all of this the magical redundancy of verse pattern serves to underscore the redundancy whereby we recognize continuities at all. Verse aids the memory, and so the truth; for the Greeks (*Hymn to Apollo,* 1.1), truth is *a-letheia,* a non-forgetfulness which is a laying-bare. In early verse, as we can still hear it in taped samples of, say, Yugoslav, Bulgarian, Xhosa, and Ainu song,[7] there is a line pause emphatically more marked than the modern reader accords to his own verse. A silence heavily underscores the redundant continuities.

4.

A poem adds the most primitive virtual and arbitrary redundancies to the redundancies of language. These specially marked linguistic features of the poem are noticeable in the meters and line breaks of oral poetry we have, as well as in the virtualized and minimalized redundancies of free verse. All these superadded redundancies constitute technique, a means of access to something. As McFarland (3) insists, this something is not exactly "content," since the denotational and narrative portions of a poem are part of its *"substantia,"* roughly, all its linguistic features, the syntax and lexical items and sound patterns of the *langue* taken together with the formalized features. Rather this something, which I am calling "myth," has an aspect of McFarland's *ens,* or subjective withness to the objective world; it has also an aspect of his *essentia,* a heightened awareness of the fusion, and the split, that the poem brings into focus between the nowness of human life, its *Dasein,* and its contrasting openness to the past and to the future, its *Existenz.* The technique of "estrangement" or "foregrounding," as McFarland implies, may be taken to bring about a separation in the poem between ordinary communication and the specially heightened, globalized message of the poem.

This heightening is the sign of access to the something of the poem, a something which in psychological terms involves a sense of primary process or the unconscious; and involves, again, the unknown forces for which mythic systems are designed to deal. Homer uses myth one way, Yeats another; and William Carlos Williams mostly takes the stance of claiming not to use it at all, except in a carefully maintained disjunction: the man Paterson only fictively stretches out as the city Paterson to have the waterfall deafening his ear. The same is the case for the HCE of *Finnegans Wake,* framed in a dream-distorted account that carries with it a metalinguistic, Viconian commentary on the function of myth. Walter Savage Landor, Pushkin, and Emily Dickinson do almost entirely without myth in any explicit sense—and yet in their poems we are brought, as we must be, into an awareness of something whose power is not only felt but felt as part of the message of the poem, a message that cannot be coded back just into its philosophical strategies of bringing *ens* into conjunction with *essentia.*

All this would be no more than to assert that "poetry is moving" or "poetry is powerful," were it not for the fact that the language of every poem, and of every literary act, contains not only a strategy of access to the realm of myth but at least an implied metalinguistic comment on the ontological relation of its own language to that realm. We learn from Homer, and from Yeats, and from Williams, the mode of this metalinguistic relation. And the general absence of explicit mythic figures in

Pushkin, Walter Savage Landor, and Emily Dickinson, means not just that they are high on *ens* and *essentia* while Pope is low, but that such an absence of mythic figures will concentrate on essences (which the fancifulness of Emily Dickinson may be taken to emphasize). It is just this concentration which Pope, in turn, holds at low voltage. There is this mode of metalinguistic comment implied in his prosiness, and also in the almost exclusive Latinity of his classicism.

The retroduction to Greek classicism in Keats and Hölderlin implies an attempt to revive and recapture a Hellenic modality of metalinguistic relation to the realm of myth. Not even these poets took this revival, or more precisely this "bracketing" of a revival, of metalinguistic relation in the poetry, to be equivalent to a revival of the social set of the admired, Greek use of myth. Hölderlin did not believe that his Rhine operates like the Achelous of Homer or the Dirce of Pindar, though the poem "Der Rhein" carries a running invocation to gods. *"Ein Rätsel ist Reinentsprungenes"* ("a riddle is the Pure-origined"), he declares in that poem and links with this the declaration that "The song is scarcely permitted to unhusk it."

"Ein Rätsel ist Reinentsprungenes. Auch / Der Gesang kaum darf es enthüllen." Keats's address to his Grecian urn also adduces a metalinguistic set, "Thou, silent form, dost tease us out of thought / As doth eternity." The nightingale's imagined disappearance brings him to the typical conclusion of an unresolved question about its modality, "Fled is that music:—Do I wake or sleep?"[8] Yeats ends "Leda and the Swan" with a comparable question, where the terms are "knowledge" and "power" instead of "truth" and "beauty."

All this is of the bare statement of the poem. Its strategies of organization, either "diffusion" or severe coherence, and its strategies of reference, or "generality" (Cook, 1967), may likewise be taken to serve a particular mode of access to, as well as a particular kind of definition of, myth.

Both stories and plays further pattern their recurrences of event so as to reconstitute some version of the cyclic ritual celebration by which primitive peoples have access to heightened awareness. In this sense art functions as religion does. The terminal question is not only a terminal proposition for Keats or Yeats; it is also a way of not closing the pattern or circle of evocations that the rhythms and statements of the poem must constitute if it is to be successful.

5.

In the psychic economy of bringing the unconscious to bear on the context of a communicative act, as Lacan defines this central human procedure of speaking, such breaks in a pattern are seen negatively. They betoken an unbridgeable gap in the circuit of reaching the Self in the self via the other in the Other. And all procedures involving images in such statements have the metaphorical character of overriding, or else the metonymic character of maintaining, the relationship between the signifier and the signified. Language is thus in this view a metalinguistic machine for working out identifications between the symbolic, the imaginary, and the real. Lacan further defines the whole psychological process in such communicative structures, building an elaborate algorithmic series on the patterns of recurrence between the presence of the symbolic and its absence.[9] The symbolic, in Lacan's structuring of significations with respect to the Freudian death-wish, always dominates the imaginary and the real; any compulsion to repetition, and therewith we may say the substructure of any redundancy, must be symbolic because of its relation to an origin in the unconscious.

In acts of literary communication, however, the symbolic is always more precisely present than in other statements, and even structures of "absence" have the positive function of leading in the direction of presence (unless they fail). Nor do they simply refer to presence; an absence in a communicative structure does that, like the embarrassed silence between patient and analyst. In literature reference and evocation are inseparable; the speech act of literature has the goal of achieving this connection, of bringing language and designative structures over into the realm of myth.

But to speak of it as "the order of symbol" (or with Bateson as an information-processing of contexts that occasionally refer to higher contexts) ultimately obscures the primacy, and urgency, of that with which literature deals. Art, to be sure, must unfailingly enlist hierarchies of contexts, as Bateson shows in his decoding of context-levels in Balinese paintings and his reference of these to modes of symmetry and complementarity in a society's social patterns. Yet the convergence permits the essential to take place, a witness or immediacy of perception.[10] The convergence of these contexts in the work of art is everything.

Looked at under the microscope of Fish's subtle and sequential stylistic analysis, the epidermis of Donne's sermons dissolves into cells and pores; the skin no longer covers the body, and Donne would seem to be denying instead of affirming his faith. But a sermon of Donne's is not a "self-consuming artifact." It is an exhortation at a certain depth, a depth that for us, and possibly for his auditors, reached the literary. Like the sermons of Bossuet and the *Confessions* of St. Augustine, it touches a ground where religion and art have something indistinguishable in common, the ground of a numinous source.

It is in the crucial area of belief for the participants in such complicated speech-acts as literary ones, and of ontological modality for the ultimate reference of a literary statement, that such discriminating discussions fall short. Taken as analysis, they increase our perception of how fine-woven the tissues of literature may be. Taken as prescript, they constitute a super-nominalism[11] whose counterpart in philosophy is the *"Mythologie blanche"* of Derrida, the referral of all signification to uncorrectable distortion.

On the side of language, a literary statement is complex enough to need the tough hermeneutic discriminations of Hirsch, and also something of the intersubjective justifications that Gadamer offers, referring the question to a network of post-Dilthey epistemological abstractions.[12] On the side of myth, the literary statement may reduce the reader to a vague statement that the poem is unparaphrasable, something that the diehard advocate of primary process will also say about the full meaning of a dream, its "navel" as Freud calls it.[13] However much the poem resembles the dream in its overdetermination, and in its utilization of the mechanisms of displacement (metonymy) and condensation (metaphor), the poem sets up a different relationship between language and unconscious process of myth than does the dream. The poet and the daydreamer, in Freud's view, use comparable psychic processes, but to different ends. The poem becomes public; it enters the world of reality to declare something about the durable interaction of reality with fantasy. The daydream is private, fantasy pure and simple, though it may feed on reality. The poem, again, really tells us not just about fantasy but about the interaction of reality and fantasy, of language and myth.

6.

What does it tell us? There is a quandary about the act of interpretation which derives from something other than the heresy of paraphrase.

On the side of language, the discrimination of structures in the poem cannot approach the myth-core in it without re-rendering it as demythologized language. Even in the psychic life the unconscious can only be known as its manifestations surface in the ego. On the side of myth, the assertion of its presence in the poem would seem quickly to result only in either exhortations of praise or crude typologies of archetype. We are caught, so to speak, between Bateson and Northrop Frye, if not between Lévi-Strauss and Freud.

But we resolve this dilemma, at least in the proposal of the question (and to ask a question is to begin to answer it), if we attend to the *interaction* between language and myth which it is the poem's main business to effectuate, on the unavoidably primary ground of a consciousness and its being-in-time.

Freud says that the spectator is "gripped" by a play (2, pp. 179–183), and that Sophocles's management (*Handlung*) of the material in *Oedipus Rex* is *comparable* (*vergleichbar*) to the work (*Arbeit*) of a psychoanalysis. Poems and stories, too, manage affective sequences in their readers, as Norman Holland discusses these in his studies of the (psycho-)dynamics of literary response. Insisting on the likeness between the terms of comparison, the temporal process of the poem and temporal process of an analysis, yields the structural similarities between the poem and the self-awareness which the *emotional* sequences of the analysis offers. At the same time there is an irreducible difference between the two, and this difference is crucial. The affective sequences in a literary work are virtual: the work refers them to a higher context of perception, where their interactions with the possible extensions of language actualized in the poem put the affective sequences at a task quite different from that of mere recursive self-reference, or even self-awareness in a psychoanalytic sense.

Bateson's recurrent example for referral to a different level may serve to throw this transumptive aspect of the language-myth interaction of a poem into relief. Dogs bite each other in play, signalling thereby not that they are about to fight, but the opposite: it is a gesture of peace. This play behavior, seen negatively, avoids combat. Seen positively, however, it establishes a ground of peace between the dogs where it is then possible for them to associate further, even to indulge in other kinds of play than mock combat. The distinctions apply, by analogy, to the communicative effect of a poem. Seen negatively, the poem in its sequences does manage the psychological sequences it evokes; it becomes an instrument

whereby the ego successfully sublimates what it might otherwise have re-
pressed. Seen positively, however, the reader, healed or well in this regard by reading the poem, takes the affective act of reading and uses it
to refer more than simply to his health.

In Jolles' terms, again, a myth is an answer to a question we do not
have; a riddle is the inverse, a question to which we do not have the
answer. A psychoanalysis turns a riddle into a myth. But in doing so it
is, in Freud's terms, "endless" (*unendliche*) not only in the sense that
it has a stubborn tendency not to terminate, but also in the sense that it
goes from a riddling datum—the stalled patient who wishes to be rid of
his stalling—to a ground of explanation in the unconscious: it moves
from riddle to myth.

And so does the poem, play, or story. But the literary work combines
that motion, so to speak, at one and the same time with the reverse. We
do not know where the lines of the poem or the action of the play or
the events of the novel will take us: it is a riddle. When we have concluded, we have a complete "answer," a myth, or the virtual equivalent
in linguistic structures for what in an earlier stage of society would have
been simply a myth. This myth, however, reestablishes its character as a
riddle. The whole text of *War and Peace* is an answer (myth); but it is
also a giant question (a riddle). Apollo, on the other hand, taken by
himself is simply an answer (referring to the ground of the unknown).
Taken in the play of Sophocles he becomes something more qualified
(and less), but also something more complicated (and less).

Literature is a temporal art, as we have known since Lessing. More
than this, however, language itself is a temporal process: it proceeds
through sequences of contrasting phonetic choices linked together in
patterns. Without the patterns, there could be no redundancy in language, and no recognition of meaning. Without the initial phonetic contrasts there could be none either. Any literary art takes these features
of language and transposes them into new patterns, new contrasts, and
therefore new redundancies: it harnesses arbitrary sequences of sound
in poems, of event in stories and plays—and of contrasts, often, in its
idea-systems, the irony practiced by Stendhal or the "paradox" which is
fundamental to at least some poetry. Image and metaphor, too, can be
seen as a transposition into what is virtualized of a relation between
signifier and signified. One no longer points exactly at a real horse or
tree in nature; the virtualized horse signifies something else, something
relatable to the numinous power earlier societies and dreams even today

invest in horses and in trees. Even the true historian, who points at real people and events, does so in order to make a larger point lurking under these linkages. In this sense we cannot improve on the definition of Hesiod, who has the Muses accuse him of making "false" (*pseudea*) statements about things in a way that makes them "like the genuine" (*etumoisin homoia, Theogony,* 27).

Being virtual, the image or metaphor has a riddling character: it suggests something else than signification. Being arbitrary, the sound sequences in poems and the sequences of evocative events in plays and stories are also riddling as well as evocative: we are not only clearly moved; we are obscurely aware of something that being moved is necessary to and not arbitrary. The riddle is only arbitrary in its significations ("What has eighteen legs and swats flies?" could seemingly mean lots of things); but the signification becomes necessary, once the solution of the riddle is offered (it necessarily signifies, in the speech-act "riddle," "a baseball team"). Such a puzzle-riddle functions somewhat as Freud says wit does, to solidify good feeling between people by having the auditors do homage to the lively verbal resourcefulness of the speaker, not to resolve tensions, as the joke does, but to create the momentary test of intellectual tension by way of celebrating the equality and conviviality of two or a few more people. In literature, the movement from the arbitrary of its virtualized structures and significations to the necessity of its Mysterious Signification does homage to the power of the message. An arbitrariness superadded to language has been made to yield significations in the area of myth, without terminating in a necessary, single solution.

This arbitrariness involves the transposition of temporal patterns analogous to those in natural language. Literature may thus be said to foreground, or to insist on, its temporal character: it calls attention to the fact that it adds rhymes or compasses the significant events of years in a few staged hours of causal linkage, thereby making the future take on the character of the past (Cook, 1976). Primitive rituals bring the celebrant into heightened awareness of a convergence of the unique, one-way pattern of his own life span with the common, cyclic progression of the seasons. Literature induces a virtualized version of this awareness (which it may enlist as part of its own awareness, a play of Sophocles at the Greater Dionysia); virtualized temporal structures in literature are made to produce a heightened awareness of a virtual convergence between the secret of one man's being and destiny (McFarland's *ens* and *essentia*) and the possibility of giving it utterance in language.

The act of writing transposes the natural temporal sequences of ordinary language onto a spatial, and external plane, as Ong has pointed out. Writing is, further, abstract—at its most abstract in Greek and Western alphabets, a one-for-one assignment of letters to arbitrary phonetic values, an assignment as arbitrary as (and parallel to) the assignment of phonetic values to semantic entities. It is, as though by a kind of analogy, the literate cultures which permit language and myth to permute their relations by standing in some disjunction one from the other.

The syllabary of Hebrew is somewhat less abstract. Without the vowels written, a triliteral root can carry any one of a number of grammatical transformations: the written set of syllabic markers ("letters") does not exactly tie down the sound of the word, and therefore does not tie down its meaning. Without taking the analogy between syllabary and myth-language relation in the Bible to the point of exhaustive correspondence, there is a kind of rightness that in the text, as it is uttered, the syllables of the quadriliteral for God—which already do not provide a distinct pronunciation—have in the tradition an entirely alien, honorific expression to be uttered when the divine name occurs, *Adonai* spoken when JHVH is written. The centrality of JHVH, and the high redundancy count of its recurrences in the text, can be correlated, if only loosely, to the fullness of reference that is felt to inhere in the syllabic shorthand. The Sanskrit *devanagari,* where the vowels are written in, handles the syllable "Om" with far fewer permutations. However, *devanagari* does not separate its words; in its texts perceptions as well as words tend to get lumped together. And the Indian tradition is more conservative in its reference to mythological personages, but more innovative in its development of abstraction (with analogy to an alphabet instead of a syllabary) than that in the Bible. Job takes JHVH a greater distance from the Pentateuch than the Upanishads take the deity from the RgVeda; but at the same time the language of the Upanishads reaches, and stays rather flatly on, a level of abstraction to which the Old Testament has no recourse.[14] In the New Testament, an alphabetic Greek subsumes and transposes the syllabic Hebrew, and JHVH retains at once the energy of *theos* and the abstraction of *logos.*

At an earlier stage, language and myth are completely fused, as in a representational system. The bison on the wall at Altamira has no phonetic character at all, and yet it must surely be Paleolithic man's sole form of writing for the word *bison.* Warburton, cited by Derrida (2, pp. 308–9, 334–37), identifies hieroglyphics and the dream-interpretation for which the Egyptians were especially noted. Freud makes a comparable comparison for the Chinese (VIII, pp. 404–05). A soundless representation would seem in Egyptian hieroglyphics (insofar as the accounts of hieroglyphics make this clear to one who cannot read them) to retain a comparable relation between the pictograph and what it signifies, and therefore between myth and language, so fully that the development of literature in our sense is scarcely possible—or at least any development that allows for more than the disjunct love lyrics of one early text, graceful but casual, and possibly lacking the charge of the Western poems that they seem to become when they are translated. The hieroglyphic pictograph for *sun* can also mean "day," "light," "time," "eternity," and other abstract notions associated so intimately with the concrete and visible sun that no distinction is possible between what is seen and what is thought (and so between what is signified in language and what is assumed in myth). These hieroglyphics combine in various ways, so that the ideogram for "feather" or "truth" can be added in a different combination, as a representation for the sounds "sw," to the ideogram for sun, and still the sun is designated. And the determinative is a separate, silent hieroglyphic.

It would seem that the Egyptian hieroglyphics never become exclusively the lexicon of significant syllables, taken by themselves, which Chinese ideograms are. As sounds, they tend to lose their significance; as free areas of signification, they can easily be divorced from sound. Nor do hieroglyphics combine the way Chinese ideograms are said to do: the idea of sun is not put together with some idea for a further idea, as, in Liu's explanation, where the ideogram for "window" plus the ideogram for "moon" give the composite character *ming,* signifying "bright."[15]

One typology of relations between language and myth may be set up according to the degree of linkage between them. Another typology is possible in terms of degree of abstraction, and still another in terms of modality of credence to be assigned a statement. One could trace any of these typologies of relation between language and myth diachronically from Neolithic times to modern (it being part of the modality of the modern to try to revive the Neolithic).

But one could also consider them synchronically, as typical of the cultural systems where each kind of relation between language and myth occurs, in loose analogy to the kind of writing system it has adopted for itself. For the Egyptian an elaborate pantheon is retained which is at once visual and abstract. Hieroglyphics are visual, and far more emphasis is accorded sculptural and painterly representation of mythical entities: the Book of the Dead was painted on coffin lids, from which we have extracted it, and Egypt still contains volumes uttered in the silent language of stone. The Chinese would seem to have had a simpler, and more hieratic mythology,[16] as far back as the Shang, and therefore to have had a writing system which admits at once of the possibility of personal poetry, in the *Confucian Anthology* (the earliest elaborate personal poetry in the world, quickly become "scriptural" within the society), and of a loose freedom from the myths. The rather simple myths themselves also had a frequent but iconographically simple representation in paint and in bronze, as the ideograms also are simple of form but quite a great deal freer in ideological combination than Egyptian hieroglyphics.

The Hebrews describe but do not preserve the temple of Solomon, let alone reproduce it widely; and on the altar stood the written book. The assignment of the whole work in the relation of myth and language to the word itself turned the mythology inward, stripped to monotheism. Hebrew is starkly simple in its verbal means, the same locution, *davar,* indicating both "word," *verbum,* and "thing," *res.*

The Greeks, after the invention of the alphabet, thereby (or at least therewith) felt free to elaborate a whole series of relations between language and myth in their literature; and at the same time to be poised in their graphic and sculptural arts to a concomitant and full "stylistic" development. To change from archaic to "classical" is not only to break free from Egypt but also to admit of the possibility that the statues could, so to speak, be seen as luxuriating in their own significations. "Breathing" in this way, they come to seem more "personal." The Greeks can then begin building temples of stone rather than wood, at just the time when the alphabet was being adopted, and the poise and reliance implicit in this act has transmitted the stone temples to us, as the wooden ones could not have been.

In the assignment of imaginative functions, those that relate language to myth within a culture, the role of literary expression is crucial. However much work literature is given to do over against painting and sculpture and architecture and (what I have mostly left aside) the inevitably pure abstractions of music, it will do that work, it will elaborate its virtual significations, by using, by indicating, and by invoking, at once its connection to the terrain of myth, and its separation therefrom. Literature is able to incorporate and transpose myths by having changed the relation between myth and language. In this case too, as Heraclitus said of his "back-bent harmony" as of a bow or a lyre, "what is borne apart is borne together."

NOTES

1. While a temporary suspension of lexical questions may clarify certain analyses of linguistic structures, no utterance can be handled, even in its structure, as though it were content-free. As Charles J. Fillmore says (Davidson and Harmon, p. 21), "given a full grammatical description of a sentence, with complete semantic descriptions of the lexical items it contains, it should be possible to 'compute' the full semantic description of the sentence, including, of course, information about what its utterers must presuppose to be true, including its utterers' imputations of presuppositions to individuals described or referred to in the sentence." The last provisos would entail giving not just a sociological or anthropological description of a speaker, but also the entire fabric of possible and actual response, conscious and unconscious, including also the area with which myth deals, the sacred. Further, as Searle says (Harman, pp. 27, 29), "What is the string of symbols that comes out of the semantic component supposed to *represent* or [to] *express* in such a way as to constitute a description of the meaning of a sentence? . . . either the readings are just paraphrases, in which case the analysis is circular, or the readings consist only of lists of elements, in which case the analysis fails because of inadequacy. . . . The glue that holds the elements together into a speech act is the semantic intentions of the speaker."

2. The Greeks connected the discovery of fire with a wide range of technical procedures, in the "Democritean" tradition that later Tzetzes centered on the figure of Prometheus (Thomas Cole, esp. pp. 20–21). Another such figure is Phoroneus, hero of the *Phoronis*, a lost Argive epic (Huxley, pp. 31ff); Phoroneus is the first man and a smith.

3. Aristotle, *Politics*, 1326b, 2–26.

4. Plato still defines "the knowable" in terms of syllable (*sullabe*) rather than letter (*stoicheion*) (*Theatetus* 203c). For Aristotle, however, the term for letters is adapted for application to constituent elements of any sort, *stoicheia*, a usage Plato himself verges on for *stoicheia* (*Timaeus*, 48).

1. Lévi-Strauss, Myth, and the Neolithic Revolution

1. In Cook (6), I have expanded these remarks into a more particular critique of Lévi-Strauss's *Mythologiques*.

2. Leaving out the sacred provides Lévi-Strauss with a very considerable gain in coherence and focus, even though he obviously feels, and argues, that "the sacred" is just a term too plenary, with too many senses, for signification. In Lévi-Strauss's view, terms like *mana* falsely pretend to cover the inexplicability and centrality of the processes of social explanation. As Girard says (p. 335),

> Tant que le sens 'se porte bien,' le sacré est absent; il est hors de la structure. L'ethnologie structurale ne le rencontre pas sur son

285

chemin. Le structuralisme fait disparaître le sacré. Il ne faut pas lui reprocher cette disparition. Elle constitue un progrès réel car, pour la première fois, elle est complète et systématique. Même si elle s' accompagne d'un parti pris idéologique, elle ne résulte aucunement de lui. Le structuralisme constitue un moment négatif mais indispensible dans la découverte du sacré. (Insofar as the sense "is in good shape", the sacred is absent; it is out of the structure. Structural ethnology does not encounter the sacred on its path. Structuralism makes the sacred disappear. We must not reproach it for this disappearance. It constitutes real progress for, for the first time, it is complete and systematic. Even if it is accompanied by an ideological *parti pris*, it derives in no way from that. Structuralism constitutes a moment negative but indispensable in the discovery of the sacred.)

This argument would presumably be extrapolable to cover Girard's own profound, but too exclusively mythic, enterprise, in which the evasion of violence explains all social processes, and notably religion (p. 439). "Seront dits *religieux* tous les phénomènes liés à la remémoration, à la commémoration et à la perpetuation d'une unanimité toujours enracinée, en dernière instance, dans le meurtre d'une victime émissaire." ("All those phenomena will be called *religious* that are linked to a remembering, a commemorating, or a perpetuation, of a unanimity always rooted, finally, in the murder of a scapegoat.") What could be disputed would not be the correctness of this highly original and probing conclusion, but rather its exclusiveness, and the implied shrinking and negativization of the social processes, including depth-psychological ones, which he insists on defining primarily with reference to it.

3. Anthony Wilden's comments are quite apposite here, that the double-bind oscillation described by Gregory Bateson becomes an unconscious repetition in Freud and Lacan (p. 3), from whom Lévi-Strauss seems at times to borrow, as in his distinctions, identical with Lacan's, between the symbolic, the imaginary, and the real (OMT; p. 68).

4. Lévi-Strauss (9, pp. 139–73) himself accuses Propp of a confusion between history and context via a formalist's confusion of form with content and abstract with concrete. In the process he points out the difference between the content-free phonemes which are combined to make words and the use by mythemes of material which already possesses content. Nevertheless, he himself oscillates between this view of the "words" used by mythemes, and the view that structural analysis reveals something that underlies a seeming content. The jaguar does tend to disappear into the functions assigned his significances in the oppositions of the tales where that animal-figure occurs.

Lévi-Strauss has, Wilden says (p. 239), "a preference for the static and homeostatic rather than for the dynamic and morphogenic."

The formulae of Propp are modified by the Soviet folklorists who follow him, Nekludov, Meletinsky, and Segal (Maranda, 1974). In so doing they revise him in the direction of what amounts to type-clusters and motifs, implying a weakness in the deep structure of his sequences.

5. A striking illustration of the indissolubility of physical and spiritual elements in myth-systems is offered by the *mudra* diagram printed in Saunders (pp. 32–34).

While this is of course a fairly late diagram, the conjunction of physical and spiritual in *mudra* is traceable to the earliest stages of Hindu religious thought.

This Japanese diagram offers a maze of attributions for the fingers of both hands. Its repertoire of categories strikingly resembles Lévi-Strauss's analyses in its fine-meshed and coordinated attributions, while differing from them in its thorough and detailed conjunction of the micro-physical and the spiritual.

We are offered in the analyses as well as in the natural groupings, oppositions of two (the left and the right hand), five (the five fingers of each hand) and ten (the two taken together). These are the very numbers that Lévi-Strauss finds are widely permuted in North American Indian classification and elsewhere (OMT, "Les decades"; pp. 269–309).

For each finger, in addition, there are seven significant positions, though only the number seven, repeated ten times or once for each of the fingers, does not enter into the reckoning of the groups of twos, fives, and tens. As in Lévi-Strauss and in myth systems generally the category "two," the binary principle, is fundamental, here used to divide the "temporal reality" (left hand, moon) from "ultimate reality" (right hand, sun)—though even here the categories are differently organized from Western ones, and for "ultimate reality" is reserved the "outer" and "observation," while "temporal reality" subsumes the "inner," "contemplation," and "blessedness."

6. This vacancy or mere relationalism of analysis for the system of myth also continues to pose a problem for the semantics of natural language. As David Lewis says (pp. 169–70),

> Semantic markers are symbols: items in the vocabulary of an artificial language we may call Semantic Markerese. Semantic interpretation by means of them amounts merely to a translation algorithm from the object language to the auxiliary language Markerese. But we can know the Markerese translation of an English sentence without knowing the first thing about the meaning of the English sentence. . . . The Markerese method is attractive in part just because it deals with nothing but symbols: finite combinations of entities of a familiar sort out of a finite set of elements by finitely many applications of finitely many rules. There is no risk of alarming the ontologically parsimonious. But it is just this pleasing finitude that prevents Markerese semantics from dealing with the relations between symbols and the world of non-symbols—that is, with genuinely semantic relations. Accordingly, we should be prepared to find that in a more adequate method, meaning may turn out to be complicated, infinite entities built up out of elements belonging to various ontological categories.

7. Lucretius' arguments against the instantaneous origin of language still hold (*De Rerum Natura*, V, 1028–55): that the process of learning language, the necessity of getting it from a social context, and the impossibility of imposing such a strange invention on those with whom one would have to communicate, all indicate that the development would have to have been a gradual process. Bailey points out that Lucretius is developing notions of Epicurus that are "closely akin to modern theories," in contradiction to the theory of Plato in the *Cratylus* (III, 1486–90).

2. The Large Phases of Myth

1. Bellah (p. 41), following Stanner on the Australian aborigines, characterizes such pre-Neolithic societies as "dreaming" the totality of their myth,

asserting that the "participation" deduced by Lévy-Bruhl—and confined by him to the Australian aborigines on the criticism of Mauss—extends to all details of living. Bellah's categories, "primitive," "archaic," and "historical," though centered on religion rather than on exchanges between myth and language, share some features of my typology of periods. On the resistance of a "first-phase" mythology to contrastive definition, Neumann's remarks are suggestive (I, 121):

> To become conscious of oneself, to be conscious at all, begins with saying "no" to the uroboros, to the Great Mother, to the unconscious. And when we scrutinize the acts upon which consciousness and the ego are built up, we must admit that to begin with they are all negative acts. To discriminate, to distinguish, to mark off, to isolate oneself from the surrounding context—these are the basic acts of consciousness. Indeed, experimentation as the scientific method is a typical example of this process: a natural connection is broken down and something is isolated and analyzed, for the motto of all consciousness is *determinatio est negatio*. As against the tendency of the unconscious to combine and melt down, to say to everything *"tat tvam asi"* "that art thou"—consciousness strikes back with the reply "I am not that."

2. The traces of likely Chinese influence on archaic Greece and even earlier (Butterworth) across the great Central Asian Plain, and the probability that North America was populated by Asiatic migrants across the Bering Strait, would provide the most difficult links in a chain connecting peoples, group by separate group, across the entire world, in the gradual migrations of Neolithic and post-Neolithic times. Such linkages would give a status of more than mere parallelism, and less than racial memory, to the predominant feminine deities of the Japanese and the Navajo, among others. Meletinsky (1979) provides additional evidence of a shared mythology between Siberian groups and Indians of the Pacific Northwest.

3. Plato (*Menexenus* 238 c) declares that woman imitates earth and not earth the woman, bringing the female half of humankind into a special relation with an encompassing Gaia. "By Hera" in Plato always accompanies statements of admiration (Dodds on *Gorgias* 448 d 5).

4. André Leroi-Gourhan (1, pp. 85–99) demonstrates that at all periods of cave wall decoration, male and female symbols, realistic or abstract, tend to be associated with each other, while animals tend not to have their sexual characteristics emphasized or even portrayed. At the same time there are no whole male figures in any distinguishable number to set beside the Venusses. Of the female symbols 91 percent are found at the central portion of the decorated walls, at the places where the cave enlarges, or else in alcoves and fissures. And female symbols, along with the aurochs and the bison associable to them, occupy more than 90 percent of the most distinguishable wall surfaces. The horned dancer outlined on the wall at Trois Frères may well be in the service of the Mother Cult. In any case he does not offer any counterbalance to the multiplicity of her manifestations. Still, a more complex possibility for interaction of male and female may be offered by the complicated positions of the humans outlined in the late Paleolithic cave drawings from Monte Pellegrino near Palermo, and by the marking of lunar periodicities deciphered by Marshak.

5. I owe a version of this idea to a lecture given by Curtis Bennett at SUNY Buffalo, Spring, 1971.

6. Of some 412 Paleolithic sites listed by Müller-Karpe, only 6 are in the Western Hemisphere, all of them in North America. All of them present finds too rudimentary for anything like the constructions about the Paleolithic in the much richer remains from the Old World, though comparable flaking techniques are observable in the artifacts. But the sites hold only the brief remains of short stays during hunting expeditions. As Müller-Karpe says (p. 11), "Da die paläolithischen Funde Nordamerikas von kurzfristigen Jagdaufenthalten herrühren, enthalten sie häufig nur einen eng begrenzten Ausschnitt des der betreffenden Population bekannten Gerätebestandes." ("Since the Paleolithic sites originate in short stays during hunting expeditions, they contain for the most part only a very limited selection of the implements known for the population in question.") Lévi-Strauss, however, does distinguish between the Neolithic in Europe and that in the Western Hemisphere by pointing out that there is little or no domestication of animals to accompany agriculture in the latter (9, p. 390).

7. The notion of a "tribe" poses many difficulties, as set forth by Morton H. Fried (pp. 154–75). And yet it seems a convenient term for characterizing societies of a certain rudimentary sort that have not developed bureaucratic procedures with indirect staff-and-line authority systems. My second phase of the relation between language and myth, for example, I am arguing, is preserved under increasing social complexity. It would cut across Service's three levels of sociocultural integration: the patrifocal band, the tribe (in his more particular use of the term), and the chiefdom, persisting even into societies like that pictured in the Homeric poems where the chiefdom is already on its way towards becoming a kingdom.

8. The word I have rendered as "dispute," *neikos, neikeiein,* has a repertoire of senses that puts many kinds of social strife under its heading, as Adkins (2, pp. 37–38) explains:

> *Neikeiein* is used to characterise Nestor's statement (*Iliad* 7.161) that not even the chieftains of the Greeks are willing to face Hector; Euryalus' remark that Odysseus does not look like an athlete, but a merchant (*Odyssey* 8.158); and a message sent from Zeus to Poseidon by Iris (*Iliad* 15.210). Now the message Zeus gave to Iris was (160ff): "Tell him to stop fighting and rejoin the other gods on Olympus, or go into the sea If not," (163ff). . . .
> Of these examples, the first appears to be a rebuke, the second an insult, and the third a sharp command combined with a threat. Yet all are *neikeiein.*

Nagy (2, pp. 109–10) codes the *neikos* of this passage into the interaction of the hero with his society. Empedocles later abstracts and universalizes this very term as a principle of dissension in the universe (*Neikos*), a counterforce to the principle of unification (*Philia*).

9. Martin Pops traces a whole series of iconographic and ideological projections of labyrinths, from Paleolithic caves to modern pop puzzles, following Rachel Levy for the former.

10. Nardi (XII, glossing *"I'mi son un che quando/amor mi spira', noto, e*

a quel modo/ch'è dita dentro vo significando," cites Richard of St. Victor on the necessity of totality to the presence of love (*De Grad charit.*, I): "*Aut totus (amor) intus est aut nusquam est . . . solus de ea digne loquitur qui, secundum quod cor dictat verba componit.*"

3. HERACLITUS AND THE CONDITIONS OF UTTERANCE

1. Pavese, p. 272 (24 April 1944).
2. Jaeger would attribute the very attempt to define *typoi peri theologias* (*Rep.* 379a) "to the conflict between the mythical tradition and the natural (rational) approach" (2, p. 4).
3. Walter Burkert points out (1962, pp. 35ff.) that Aristotle criticized the numbers of Pythagoras and Plato as not being the same as those of a process of calculation (*Rechenprozess*); Aristotle calls them "not associable" (*asymbletoi, Metaphysics* 1080 A, 29, 1081 A, 1–2). "The relationship of these numbers to the mathematical ones remains uncertain." Pythagoras confuses, Burkert says, the four functions he assigns to numbers: In his system they act as symbols of order, as points in a series, as determinations in space (the image of pebble-lots is used [*psephoi*]), and as a law of nature.
4. Among those who reserve their fullest rigor for the questions of "flux" and "fire" are Jean Bollack and Heinz Wismann, W.K.C. Guthrie, Charles H. Kahn, G.S. Kirk, M. Marcovitch, Karl Popper, Karl Reinhardt, Gregory Vlastos, and W.J. Verdenius.

Almost all of them attempt in some way to connect *logos* and flux or *logos* and fire. We may remain convinced that such a connection obtains, and yet we cannot define it in the face of such small overlap between any pair of these terms in the statements of Heraclitus we do have. Of some one hundred and forty-seven B fragments in Diels, only ten at most mention fire, and only five mention it outright; the larger total counts emendations, compounds (*purkaie, prester*), and verbs that imply fire (*haptesthai*). Of all those there is only one that mentions *logos*, B 31, and the connection is by no means firmly deducible in its exact effects there. There are at least eleven fragments where *logos* or its verb occurs, and another twenty-four mention such arguably relatable notions as *hen, noos, onoma, gignosko,* and *eidenai*. There is next to no mention, direct or indirect, of fire in all these thirty-five statements nor does any one of them mention the three flux fragments, nor is there any overlap at all between "flux" fragments and "fire" fragments. To use the terminology of modern information theory, this lack of overlap offers far too much "noise," and far too little "redundancy" to offer a message; a ratio of 50 percent would usually be needed for defensible decoding, and the language here—though the ratios could be variously tabulated—offers on any tabulation only a minute fraction of that requisite ratio.

This verbal-phenomenological fact should stand as a massive caveat against those who would construct some specific physiological doctrine for Heraclitus as the supposed heir of the Milesians, whom he does not even mention. Moreover, as Cherniss points out (1935; p. 380), Plato never once mentions Heraclitus and fire. (Still, in a context where he will soon mention flux—hōs hoi sophoi phasin aei gar hapanta anō te kai katō rei [*Philebus* 43a]—Plato does touch on the doctrine of universal conflagration without mentioning Heraclitus specifically [29 b-c]. Moreover, *harmonia*, a notable term in Heraclitus, is introduced as an organizing principle shortly thereafter [31 a-d]).

Cherniss, like many others, makes a qualifying statement (p. 381), "Heraclitus did not distinguish between the sign and the thing signified; fire is both a token for exchange like gold in trade (fgt. 90) and is involved in change itself (fgts. 76, 126)." Kahn takes back what he gives away when he first distinguishes Heraclitus from the Milesians and then defines Heraclitus' doctrine in what are really their terms. Karl Reinhardt says in a footnote (1959; 196n), "and finally I believe that in Heraclitus the world-fire generally plays a much more subordinate role than is usually supposed." Kirk himself pauses before the hard facts (1974, p. 193), "Strangely enough, however, we do not find that Heraclitus used his discovery of the unity of opposites in any obvious way at any rate, to explain cosmological phenomena." If so, what is strange is our trying to use Heraclitus' views to do just that. M.L. West (1971) convincingly raises the whole question of the ascription of any doctrines to Heraclitus, though his skepticism throws out the baby with the bath water when he asserts, against the evidence of Heraclitus' thrust as taken by antiquity and also against the very breadth of senses in the word *logos*, that there is no such thing as a *logos* doctrine in Heraclitus' work.

5. Aristotle, *De Mundo* 5 396 b 20, and Strabo in Diels 22.A 3a.

6. Vlastos sees the reference to *dike* in B 80 especially as an echo of Anaximander, and B 30 as a criticism of his doctrine of eternal worlds, while the references to thunder and lightning combine Anaximander and Anaximenes. On the other hand Vlastos admits that Heraclitus is "ignored in Ionia" (p. 368), by Anaxagoras and Leucippus if arguably not by Parmenides and Empedocles. Walter Bröcker, in addition to the *dike* references (B 23, B 80, B 94, B 102), reasons on the basis of a single archaic word in B 126, that the references there to hot, cold, wet, and dry in transformational conjunction are quoted from Anaximander. All we can confidently assert here is that there is a large area of cosmological discourse which Heraclitus inherits from the Milesians and on which he very occasionally touches.

7. See von Fritz (1947) on this point, who cites Snell (1924). It is hard not to see in this aphorism an amplification of half of Archilochus' statement (201 West), *poll oid' alōpēx, all' echīnos hen mega.* "The fox knows many things, the hedgehog one big thing."

8. Liddell and Scott, *sub voc.*

9. To this it might be added that each figure differs from the other three: Pythagoras alone left a cult, Hesiod alone stays close to the Homeric tradition, Xenophanes alone complements a critical attitude towards the gods with a search for philosophical unity, and Hecataeus alone occupies himself in sober prose with presumably verifiable facts.

10. Vlastos, *op. cit.*

11. It may indeed be that those aphorisms were rank-ordered, or put into some other kind of systematic order. But they would have to be regarded as standing free whether they were rank-ordered or not. Otherwise we would be returning them to a form of the continuous discourse from which it was Heraclitus' masterstroke to liberate them. If they were rank-ordered or ordered in some other kind of sequent argument—if Heraclitus were a sort of archaic Wittgenstein—then his book would be a uniquely anachronistic document. It would be hard, if not impossible, to find a parallel at any equiv-

alent stage of any culture, to say nothing of Greek culture. Charles H. Kahn argues that the ambiguity of the word *logos*, together with the plausibility of there having been a doctrine, argues for an ordering of the aphorisms; and he proceeds not exactly to produce one, but to provide, as usual, a doctrine. *Logos* can mean, "on the one hand, a specific utterance, on the other hand, an orderly relationship between things which is reflected in discourse" (p. 192). But even the presence of these two (and many other) meanings in the word *logos* as used by Heraclitus does not argue for a stitching together of the aphorisms. Kahn's point is logically neutral. The fact that *logos* sometimes means "gathering" or "ordering" does not imply that the doctrine of unification (B 32, *hen to sophon*) would have to be expressed in any utterance longer than a single discrete sentence. The absence of any unit even so large as a paragraph in the 147 B fragments we do possess is a considerable counter-argument in favor of the conventional view that the aphorisms stand free. The kind of elaborate rhythmic pattern that Deichgräber repeatedly finds in single aphorisms would also argue for their discreteness: in language a marking of phonological discreteness is also a marking of semantic discreteness. One could, in fact, on this principle, use Deichgräber's analysis to substantiate the discreteness of the aphorisms, though not, as he implicitly does, to argue for the presence in them of a rhythmic pattern more marked than one would find in any well-formed and well-balanced sentences. Alternatively, if one argues for a continuous prose discourse which has somehow been broken up, only at most two or three of the existing 147 "fragments" have such a flow. For the others to have been preserved by chance as distinct and separable utterances would present a situation unparalleled by few if any writers in the whole history of the accidents of literary transmission.

12. Homer's tendency to schematization, especially in the *Iliad*, is discussed in Cedric Whitman, and somewhat differently in Cook (1966).

13. On this point Robert Lowth and Samuel Levin are especially apposite. For reasons no doubt related to the emotional patterning of sound structures in language, there is a permanent tendency for a tradition of prose to develop itself on the assumption of a poetry that it is superseding or supplementing. As Lotman says of Russian literary history, "artistic prose developed on the basis of a defined poetic system, *as its denial*" (italics Lotman's).

It would not be too much to say that all Western practice in prose could be deduced from Heraclitus. This is almost what Eduard Norden does, who locates in Heraclitus the beginnings of balanced rhetorical cola in prose. He then demonstrates how Gorgias may be seen as a specialized version of Heraclitus and goes on to derive all of Western rhetoric, ancient, medieval, and Renaissance, from Gorgias—when in fact he has done so from Heraclitus.

14. Timon of Phlius as cited by Diogenes Laertius, IX, 6 (Diels 22.A1). The word *ainigma*, it is worth noting, occurs first in Heraclitus' slightly younger contemporary Pindar (fgt. 177).

15. As Gregory Vlastos (*op. cit.*) points out, *palintropos* is to be preferred to *palintonos* as the *difficilior lectio*, and the word is also repeated in Parmenides (B 6.9).

16. The identification of oracle with riddle is made twice in the *Agamemnon*: 1112, 1183.

17. *Poetics*, XXII 51.1458a. "The idea of a riddle is to fit the things said together in impossible combination. And it is not possible to do this according to the regular collocation of words, but it can be done according to meta-

phor, as 'I saw a man stick bronze on a man with fire,' and the like." (The answer is a cupping bowl.)

18. See Kranz. Comparable connections about B 93 are made by Uvo Hölscher. Homer, too, prefers the simile; Pindar will rely on metaphor.

19. The elenchic procedure may be said to harness negation in what Bollack and Wismann (18) call the *"antiphrase."*

G.E.R. Lloyd shows Heraclitus as using both polarity and analogy in combination (p. 96), "Two features of Heraclitus' philosophy are especially important . . . (1) his apprehension of the analogy between different examples of opposition, and (2) his alleged violation of the Law of Contradiction." Lloyd's point (1) here has Heraclitus effectually cut across and comprehensively combine the two principles he so amply documents.

20. Bruno Snell begins to make such a distinction that implies an *elenchos* by stressing Heraclitus' emphasis on opposites, remarking on Heraclitus' point of departure from his own consciousness, *"Heraklit geht bei seinem Denken aus von den Zuständen des eigenen Ich . . . hinaus projiziert"* (1924; p. 135). Snell posits (1924, p. 141) a questioning in Heraclitus of the fit between word and thing, especially in B 15, B 32, and B 48. He thus says, suggestively —though this is still not fully an *elenchos*—*"So ist denn die Spannung in dem Wortspiel wohl grösser als man auf den ersten Blick annehmen möchte"* (143).

21. It is perhaps significant that the root *lig* (Pokorny, sub voc.), meaning "gather," appears perhaps first in Greek rather than Sanskrit, its other early occurrences being in Old Persian, Albanian, Latin, and Anglo-Saxon. Guthrie (*op. cit.*, pp. 420–24), lists eleven major senses for *logos*, all of which apply in some degree to Heraclitus: (1) anything said, (2) worth, (3) taking thought or holding a conversation with oneself, (4) reason, argument, (5) the real reason, (6) measure, (7) correspondence, relation, proportion, (8) general principle of rule, (9) the faculty of reason, (10) definition or formula (common in the fourth century but "difficult to pinpoint" in the fifth), (11) idiomatic periphrasis for "say" or other senses. Under each of these headings there is a considerable array of sub-senses, as also in the Liddell and Scott entry for the word, and more elaborately in a source Guthrie cites, Hans Boeder.

22. This is just the example Aristotle uses (*Rhetoric* 1407 b) when he criticizes as not *euphraston*, as though it were a minor stylistic fault of failing to "punctuate" (*diastixai*), this fundamental stylistic practise of Heraclitus. ". . . when the punctuation is hard, as in the writings of Heraclitus. For it is hard to punctuate Heraclitus' writings, since it is unclear to which word another belongs, whether to the preceding one or to the following one, as at the beginning of his book; for he says, 'The word being this always men are ignorant,' where it is unclear whether 'always' should go with 'being' or with 'ignorant' in its punctuation."

23. Kirk (1964; p. 398) offers four initial interpretations of this puzzling aphorism, (i) wisdom is separated from all men; (ii) wisdom is separated from all things; (iii) the wise (cf. *hen to sophon mounon* in fr. 32) is separated from all men; (iv) the wise is separated from all things." His exclusions of i and iii are not finally convincing. Bollack and Wismann add the word "art" in their translation, offering a fifth interpretation, that the art of discourse (*logous*) is in question.

24. The Heraclitean simile always involves primarily a logical rather than a physical comparison, and by this practice it inverts that of the Homeric

simile, wherein a physical comparison can always be detected (Cook, 1966, 98–106). Heraclitus uses similes much more often than Empedocles does, though Empedocles writes in verse; Walther Kranz counts only eleven in the much greater extant body of Empedocles' work. Eberhart Jüngel demonstrates how fully Heraclitus works the logic of his comparisons.

25. Plato, *Cratylus* 402A; Diels 22.A6; also B 12, B 49a.

26. There are traces of a tradition that has Thales asserting the unity of opposites. Diogenes Laertius I, 35 (Diels 11.a1) quotes him as saying "Death is not different from life," the subject and proposition of Heraclitus B 62. Thales is also quoted as declaring night to be prior to "any single day."

27. Evidence from vases and elsewhere as to the chthonic character of Dionysus is discussed in Jane Harrison, 404–411.

28. Jean Bollack, (1971, 67–120) distinguishes poets from theologians in glossing Aristotle Met. 983b27–984–a3, and points out that later in 1074d38–b14 myth is distinguished from an earlier stage. "*Erst dem Philosophen wird daher die Metapher als solche sichtbar.*" (p. 95). However, with Heraclitus, we may say, the metaphor has become invisible rather than visible, and therewith so has the myth.

29. The Zeus of B 120 is an astronomical figure, "God of the bright sky" in A.B. Cook's title phrase.

30. *Rg Veda* 2.12; 10.121, as cited in S.N. Kramer, *Mythologies of the Ancient World*, New York, 1961, 286.

31. Jane Harrison, p. 153. Herodotus (2.47) mentions an Egyptian pig sacrifice involving fire, which he says it is not fitting for him to tell.

32. W.K.C. Guthrie. I follow Bollack, however, in refusing to emend the text by inserting a "not" before *kinoumenos*, a reading which confuses Guthrie's point.

33. Of *theion* and *ethos* as contrasted with *anthropeion* in B 78 and B 14, Shirley Darcus concludes "the human (*anthropeios*) and the divine (*theios*) were seen by Heraclitus as distinct but related states."

34. *Hoteo*, a relative pronoun that goes with either or both alternatively, functions as a metalinguistic qualifier, like the repeated *ekeinon* in B 62.

35. Deichgräber (p. 483) goes so far as to say that *akouein* in Heraclitus' usage amount to *anagignoskein*, "read." His argument, however, rests on a fairly restrictive reading of B1 and other fragments. Elsewhere Liddell and Scott does not attest *akouein* in the sense "read" before Polybius.

36. Diels 3.A2. What is said of Epimenides' writings, allowing for the greater closeness to Homer implied in *epikos*, sounds somewhat like Heraclitus in its inclusion of mysteries and purifications, and its "enigmatic" form: "He wrote much epically, and in prose about certain mysteries and purification and other riddling matters."

Epimenides was sometimes included in the list of the Seven Wise Men, most of whom were lawgivers, like Solon, the Bias of B 35, and the Hermodorus of B 121. Chadwick (I, p. 494) reminds us that "Written literature usually begins with the writing of the laws," and he gives evidence from England, Sweden, Denmark, Norway, and Iceland, which could be amplified by the cases of Greece, Israel, Babylonia, and perhaps also the India of the *Manavadharmshastra*, the China of Confucius, and others.

37. Following the *difficilior lectio, palintropos*. See note 15 above.

38. Again the possibility of precise and complex alternate interpretation for Heraclitus' aphorisms is illustrated by Flora R. Levin's reading (personal

communication) of the verbs in B 51 together with the lyre especially, 'how what is different agrees with itself'—has to do with the lyre; while 'borne apart,' etc., has to do with the bow. Heraclitus could be talking about the *octave* or *harmonia* (in the sense of Pythagoras), in which the 'same' note is emitted in a 'different' register. Thus A is 'borne apart' to A1 like the contrary force of the bow string.

"Hence, in what way can a thing that is borne together be at the same time borne apart? Answer, a bow or lyre tuned to an octave (like Terpander's) so:

tension	slackening	bow
high	low	lyre
forth	back	both
different	same	both*

*all in *palintropos*"

39. Plato, indeed, applies the principle of change much discussed among the followers of Heraclitus to their mode of utterance and argument (*Thaeatetus*, 179e–180b):

Theodorus . . . in Ionia the sect makes rapid strides; the companions of Heraclitus powerfully lead the chorus of the doctrine.

Socrates Then we are the more bound, my dear Theodorus, to examine the question from the foundation as it is set forth by themselves.

Theodorus Certainly we are. About these speculations of Heraclitus, which, as you say, are as old as Homer, or even older still, the Ephesians themselves, who profess to know them, no sooner talk about them than they are stung to madness. For, in accordance with their books, they are absolutely carried along; but as for dwelling upon an argument or a question and quietly asking and answering in turn, they can do that worse than anything; or rather, the determination of these fellows not to have a particle of rest in them is more than the utmost powers of negation can express. If you ask any of them a question, he will pull out, as from a quiver, little riddling utterances, and shoot them at you; and if you inquire the reason of what he has said, you will be hit by some other new-fangled word, and will make no way with any of them, nor they with one another; their great care is, not to allow of any settled principle either in their arguments or in their souls, conceiving, as I imagine, that any such principle would be stationary; for they are at war with the stationary, and do what they can to drive it out everywhere.

(—Jowett, revised)

It may be that the term "souls" (*psychas*) and the metaphor of the bow are both ironic and oblique references to Heraclitus.

As a forerunner in the great philosophical tradition that Plato would transmit, Heraclitus has already performed upon mythic thinking a large share of the work that Walter Hirsch attributes to Plato, and his formulations (p. 167) could be applied to Heraclitus with little adjustment, *"Die Schwierigkeit im Übergang zum Mythos ist für die Philosophie Platons das Problem, ihn an den Logos zurückzubinden. Die Lösung dieser Aufgabe wird vorbereitet durch den Versuch, dem Logos das ihm Mögliche an Beweglichkeit abzugewinnen—eine Denkweise, die im platonischen Entwurf Dialektik heisst."* (The difficulty in the transition to *mythos* is for Plato's philosophy the problem, to connect it back to the *logos*. The solution of this task is prepared for in the attempt to win for the *logos* a maximum mobility—a mode of thinking that is called dialectic in Plato's project.)

4. PINDAR: "GREAT DEEDS OF PROWESS ARE ALWAYS MANY-MYTHED"

1. All citations are from the edition of Snell (1964).

2. Here the "fourth labor among three" (60) probably refers to the whole system of traditional punishments, to Tantalus' fellow offenders whom Pindar does not name in this ode, though he does elsewhere: Ixion (*P*.1.21), Tityos (*P*.4.46, 90), and Sisyphus (*O*.13.52; fgt. 5). Pelops himself gives his name to the entire Peloponnesus, and the "six sons" mentioned but not named in the last clause about him before the present reference to his tomb could be related to the complex myths of other heroes whom Pindar also mentions elsewhere, however the list is given: Atreus, Thyestes, Pittheus, Alcothoos, Pleisthenes, Chrysippus (or Hippalkmos and Dias. *Scholia*, Drachmann, *ad loc*). Through Atreus and Thyestes we ultimately get the Trojan war, through Chrysippus the Theban legend, through Hippalkmos the voyage of the *Argo*.

3. Some scholars such as Bundy (p. 37), have read the passage, "one race of gods, one of men" as indicating separate races. If so, the "one mother" would be abrupt and the "wholly differentiating power" would lack its contrast. Again, Hesiod in the *Works and Days* (*homothen*, 106) stresses the common origin of Gods and Men.

4. David C. Young's survey, "Pindaric Criticism," shows that since Dissen's work over a century ago the question of "unity," of a central thread in an ode and the relation of individual myths, apophthegms, or even single words thereto, has been a persistent and dominant preoccupation of studies of Pindar. That a dynamic instability obtains of the relations between one myth and another in an ode, and between myth and victor, is attested to by such prolonged and various perplexities of interpretation.

5. Among those who discuss Pindar's "ring composition" are Finley; Schadewalt, who speaks of *"die oft bei Pindar zu beachtender 'Ringkomposition' der erzählenden Teile"* (p. 308, n.1); L. Illig; R.W.B. Burton; and David C. Young.

6. Metaphors about ships and voyages in Pindar's work are extensive enough to have occasioned a book-length study: Jacques Péron, *Les Images maritimes de Pindare*. And he says (p. 23), *"Pour Pindare la poésie est avant tout mouvement; ses odes, comme il le dit dans la IIe Isthmique, il ne les a pas faites pour qu'elles restent en place."*

7. *O*.1.116; *O*.9.38; *P*.1.12; *P*.4.248; *P*.6.49; *N*.6.23; *I*.7.18; *Pa*.7B.20. *Sophos* = poet, *P*.3.113; *I*.1.45; *Pa*.18.3; *O*.1.9; *P*.9.78; *P*.10.22; *I*.8.47; Fgt. 35b.

8. Gildersleeve offers one example (pp. 301–302): "Who is the oak? Iason. But as Iason would be the type of Damophilos, Arkesilas would be Pelias, which is monstrous."

9. *P*.5.14,55,102; also *P*.4.141, 255.

10. Farnell (*ad loc*, II, p. 182) calls the word "almost intolerable," and says correctly that Wilamowitz's defense of the text (p. 383, n.1) "lacks clearness." There would, further, seem little justification for Wilamowitz's assertion here: *"chronos ist ja immer so zu sagen eine Linie, kairos ein Punkt."* Bowra rejects the repeated manuscript reading *"chronon"* for Bergk's taming emendation, *chloan*, a word otherwise unexampled in Pindar.

The scholiast (Drachmann, II, 191) twice uses the word in explaining the four lines generally, but he does not specifically so gloss.

11. Nilsson (1906) came to the conclusion that secularism dominated the

Pythian festival, *"Uber die Pythien kann ich mich kurz fassen da die agonistische Bedeutung die religiose völlig verdrangt hat."*

12. Cook (1971, pp. 5–6). "So, in the myth to begin with, the emotion attendant on bringing together the general of the group and the particular of the individual reconciles, as merely differences of emphasis, such seemingly contradictory assertions about the function of myth as Freud's insistence on the individual on the one hand (1955; p. 153) ("The myth is then the step by which the individual moves out of the psychology of the mass") and Lévi-Strauss' group-language definition of myth on the other (L–S 4, p. 36) ("Music exposes to the individual his own physiological roots; mythology, his social roots. One takes us in the guts; the other, if one may dare to say it, 'in the group' ").

13. Young (p. 122) elaborates *Olympian* 1 into a ten-fold circular pattern with exactly matching line-lengths for the corresponding sections of the ode —a pattern not congruent with the colametric structure.

14. The verbs are *agallo* (*agalma*) *agamai, aglaizo, aineo* and *epaineo, amphaino, arnumai, atuzomai, boao, gegoneo, daidallo, daizo, dainumi, damazo, elelizo, elpomai, ereido, erizo, euchomai, thuio, iaino, kainumai, kamno, keladeo, klazo, kraino, maiomai, marpto, marnamai, nikao, olophuromai, horizomai, orthao, hormao, pertho, pelamai, piaino, ripto, saino, speudo, tarasso, teleo,* and *orouo, tello, timao, phaino, phrisso, cheo.* All these verbs suggest a constantly energetic and creative action.

15. To the adjectives already listed may be added: *habros, aidoios, aithon, hapas, atrekes, aphneos, bathus, dnopheros, exochos, eslos, euthus, eurus, euphron, zatheos, thama* (adv.), *thaumastos, thrasus, kalos, karteros, kleennos, kleitos, klutos, kraipnos, kratistos, labros, leukos, liparos, malthakos, megas, xanthos, obrimos, holos, oxus, orthos, peran* (adv.), *pikros, polus, potanos, potnia, saphes, tachus, trachus, phthoneros, philos, okus.*

16. Detienne (1967) finds *aletheia* always entangled at this period in a context of myth.

17. Pindar touches here and there on the chthonic maternal deity who appears through Greece as Artemis, Cybele, Demeter, Persephone, and at one point in his work simply as "the Mother": "But I wish myself to offer a prayer/To the Mother, the holy goddess whom maidens before my door/Sing at night, and with a prayer to Pan" (*Pythian* 3.77–79). Young believes (pp. 45ff) that this invocation to the Great Mother, as a substitute for Asklepius, is made because of her accessibility, rather than for some specific healing function—an interpretation which substantiates the comprehensiveness of her figure. The mention of Pan here preserves the association of Dionysus and related deities to a problematic female element in the Dionysiac procession, and in the birth and bearing of this god. And Demeter is linked with Dionysus at the beginning of *Isthmian* 5.(105); as the Great Mother Goddess with Pan (fgt. 96).

At another point Pindar wishes a group of Theban legendary heroines to make a night procession in honor to the shrine of a local goddess, Melia (*Pythian*.11.1–16) with an emphasis on the feminine element that Méautis stresses (pp. 264–65). While, for example, Empedocles' evocation of this chthonic deity (*Katharmoi*, B 128 Diels) is more prolonged and detailed than any Pindar offers us, Pindar's very inclusions are significant in the light of the primarily, if not exclusively, male character of the athletic contests and celebrations. Pelias insults Jason by asking him "who of earth-born men (*chamaigeneon*) brought you forth from her hoary womb?" (*Pythian* 4.98), and we cannot speak here with Lévi-Strauss in his analysis elsewhere of chthonic overvaluation, either pro or con, but rather simply of a sensitizing to the terms. The Mother is linked with Pan in fgt. 96, and other references to her by that name occur in *O.*7.38; *N.*6.2; fgt. 80; and Dithyramb 2.9 (fgt. 70b). The cult figure of a goddess associated with trees whom we may seem to recognize from Minoan and Mycenean seals is evoked at *P.*4.74, of an oracle to Pelias "spoken at the mid-navel of the mother with fine trees (*eudendreos*)." Pindar names Demeter three times, Earth (*Gaia*) five, and Hera twenty-two—not to speak of the Muses (about sixty times).

The opening of *Isthmian* 5 addresses "Mother of the Sun, the Divine (Theia) of many names." While this particular designation, Theia, is borrowed from Hesiod (*Theogony* 371), the term is vague, with a general and inclusive force which Wilamowitz (pp. 201–203) emphasizes. Farnell (1907, III, pp. 289–307) provides a large context in archaic Greece for the cult of a Mother Goddess.

G.L. Huxley points out a divergence between Homer (*Iliad* 5.370ff and 428) and Hesiod (*Theogony*, 353) as to Dione and the birth of Aphrodite, indicating an instability about origins. This instability is paralleled, in Hesiod, by an implicit instability of focus: the *Erga* offers a pattern for almost exclusively male enterprise, while the *Eoiai*, taken in antiquity to be Hesiod's, is concerned exclusively with females.

18. *O.*1.30; *O.*2.50; *N.*9.54; *I.*5.21.

5. INQUIRY: HERODOTUS

1. George Thomson (1, p. 83), emphasizing the use of *isocola* in Gorgias and Heraclitus, links both through this formal practice to the ritual of the dirge. He says of Heraclitus "all the elements of his dialectic are embedded in primitive religion."

2. Aristotle uses the word *arrhythmon* in connection with him (though verse echoes have been found in him at least since Demetrius [181]).

Here one must contradict Aristotle's assertion that "Herodotus could be put into meters and he would be no less history with meter than without meters" (*Poetics* 1451 G.3).

Aristotle characterizes the paratactic style by quoting the opening of Herodotus, and his terms are suggestive for more than style (*Rhetoric* 1409a; 1404a):

The strung (paratactic) style is the old one: "Of Herodotus of Thurium's inquiry this is the exposition" . . .

Since the poets in saying pleasant things by means of style thought they were providing a notion, in this way there came to be a poetic (prose) style, as that of Gorgias.

3. As Fritz Schulz says (p. 25), "Important legal acts were indeed recorded in writing as early as the Sixth Century B.C. (in Rome), but the writing was purely evidential, the record of an already fully accomplished legal act; at most the document might serve to simplify the spoken formula by being referred to in it as containing details . . . The same appears to hold of Greek law in pre-Hellenistic times."

4. *Aitia*, a noun roughly meaning "cause" (where the adjective *"aitios"* in Homer means "guilty"), occurs in Pindar, *Olympian* 1.35, and here and there in the pre-Socratics, though not often before Democritus, unless Anaximander's doctrine as phrased by Plutarch (Diels 12.A10) be taken for the words of the early writer.

5. Choruses of women who utter rebukes (*kertomioi*) are also described in Herodotus 5.83.

6. On the question of what lurks under the story, Aristotle makes a distinction, unfortunately given honorific currency by Sidney and others in the Renaissance, that is quite simply too easy. He distinguishes between a *historia* that tells events as they happen and a *poiesis* that tells essential events as they might happen, *poiesis* telling the general and *historia* the particular:

> From what has been said it is clear too that the poet's job is not to tell what has happened but the kind of things that can happen, i.e., the kind of events that are possible according to probability or necessity. For the difference between the historian and the poet is not in their presenting accounts that are versified or not versified, since it would be possible for Herodotus' work to be put into verses and it would be no less a kind of history with verse than it is without verses; rather the difference is this: the one tells what has happened, the other the kind of things that can happen. And in fact that is why the writing of poetry is a more philosophical activity, and one to be taken more seriously, than the writing of history; for poetry tells us rather the universals, history the particulars.
> (*Poetics* 1451b 2–3)
> Translated by Gerald F. Else

Aristotle makes this last remark to amplify what he had just said about Herodotus' being characterized by content and not by metrical form. Yet "the universals" and "the particulars" as well as "the kind of things that can happen" are either so obvious as distinctions—and themselves so universal—or so particularly bound up with the terms of Aristotle's system, that they cannot serve other than to beg the question of what might lurk under the story. In any case, as Longinus implicitly reminds us, Herodotus is also poetic; and we know that Homer is also historical. And so the crucial sanctimonious remark embedded in this discussion, "therefore *poiesis* is both more philosophical and nobler than *historia*," is not only gratuitous but obscures important points.

7. See note 21, chapter 3. Related logical difficulties make the word *logioi* hard to interpret (Thomas Cole, p. 58, n.34).

8. Powell, sub voc.

9. The case of Cleobis and Biton, in its references to the religion of a mother deity, must contain for the modern anthropologist echoes of the sort of mother-cult, Cybele and other, on the terrain of Asia Minor rather than Argos, where the cart in which the goddess rides is drawn or at least worshipped by enfeebled male devotees. There is also for us the psychoanalytic pattern of a sibling rivalry totally sublimated, to the death, in a superego service to the mother. And it is a fact, shocking to us if not to Solon and Herodotus, that the mother was only overjoyed (*perichares*) and the other Argive women only congratulated her on her good fortune in having such sons. But of course these extrapolations into myth or depth psychology are not possible in Herodotus, even so much as they would be in Homer, because

this story exists as an exemplum, coordinate with and complementary to the story of Tellus (one father, one mother; two sons, two daughters).

10. Benardete trenchantly arrays the detail of this comparison, and I am here generally following his lead.

11. The Greeks developed early a curiosity about the specific origins of their peoples, as distinct from the common tribal question about the origin of humanity in general. The five ages of man in Hesiod's *Erga* try to satisfy this curiosity with a systematic account, and the question is touched on by Pindar and Empedocles, as well as by Thucydides. Plato's account of the age of Kronos in the *Politicus* and of Atlantis in the *Timaeus* are in the same vein. There, in fact, he may be said to parallel Herodotus, since he offers an account of word-of-mouth tradition through sources comparable to Herodotus': a third-hand auditor of Solon recounts what an Egyptian priest told him about the destruction of Atlantis by earthquake (27–28), leading first to some ethnographic data, then to a creation story, and finally to an abstract redefinition of the cyclic, time as the moving image of eternity (38a–b).

12. This one passage would seem to be sufficient answer both to the separatists who urge that the *Egyptioi logoi* are detachable enough to have been written at some other time, and the unitarians who argue a tight and elaborate coherence of the history at all points. Both are right, and neither; Herodotus' own conception of *historie* rules out the exclusiveness of either view.

13. Invisibility has powerful connections in itself with bureaucracy, the new abstractions of money, law, and philosophy, as Marc Shell argues in "The Ring of Gyges."

6. OVID: THE DIALECTICS OF RECOVERY FROM ATAVISM

1. Ovid handles the Muses as intricately as he does his other materials. In Books IV and V of the *Fasti* he imagines them discussing which should guide his poem, and disagreeing (V, 9, "*dissensere deae*"). He himself feigns (V, 1–8) not to know which of several directions to take, though of course, given the framework of his poem, he knows he must at this point deal with Maia and with the first of May. He then has Polyhymnia and Urania speaking in alternation, with Thalia and Clio approving (a procedure it would be easy to read allegorically). Fränkel (1945, p. 240) points out that Callimachus, too, has his muse conversing with him, and yet it would not be so elaborately.

In the *Ars Amatoria* Ovid contrasts the Muses with experience and says his aim is to speak truth, distinguishing himself from Hesiod (*Ascra*):

> Nec mihi sunt visae Clio Cliusque sorores
> Servanti pecudes vallibus, Ascra, tuis;
> Usus opus movet hic: vati parete perito;
> Vera canam: coeptis mater Amoris ades!

> Clio and Clio's sisters have not been seen by me
> As I was minding my flocks, O Ascra, in thy vales;
> Use moves this work: appear to an experienced bard;
> I shall sing the truth: mother of Love, be here as I begin!
>
> (I, 27–30)

The charge surrounding the Venus whom the last trope names is considerably reduced from that which Lucretius accords the *alma Venus* of his invocation, though Ovid diverges from the "lying" Hesiod in the direction of truth, as

Lucretius claims also to have done. Yet the very last words of the *Metamorphoses* assert that their function is to bring fame to the poet, and the last word of all is *vivam*, "I shall live."

Later, in the *Fasti*, he declares his impartiality before the individual Muses

> turbae pars habet omnis idem.
> gratia Pieridum nobis aequaliter adsit
> nullaque laudetur plusve minusve mihi

> Each part of the throng has the same;
> May favor towards the Pierides be equally present in us,
> and may none be praised more greatly or less by me.
>   (V, 108–110)

In the *Tristia* poetry is described as a sort of obsession, "perhaps the way the beaten gladiator seeks out the sand again," "scilicet ut victus repetit gladiator harenam" (II, 17), though he also soon speaks of the power in song to invoke great gods, "exorant magnos carmina saepe dios" (II, 22). It is hard not to see both casualness and freedom in these diverse attitudes towards the Muses.

2. For Lucretius the parts of the body are not composed of Aristotelian elements but of rather volatile forces: air, heat, breath, and a fourth part, "mixta latens animi vis est animaeque potestas," "a mixed hidden force of animus and power of anima" (III, 277).

3. As Bateson forcefully demonstrates, tone is not simply overtone. Rather, in literature and in natural language, it is always philosophically extensible. Ovid often confects a situation in which he is bantering with his gods or muses. On the one hand he cannot be disengaged from some form of belief even in the deified emperor, a credence with which many modern interpreters have struggled, sometimes trying to undermine it by applying to it the modality of the irony which Ovid does in fact apply to all sacral entities in his poem. He would seem, for example, to take at face value the descent of the shield from the sky: "Credite dicenti; mira sed acta loquor"/"Believe me when I speak: I tell of wonders but ones which were done" (*Fasti* III, 370). And very soon in the same poem, speaking of the emperor's accession to "pontificalis honor," he assigns an equally firm credence to the divine *numen* of the emperor in a way we find equally difficult to understand, given his irony: "ignibus aeternis aeterni numina praesunt/ Caesaris: imperii pignora iuncta vides." "Over eternal flames the divine powers of eternal Caesar/Preside: of empire you see the pledges unified." (*Fasti* III, 421–22).

4. In the *locus amoenus* trees are always shady, streams purling, meadows flowery, waterfalls crystalline. We do have these "pleasant" attributes, for example, in the *Fasti*'s description of Henna where (III, 420–44) Pluto abducts Proserpina: "valle umbrosa, aspergina multa/uvidus . . . prata," and the set-piece of flower descriptions (430–44). The delineation, however, has opened with some "unpleasant" non-pastoral terms: *vastum, scopulis* (419), touching on the same note once again in *inanis* (433). The uniformly "pleasant," and lingering, flower description is suddenly interrupted by the act of abduction, rendered swiftly in a single line so summary that it contains no adjectives but only the adverb of that manner: "hanc videt et visam patruus velociter aufert," "There saw her and, seen, her uncle rapidly snatched her off" (445). This line is immediately followed by the striking use of an ominously "pleasant" adjective. It is the only one in its line, which its four syllables dominate: "regnaque caeruleis in sua portat equis," "and car-

ried her on cerulean horses to his kingdom" (446). The dark blue, coming so soon after the flowers, has a pleasant air, and it suggests the beautiful visible attributes away from which Proserpina will be carried. But it anticipates the cancellation of those attributes under the earth; and *caeruleus* is also used of rain at night, the altars of the Manes, etc. Since *caeruleus* is a standard epithet for Neptune and the sea, and since Neptune has horses, the third brother is briefly touched metonymically into this picture (Jupiter is implied by the relationship of *patruus*, 445); the horses will soon be under the earth —they cannot stand the sunlight—and the "pleasant" connotations of *caeruleus* will fall away. Meanwhile both pleasant and unpleasant associations with the terms in the immediately preceding lines of the poem are gathered up into the one word *caeruleis*, the pleasant ones destined, as Prosperina is herself, for rapid change.

In the *Metamorphoses* the "unpleasant" elements of the landscape are dwelt on more fully, and the same story itself is coded for more complex connections: it is told by the Muses as Calliope's winning entry in a contest between the Muses and the bird-changed Pierides, as a result of which the Muses take over the springs on Helicon. These have sprung up under the hoof of Pegasus after he was released through the death of Medusa by Perseus. Minerva is told the Persephone story because she is now free of the long job of protecting Perseus and has gone there precisely because news of the springs had reached her ears (*Metamorphoses* V, 230ff).

5. Otis summarizes the metrical attributes of their respective styles (pp. 74–75): "Hence the un-Virgilian character of Ovid's metric: he sacrificed most of the weight, gravity and *ethos* of Virgil's hexameter to rapid and unbroken movement. By increasing the number of dactyls, regularizing the pauses and, above all, reducing the elisions, he made his lines move at a very accelerated pace. . . . the proportion of elisions to the total of lines in the whole Aeneid and Metamorphoses is 15.6% for Ovid and 50.3% for Vergil."*

6. Albrecht discusses the play of tone in the *Metamorphoses*; D'Elia, that in the *Fasti*. As Walther Kraus says of the *Metamorphoses*, "The scope extends from hard tragedy (6.589ff) to keen comedy (1.415ff, 2.36ff)."

7. The lightness of the interwoven verbs, and in a divine conversation, may lead to an outright joke, as in these words of Jupiter to Numa: "addidit hic 'hominis': 'sumes' ait ille 'capillos.'/postulat hic animam, cui Numa 'piscis' ait." "The latter added '(head) of a man': 'you will take' said the former 'hair'./He demanded the life, and to him Numa said 'fish'" (*Fasti* III, 341–42). Here we are given a kind of sub-riddling request on the god's part and a weaseling, but effective, reply from the legendary king. The verbs wind down for the final answer, though a touch of their complexity still clings to Numa's one-word answer, since *piscis* could be taken either in the nominative or the genitive.

8. Lucretius touches from time to time on allegory, as when he argues that Tityos, Tantalus, etc., are to be understood not as legendary figures in the afterlife but as *exempla* for activities in this life (III, 979ff).

9. The *Thesaurus Linguae Latinae* lists most of these uses of *concelebro* as preceding Lucretius. Plautus (*Pseud.* 165) and Lucilius (790) use the word in the sense of celebrating a festival day (Greek *suneortazo*), Plautus (*As.* 799) and Terence (*Phormio praef.* 3.4) in the sense of inhabit or fill,

---

*See A. Siedow, *De Elisionis usu in hexametris Latinis* (1911), p. 55.

and Plautus also in the senses of causing to abound (*Ca* IV, iii,2) and of solemnizing (*Ps.* I,ii,32).

7. BETWEEN PROSE AND POETRY: THE SPEECH AND SILENCE OF THE PROVERB

1. Various deductions about the necessity of presupposition for the structural rules of some statements are made by Richard Garner, George Lakoff, Robin Lakoff, Edward L. Keenan, and Arnold M. Zwicky in Fillmore and Langendoen. As George Lakoff says (p. 69),

> certain sentences will be grammatical only relative to certain presuppositions and deductions, that is, to certain thoughts and thought processes and the situations to which they correspond. This seems to me wholly natural.
> The consequences of these observations are important for both linguistics and natural logic. Logic, as it is normally studied, involves a formal system containing axioms and rules of inference which are not constrained with respect to either form or content by empirical linguistic considerations. But these observations show that natural logic must be so constrained, at least with respect to the form of expressions.

2. The ancients classified such locutions as proverbs. For example, "hang by a hair," Diogenianus 4.40 and "write on water," *ibid.* 5.83 (in Leutsch and Schneidewin, i, pp. 238, 267).

3. Chinese is rich in such locutions, as Arthur H. Smith demonstrates.

4. This is also independently declared at 1 Kings 5:12, "And he spoke three thousand proverbs."

5. Aristotle couples Stesichorus and Aesop as producers of maxims (*Rhetoric* 1393b) which he goes on to define (1394a2), "it deals . . . with the objects of human actions, and with what should be chosen or avoided with reference to them. As the enthymeme is, as we may say, the syllogism dealing with such things, maxims (*gnomai*) are the premises or conclusions of enthymemes without the syllogism."

6. Dümler, ed., *Epistulae Karolini Aevi*, IV, No. 132, as cited in Boas, pp. 8–9.

7. Gordon, 2.125, p. 265, "Their pleasure, their discomfort; their discomfort, their pleasure." This is deduced to mean "One man's meat is another man's poison."

8. Gordon, 1.154, p. 121: "*Dam-nu-gar-ra e-a ti-lam-am/a-sag-a-sag-e dirig-ga-am.*" "A thriftless wife surviving in a household is afflicted with all the sickness (demon)s." This implies the same general ethic, though put in negative rather than positive terms, as *Many a mickle makes a muckle*. It is highly wrought, with many rhymes and assonances. The language is firm, and the idea has a comparably firm position in a society hierarchical enough for more than marginal differences to show in the household management of a storage economy, which is here reflected on. The Protestant ethic of *Many a mickle makes a muckle* would be just a special development of such a reflection.

9. Greek offers a special grammatical category for the verbs of the proverb, the gnomic aorist. Gesenius lists no corresponding form in Hebrew, but the combination of the repetitive imperfect and the jussive imperfect offers something comparable, as for example in Proverbs 2:6, "For the Lord gives

wisdom," where "gives" is in the imperfect rather than in the normal (present) perfect form, (*Az JHVH yiten chokhmah*). There seems to have been no gnomic aorist in Sanskrit, which may correlate with the fact that at a corresponding period there are no separate collections of proverbs in Sanskrit.

10. Searle (p. 41) follows the tradition of Kant in distinguishing between regulative rules and constitutive rules. The first "regulate antecedently existing forms of behavior; for example, the rules of etiquette regulate interpersonal relationships, but these relationships exist independently of the rules of etiquette. Some rules on the other hand do not merely regulate but create or define new forms of behavior." The proverb has both regulative and constitutive features.

11. William Alston characterizes a fair share of "linguistic acts" as "rule-recognition acts." In saying "open the door" I imply that the auditor knows my statement will conform to the rules for this command, that there is a door, that the door is not open, that it is possible for the auditor to open it, and that I wish it open. In this light, too, the proverb is metalinguistic. It frames for recognition a general rule that could be applied to the specific circumstance in which it is uttered: it at once constitutes and comments on a linguistic act, being thereby metaphysical even when not explicitly metalinguistic.

12. Margot Norris spells out some philosophical consequences of Joyce's linguistic manipulations. See also Cook, 1967.

8. THE SELF-ENCLOSURE OF THE RIDDLE

1. In some respects the interchange pattern of the riddle resembles that of the witticism, a verbal sequence brought to an explosive climax by the speaker to create an effect in the hearer. The interchange might well be subjected to versions of the libido analyses which Freud accords the witticism. But the riddle has to do with death as well as some sublimated form of sexuality; the riddle was a death-test in early cultures, presented to Oedipus by a powerful sex-icon, the Sphinx. Even in ordinary conversation, as Martin Pops says (personal communication), the riddle produces

> discomfiture . . . no matter what the answer [one is] disappointed . . . riddles are like magic tricks, as indeed they are tricks in language. . . . Almost everyone gets the point of a joke—a small (and perhaps self-deceiving) accomplishment which prompts a joke in return. Is the reason one hardly ever tells a riddle in return because one hardly ever "gets" one, on one's own? To tell a riddle in return, then, is a kind of revenge (i.e., an act of unseemly earnestness, not playful reciprocity).

Lévi-Strauss (10, pp. 32–35) connects the riddle as a form of expression and the incest taboo for cultural conjunction and some structural homology, noting, after Boas, that the North American Indian tradition tends to lack both riddles and proverbs. The relative absence of these forms would substantiate my own assignment of them to a second phase, and also my attribution of the growth of riddle and proverb to the inception of the third phase —though in fact the Athabascan languages are supposed to have a riddling tradition. These peoples, however, border on the Eskimos and their rich culture.

2. Tryphon (*Rhetores Graeci*, III, 90) gives six types of riddle: like, opposite, coincidence, history, homonymy, and language.

3. "You speak enigmas, my good man, or do you compose riddles? For uncommonly like Apollo you make nothing clear."

4. Borges makes a similar point.

5. The earliest form of the riddle of the Sphinx comes from Asklepiades of Tragilos, a fourth-century compiler, as quoted in the scholia on Euripides' *Phoenissae* 45 (Robert, p. 56), and as quoted in Athenaeus, X, 456b. Robert conjectures that five broken letters on a fifth-century vase may be a quotation from the riddle.

Variants of the Sphinx riddle appear in Thompson's *Motif-Index of Folk-Literature* under H 761.

9. PARABLE

1. Jeremias, 1966, p. 10, "Jesus' parables are something entirely new. In all the rabbinic literature, not one single parable has come down to us from the period before Jesus; only two similes from Rabbi Hillel (c. 20 B.C.), who jokingly compared the body with a statue, and the soul with a quest. It is among the sayings of Rabban Jochanan ben Zakkai (d. c. A.D. 80) that we first meet with a parable. . . . As its imagery resembles one of Jesus' parables, we may well ask whether Jesus' model (together with other factors, such as Greek animal fables) did not have an important influence on the rabbi's adopting parables as a narrative form."

2. Ibid., p. 102.

3. Hauch (Kittel, x V, p. 751, sub voc *parabole*) quotes Jeremias on the "zweifache Sitz im Leben" of the parables. He goes on to discuss their tendency to shift the context of their auditors, and to alter their allegorical bearing in mid-narration.

4. Matthew 13:1–52, 20:1–16, and 24:32–25,30. Mark 4:1–34. Luke 8:4–18, 10:25–37, 13:6–21, 15:11–16.31, and 18:1–19:27. John 10:1–18.

5. Details on these are given in Bolte and Polivka, 1, pp. 41–45.

10. METAPHOR: LITERATURE'S ACCESS TO MYTH

1. Von Franz (pp. 9–10) diagrams the interconnections between the tree, as an example of a central symbol, and spring, death, bird, mother, moon, sun, sun god, ancestor, phallus, bull, and father.

> The sun myth and the tree myth are connected, for in the morning the sun is born in the east out of the tree . . . every Christmas the tree gives birth to the new light in the moment of the winter solstice . . . the tree is also a mother . . . in Saxony, even now, it is said that beautiful girls grow under the leaves of trees . . . the souls of unborn children rustle under the leaves. . . . But the tree is not only the mother of life but also the death mother, because from trees coffins are made, and there are the tree burials . . . Under every tree there is a spring. There is the world-ash Yggdrasil with the Urd well underneath. . . . As the mother the tree is feminine, but it is also the father because the tree is a phallic symbol; for instance, in the Aztec chronicles the word for the original land where the Aztecs and the Mayans emigrated represents a broken-off tree. . . . There

are stories of a woman passing a tree and a seed from the tree entering her womb. Therefore clearly the tree is a father, and that links up with the tree being the sun, which is a father-figure.

2. "Children do not learn to speak metaphorically as a kind of crowning achievement in the apprenticeship of language-learning. Rather they use metaphors naturally from infancy onwards, and have gradually to learn—with respect to each noun, verb, adjective or adverb—how to speak literally. 'The car shouted at me,' says the child. 'No, it hooted at you,' corrects the parent. It is psychogenetically more illuminating to view literal patterns of word-use as the result of imposing certain restrictions on metaphorical ones, than to view metaphorical patterns as the results of removing certain restrictions from literal ones. The deliberate utterance of metaphor, in the awareness that it is such, is no doubt a phenomenon of adult *parole*. But metaphorical sentences are as much part of the *langue* that children acquire as are non-metaphorical ones." (723)

3. The Opies sketch a history for the nursery rhyme that remarkably parallels that for riddle and parable, and to a lesser extent that for proverb (pp. 6–9): a few references in antiquity, a few in the Middle Ages, and a sudden burgeoning and blossoming in the sixteenth century. Again, a comparable phenomenological set towards the world of myth, taken together with a related conception of what a human futurity, and so childhood, may be, would allow for the generation of this particular blend of art song, folk song, proverb, riddle, and parable—again without any reference more than residual to mythic structures.

4. Derrida 4, p. 323:

> La métaphore est donc determinée par la philosophie comme perte provisoire du sens . . . C'est pourquoi l'évaluation philosophique en a été toujours ambigu. La métaphore est menaçante et étrangère au regard de *l'intuition* (vision ou contact), du *concept* . . . , de la *conscience*; mais elle est complice de ce qu'elle menace . . . L'opposition de l'intuition du concept et de la conscience n'a plus, à ce point, aucune pertinence. [So metaphor is determined by philosophy as a provisional loss of sense. . . . That is why its evaluation by philosophy has always been ambiguous. Metaphor is menacing and strange in face of the intuition (vision or contact) of the *concept* . . . , of *consciousness* but it is always in complicity with that which it menaces. The opposition between intuition and concept, and consciousness, has at this point no longer any pertinence.]

5. Pound's massive displacement of the political and cultural history into image-points and anecdote-points may be illustrated by his handling in these lines of so little in what we might find to be important for the Ch'in dynasty (his"Tsin"). As he continues:

> Wall rose in the time of TSIN CHI
> TCHEOU lasted eight centuries and then TSIN came
> and of TSIN was CHI HOANG TI that united all China
> who referred to himself as the surplus
> or needless bit of the Empire
>   and jacked up astronomy
> and after 33 years burnt the books
>   because of fool literati
>   by counsel of Li-sse
> save medicine and on field works
>   and HAN was after 43 years of TSIN dynasty.

That is all Pound gives us for what Goodrich narrates in a "Short History" already far more succinct than the eight French volumes on which Pound bases his verses:

> Scorned by the other states for their uncouthness and barbarity, the people of Ch'in absorbed some of their critics' culture and over-looked no opportunity to improve their military fitness. The teach-ings of a succession of statesmen who followed the Lord of Shang had made their government the best disciplined and most purposive of any east of the Gobi. In 318 the Ch'in, who dominated the north-west, moved into Szechuan and seized control of the great food-producing plain. The huge irrigation system which the governor and his son reputedly began there about 300 has banished serious floods and droughts for twenty-two centuries and is still in existence. A canal nearly one hundred miles long was cut across Shensi in 246 to enrich the alkaline soil with water laden with silt. The produc-tivity of this region, says the annalist, promptly increased about twenty-eight pecks per square mile. Having thus assured a food supply, the authorities erected a grain station near modern Kaifeng to provision their troops. To break up the feudal system no fief was granted after 238. To guard against rebellion in the rear and to provide labor there was considerable transfer of the population from one province to another during 239–235 B.C. Powerful fam-ilies—120,000 in all, according to the annalist—were required to move to the capital at Hsien-yang in modern Shensi. By 234 Cheng, who as a young boy had become head of Ch'in in 247, was ready to put his armies in the field and by 222 he had vanquished the last of the rival states. The combination of excellent preparation, con-stant pressure, and superb mastery of the newest arts of war, es-pecially cavalry, proved too much for his enemies. He promptly created the first empire and assumed the title of First Emperor (Shih-huang-ti); his system of government lasted till the twentieth century." (31–32).

Goodrich goes on to outline that system of government and to describe what Pound mentions in just one word, the building of the Great Wall.

6. Angus Fletcher's book on allegory is thus always on the verge of trans-forming most literary works into allegories and literary theory in general into the theory of allegory. So his "demonic agent" accounts for the incorporation of myth-forces into allegories (and literary works generally); and his "cosmic image," with its many references to novels, is extensible to the treatment by any literary work of a comprehensive notion of reality: "For naturalistic fables the range of the imagery would be nothing less than the range of nat-ural phenomena itself, and at that point the loosening-up of the term *kosmos* would be complete" (p. 146).

11. Language and Myth

1. Was it just accidentally that Mallarmé wrote a long-projected school textbook on myth, *Les Dieux Antiques*?

2. Even an emphasis on semantic questions entails such a concern. As Donald Davidson says (p. 248), "But meaningfulness is only the shadow of meaning; a full-fledged theory should not merely ticket the meaningful ex-pressions, but give their meanings. The point is acknowledged by many lin-guists today, but for the most part they admit they do not know how to meet this additional demand on theory, nor even how to formulate the demand."

3. "I wrote Leda and the Swan because the editor of a political review asked me for a poem. I thought, 'After the individualist, demagogic movement, founded by Hobbes and popularized by the Encyclopaedists and the French Revolution, we have a soil so exhausted that it cannot grow that crop again for centuries.' Then I thought, 'Nothing is now possible but some movement from above preceded by some violent annunciation.' My fancy began to play with Leda and the Swan for metaphor, and I began this poem; but as I wrote, bird and lady took such possession of the scene that all politics went out of it, and my friend tells me that his 'conservative readers would misunderstand the poem.' " (Quoted in Ellmann and O'Clair, p. 134.) Yeats sets the whole in a narrative (Yeats, pp. 50–51; Michael Robartes and Owen Aherne are mysterious visitors): " 'Or transformation,' Aherne corrected once more. 'If you had answered differently,' said Robartes, 'I would have sent you away, for we are here to consider the terror that is to come.' "

4. That adding meter to language defines poetry is a topos in Plato (Gorgias 502c): "If one took the song and the rhythm and the meter from the whole of poetry, would there be anything left but statements?" And Gorgias said it too (Helen 9): "I think and name all poetry to be a statement possessing meter."

For another line of argument, in Ṛgveda III, 38, Indra enjoins poets to contemplate him. In X, 71, the act of naming is a function of revealing through love what is hidden inside the poet.

5. *Parabole* was also the word used in the Septuagint to translate the Hebrew *mashal*, "proverb."

6. Brian Caraher, in an unpublished paper on the riddles of the Exeter Book, finds them to be characteristically involved in mediating the contradictions of existence as exemplified in the single figure of a riddle in question. This is an intermediate stage, as the riddle form preserves some of the sacral context from which it separates itself by combining with the "poem" form.

7. I heard samples of all these played at the University of Michigan conference on Oral Literature and the Formula, November, 1974.

8. Something of this modality is implied in what Hartman (2) calls "Hesperian" poetry, using the "Ode to Autumn" as a chief example.

9. Lacan presents a hierarchy of four sets, each re-ordering the one below, for the sequences of alternating presence and absence of "the symbolic," as it functions in a person's determination of the significations he uses (1, pp. 6–61). He thus makes a calculus out of Freud's repetition-compulsion and Kierkegaard's principle of repetition (both examples his). As he asserts (p. 46), "Cette répétition étant répétition symbolique, il s'y avère que l'ordre du symbole ne peut plus être conçu comme constitué par l'homme, mais comme le constituant." It would not be difficult to translate "le constituant," since it is "l'ordre du symbole," into the ground of myth and the unknown; *ethos anthropo daimon.*

10. Bateson, like Lévi-Strauss and in a way parallel to Lacan's, translates the component of feeling in human affairs into a cybernetic system of levels of communication. He keeps quoting Pascal on the reasons of the heart, leaving the heart nothing but its reasons. It is to be expected that he would feel Lévi-Strauss to be misunderstood (pp. 138–39). "They say he emphasizes too much the intellect and ignores the feelings. The truth is that he assumes that the heart has precise algorithms." And of feelings he himself says,

"Among Anglo-Saxons, it is rather usual to think of the 'reasons' of the heart or of the unconscious as inchoate forces or pushes or heavings—what Freud called *Trieben*. To Pascal, a Frenchman, the matter was rather different, and he no doubt thought of the reasons of the heart as a body of logic or computation as precise and complex as the reasons of consciousness."

In all this he puts the reader in what might appropriately be called a double bind. Since he at once praises the unconscious and offers important insights into its function as a communicative system, he would seem to be enlisting the proponents of art, humor, interplay, and freedom on the side of an argument that can neither be accepted nor rejected—without laying oneself open to the accusation of Anglo-Saxon ethnocentrism which the Anglo-Saxon Bateson has generously taken the lead in leaving behind.

11. I owe this term to Gary Gabriel. Derrida himself well characterizes the tendency of philosophy to get caught in mazes when facing metaphor, though he does not, characteristically, commit himself as to the possibility of issuing therefrom (See Chapter Ten, Note 4). His lack of commitment, of course, is part of a "deconstructive" strategy, undertaken with impressive subtlety and consistency, to "ruiner par aporie le discours métaphysique" in the words of Paul Ricoeur (1975, 365). As Ricoeur shows, by maintaining a distinction that Derrida overrides between live metaphor and dead, "parler métaphoriquement de la métaphore n'est aucunement circulaire dès lors que la position du concept procède dialectiquement de la métaphore elle-même." Moreover, identifying metaphors, live or dead, on the significative surfaces of texts can never reach the modality of their function within the whole speech act of philosophical statement or poem—categories which must be prior, for utterance to take place, to the specific manifestations of figures within such utterances. In such a deconstructive attention to language, the function of myth in poetry and the establishment of assent in philosophy, necessary to the transfer of communication, become obscured. See also Cook (7).

12. The differences between Hirsch and Gadamer (as both change positions) may be seen not just in their agreement on specific hermeneutic issues but also in the emphases implied by their leading terms.

13. Emphasis on this term, and the possibility of elaborating this point, I owe to Samuel Weber.

14. Recent commentators have stressed the distinctiveness of the Old Testament vision in its emphasis on a *deus absconditus* against the prevailingly myth-enmeshed systems of the Mediterranean countries surrounding Israel. As Herbert Schneidau well puts it, for example (p. 4), "literature differs from analogues such as myth by virtue of its self-conscious relation to culture. In the Bible this relation finds expression . . . in a great image . . . in which the absolute gulf between God and his creatures manifests itself."

15. Liu (pp. 4–5) lists this as *Huei-yi*, "understanding the meaning," a third type of composite character in which the simple character for "field" and the simple character for "strength" are combined to give the character *Hsiang-hsing*, signifying "man." Of all his six classes only the first three would have functions paralleling Egyptian hieroglyphics: *Hsiang-hsing*, "imitating the form," where a picture of the sun stands for "*jih*," "sun"; the second, *Chih-shih*, "pointing at the thing," where a simple grapheme stands for a number or the pictogram for tree is altered by one stroke to mean "tree-top" and by another to mean "tree-root" or "pen"; and the third, *Hsieh-cheng*,

"harmonizing the sound," where the composite phonogram is used as a component of the sound of another.

As Needham says (1, p. 32), "Of the 49,000 characters given in the great dictionary Khang-Hsi Tzu Tien of +1716 not more than five percent are pictographs and symbols; all the rest are of the sixth class (*Hsing-Sheng*, "picture plus sound")."

As for the relation between the development of science and the form of writing, he says (4, xxiv), "Chinese mathematics was indelibly algebraic rather than geometrical," whereas, for Greece, in Lasserre's view (p. 64), "If we leave aside the identification, construction and calculation of the areas of figures, this geometry directed all its efforts towards one goal: the study of relations." Greek geometry—which was all of Greek mathematics up to Plato's time—concerned itself with problems which might have been phrased in other than geometrical terms. The careful, abstract spatialization of an alphabet could be related to this tendency, for it was also the period of Democritus' atomic theory. And as Needham goes on to comment (4, p. 30), "Now it is a striking, and perhaps significant, fact that the languages of all those civilizations which developed atomic theories were alphabetic."

16. The term "Chinese mythology" is probably too global for the early period, however. As Eberhard cautions (p. 14), "The area of modern China was the seat of more than ten sharply outlined cultures."

LIST OF WORKS CITED

Adkins, A. W. H.
    (1) *Merit and Responsibility: A Study in Greek Values.* Oxford: Clarendon Press, 1960.
    (2) *From the Many to the One.* London: Constable, 1970.
Adorno, Theodor W.
    (1) *Noten zur Literatur* I. Frankfurt: Suhrkamp, 1958.
    (2) *Philosophie der neuen Musik.* Frankfurt: Ullstein, 1958.
Albertz, D. M.
    (1) *Botschaft des Neuen Testaments.* Zurich: 1947–52.
    (2) *Die synoptische Streitgespräche.* Berlin: 1921.
Albrecht, Michael von. "Ovids Humor und die Einheit der Metamorphosen." In Albrecht and Zinn.
Albrecht, Michael von, and Zinn, Ernst, eds. *Ovid.* Wege der Forschung, 92 Darmstadt: Wissenschaftliche Buchgesellschaft, 1968.
Alston, William P. "Linguistic Acts." *American Philosophical Quarterly* 1 (April 1964):138–46.
Ariès, Philippe. "At the Point of Origin." *Yale French Studies* 43:15–23.
Austin, J. L. *How to Do Things With Words.* Oxford: Clarendon Press, 1962.
Bachelard, Gaston.
    (1) *La psychanalyse du feu.* Paris: Gallimard, 1949.
    (2) *L'eau et les rêves.* Paris: José Corti, 1963.
Badian, Ernst. "Ennius and His Friends." In *Entretiens sur L'Antiquité Classique* XVII. Vandoeuvres (Geneva): Fondation Hardt, 1972.
Bailey, Cyril. *Titi Lucreti Cari De Rerum Natura.* Oxford: Clarendon Press, 1947.
Barthes, Roland.
    (1) *Critique et vérité.* Paris: Seuil, 1966.
    (2) *S/Z.* Paris: Seuil, 1970.
Bataille, Georges.
    (1) *La Part maudite.* Paris: Minuit, 1967.
    (2) *L'Erotisme.* Paris: Minuit, 1957.
Bateson, Gregory. *Steps to an Ecology of Mind.* New York: Ballantine, 1972.
Bellah, Robert N. "Religious Evolution." In Lessa and Vogt.
Benardete, Seth. *Herodotean Inquiries.* The Hague: Nijhoff, 1969.
Bernbeck, Ernst Jürgen. *Beobachtungen zur Darstellungsart in Ovids Metamorphosen.* Münich: C. H. Beck, 1967.
Bettelheim, Bruno. *The Uses of Enchantment: The Meaning and Importance of Fairy Tales.* New York: Knopf, 1976.
Binns, J. W., ed. *Ovid.* London: Routledge & Kegan Paul, 1973.
Bischoff, Heinrich. "Der Warner Bei Herodot." In Marg.
Black, Max. *Models and Metaphors.* Ithaca: Cornell University Press, 1962.
Boas, George. *Vox Populi.* Baltimore: Johns Hopkins University Press, 1969.

Boeder, Hans. *Archiv für Begriffsgeschichte,* 1958, as cited in Guthrie, pp. 82ff.

Böhtlingk, Otto. *Indische Sprüche.* Osnabruck: Zeller, 1966 (1870–1873).

Bollack, Jean. "Mythische Deutung und Deutung des Mythos." In *Terror und Spiel,* edited by Manfred Fuhrman. Munich: W. Fink, 1971.

Bollack, Jean, and Wismann, Heinz. *Héraclite ou la séparation.* Paris: Minuit, 1972.

Bolte, Johannes, and Polivka, Georg, eds. *Anmerkungen zu den Kinder und Hausmärchen der Brüder Grimm.* Leipzig: Dieterich'sche, 1930.

Bömer, Franz. "Ovid und die Sprache Vergils." In Albrecht and Zinn.

Borges, Jorge Luis. "The Kenning." *The New Yorker,* 26 January 1976, pp. 35–36.

Bowra, C. M., ed. *Pindari Carmina.* Oxford: Clarendon Press, 1935.

Brandt, Per Aage. "The White-Haired Generator." *Poetics* 6 (1972):72–83.

Breton, André. *Clair de terre.* Paris: Gallimard, 1973 [1932].

Bröcker, Walter. *"Heraklit Zitiert Anaximander." Hermes* 84 (1956):382–84. Reprinted in Gadamer.

Brooke-Rose, Christine. *A Grammar of Metaphor.* London: Secker and Warburg, 1958.

Brown, John Pairman. "Techniques of Imperial Control: The Background of the Gospel Event." *Radical Religion* 2, no. 2 (1975):73–83.

Budge, E. A. Wallis. *The Egyptian Book of the Dead.* New York: Dover, 1967 (1895).

Bultmann, Rudolf. *The Theology of the New Testament.* New York: Scribner's, 1951.

Bundy, Elroy. *Studia Pindarica* I, II. *University of California Publications in Classical Philology* 18 (1962):1–34; 35–92.

Burkert, Walter.
    (1) *Weisheit und Wissenschaft.* Nuremberg: H. Carl, 1962.
    (2) *Homo Necans.* Berlin: De Gruyter, 1972.

Burton, R. W. B. *Pindar's Pythian Odes.* Oxford: Oxford University Press, 1962.

Bury, J. B. *Ancient Greek Historians.* New York: Dover, 1958.

Butterworth, E. A. S. *Some Traces of the Pre-Olympian World in Greek Literature and Myth.* Berlin: De Gruyter, 1966.

Calder, William M. III, and Stern, Jacob, eds. *Pindaros und Bakchylides.* Wege der Forschung 124. Darmstadt: Wissenschaftliche Buchgesellschaft, 1970.

Campbell, Joseph, ed. *Man and Time.* Eranos Yearbooks 3. New York: Pantheon, 1957.

Capovilla, Giovanni. *Callimaco.* Rome: L'Erma, 1967.

Caraher, Brian. See Massey.

Cassirer, Ernst. *Language and Myth.* New York: Harper, 1946.

Cerri, Giovanni. See Gentile.

Chadwick, H. M., and Chadwick, N. K. *The Growth of Literature* I. Cambridge: Cambridge University Press, 1932.

Chantraine, Pierre. In *Mélanges Henri Grégoire.* Brussels: Annuaire de L'Institut de Philologie et d'histoire orientales et slaves, 1949, IX.

Charbonnier, Georges. *Entretiens avec Claude Lévi-Strauss.* Paris: Plon, 1961.

Chatman, Seymour, ed. *Literary Style: A Symposium*. London: Oxford University Press, 1971.

Cherniss, Harold. *Aristotle's Criticism of Presocratic Philosophy*. Baltimore: Johns Hopkins University Press, 1935.

Chomsky, Noam.
    (1) *Syntactic Structures*. The Hague: Mouton, 1957.
    (2) *Aspects of the Theory of Syntax*. Cambridge: MIT Press, 1965.

Cohen, L. Jonathan, and Margalit, Avishai. "The Role of Inductive Reasoning in the Interpretation of Metaphor." In Davidson and Harmon.

Cohen, Marcel. *La Grande invention de l'écriture, et son évolution*. Paris: Imprimerie Nationale, 1958.

Cole, Thomas. *Democritus and the Sources of Greek Anthropology*. Cleveland: Western Reserve University Press, 1967.

Collingwood, R. G. *The Idea of History*. Oxford: Clarendon Press, 1946.

Cook, A. B. *Zeus*. Vol. 1 Cambridge: Cambridge University Press, 1925.

Cook, Albert.
    (1) *The Meaning of Fiction*. Detroit: Wayne State University Press, 1960.
    (2) *The Classic Line*. Bloomington: Indiana University Press, 1966.
    (3) *Prisms*. Bloomington: Indiana University Press, 1967.
    (4) *Enactment: Greek Tragedy*. Chicago: Swallow Press, 1971.
    (5) *Shakespeare's Enactment*. Chicago: Swallow Press, 1976.
    (6) "Lévi-Strauss and Myth: A Review of *Mythologiques*." MLN 91, no. 5 (October 1976):1099–1115.
    (7) "Aspects of Image: Some Problems," *Journal of Aesthetics and Art Criticism*, Spring 1980.

Cox, Harvey. *The Secular City*. New York: Macmillan, 1965.

Dale, A. M. "The Metrical Units of Greek Lyric Verse." *Classical Quarterly* 44 (1950).138–51; n.s. 1 (1951):119–29.

Daniélou, Jean. *Sacramentum Futuri*. Paris: Beauchesne, 1950.

Darcus, Shirley. *"Daimon* and *Ethos* in Heraclitus." *Phoenix* 28, no. 4 (1974): 390–407.

Davidson, Donald. "Semantics for Natural Languages." In Davidson and Harmon.

Davidson, Donald, and Harmon, Gilbert, eds. *Semantics of Natural Language*. Dordrecht: D. Reidel, 1972.

Davies, W. D. *The Setting of the Sermon on the Mount*. Cambridge: Cambridge University Press, 1966.

De George, Rand F., ed. *The Structuralists from Marx to Lévi-Strauss*. New York: Anchor, 1972.

Deichgräber, Karl. *Rhythmische Elemente im Logos des Heraklit*. Wiesbaden: F. Steiner, 1962.

Deleuze, Gilles. *L'Anti-Oedipe*. Paris: Minuit, 1972.

D'Elia, Salvatore. "Die Ironie in Ovids Fasten." In Albrecht and Zinn.

Dentan, Robert C., ed. *The Idea of History in the Ancient Near East*. New Haven: Yale University Press, 1955.

Derrida, Jacques.
    (1) *De la Grammatologie*. Paris: Minuit, 1967.
    (2) *L'Ecriture et la différence*. Paris: Minuit, 1967.
    (3) *La Dissémination*. Paris: Minuit, 1970.

(4) *Marges*. Paris: Minuit, 1972.

Detienne, Marcel.

(1) *Les Maîtres de vérité dans la grèce archaique*. Paris: Maspero, 1967.

(2) *Les Jardins d'Adonis*. Paris: Gallimard, 1972.

Diamond, Stanley. *The Search for the Primitive*. New York: E. P. Dutton, 1974.

Diels, Hermann. *Herakleitos*. Berlin: 1909.

Diels, Hermann, and Kranz, Walther. Diels, *Die Fragmente der Vorsokratiker*. 3 vols. Revised by Walther Kranz. Berlin: Weidmann, 1960 (1903–51).

Dirringer, David. *Writing*. New York: Praeger, 1962.

Dissen, L. *Pindari carmina quae supersunt*. Gotha and Erfurt: 1830.

Dodds, E. R. *Plato's Gorgias*. Oxford: Clarendon Press, 1959.

Drachmann, A. B. *Scholia Vetera in Pindari Carmina*. Amsterdam: Hakkert, 1964 (1910).

Driver, Samuel R. *An Introduction to the Literature of the Old Testament*. New York: Meridian, 1956 (1897).

Dronke, Peter. *Medieval Latin and the Rise of European Love Lyric*. 2 vols. Oxford: Clarendon Press, 1966.

Duchemin, Jacqueline. "Essai sur le symbolisme Pindarique: or, lumière et couleurs." In Calder and Stern.

Dumézil, Georges.

(1) *Mythe et épopée*. Paris: Gallimard, 1968.

(2) *La Religion romaine archaique*. Paris: Payot, 1974.

Durand, Gilbert. *Les Structures anthropologiques de l'imaginaire*. Paris: Presses Universitaires, 1963.

Eberhard, Wolfram. *The Local Cultures of South and East China*. Leiden: Brill, 1968.

Eco, Umberto. *A Theory of Semiotics*. Bloomington: Indiana University Press, 1976.

Ehwald, Rudolf, and Haupt, Moriz. *P. Ovidius Naso, Metamorphosen*. Zurich: Weidmann, 1966 (1853).

Eliade, Mircea.

(1) *Aspects du mythe*. Paris: Gallimard, 1963.

(2) *Le Sacré et le profane*. Paris: Gallimard, 1965.

Ellman, Richard, and O'Clair, Robert, eds. *The Norton Anthology of Modern Poetry*. New York: Norton, 1973.

Else, Gerald F. *Aristotle's Poetics: The Argument*. Cambridge: Harvard University Press, 1963.

Farnell, L. R.

(1) *The Cults of the Greek States*. 5 vols. Oxford: Clarendon Press, 1896–1909.

(2) *The Works of Pindar*. 3 vols. London: Macmillan, 1930–32.

Farrar, Austin. *A Rebirth of Images*. Boston: Beacon Press, 1963 (1949).

Fillmore, Charles J., and Langendoen, D. Terence, eds. *Studies in Linguistic Semantics*. New York: Holt, Rinehart and Winston, 1971.

Finley, John H. *Pindar and Aeschylus*. Cambridge: Harvard University Press, 1955.

Fish, Stanley. *Self-Consuming Artifacts.* Berkeley: University of California Press, 1972.

Fletcher, Angus. *Allegory.* Ithaca: Cornell University Press, 1964.

Fontenrose, Joseph. *Python: A Study of Delphic Myth and Its Origins.* Berkeley: University of California Press, 1959.

Foucault, Michel. *Les Mots et les choses.* Paris: Gallimard, 1966.

Fränkel, Herman.
  (1) "Pindar's Religion." *Die Antike* 3 (1927):39–63. Reprinted in Calder and Stern.
  (2) "A Thought Pattern in Heraclitus." *American Journal of Philology* 59 (1938):214–28. Reprinted in Mourelatos.
  (3) *Wege und Formen Frühgriechischen Denkens.* Munich: C. H. Beck, 1960.
  (4) *Ovid: A Poet Between Two Worlds.* Berkeley: University of California Press, 1945.

Frege, Gottlob. "Sense and Reference." 1892. Reprinted in *The Philosophical Review* 57, no. 3 (May 1948):207–29.

Freidenberg, Olga M. *Mif i literatura drevnosti.* Moscow: Nauka, 1978.

Freud, Sigmund.
  (1) "Massenpsychologie und Ich-Analyse." In *Gesammelte Werke,* Vol. 13, pp. 71–162. London: S. Fischer Verlag/Imago, 1955 (Frankfurt: S. Fischer Verlag, 1921).
  (2) *Die Traumdeutung.* Vienna: Deuticke, 1899.

Fried, Morton H. *The Evolution of Political Society.* New York: Random House, 1967.

Friedlaender, Paul. *Plato.* Translated by Hans Meyerhoff. Bollingen Series. Princeton: Princeton University Press, 1958.

Furley, David H., and Allen, R. E., eds. *Studies in Pre-Socratic Philosophy.* New York: Humanities Press, 1970.

Furth, Montgomery. "Elements of Eleatic Ontology." *Journal of the History of Philosophy* 6, no. 2 (April 1968):111–32. Reprinted in Mourelatos.

Gadamer, Hans-Georg, ed.
  (1) *Wahrheit und Methode.* Tübingen: Mohr, 1960.
  (2) *Um die Begriffswelt der Vorsokratiker.* Wege der Forschung 9. Darmstadt: Wissenschaftliche Buchgesellschaft, 1968.

Gardiner, Patrick, ed. *Theories of History.* Glencoe, Ill.: Free Press, 1959.

Garner, Richard. " 'Presupposition' in Philosophy and Linguistics." In Fillmore and Langendoen.

Gelb, I. J. *A Study of Writing.* Chicago: University of Chicago Press, 1952.

Gentile, Bruno, and Cerri, Giovanni. "Strutture communicative del discorso storico nel pensiero storicografico dei Greci." *Il Verri,* June 1973, pp. 52–78.

Giedion, Siegfried. *The Eternal Present.* New York: Pantheon, 1962.

Gigon, Olof. *Der Ursprung des Griechischen Philosophie von Hesiod bis Parmenides.* Basel: Benno Schwabe, 1945.

Gildersleeve, Basil L. *Pindar: The Olympian and Pythian Odes.* New York: Harper and Brothers, 1885.

Gimbutas, Marija. *The Gods of Old Europe.* London: Thames and Hudson, 1974.

Girard, René. *La Violence et le sacré.* Paris: Grasset, 1972.

Gluski, Jerzy. *Proverbs.* Amsterdam: Elsevier, 1971.

Gogarten, Friedrich. *Der Mensch Zwischen Gott und Welt.* Stuttgart: Friedrich Vorwerr Verlag, 1956.

Gomme, A. W. *A Historical Commentary on Thucydides.* Oxford: Clarendon Press, 1956.

Goodrich, L. Carrington. *A Short History of the Chinese Peoples.* New York: Harper, 1959.

Gordon, Edmund I. *Sumerian Proverbs.* Philadelphia: University Museum, 1959.

Gottschalk, Walter. *Die Bildhaften Sprichwörter der Romanen.* Heidelberg: Carl Winter, 1935.

Graves, Robert. *The White Goddess.* London: Faber, 1949.

Grimal, Pierre, ed. *Larousse World Mythology.* New York: Prometheus, 1965.

Grimm, Jacob. *Über Deutsche Runen.* Göttingen: 1821.

Guthrie, W. K. C. *A History of Greek Philosophy.* Vol. I. Cambridge: Cambridge University Press, 1962.

Hainsworth, J. B. *The Flexibility of the Homeric Formula.* Oxford: Clarendon Press, 1968.

Hamilton, Richard. *The Epinikion.* The Hague: Mouton, 1974.

Harman, Gilbert, ed. *On Noam Chomsky.* New York: Doubleday, 1974.

Harrison, Jane. *Prolegomena to the Study of Greek Religion.* New York: Meridian, 1957 (1903).

Hartman, Geoffrey.
   (1) *Beyond Formalism.* New Haven: Yale University Press, 1970.
   (2) *The Fate of Reading.* Chicago: University of Chicago Press, 1975.

Haupt, Moriz. See Ehwald.

Havelock, Eric. *Preface to Plato.* Cambridge: Harvard University Press, 1963.

Hawkes, David, trans. *Ch'u Tzu, The Songs of the South.* Oxford: Clarendon Press, 1959.

Hegel, Friedrich. *Aesthetik.* Frankfurt: Europäische Verlagsanstalt, n.d. (1842).

Heidegger, Martin.
   (1) *Vorträge* III. Pfullingen: G. Neske, 1954.
   (2) *Unterwegs zur Sprache.* Pfullingen: G. Neske, 1959.

Heinze, Richard. "Ovids elegische Erzählung." *Berichte der Sachsischen Akademie der Wissenschaft* 71, no. 7 (1919).

Hexter, Jack. *Doing History.* Bloomington: Indiana University Press, 1971.

Hirsch, E. D. *Validity in Interpretation.* New Haven: Yale University Press, 1967.

Hirsch, Walter. *Platons Weg zum Mythos.* Berlin: De Gruyter, 1971.

Holland, Norman N. *The Dynamics of Literary Response.* New York: Oxford University Press, 1968.

Hollis, A. S., ed. *Ovid: Metamorphoses Book VIII.* Oxford: Clarendon Press, 1970.

Hölscher, Uvo.
   (1) *Anfängliches Fragen.* Göttingen: Vandenhoeck und Ruprecht, 1968.

(2) "Paradox, Simile and Gnomic Utterance in Heraclitus." In Mourelatos. Reprinted from *Anfängliches Fragen.*

How, W. W., and Wells, J. *A Commentary on Herodotus.* Oxford: Clarendon Press, 1912.

Huxley, G. L. *Greek Epic Poetry from Eumelos to Panyassis.* London: Faber, 1969.

Illig, L. *Zur Form der Pindarischen Erzählung.* Berlin: Junker und Dünn-
haupt, 1932.

Jaeger, Werner.
   (1) *Paideia,* 1935. Translated by Gilbert Highet. New York: Oxford
      University Press, 1965 (1939).
   (2) *Theology of the Early Greek Philosophers.* Translated by S. Robin-
      son. Oxford: Clarendon Press, 1960 (1947).

Jahn, Jahnheinz. *Muntu.* New York: Grove Press, 1961.

Jeffery, L. H. *The Local Scripts of Archaic Greece.* Oxford: Clarendon Press,
1961.

Jeremias, Joachim J. *Rediscovering the Parables.* New York: Scribner's,
1966.

Jolles, André. *Einfache Formen.* Tübingen: Niemeyer, 1968 (1930).

Jowett, Benjamin. *The Dialogues of Plato.* New York: Random House, 1937
(1892).

Jüngel, Eberhard. *Zum Ursprung der Analogie bei Parmenides und Heraklit.*
Berlin: De Gruyter, 1964.

Kafka, Franz. *Briefe an Felice.* Hamburg: S. Fischer, 1970.

Kahn, Charles H. "A New Look at Heraclitus." *American Philosophical
Quarterly* 1 (1964):189–203.

Keenan, Edward L. "Two Kinds of Presupposition in Natural Language." In
Fillmore and Langendoen.

Kenney, E. J. "Style in Ovid's *Metamorphoses.*" In Binns.

Kirchberg, Jutta. *Die Funktion der Orakel im Werke Herodots.* Göttingen:
Vandenhoeck and Ruprecht, 1965.

Kirk, Geoffrey S.
   (1) "Natural Change in Heraclitus." *Mind* 60 (1951):35–42. Reprinted
      in Mourelatos.
   (2) *Heraclitus: The Cosmic Fragments.* Cambridge: Cambridge Uni-
      versity Press, 1962.
   (3) "Popper on Science and the Pre-Socratics." In Furley and Allen.

Kittel, G., and Friedrich, Gerhard. *Theologisches Wörterbuch zum Neuen
Testament.* Stuttgart: Kohlhamer, 1927–1973.

Köhnken, Adolf. *Die Funktion des Mythos bei Pindar.* Berlin/New York:
De Gruyter, 1971.

Kramer, Samuel N., ed. *Mythologies of the Ancient World.* New York:
Doubleday, 1961.

Kranz, Walther. "Gleichnis und Vergleich in der Frühgriechischen Philosophie." *Hermes* 73 (1938):99–122.

Kraus, Walther. "Ovidius Naso" in *Der Kleine Pauly.* Münich: Druckemüller,
1972.

Lacan, Jacques.
   (1) *Ecrits.* Paris: Seuil, 1966.
   (2) *Le Séminaire* I. Paris: Seuil, 1975.

Lafaye, Georges. *Les Métamorphoses d'Ovide et leurs modèles grecs*. Hildesheim: Olms, 1971 (1904).

Lakoff, George. "The Role of Deduction in Grammar." In Fillmore and
Langendoen.

Lakoff, Robin. "Ifs, Ands, and Buts about Conjunction." In Fillmore and
Langendoen.

Latte, Kurt. "Die Anfänge der Griechischen Geschichtsschreibung." In *Entretiens sur L'Antiquité Classique* IV. Vandoeuvres (Geneva): Fondation Hardt.

Leroi-Gourhan André.
> (1) *Les Religions de la préhistoire*. Paris: Presses Universitaires, 1964.
> (2) *Le Geste et la parole*. Paris: Albin Michel, 1965.

Lessa, William A., and Vogt, Evon Z. *Reader in Comparative Religion*. New
York: Harper and Row, 1972.

Leutsch, E. L., and Schneidewin, F. G. *Corpus Paroemiographorum Grae-
corum*. Hildesheim: Olms, 1965 (1839).

Lévi-Strauss, Claude.
> (1) *Anthropologie Structurale*. Paris: Plon, 1958.
> *Structural Anthropology*. New York: Doubleday, 1967.
> (2) *Tristes Tropiques*. Paris: Plon, 1955.
> *Tristes Tropiques*. New York: Atheneum, 1974.
> (3) *La Pensée Sauvage*. Paris: Plon, 1968.
> *The Savage Mind*. Chicago: University of Chicago Press, 1966.
> *Mythologiques*
> In the text, I indicate the *Mythologiques* by initials (English initials in
> the case of works that have been translated into English).
> (4) *Le Cru et le cuit*. Paris: Plon, 1964.
> *The Raw and the Cooked*. New York: Harper and Row, 1970 (RC).
> (5) *Du Miel aux cendres*. Paris: Plon, 1966.
> *From Honey to Ashes*. New York: Harper and Row, 1973 (HA).
> (6) *L'Origine des manières de table*. Paris: Plon, 1968 (OMT).
> (7) *L'Homme nu*. Paris: Plon, 1971 (HN).
> (8) Introduction to *Sociologie et anthropologie,* by Marcel Mauss.
> Paris: Presses Universitaires, 1968.
> (9) *Anthropologie structurale deux*. Paris: Plon, 1973.

Lévi-Strauss, Claude, and Jakobson, Roman. "Let Chats de Baudelaire." In
De George.

Levin, Samuel R.
> (1) *Linguistic Structures in Poetry*. The Hague: Mouton, 1962.
> (2) *The Semantics of Metaphor*. Baltimore: Johns Hopkins Univer-
> sity Press, 1977.

Levin, Saul. "Know Thyself: Inner Compulsions Uncovered by Oracles." In
Fons Perennis, Saggi Critici in Onore di Prof. Vittorio D'Agostino.
Turin: Baccola and Gili, 1971.

Levy, Rachel. *Religious Conceptions of the Stone Age*. New York: Harper,
1963 (first published as *The Gate of Horn*, 1958).

Lewis, David. "Natural Semantics." In Davidson and Harmon.

Liddell, Henry G., and Scott, Robert, eds. *A Greek English Lexicon*. Revised
and augmented by Sir Henry Stuart Jones and R. McKenzie. Oxford:
Clarendon Press, 1968.

Liu, James J. Y. *The Art of Chinese Poetry*. Chicago: University of Chicago Press, 1962.

Lloyd, G. E. R. *Polarity and Analogy: Two Types of Argumentation in Greek Thought*. Cambridge: Cambridge University Press, 1966.

Lotman, Juri M. *Lektsii po struktural'noe poetike*. Providence: Brown University Press, 1968 (1964).

Lowth, Robert. *De Sacra Poesi Hebraeorum Praelectiones Academicae*. London: 1753.

Lüthi, Max. *Das Europäische Volksmärchen*. Bern: Francke, 1947.

Mack, Dorothy. "Metaphoring as Speech Act." *Poetics* 4 (1975):221–56.

Mallarmé, Stéphane. *Oeuvres complètes*. Paris: Gallimard (Pleiade), 1945.

Maranda, Elli Köngas. "The Logic of Riddles." In *The Structural Interpretation of Oral Literature*, edited by Pierre Maranda and Elli Köngas Maranda. Philadelphia: University of Pennsylvania Press, 1971.

Marcovitch, M. *Heraclitus: Editio Maior*. Mérida, Venezuela: Los Andes University Press, 1967.

Marg, Walter, ed. *Herodot*. Münich: C. H. Beck, 1962.

Marouzeau, Jules. "Ein Verfahren Ovids." In Albrecht and Zinn. "Un procédé Ovidien." *Ovidiana*, Paris, 1958, 101–105.

Marshak, Alexander. *The Roots of Civilization*. New York: McGraw-Hill, 1972.

Massey, Irving. *The Gaping Pig*. Berkeley: University of California Press, 1976.

Massey, Irving, and Caraher, Brian. *Literature and Contradiction: Occasional Papers*. SUNY at Buffalo, New York: 1974. Mimeographed.

Mauss, Marcel. *Sociologie et anthropologie*. Paris: Presses Universitaires, 1968.

McFarland, Thomas.
    (1) "Poetry and the Poem: The Structure of Poetic Content." In *Literary Theory and Structure: Essays in Honor of William K. Wimsatt*, edited by Frank Brady, John Palmer, and Martin Price. New Haven: Yale University Press, 1973.
    (2) *Shakespeare's Pastoral Comedy*. Chapel Hill: University of North Carolina Press, 1972.

McLuhan, Marshall.
    (1) *The Gutenberg Galaxy*. Toronto: University of Toronto Press, 1962.
    (2) *Understanding Media*. New York: McGraw-Hill, 1964.

Méautis, Georges. *Pindare le Dorien*. Neuchâtel: La Baconnière, 1962.

Meletinsky, E. M.
    (1) *"Edda" i rannie form'i eposa*. Moscow: Nauka, 1968.
    (2) *Poetika Mifa*. Moscow: Nauka, 1976.
    (3) *Paleoaziatskii Mifhologicheskii Epos*. Moscow: Nauka, 1979.

Meyer, Eduard. "GeschichtsAuffassung." In Marg.

Mourelatos, Alexander P. D., ed. *The Pre-Socratics*. New York: Doubleday, 1974.

Müller-Karpe, Hermann. *Handbuch der Vorgeschichte, Die Altsteinzeit*. Munich: C. H. Beck'sche, 1966.

Myres, John L. *Herodotus: The Father of History*. Oxford: Clarendon Press, 1953.

Nagy, Gregory.
    (1) *Comparative Studies in Greek and Indic Meter*. Cambridge: Harvard University Press, 1974.
    (2) *The Best of the Achaeans*. Baltimore: The Johns Hopkins University Press, 1979.

Namier, Lewis. *Vanished Supremacies*. New York: Harper, 1963.

Nardi, Bruno. *Dante e la cultura medievale*. Bari: Laterza, 1949.

Needham, Joseph. *Science and Civilization in China*. Vol. 1 and Vol. 4. Cambridge: Cambridge University Press, 1954.

Neihardt, John G. *Black Elk Speaks*. Lincoln: University of Nebraska Press, 1961.

Neumann, Erich. *The Origins and History of Consciousness*. New York: Harper, 1962 (1949).

Nietzsche, Friedrich. "Zur Geschichte der theognideischen Sprachsammlung." *Rheinisches Museum* 22 (1867):161–77.

Nilsson, Martin P.
    (1) *Griechische Feste*. Leipzig: Teubner, 1906.
    (2) *A History of Greek Religion*. New York: Norton, 1962 (1925).

Nock, Arthur Darby. *Conversion*. Oxford: Clarendon Press, 1933.

Nock, Arthur Darby, and Festugière, A. J. *Corpus Hermeticum*. Paris: Budé, 1945.

Norden, Eduard. *Die Antike Kunstprosa vom sechsten Jahrhunderte bis in die Zeit der Renaissance*. Leipzig: Teubner, 1915.

Norris, Margot. *The Decentered Universe of Finnegans Wake*. Baltimore: Johns Hopkins University Press, 1976.

Nussbaum, Martha C. *"Psyche* in Heraclitus." *Phronesis* 17(1972):1–16; 153–170.

Ohmann, Richard. "Speech, Action and Style." In Chatman.

Olson, Charles.
    (1) *Bibliography on America for Ed Dorn*. San Francisco: City Lights, 1964.
    (2) *The Maximus Poems* IV, V, VI. London: Cape Goliard, 1968.

Ong, Walter J., S.J. *The Presence of the Word*. New Haven: Yale University Press, 1967.

Opie, Iona, and Opie, Peter. *The Oxford Dictionary of Nursery Rhymes*. Oxford: Clarendon Press, 1951.

Otis, Brooks. *Ovid as an Epic Poet*. Cambridge: Cambridge University Press, 1966.

Parke, H. W. *Greek Oracles*. London: Hutchinson, 1967.

Pauly, August; Wissowa, Georg; and Kroll, Wilhelm; eds. *Realencylopädie der Klassischen Altertumswissenschaft*. 24 vols. Stuttgart: Druckenmüller, 1894ff.

Pavese, Cesare. *Il Mestiere di Vivere*. Turin: Einaudi, 1952.

Paz, Octavio. *Claude Lévi-Strauss: An Introduction*. Ithaca: Cornell University Press, 1970.

Péret, Benjamin. *Le Grand jeu*. Paris: Gallimard, 1968 (1928).

Péron, Jacques. *Les Images maritimes de Pindare*. Paris: Klincksieck, 1974.

Pfeiffer, Rudolf, ed. *Callimachus*. Vol. I, *Fragmenta*. Oxford: Clarendon Press, 1949.

Phillips, Margaret Mann. *The 'Adages' of Erasmus.* Cambridge: Cambridge University Press, 1964.

Phillipson, Paula. "Genealogie Als Mythische Form." In *Hesiod.* Wege der Forschung 44. Darmstadt: Wissenschaftliche Buchgesellschaft, 1966.

Podlecki, Anthony J. "The Language of Heroism from Homer to Pindar." In *Classics and the Classical Tradition: Essays Presented to Robert E. Dengler.* State College, Pa.: The Pennsylvania State University Press, 1973.

Pohlenz, Max. *Herodot.* Darmstadt: Wissenschaftliche Buchgesellschaft, 1961.

Pokorny, Julius. *Indo-germanisches Etymologisches Wörterbuch.* Bern: Francke, 1959.

Polivka, Georg. See Bolte.

Popper, Karl. "Back to the Pre-Socratics." In Furley and Allen.

Pops, Martin. "Labyrinths." *Salmagundi,* Fall 1974, pp. 94–111.

Pouillon, Jean. "Sartre et Lévi-Strauss." *L'Arc* 26 (1965):55–60.

Pound, Ezra. *Confucius.* New York: New Directions, 1951.

Powell, J. E. *A Lexicon to Herodotus.* Hildesheim: Olms, 1966 (1938).

Pritchard, James B. *Ancient Near Eastern Texts Relating to the Old Testament.* Princeton: Princeton University Press, 1955.

Propp, Victor. *Morphology of the Folktale.* Bloomington: Indiana University Press, 1958 (1928).

Pucci, Pietro. *Hesiod and the Language of Poetry.* Baltimore: Johns Hopkins University Press, 1977.

Puech, Henri-Charles. "Gnosis and time." In Campbell.

Rahner, Hugo. *Griechische Mythen in Christlicher Deutung.* Zurich: Rhein, 1966.

Reinhardt, Karl.
(1) *Parmenides.* Frankfurt: V. Klostermann, 1959.
(2) *Vermächtnis der Antike.* Göttingen: Vandenhoeck und Ruprecht, 1966.

Ricoeur, Paul.
(1) *De L'Interprétation.* Paris: Seuil, 1965. *Freud and Philosophy: An Essay in Interpretation.* New Haven: Yale University Press, 1970.
(2) *La Métaphore Vive.* Paris: Seuil, 1975.

Robert, Carl. *Oedipus.* Berlin: Weidmann, 1915.

Robinson, Richard. *Plato's Earlier Dialectic.* Oxford: Clarendon Press, 1953.

Rohde, Erwin. *Psyche.* Tübingen: 1925.

Rosenmeyer, Thomas. "Hesiod and Historiography." *Hermes* 85, no. 3 (1957):257–85.

Ross, James F. "Analogy as a Rule of Meaning for Religious Language." *International Philosophical Quarterly* 1 (September 1961):468–502.

Rudberg, Gunnar. "Zu Pindaros' Religion." *Eranos* 43 (1945):317–36. Reprinted in Calder and Stern.

Russo, Joseph. "Is 'Oral' or 'Aural' Composition the Cause of Homer's Formulaic Style?" In *Oral Literature and the Formula,* edited by Benjamin A. Stolz and Richard S. Shannon. Ann Arbor: Center for the Coordination of Ancient and Modern Studies, 1976.

Sahlins, Marshall. *Echanges et communications*. The Hague: Mouton, 1970.

Sartre, Jean-Paul. *L'Etre et le néant*. Paris: Gallimard, 1943.

Saunders, E. Dale. *Mudra*. Bollingen Series. Princeton: Princeton University Press, 1960.

Schadewalt, Wolfgang.

    (1) *Der Aufbau des Pindarischen Epinikion*. Halle: 1928. (*Schriften der Königsberger Gelehrten Gesellschaft geisteswissenschaftliche Klasse 5*, no. 2:259–343.)

    (2) "Das Religios-Humane als Grundlage der geschichtlichen Objektivität bei Herodot." In Marg.

Schneidau, Herbert. *Sacred Discontent*. Baton Rouge: Louisiana State University Press, 1976.

Schrijvers, P. H. *Horror ac Divina Voluptas*. Amsterdam: Hakkert, 1970.

Schulz, Fritz. *History of Roman Legal Science*. Oxford: Clarendon Press, 1946.

Schwartz, Murray M. "*The Winter's Tale*," *American Imago* 30 (Fall 1973): 250–73; and 32 (Summer 1975):145–99.

Searle, J. R. "What Is a Speech Act?" In *The Philosophy of Language*, edited by J. R. Searle. Oxford: Oxford University Press, 1971.

Segal, Charles Paul.

    (1) "God and Man in Pindar's First and Third *Olympian* Odes." *Harvard Studies in Classical Philology* 68 (1964):211–68.

    (2) "Pindar's Seventh *Nemean*." *Transactions and Proceedings of the American Philological Association* 98 (1967):432–80.

    (3) Review of Thummer in *The Classical Journal* 64 (April, 1969): 330–33.

    (4) *Landscape in Ovid's Metamorphoses*. Hermes' Einzelschriften, Heft 23. Wiesbaden: Steiner, 1969.

Serres, Michel. *La Naissance de la physique dans le texte de Lucrèce: fleuve et turbulence*. Paris: Minuit, 1977.

Service, Elman R. *Primitive Social Organization*. New York: Random House, 1962.

Seznec, Jean. *The Survival of the Pagan Gods*. New York: Harper, 1961 (1940).

Shell, Marc. *The Economy of Literature*. Baltimore: Johns Hopkins University Press, 1978.

Sherwin-White, A. N. *Roman Society and Roman Law in the New Testament*. Oxford: Clarendon Press, 1963.

Shklovski, Victor.

    (1) "*L'Art comme procédé*." In Todorov.

    (2) *O Teori Proz'i*. Moscow-Leningrad: Krug, 1925. Sections translated in Todorov.

Shumaker, Wayne. *Literature and the Irrational*. Englewood Cliffs, N.J.: Prentice-Hall, 1960.

Simpson, R. Hope, and Lazenby, J. F. *The Catalogue of the Ships in Homer's Iliad*. Oxford: Clarendon Press, 1970.

Slater, Philip. *The Glory of Hera*. Boston: Beacon Press, 1968.

Slater, William J. *Lexicon to Pindar*. Berlin: De Gruyter, 1969.

Smith, Arthur H. *Proverbs and Common Sayings from the Chinese*. New York: Dover, 1965 (1914).

Snell, Bruno.
  (1) "Die Ausdrücke für den Begriff des Wissens in der Vorplatonischen Philosophie." *Philologische Untersuchungen* 29 (Berlin, 1924): 72ff.
  (2) "Die Sprache Heraklits." In *Gesammelte Schriften.* Göttingen: Vandenhoeck und Ruprecht, 1960 (1926).
  (3) *The Discovery of the Mind.* Translated by Thomas G. Rosenmeyer. New York: Harper, 1960 (1953).
  (4) *Griechische Metrik.* Göttingen: Vandenhoeck und Ruprecht, 1962.
  (5) ed. *Pindarus.* Vol. I, *Epinikia;* Vol. II, *Fragmenta.* Leipzig: Teubner, 1964.
Snodgrass, A. M. "An Historical Homeric Society?" *Journal of Hellenic Studies* 94 (1974):114–25.
Snyder, Gary. *Earth House Hold.* New York: New Directions, 1968.
Spengel, Leonard, ed. *Rhetores Graeci.* Leipzig: Teubner, 1856.
Stevens, Wallace. *Opus Posthumous.* London: Faber, 1959.
Symonds, John Addington. *The Greek Poets.* New York: Harper, n.d.
Taylor, Archer.
  (1) *The Proverb.* Cambridge: Harvard University Press, 1931.
  (2) *The English Riddle.* Berkeley: University of California Press, 1951.
Thompson, Stith. *Motif-Index of Folk-Literature.* 6 vols. Bloomington: Indiana University Press, 1955–58.
Thomson, George.
  (1) "From Religion to Philosophy." *Journal of Hellenic Studies* 73 (1953):77–83.
  (2) *Greek Lyric Metre.* Cambridge: Heffer, 1961 (1929).
Thummer, Erich. *Pindar: Die isthmischen Gedichte.* Heidelberg: Carl Winter, 1968.
Tilley, Morris P. *A Dictionary of the Proverbs in England in the Sixteenth and Seventeenth Centuries.* Ann Arbor: University of Michigan Press, 1950.
Todorov, Tzvetan.
  (1) ed. *La Littérature du fantastique.* Paris: Seuil, 1971.
  (2) ed. and trans. *Théorie de la Littérature, Textes des formalistes russes réunis, présentés et traduits.* With a preface by Roman Jakobson. Paris: Seuil, 1966.
Tolkien, J. R. R. "On Fairy Stories." In *The Tolkien Reader.* New York: Ballantine, 1966.
Turner, Victor. *Dramas, Fields and Metaphors.* Ithaca: Cornell University Press, 1974.
Van Dijk, Teun A. "Formal Semantics of Metaphorical Discourse." *Poetics* 4 (1975):173–98.
Van Gennep, Arnold.
  (1) *Les Rites de passage.* Paris: E. Nourry, 1909.
  (2) *Manuel de folklore Français contemporain.* 3 vols. Paris: A. Picard, 1946–58.
Verdenius, W. J. "Heraclitus' Conception of Fire." In *Kephalion,* edited by J. Mansfeld and L. M. de Rijk. Assen: Van Gorcum, 1975.
Vermeule, Emily Townsend. *The Art of the Shaft Graves of Mycenae.* Norman: University of Oklahoma Press, 1975.

Vernant, Jean-Pierre. *Mythe et Pensée chez les grecs*. Paris: Maspero, 1966.

Vivante, Paolo. "On Myth and Action in Pindar." *Arethusa* 4, no. 2 (Fall 1971):119–35.

Vlastos, Gregory. "On Heraclitus." *American Journal of Philology* 76 (1955): 337–68.

Von Franz, Marie-Louise. *An Introduction to the Psychology of Fairy Tales*. Zurich: Spring Publications, 1973.

Von Fritz, Kurt. *"Nous, Noein,* and Their Derivates in Pre-Socratic Philosophy (Excluding Anaxagoras)." *Classical Philology* 40 (1945):223–42; 41 (1946):12–34. Reprinted in Mourelatos.

Von Wilamowitz-Moellendorff, Ulrich. *Pindaros*. Berlin: Weidmann, 1966 (1922).

Weber, Max. *Basic Concepts in Sociology*. New York: Philosophical Library, 1962.

Weber, Samuel. *Die Legenden Freuds*. Berlin: Ullstein, 1977.

Weiler, Ingomar. *Der Agon im Mythos*. Darmstadt: Wissenschaftliche Buchgesellschaft, 1974.

West, M. L.
    (1) *Hesiod: The Theogony*. Oxford: Clarendon Press, 1966.
    (2) *Early Greek Philosophy and the Orient*. Oxford: Clarendon Press, 1971.

White, Morton. "Historical Explanation." In Gardiner.

Whitman, Cedric H. *Homer and the Heroic Tradition*. Cambridge: Harvard University Press, 1958.

Wilden, Anthony. *System and Structure*. London: Tavistock, 1972.

Wissowa, Georg. *Religion und Kultus der Römer*. Münich: C. H. Beck, 1912.

Wyatt, A. J. *Old English Riddles*. Boston: D. C. Heath, 1912.

Yeats, William Butler. *A Vision*. New York: Macmillan, 1961 (1938).

Young, David C.
    (1) *Three Odes of Pindar: A Literary Study of Pythian 11, Pythian 3 and Olympian 7*. Leiden: E. J. Brill, 1968.
    (2) "Pindaric Criticism." *Minnesota Review* 4 (1964):584–641. Reprinted with minor additions in Calder and Stern.

Zinn, Ernst. See Michael v. Albrecht.

Zuntz, Günther. *Persephone*. Oxford: Clarendon Press, 1971.

Zwicky, Arnold M. "On Reported Speech." In Fillmore and Langendoen.

INDEX

Adkins, A. W. H., 289*n*
Adorno, Theodor W., 15, 268
Aeneid, 190
Aeschylus, 5, 6, 36, 190, 199, 204
Aesop, 215, 235, 244, 267, 272, 303*n*
Ainu, 272
Akkadian, 51
Albertz, D. M., 239
Albrecht, Michael von, 202
Alcman, 135
Alcuin, 216
Alston, William P., 304*n*
Altamira, cave paintings of, 41, 280
Alvissmol, 270
Ambrose, Saint, 7
Anaxagoras, 291*n*
Anaximander, 70, 72, 74, 78, 95, 151, 157, 171, 187, 291*n*, 299*n*
Anaximenes, 72, 78
Anglo-Saxon riddles, 227–31
Anna Karenina, 155
Arawak, 30
Archilochus, 75, 116, 132, 138, 149, 215, 267
Archpoet, the, 267
Aristagoras, 151
Aristotle, 5, 6, 8, 51, 56, 70, 71, 81, 90, 107, 189, 221, 250, 252, 261, 285*n*, 290*n*, 291*n*, 292*n*, 293*n*, 298*n*, 299*n*, 303*n*
Arkesilas, 116, 118, 120, 123, 125
Assyria, 160
Assyrioi, 165
Athenaeus, 305*n*
Athens, 139, 152, 156, 186
Atlantis, 300*n*
Atun, 30
Atys, 159
Augustine, Saint, 59, 60, 276
Augustus, 190, 192
Austin, J. L., 251

Averroes, 57
Aztec, 21, 30, 32, 43, 50, 51, 305*n*

Babylonia, 24, 39, 98, 146, 160, 164
Bacchus, 199
Bacchylides, 70, 125–26, 130, 132
Bach, J. S., 36
Bachelard, Gaston, 248, 272
Bacon, Francis, 211, 216
Badian, Ernst, 193
Bailey, Cyril, 287*n*
Balinese, 275
Balzac, Honoré de, 155
Barthes, Roland, 180
Bataille, Georges, 1
Bateson, Gregory, 2, 275, 277, 286*n*, 301*n*, 308*n*
Baudelaire, Charles, 32
Beckett, Samuel, 267
Bede, 180
Bellah, Robert N., 209–10, 287*n*
Benardete, Seth, 146, 151, 154, 167, 177, 300*n*
Bennett, Curtis, 289*n*
Beowulf, 244
Bergk, Theodor, 296*n*
Bernbeck, Ernst, 200, 205
Bettelheim, Bruno, 247
Bias of Priene, 77, 168, 169
Bible, 33, 60, 61, 62, 212, 213, 216, 226, 229, 230, 253, 270, 280, 309*n*
Bischoff, Heinrich, 310
Black, Max, 250
Blake, William, ix, 57, 59, 60–62, 66, 107, 222, 228, 251–53, 257
Boas, George, 304*n*
Boeder, Hans, 293*n*
Boethius, 258
Bollack, Jean, 73, 75, 87, 88, 92, 290*n*, 294*n*
Bolte, Johannes, 305*n*

325